BUBBLEGUM YONIS FR(

copyright 2020, 2021 by John Landau

The front and back images are public domain images creatively combined.

Other books of poetry by John Landau :

Hymns for Brueghel (2005)
Trust the Living Chaos (2005 - 2008, 2011)
Foliage for Francesca (2009)
Fleurs for Francesca (2010)
Arrest This Night! (2011)
Nights of Bliss, Apparitions of Wonder (2011)
Icarus Rising : His Waxen Wings Ablaze (2011)
Stolen From Cupid's Quiver (2012)
Sylph of Moonlit Pomegranate (2013)
Caviar Calls : Salmon, Come Home (2014)
Epistles of the Spring (2014)
Spiderman in Iambic Pentameter (2015)
Some Druglike Words (2015)
San Francisco Prelude (2016)
Spiderman : Of Birds of Prey & Creeping Things (2016)
Gilgamesh and Enkidu (2017)
Hubris To Delight the Angels' Pluck (2017)
Spiderman : Of Lords of Crime & Greedy Kingpins (2017)
The Play of the Rhythmic Mind (interview, 2018)
Beauty From The Swamp (interview, 2018)
World Beyond Apocalypse (2018)
April Fools and Other Gestes (2019)
Doubling Down (2019)
Sirenade of Slinky Selkies (2019)

Bubblegum Yonis from Saturn's Rings

APHRODISIAC RHYME & LILTING RHAPSODY

by

JOHN LANDAU

Dedication

To the loved ones who have cared for me in my convalescence, the year my knees failed, my parents, my family, my friends, and Elizabeth of Night. Your devotion and persistence has kept me going. All my love.

To William Shatner, to Peter Jackson, to Bill Bixby and Lou Ferrigno, to Kate Mulgrew and Tim Russ, to George Peppard, Mr. T, Dwight Schulz, and Dirk Benedict, to Danny Elfman, and all who entertained me as I was confined to bed. You made of cloister bedknobs and broomsticks. And to Saint Clare for epistolary yeshiva to keep my mind occupied away from pain. To Echo and the Bunnymen for their delightful poetry.

To all those who so arranged it that the monstrosity was defeated and ousted, whether legitimately or illegitimately of no matter. What matters is his wonderful absence. Hallelujah! Now, let's refind our center and knit together the ripped connections.

To all who suffered under the plague, whether in sickness or in loss of loved ones or the torments and starvations of quarantine. May we all regain our poetry from this stumbling and lame age of prose. From the plague to Boccaccio, I cry!

To my gallery of Muses, if Elizabeth, or Lucy, or Myathiwiz, or Anaid Olixip, or Moonlit Sylph, or Brooke Murphy, keep on the inspiration and the flow. To Dame Darcy, for her kind encouragement.

To the friends who fell in battle : Eve Ghost, Jim Bennett, and others struggling in the moor to regain their loyalty's footing. You are welcome when you are ready to return. My heart is open and generous.

To Lenin and his successors, to Mao and Avakian, to all who have kept the Gospel alive in troubled and dark times. And let us mention Norman Gottwald, and Theodore Jennings. To our fallen and intrepid journalist, Andre Vltchek, who warmed the hope of humanism in chilling hours. To Michael Parenti, who has no equal in this generation. And to the best-dressed man in politics, the Colonel, ten years have not forgotten you or your eccentric glamour.

To the Ancestors, to the Trees, to the Earth, to all that has Soul and lives in Soul in faith. Namaste.

CONTENTS

Preface	1
grasp the novel in these times	12
wild, sprawling Russian novels	13
this dirty rag	14
I ought to jester in my doddering	15
blood pressure	15
be my ecstasy	16
dilation's drops	16
pastry-frosting canopies of flair	16
in Jubilee is your Palladium	17
the bullies and the bootlickers have won	20
the rapists and the torturers have crowns	21
gorgeous things of awe	21
I've earned such irresponsibility	21
everyone is happy when you grin	22
today feels like a Messianic day	22
that empty field I loved	23
but baby, stay	24
let quietude have reign	24
bubblegum yonis from Saturn's rings	25
I've lost the subtlety of struggle's good	26
they will play you virtuoso	27
love that loves delight	28
feather freak of fond oblivion	28
the ecstasy of we	31
we all must have gone mad	33
I lost somewhere the essence of my fun	34
some angel holds my feet before the line	35
my most authentic me	35
guard the gates of childhood	37
in sobriety is liberty	38
everyday of their lives	38
it wasn't theoretical	39
a boy's shalom	40
escape this ponderous self	40
times are good	41
slosh you	41
ten thousand steps	41
classrooms of the creekbed	43
not man's best friend	44
possums	45
a meek Messiah bundled babe in flesh	45
I will fly in dreams	46
your crinkling lips	46
where Moses has no worth	47
ten summa of the dignity of men	49
better listen to Charles Ives	51
the swelling mediocrity of fools	52
the boy who wished he was a kite	52
skulking in our jingoistic caves	57
keep the curtains closed	58

nipping at my flowery heels	58
grenade within the garden rows	58
the way is careful and conservative	59
see beyond our sights	62
a little bit of beatnik is a boon	63
broke the dirty spell	63
we tend	65
endurance	65
groundskeeper of Muses' shrine	65
deliciousness of me	66
my niches	66
everywhere may be a school	66
working out the thorns	69
still and silent beauty's divinity	69
Bomba-bin-bal	70
Pelosi ripping up the manuscript	70
Spenglerian Cathedrals of the Wode	71
invitation improvising brings	71
hives of proletarian honey	72
I shall not trade my liberty in vain	72
Cassandra bound	73
if sobs were dollars	73
Marty in the darker '85	73
not a penny in the bank	74
O bugle, blow!	74
the great, abiding works	75
make room for others	76
there a thousand sins may be redeemed	77
only the future	77
a thousand different chains	78
to compost soil	78
my machismo wars on yours	78
our substance is more of love than flesh	79
secret weapons	83
out of a ship	84
Goddamn, this pig	86
pissing gently on the ivory	87
your awful arms	87
I huddle broken bones in hovels	87
the diplomats of Night	88
currents of the widest breath	90
an angel of a man	90
soft lily besos	91
just give it time	91
still tiptoe in the willows and sycamores	92
Our Lady of the Petal-Paths	92
flirts and champagne socialists	93
by one's weariness alone	94
aloof	94
unfamiliar wakened ones	94
ten-sided dice on fingernails	95
jackrabbit's slippers	95
old Tom Hatten Family Films	97
Taoist cowboy	98

hilltops float in fog	98
mosques of goddess modesty	98
the red-tailed hawk is beautifully oblivious	100
Naxalite forests	101
in the cleft vagina of the soil	101
smooth hexameters upon a scroll	101
Babylon may weep midst of her smoke	102
July, 64 a.d.	104
today it's Africa	105
nothing makes me superior	106
the better of us sentient swims the sea	106
a wonderment of animals	107
I am a rainforest	109
in fragility	110
we are the friend we would be to our soul	110
strangers sharing tea and thoughts	111
favor from her violet hair	112
I'm Jagger in his supple strut	112
fuck the human race	113
in gratitude and grace	113
ruckus is necessity	116
soul doesn't care	116
walls of quarantine come down	117
back in the game	118
decoctions from the sky	119
nothing but facts	120
no Vandals at our doorsteps	120
hovering swarm of rose petals	121
sunlight once was sparkling caviar	122
a cocktail rare and dizzying	123
disappointment made into a god	124
friendship of dreams	124
her title on the scrip of soul	128
it's tangled through with you and me	129
the walnut	131
exit the newspaper	131
get on through	131
the Chattanooga barber	132
disaster this! disaster that!	132
aloofness is the savior of my life	133
corrodes the pitch between the plumes	133
there I once was young	133
erastes and eremenos	134
giddy Oz	134
I brought up beauty from the toiling deep	137
cheating scars the heart	138
someone else has all her eyes	139
drinking in the accolades at last	139
my liturgy of this your bust	140
just know they'll flee	140
the testament of Spring	141
the sins of heroes	141
my body once anemone	143
sociopaths to our own soul	144

speak cryptic and we love you	145
somatic moseying through time	145
riddle through their mouth	146
an animal at risk	147
settled bureaucrat of life	149
bric-a-brac of rumble-tumblement	150
trained the ladybugs	151
the unfinished cathedral	152
mist by some oasis font	152
imitate flamingos	153
an amazing kingdom on its way	153
such an evil bitch	156
we have the right to never bow	156
life as my defiant fist	157
a simple, pious sip	157
in Notre Dames of sun-swept forest floors	158
our reveries have truth	159
impressions	159
how far will we allow this Faust?	160
my sighs have fled like butterflies	169
the hamadryad anima	169
giving it one eye	171
the enemies of reason	171
we must assemble	171
ill words have no worth	172
to labyrinth within	173
nothing but drifting mind	174
surely I withdraw	174
she weaned me off my gothic craze	175
surrender is the best of paths for men	175
fuck rock and roll	175
Lucretius, ah!	176
frozen glide over the lake	177
crystal carousel of molecules	177
this bold capacity to understand	178
whipped cream of dreams	178
a trail of apples with a single bite	178
fireworks in lockdown storage	179
the problem is the liberals	180
fingers in Kidron's waters	181
too far the jungle law still lingers	182
invested in a single drop of good	183
divided from our neighbors	184
the reason many rouse themselves at dawn	184
yet you do	184
one never gets credit	185
a Sidhe in shimmering	185
Munhumutapa	186
raindrop-fall as mist on me	186
these chants	186
from floe to floe on icy seas	187
Monica	187
you are here when you are not	189
second Baudelaire in mystic robes	190

this vast collage	191
demammals us of sense	192
libido dominandi	192
forbid ye not the Dionysia	193
the canyon holds the vulva of the town	193
the lurid spa of afternoon	194
becomes new rhyme	195
giggling in their leaves	196
hobo hum by phantom night	196
such shape as will bewitch the heart	196
the temples Theodosius forbade	197
perfect stillness of a moment's breath	197
this suite that lilts my ears	198
let me be crying swan	198
buxom moaning murmurings	198
she dines with Petrarch in the attic space	199
a silent snake	200
doe-eyes to human-eyes	201
that's the shit that man can be to man	201
the wonder of the stubbornness	203
plaintive sermons to the bears and sheep	204
the only life for me	205
shuts me from the holy of holies	205
why I wake and dream	206
the old man who had strangled sons	206
if masters did not contradict, no gain	207
ode to a mosquito	207
surging in the vital jazz	208
so very woman at the well	208
a woman in her all	210
in severalty of orgy	210
in software's slits	211
leches bite the dust	211
doldrum on	211
we all must lick the curb	212
tirades on tap	212
I am forever we	213
a we without the me is a scam	214
a bard has duties to the warriors	215
Sophia	216
the hope of liberty	216
the angel in the animal	217
a dark ages would heal	218
we aren't streams of data	219
Torquemadas lurk in every age	219
the hillbillies' instincts	220
we've lost a man	220
Russian roulette for Black people	221
honor bonds of youth	221
cast me out of court	221
inhibited by narrow minds	221
burning every bridge	222
let your care be where it wants to be	222
a more ambitious prick	223

never really cared	223
into betweenity	223
precious sacraments	224
like cobwebs' dust	224
in midst of blackest pitch no light at all	225
the little bunker bitch	225
hope at last goes viral	226
woven in our very fibers	226
my soul alone suffice	227
heaven's dulcimer to ears	228
right wing, left wing	228
now burn it down	228
wet as yet from womb	230
the dojo of the ocean	231
the classic ages living in their bones	232
beauty involute in holiness	232
a little grace	233
fall to the ground	233
the modern Minneapolis Bastille	234
spoiler eager for the chance to wreck	234
epitome of Romans 13	235
proverbs from the sinews of their gut	235
the sabbath is for man	236
shalom	237
ease and oil	240
smoke screen	241
seanced with the proletariat	243
a limestone rabbinate	244
assert astonishing taboos	245
slow geology of generations	247
you strike a bully back, you win the fight	247
whisked away	248
neither tasted nor betrayed	249
thick like butter	250
to funk the summer eve	250
I often shower but to weep alone	250
the greater sin	251
yet I rise	253
he had the tune	254
every fruit	254
high and dry	255
unnoticed were my fruits	255
slithering reptilian	256
come, vandals!	257
they outlaw this my heart	259
two thousand years ago	260
Oscar to Bosie	262
stern rebuttals	262
John Brown is in my breast	263
a little less than best	264
just pinch your nose and eat	265
Aphrodite knows no color walls	265
the sacred temple grounds	266
fear is political	266

or you will have it shut	267
peacocks now reclaim philosophy	268
the mystic merchant	268
your sweet vagina's made of subtle lace	270
Neapolitan at heart	271
the Dresden of the everyday	271
deliver me to sages' feet	274
disciplines of delicacy	275
a glimpse of Halloween	276
because of these, I stayed	276
a meal is blessing by itself	277
a simple puppy dog	281
she is Oshun	282
this poem now shall hold her	282
reflecting foliage	283
the brimstone in the human heart	283
unanswered letters	284
I lived inside the angels' minuet	284
fetalize your newborn eyes	285
Mephistopheles of silicon	286
to Eleanor of Aquitaine	287
this Machiavelli of the comedy	288
in thickets of Topanga	290
hollow to my hungry lips	291
currency of fire	291
right from wrong	292
gaslighting is the norm	292
champagne brooded on seas	293
my soul is Scottish	294
you always might be wrong	294
you really don't know half	295
gossiping inside a burning house	295
poetry is truth	296
oblivion is best	296
carnation is salvation	297
let's get out of here	297
walking wounds	297
to the heart of me!	298
let it begin in me	299
a cantrip in a carousel of stars	300
so much I have to marshal	301
perhaps an elemental	302
to wild air	302
you orthinate my seeking soul	302
yet I got a ride	303
let's get to work	304
swindled from our feet	305
a love affair with public space	305
assholes are our saviors now	307
denizens of grey who hate all joy	307
a truce for Carnival and Lent	307
down to the very bone	308
chapel of the moonlit-webbed sky	308
feathers pink and haughty	309

lucky skits of children	309
they'd look like this	310
lurid blue of sky voyeur	310
from the heights	311
dancing with the dragon	311
an asshole for one's love	311
the cannibals of men	312
carve out canyons	312
lay aside the hero's tale	313
fragrant, subtle calendars	313
Jerry Springer of the web	314
your palms pulse Handel	314
rusting me with fiery tears	314
my Roman friend of old	316
the essence of my happiness	317
eyes have yet to see the far-off light	317
a curse without the dance	318
Acts 4:36-7	318
fluids are Messiah's hidden prayers	320
shrieks of all the shanty towns	320
your naked reveries	320
the utter Aphrodite of your flesh	321
roasting marshmallows	321
an angel that I heed	322
a Stradivarius	322
beloved nudity of ghosts	324
an entourage of elegance	325
a pantheon of light	326
nickeled dimes	326
malfeasance	327
a ballerina through the swamp	327
tethered to angst	328
farewell my pouts	328
my windows boarded up	329
the rolling bath of Ranch dressing and dill	329
gumball machine	331
subterranean and lewd	331
architecture of the damned	331
syrup on the page	332
fuck these damn fluorescent lights	333
a gaggle's fluff	333
aebelskievers made of verse	334
glassy snow-globe	334
sugar oyster	336
I felt beautiful again	336
votary of fleet Atargatis	336
jello of collective dung	338
turns my skin into a wonderland	338
birds would cease to sing	338
straitjacket of skin	339
careless play of innocents	339
measure out the deep	340
captive creatures of our awe	340
savor of the shade	341

how her vineyard tastes	341
the first temptation	342
the second temptation	343
the third temptation	348
idolize the gutter	352
lotuses from mud	352
a long and brutal brooding	357
something we might yet become	357
anything at all is doable	358
struggling to emerge from a latrine	361
unclassifiable	361
wrath in spasm ate at me	362
the country lost its flippin mind	362
a sacred shrine to self	363
your sweetest joy is mine	365
heirloom's gallery	365
allow no goblins to reside	366
I could be bubblegum	367
a scar I caress in lieu of you	368
my paramours, the angels	369
symphony of noise and beauty	370
a thousand terrible distractions	371
the glass of placid Taedong	372
my nightingale	372
song is the connubium of us	372
pick up a gun	373
just the pigs they are	374
the bed became a town of ghosts	374
flamingo	375
the priceless value of his work	376
an elfin breath that swift enchants	376
children of the zephyrs	377
thirsty for the open sea	377
gizzard breweries	378
no patience for wasted work	378
council of the gods	378
lantern-lucent on my blessed bed	380
filet mignon of his nobility	380
fond allures	381
fond and yet forlorn	382
let the puritans complain	382
no Mother Earth, no true theology	383
I was made for old guild workshops	384
a Grecian tholos	385
too flowery for you? go fuck yourself	387
just once within all time	388
skein in skiff	390
waiting for the cavalry to come	390
a cow's life	390
Lenin but not Dherzinsky	391
wet for the wonder	391
leaf collage in breeze	391
the muddled labyrinth of life	392
ink wet upon the page	392

November 3, 2020	393
to sip the silence as its wine	393
the common touch of the divine	393
that is the sad of it	394
the mountains know me	394
the gutter as our citadel	395
the citizens of sewers	395
somatic whalesong in my suit of skin	396
so soft it sifts the heavens	396
mahogany in moonlit dew	396
marinade of silence	397
Francis in the chaparral	397
lips are goblets dipped	397
garden of monoliths	400
quicksilver night conceals	400
puttis	401
Tiffany of poets	402
shakespeare's sonnets redux	403
another Paris, and another Helen	404
shy and flighty doe-eyed thing	405
taking a shit to Sinatra	407
the coal, the stone, the geode lair	407
to gaze at mammaries	408
we must discover deeper roots	408
reminders of the angels	409
leotard of birth	410
have mercy on my bruises	410
dormancies but dream in depths below	411
the poetry of adipose and skin	416
makes my heart to glide	417
Glèndalê	418
to each a time, a pinnacle, a peak	419
myrhh of heaven	419
I've known the very vamps	420
wonderment a child knows	421
a room of puppy dogs	421
single sip of drunken fingertips	423
chrysanthemum	424
how soft we all might be	424
success	425
the People's Chamber Halls	425
traitors and retards	426
a species of champagne and opium	426
delicious poltergeist of haunting beauty	427
world's burlesque	427
allodial of fraud	427
this is our birthright	428
in Eden's primal lens	430
the fire and the lace	431
the sugar of the sky	432
my Peter Pan is weathered but alive	432
in shadows I was wounded	433
rippling plum	435
the darling daredevil	436

let the face talk	437
a diva in the heart of dwarves	437
perceive the colt and not the man	437
the angel-glimpse	438
Oak and Avena	438
your beauty shrinks from me	439
between a son and mother	440
ideals have proven inconvenient	440
auctioning Messiah's clothes	442
that ruffle round the whorl	442
restored, released, renewed	442
sunset's cobweb scene of fading flames	443
army of a man	443
the foxes still roam freely	445
makes reason validate his wickedness	445
misty strip-tease on a summer's night	446
papyrus singing birdsong	447
O for a slam-pit	448
San Francisco	449
plaster putto	450
the frolicsome brocade	451
night restores	451
apple-sweet	452
Phidias in rue	453
song aplenty in the blood	454
from soil such as this	454
Platte Bridge	455
Eucalyptine masques	455
sonnet her immortal to the nations	456
possessed by purple	459
midnight masques in candelabra glow	460
I miss the Castro like I miss my life	461
the Belladonna belle of yesteryear	463
Easter, 1995	464
a playboy and a loon	465
a handkerchief to wipe my tears	466
a little Eden now, tomorrow more!	467
Negar	467
Our Lady of Conculia Capilli	468
surely I were Catholic	469
the wisps of jellyfish of sky	469
our star, how patiently it spins	470
miserable and comfortable	472
lackadaisicality on wing	472
invisible and winged	472
your ugly, shitty soul	473
topsy-turvy land	473
I live emotionally as I will	474
bring me the feminine	474
homeland of the foam where toes first danced	475
Svipdag's descent to win the sword	477
her skin is tamarind	486
a new bounce to her gait	486
this grudging world has cleaved us	488

something giddy reigns	491
a worldwide technocratic takeover	491
such wonders are of Antichrist	492
has-been hack	492
where now stands praise we yearned	492
emotion on emotion	493
a lion	493
Lesbia	494
as delicate as flight	494
if I were rose	495
the daughter Beauty had with Grace	495
morning canticle of winged ones	496
peacocks as my entourage	496
who cannot trust himself, let no one trust	498
whirlwind made of leaves	498
caressers	500
carnival of sylphs	501
feather-fall of snow-drift fuchsia	503
every open way	503
a moth to every Muse's torch	504
the age's total mockery of faith	505
thank God for Spiderman	505
farewell to Baals	506
she had the eldritch air	507
the world is wet from embryo	511
eager for life's diorama	512
now broken up with grass	512
the mead of thirstiness	513
Wild Eadric	513
one yearns to touch that softest skin	518
ghosts in command	518
now but copper change	519
I chant shalom	520
nectar of the springs	523
a duchess of abalone	523
sighs are snowfall	523
rainshower of peonies	524
not the rind	524
never have doubt	525
icicles like cigarettes	526
this living silk as gift	526
a princely fish	527
happiness were deep-sea fish	528
sap asleep by night	528
falling gamelan to mud	529
just a little craze	529
maiden hidden in the soap	529
Dialogue Between A Monk and Mage	530
you're in cactus	537
effeminate and lovely Son of God	538
we get the Puritans that we deserve	539
800 million	540
taste of peach	540
the scars a tribesman sports	541

Artemis in bronze	542
silliness were brandywine	543
scent of inner sinews	544
poem on a toilet roll	544
naked, warm, and dolphin-wet	544
duty and beauty	545
to feed you mint	546
lads of butterscotch-sunlight	547
baptismal on aching flesh	547
oysters yielded but reluctantly	547
the rabid poisons raped	549
Verdugo	550
illusions that you love	550
just dump her	551
columnar-sculpted like a forest glade	551
as many of them as I can	552
two curly-haired Davids	553
Mystery weeps	553
worms delight in gnawing at the roots	554
stretch the worse to seem the better	554
Roxanne	555
the realm of prayer	555
epiphany of Aphrodite	555
the roses purr	556
Aubrey Beardsley wings	557
enlist in Starfleet	557
to dance in zero gravity	557
behold you loving me	558
tribal chief	558
Indigenous America	559
the red-legged partridge	559
the cosmic cure	560
you will at last command	560
wish upon the tip of tongue	561
has name of love	562
monuments of mirth	562
consummated	562
Mike Monahan	563
an aquaman upon the land	563
sweet sorbet	564
upwards to the skies	565
more to sleep as life	565
canteloupe exposed to milky view	565
a mountaintop of cream	566
show us the way to 2022	566

Preface

Fox News needs to be shut down. There needs to be a relentless campaign to get it off the air. And anyone who repeats its talking points needs to be gagged. Literally. I would support a law to mandate gagging of such rabid and frothing jingoism.

And Israel needs to unilaterally withdraw from the Occupied Territories and allow the Palestinian Authority the state power necessary to evict all settlers from the Territories. That single act, bringing peace at last, would prove redemption for Israel, and ultimately the world, for Israel's right-wing mentality has corrupted almost all of Judaism, which has always been a world force for progress and liberalism, but has gotten culdesacked into terribly compromising reactionary deadends that began with Israel alone, but have had time to worm their way in to the heart of practice and contemplation everywhere, and sideswipe the tradition off its prophetic path. Get Judaism back on those tracks, and the entire world will become a more hopeful place in one fell swoop. *I want my real Judaism back.* Authentic, messianic, prophetic Judaism. Poetry will flow again.

Now, this was meant to be whimsical, but then the year itself intervened. *Bubblegum Yonis from Saturn's Rings?* Delight and surrealist intrigue. That is the silver coin I tossed into the pond. Sulfurous belch is what emerged from the marsh. I respond somewhat sourly, and hope you will take a rain-check on that promise of pure wonderland. That said, you will find *creme brulee* here nonetheless, stashed away in a survivalist cave hidden behind cactus.

The claustrophobic angst of the ensnaring compaction of the private domain threatens on all sides to diminish our breadth of audience, the reality of the larger scope, and to collapse our hopes into a diminished catacomb. To maintain the vision of the larger audience in the midst of suffocating isolation, and keep one's voice alive as it reaches out to touch at the civilizational level when one's personal situation is of social burial becomes more strangled as time moves onwards without any encouragement and the sense that one's audience is nothing but a farce invented by a delusional mind. With this disillusionment, which is itself an illusion, yet as an illusion disillusionment always carries itself as absolute truth, to maintain the dignity and elevation of one's voice, the very quality one came into the world to develop, takes on a Herculean level of endurance, and one wonders in a sense, is obscurity but a slow way to asphyxiate a voice that cries out to be heard?

My model is Chagall, for he was oblivious to the critics demanding constant innovation. He was a true craftsman, which means, he did what he loved, and he threw himself into the art of the refrain, repeating theme after beloved theme in endless combinations. Does one Chagall painting look like another? Often. It is lovely to be that in love, and I am of his ilk.

Poetry is at low ebb. It can be nothing other in a time of disillusion, hopelessness, and the overturning of all decency that has signaled the werewolves to come out of the closet and run rampant with their cruelty and callousness. My verse is on life support. How much further can we go with this almost universal bleakness? Never before have I seen the worst elements so empowered, so emboldened, so triumphant. That means Christianity has taken a hit and has failed to work its alchemy, for the crucifiers of Christ are now the loudest wavers of that cross. Truly this is a carnival for Antichrist.

Saxo's King Frodi, Harbinger of Harvests, Sweet Love, and Freedom, Messiah of a Great Peace won at the cost of terrible war against a giant troop of savage despots, has an ally in a strange corner, a General from the North who has abandoned his trollkin to fight the Messianic fight, Starkad, the grim, grizzled, deformed colossus of combat, whose songs are litanies of blood. As faithful and fanatical to the cause as he is apathetic to the collateral damage, Starkad is a devoted convert to Frodi's green dreams of expanded brotherhood. Starkadr does not quite understand this beautiful enchantment for which he fights, and yet it is so wondrous, there is little count of sacrifice he would balk towards its favor. I have suggested before that Starkadr may be painted as the mythic type of Stalin, giving archetypal undertones to history.

But the image of Starkadr, that the West alone seems capable of seeing, does not exhaust this figure. There was a calm and collected energy to him, the gatherer of the councils' drones, the ear attentive in the caverns, the mind contemplative of mines and forges, the dwarven wisdom of the deep, whose riddles rough were offered up as ore as yet unpolished. He held the heritage of Durin and Dvalin in his blood, and brought forte from below to Handel's suite, bestowing untamed gemstone-garlands on the Messianic altar, the bulky dwarven piety of gravitas, as best he knew, the meeting of the goblin fathoms with the Saoshyant, rough, sincere, proud, and rude. If these qualities are not grasped and integrated, the picture becomes mere caricature, convenient villainizing to absorb our own unowned shadow. There is enough shading in the chiaroscuro here without adding our own. The call of Mashiach echoed in the caverns of the mountains; a new Ulfilas crafted glyphs for hidden Goths, whose response to the strange gospel, nuance lost in translation, was as devoid of guile as it was still storming with barbaric hordes, their wild horses snorting fire. A latter day throng of Arius, a mixed multitude of Sarmatians and Alani, Russ and Turk, heretical but devoted to what light this cryptic rough-hewn gospel might bring their dark abysms.

    Here caricature begins to graduate into authentic symbol, rich and redolent with promise as well as threat, bypassing the honey monocultures of moral dramas for the far more varied flavors of the full palate of history, with sufficient saltiness, fishiness, bitterness, and sweet and sour. We meet with CS Lewis here, introducing us to a far and distant tribe of ruffians and troglodytes, living close to the inner heat of the earth in scraped tunnels and rustic labyrinths, bristly-haired sylvestri who have heard rumor, passed through many tongues altering the form but keeping the savor of the gist, of wondrous good news, news worthy of a gamble, of a go, of a struggle, of a forging. A forging as sooty and full of ash and fire as any smithing, a gamble as rocky and full of brawl as stony hearts may rumble, a fool's errand sweet melody to hooligans and oafs devout as they are bellicose. Here angels' gossip whispered by serpents slithering in the burrows was heard not by saints but hulking brutes whose hearts were as pure as their tempers were perilous, bouldery sinners enchanted with a dream, and heading this dwarven endeavor, a half-breed king the scion of dwarves and giants, a brillo-smith work ethic and the raucous get-it-done ravageries of trolls, who would lead them on come hellfire or war, the stubbornness of the stomping bull, and the devil take the china shop. All of that is summed up in Stalin, and if you don't get that, you've got nothing but dust in your hands, the soot left over from a magnificent forge. It may lie rusting now, but it was once the citadel the workers of the underneath held as their own.

    Did Moses drown Egyptian hordes with single thump of staff? Did Levites at his heed come Sicarii throughout the camp, and down the thousands? Did fire burn the discontent in deserts of the Sinai? Wonder not the dwarf-king hailed as leader of the Exodus! And while these wild buffalo stampeded, treading out the plains to storm the very gates of the millennium, the pious citizens of Mammon slept upon their Bibles, content to babble in church inane hymns they dreaded ever bringing forth to pass, so exacting yet in Pharisaical precision, they looked with disdain down their empty lips' service on those who were — doing it all wrong!! — while they sat on their asses and called out Jesus' name as the poor starved about them. Jesus on a popsicle stick, dollar signs in mandala of eyes. Those with clean and lily-white Bibles; those with the snare-drum soot of a marching gospel, learning by doing, learning by failing, learning by falling in the millions to stop the Nazi hordes. And your silver-spooned lips fed sips of brandy by simonist priests overseeing labor camps in the colonies dare to utter stale and fetid words of contempt? Look in the mirror, hypocrite! You've got your own mustache to deal with, much more trim and Charlie Chaplin than the mustachio you slander.

  This is not a rehabilitation, but a reception of blood-and-ash-stained jewels salvaged from the smithies of war and Herculean jihad, a torn but priceless heirloom from the battlefields. Would you have all that sacrifice be in vain? Would you learn nothing? Are you incapable of receiving dark grandeur clothed magnificent and terrible in robes of horror, yet from which some dull but fairy gleam still shines? Only myth can delve these depths. The rest may be propaganda, either side, but something martial and astounding still smokes in the ruins. A poet is remiss to leave this fallow; a bard's as good indicted if he does. So I will utter unpopular sagas in foreign tongues that scrape against the grain, and offer hair-shirts itching at patriotic skin. I am but a chronicler of stark campaigns, a Smith with seeing stones peering back to battles of Lamanites and Nephites. Epic hurricanes of spears, and melee-gales of iron darts in ages past, all cast to grasp a single glance on Apostolic fellowship. There's little more the splendorous than true and glorious failures. Tragedies that reached for heaven's heights may be new psalms.

  Because the paranoids think there is a snake underneath every rock, they are unable to anticipate a wildflower or fascinating insect or anything in the least interesting, because the sinister is the only thing that draws their awareness. Truly, they are beyond awareness (para-nous), and besides themselves. Certainly it is a sin to have too little wonder in a universe as full of marvel as this, and there is something scatalogical about slandering what ought to be praised as entirely depraved, which is one of the reasons why Calvinism, beyond being an amusing on-the-one-hand shtick, can never be truly convincing. It might please our soul to take the dour pose from time to time, but little does the brimstone please the singing angels.

  I know paranoids well, and I've known many over the years, and learned much from them. I've met them at Dennys, and backwoods cafes, and conversations on the sides of the road, all usually manic and with pressure of speech more attuned to the monologue and diatribe than the interflow of dialogue. They are a kind of native resource, our indigenous, from-the-bramble sages, who in their various suspicions and deep research have uncovered many connections. For this they should be valued --- entirely on the one hand. For the fact of the matter is that no matter how much I have appreciated these grizzled old souls, I cannot live by their gospel. An appreciation of the depths and breadths of evil may be a necessary antidote to naivete, but every medicine depends on its dosage, and there are dosages too high for *sophrosyne*.

There is more on heaven and earth than is dreamt of in any paranoid's imagination. Paranoids are invested in a world supercharged with significance, which might be something wonderful, even if it does egregiously set aside the obvious banality of the largely quotidian world, if it were not that the only significance sought is disillusionment taken to its highest power of nihilism. The degree to which these backwoods sages are addicted to disillusionment as if it were some mystery initiation can be astonishing.

Not that there is no value in some schooling at their school. In fact, I would dare to say that any who remain naive to at least some familiarity with covert operations and black ops is somewhat less than an adult. I have studied long at the schools of the best of these polymath curmudgeons, and would dare to say that if I had a manhood initiation, it was not in any physical ordeals, but passing through the harsh mental disciplines of coming to terms emotionally with the clearly evident prevalence of evil in the world they so skillfully muckrake. But I have no desire to make a home in that bootcamp.

While a certain level of skepticism certainly does fund intellectual inquiry, so does a certain quantum of giving benefit of the doubt, and both cognitive and emotional distortions are consequent upon always looking for the worst. The way to approach paranoia is to be aware that much of it is simply convincing bullshit, a skillfully told thriller genre, that has some, but certainly not all, of the truth the teller thinks, but which allows the holder to feel they are special by having privileged access to the scoop that others hardly suspect. Of course, there is some basis to this. No tale can be spun plausibly without some basis from which to elaborate, but of course, it is always in the elaboration that one must be careful not to mistake the exciting entertainment for reality itself. It is one lens on reality, and frequently, a mistaken one. All too often sloppy, mere associational thinking is at work, and oddly, despite the frequent dosage of skepticism, there is too much certainty about what may be possible, without enough of the healthy shrug, and certainly with far too little skepticism towards skepticism itself.

Knowing things can go wrong can make it hard to trust good things, and some prefer the permanent security of the pout to the adventure of faith. It is easier to assume that everything can go wrong and will than to stay in agnostic expectation of surprise. One can then anticipate all the bad surprises, but one loses out on the possibility of good surprises. And the strategy overall leaves one with surplus pessimism, often in toxic quantities, a pessimism far, far outstripping the worst of prospects and realistic disillusionment. And after all, one should not abuse the little mouse inside one's mammalian brain which is so easily spooked. It's not kind to frighten oneself unnecessarily when logic suggests the universe is so much more often boring and hohum than it is any valence above or beneath that.

Here I proudly embrace a new didactic. I take no bashfulness in expounding what prudence I have eked from full but careful living. One seldom hears such a truthful amalgam in our worship of the impetuous: "full" but "careful" living. To piss off the reckless is joy, and to thumb one's nose at inadvisable moronities humbugged as freedom or adventure is just good, sarcastic sense. Youth need to hear frank, unsugared wisdom that comes from depth and ample breadth of experience. I've lived my life as an experiment, and I know many of the pitfalls, and prudence — as unattractive as that word sounds, as unsexy as it seems — is precisely the medicine we need, but a prudence grounded in contact and vitality, exploration and curiosity, and not avoidance of life.

The only authority is the center. When you've found that center, entrust the whole circle to it, and spurn those who find focus too much control : they are lost. External authorities may be very useful to help one triangulate where the center is; where they show fidelity, follow them; where they're lost, follow the law that leads to center without them.

Look, positivists are full of shit. They're subtractionists who lack fidelity to lived experience because they edit out elements of life which don't jive with their rigid ideology, and it's always the most soulful aspects. I have zero respect for positivism. There are epiphanies in life, and I'll go further, there are theophanies of grace, the touch of the goddess in your life, a sudden spread of petals from your hair in your life at just the right moment refreshing your existence. Anyone who looks that gift horse in the mouth and tries to explain it away or dissect it out of existence is an impious and ungrateful lout who needs to get the fuck out of my life, because I don't want your spoilsport ass in it. The blind have no place dictating to the sighted what is real, and those who choose to blindfold themselves even more. And if you are so impoverished as you've never had such moments of beauty gently inbreaking into your life, maybe you should learn from those who have what are the graces which they have integrated into their lives, the poetic etiquette that cultivates beauty, which have a tendency to woo the graces, instead of disparaging what you don't understand. In Platonic and Aristotelian terms, these are arts, arts of life and love, where it is less a skill to be passed on, and more of a knack. As Osho might put it, it is a perfume, an aroma that exudes from one who knows, that if one participates in with enough devotion, one may pick up.

     If I strike a Polonius here, that is a venerable role I won't disdain. There are many costumes in my wardrobe. The Polonial is an honorable genre to which I am pleased to contribute. Rest assured, though, there will be rhapsodies.

     Recently I wondered whether my lines had become long-winded, but I wouldn't call myself "long-winded", but full of deep capacity for breath and song. The oratorio extends, the notes sustain, the breath of thought is broad and German in its clauses. This is good. Such fiber in such meal is nourishing, still full of flavor, fills the gut with plenty. This is feast, and fuller for it. Not to everybody's taste perhaps, but here's the table, rich with nurturance and taste.

     There are two ways to evaluate work, each valid in their own domain. The first is Olympic, in which supremacy in masterpiece is ever sought. Here's aspiration, and the spirit thrives in such. All well. But then there is the inveterate craftsman, the guildmaster too consumed in the work and its ever-evolving textures to concern himself too much with the prospect of accolades, which are but assumed, which have already become foundation, assimilation of confidence. For the guildmaster, Olympics are for youth, however glorious. Good work's good work with prize or not. It's solid without need for such applause. It's diligence that matters here, resistance to acedia, rolling the sleeves up day in and day out to make of the workshop a temple, and see what the wood, the wood itself, in tandem with the hand, will yield today, and that is harvest of the day. The day is good, and every day is different. Not everyday's Olympic. When grain and texture lead the knife to sculpt ascent, the guildmaster follows, but is far beyond the adolescent need to make everything about the highest hill. Such callow rivalry for the next and best gives way to the fertile humility of steady work, with all its ample Daedalean curiosity. The masterpieces come when they may will, and he already has several under his belt. They aren't the only pieces that matter. In fact, they're but a minor flourish, the capstone on a far more immense work, in which each piece is allowed to come into its own. Work good or bad is still work, and work is worth.

 To me, a book of poetry is not a gallery. It's an invitation into the workshop. There's sculptures and paintings everywhere, dust, stains, paint, shards, tools askance, a marvelous grotesquery of pieces beautiful and monstrous, finished, still in progress, left undone intentionally, and all the shades between. It should smell of plaster and sawdust, clay and old stained wood. A guildmaster offers no apologetics for the Muses' work, but discovers, upside down in his own Yiddish kvetchings, as a reflection in a pond of clouds above, the rationale hidden in each work. Long-winded? No, long-breaths! Pedantic? No, a backwoods aviary full of tangled riddles in birdsong. Prosaic? Testament to everyday texture. Turn a criticism upside down, it tells the truth. Good steaming shit is always fresh manure. I worry about flippant fiddlings. If a poet gives a shit, that's contribution. Something will grow in that shit. Maturity is realization of fecal wisdom; Luther writes treatises on the can.

 One will note my fancy for Anchises, father of Aeneas, in this volume. Indeed, I am intrigued by this young shepherd whom Aphrodite fell in love with, and it has provided much grist for my poetic mill : what is it like for a mortal to suddenly find himself in love with a goddess? What does that feel like? The theme is endlessly (as you will see) fascinating.

 My masters are Shakespeare, Pound, and Hopkins. Their sensibility and craft forms the essence of my core style. My fairy godmother would of course be Milton, my great-uncle Whitman, my old schoolteacher Wordsworth, and I'd be hard pressed to think of anyone more recent than these greats. The present is overglutted with utter mediocrity and rubbish. I'm writing world-class literature, not parleying with the poetaster buffoons of poetry readings. Aristocracy is now as egalitarian as simply aiming for something high, so I'll let the catfish bottom-feed to their hearts' content.

 Milton's prime virtue was his absolute aristocratic insistence when it came to his bearing and talent, and egalitarian spirit in other matters. He knew he was the best and the brightest of his generation and he would come under the yoke of no false modesty in that regard. As such, he sets an example for those of us who are brilliant, that we don't need to pander ourselves to the gutter mentality of what uncultivated boors find amusing. We can carry on with our dignity from the eagle's aerie.

Wordsworth's virtue is retreat, withdrawal from the world and back into the wild landscapes of childhood, there to make eternal the reflected essence of those heartkeen wonders. And in this age of sensationalism, where fear panders to the worst and the worst in us, we all need such quiet withdrawal to regain our aplomb, and rediscover the child within.

This particular yield is the winepress of raisins, the droplets eked in drought, the constructions possible in the dungeons of despair, the precious juice squeezed from the salt. I offer no apologies for the meagre fruits of poverty. That anything grew in the garden at all, dessicated and shriveled though it may be, astonishes me. In my pursuit of righteousness, the cynical adage of a wicked age, you can be right or you can be liked, has proven its mettle to my detriment, and old friends have determined to make it go hard, as I stand surprised before a reality even I did not think would go so low below the belt to impoverish what is cherished. Every scar you see on me has been paid in full, and the idealism left in my grizzled flesh has been purchased with barrels of brine. If Enlightenment still held currency -- we have strayed -- we would have lowered the costs of moving against the tide, the pressure-front where progress is made. Those comfortably on the sides of the stream enjoying the fruits of former progress have no idea. We have largely replaced the Inquisition with emotional famine as the penalty for refusing conformity. Progress is slow when we are desperate simply for restorations of what was taken rather than excited about new advances. But from the midst of this desert, I bring you prickly pears, succulent and tart. It is true, they still have a few thorns, but those are easily removed to get at the refreshing pulp. I bid you enjoy.

The age is both petty and vindictive, petty in its vindictiveness, vindictive in its pettiness. But every Renaissance stems from gardens cubbied in the texture of tyrannies. And I reach out to future friends far beyond the fickle ones who have disgraced the honor of their loyalties, for the future is full of friends. If Kirk and Spock have taught us anything (alas, an ailing Nimoy could not live up to) in figure, it is that. I reach out to that future whose citizens are puzzled at the ease with which our age betrays itself to pessimism, even at times, alas, I. What happened to that faith, they will wonder, supposedly built up in huge treasuries over the centuries, from irrepressible and irrefutable optimists staring right into the heart of overwhelming odds and seeing the seeds of triumph in the mulch of defeat? How readily we bow before the idols of doom; how little we wrestle with disheartenment. Though the Mohave withered my fruits, I gardened through all the same. I hoed in the winter of Fukushima. I weeded as

725 5th Avenue werewolfed into 1600 Pennsylvania Avenue, and out the other side. I plucked the humble raisins as my knees gave way and all the splendors of public life whistled into ghost towns. And these small but piquant treasures eked from the dry winds I place in your hands. A shriveled rose by any name may not smell quite as sweet, but I have secret perfumes stashed away with which I have impregnated these petals all the same.

      There are vulgar chum too jerkied by rough blows to appreciate confectionary, but rest assured, if I write sweetly, I'm overwriting the bitterness of pain, in whose clutches I am too often caught, and summoning desserts upon my tongue in swirling ink brings me some consolation. May it bring you some too.

      – John Landau, L.A., Year of the Plague, Year of the Crippling

grasp the novel in these times

Come then and grasp the novel in these times,
The mat of moss and lichen under roads,
The matrix in the flotsam, and the hand,
The gentle hand of Nature in her soft
Impressions moving through the wagon trails
Around the bush and tangles through which sun,
A simple twinkling peek, speaks forestries
Of evolutionary light on eyes,
Whose dream-collecting under-membranes know
Just how to read the gilded lettering .
Come drink liqueurs of wild quenching sap,
Each drop of which a decade sets its path
And plan inchoate in the starlit dark,
And feel the tender tendrils saga spins
From wisps, and know a guiding artistry,
In gossamer and mild undertones,
Weaves meekly in the tangles of our roots,
Leaving scrawled messages of wonderment
And love. Therein some reassuring sense
Of purpose in the plethora appears
But as a glimpse, and now this chapter new,
So lately all-bewildering for all
It scattered of the old familiar ways,
Reveals a hint of still-enwombed plot,
A flash of brief significance still young
And rascal-souled but promising in time,
So now the senselessness, which had not yet
Its ordering achieved, comes into light
As Monet scattering of colorfields
In which some new emergence shall its time
Behold. We mourned, for all the meaning once
The sustenance of us seemed fled and lost,
Betrayed to nothingness, but that was swipe
Of slate to clear the landscape clean for bold
Adventures unanticipated in
The blur our weeping cast. That dreaded end,
Reshuffling of purposes, was new
Embodiment of possibilities,
Delight now reembedded in the world,
Aware of sheer magnificence amidst

A seeming chaos more the fluttering
Of pageant-play of history and time.
A game is yet afoot amidst the depths,
Where death is but a strange renewal come
To awe now shedded of its fleshly husk,
In soma of the renaissance of life,
Her character an influence in heart
Of simmerings whose pattern is surprise,
A festive calendar where tragedies
At last their epilogue of laughter find.
We thought the petty cast of characters
The moment pulsed so grand, dispersal stood
Irrevocable in its emptiness,
But new ensembles still incipient
Gather amidst the rhizomes of our time,
And passing is the turning of a page,
A fresh and startling canvas life will paint.
Come now into fond realism renewed,
Reality more freshening and full,
More promising, in which tales shall be told,
Unknown as now but classic come the day.
Come open to that opening within.

wild, sprawling Russian novels

Where pain presided, you have substituted
Pleasure — all illusory and false.
Remember how excruciating all
That sad malarkey and its wounding was.
You've made it into art and given it shape,
To please, but don't forget reality
For craft : where wonder is, was misery.
Those maidens had no boundaries, no sense.
It less excited than it terrified.
Was one gigantic pageant of bullshit
You've turned into an ecstasy to make
Your past conform to what it ought have been.
You've healed the is with ought but is remains.
And what remains of that? Your memory
And dust. To them, but discards. They have not

The will for wild, sprawling Russian novels,
Full of life and varied characters,
That overspill a single simple plot,
Embracing rampant love's diversity
And juicy messiness, but chase the One,
The fleeting One who never quite arrives,
And lose the many meaningfuls that come.
We are not authors of this unfolding plot,
However we may flatter our control,
Or simulation of control, but have
A guiding hand in how we will respond
To richness in the rubbish of this life.
That makes the difference. Have courage then
In what upending shapes this dalliance
To keenly search in order to discern
The newer outlines slowly finding self
In what as yet seems meaningless and vain.
If once in picaresque of capers bold
And tragically ridiculous, you found
Some residue of promise in the pain,
Give time for slower purpose to emerge.
In ash excitement takes its time to sprout,
From fires lately made the char of land,
And more to strengthen in its sapling rise.
No more confusing than it ever was.
No less of promise in new awe than was.
The fire asks for patience in new soil.

this dirty rag

O let me leave this full, this too full head,
And vacate, drifting, far from all my cares —
I need to leave, to leap, to throw these chains
Of cluttered mind — to just be dumb a time,
To sit and smell the meadow flowers' scents,
To skate the glaciated rivers down
To snowflake-whitened dales through nippy winds.
O wash this dirty rag of feelings clean!

I ought to jester in my doddering

So boggled in the swamp, each moment slips
Away, and I play catch-up in the midst,
Bewildered and demoralized, then sprung
Into eureka, blushing. I was swift
Upon a time, I danced upon the edge,
Cavorting in exhilaration. Now
The wreckage of the tabloidage appalls;
I know not sense in newer generations'
Rages, somewhat startling and off,
Each scattered to a tangent ill-advised;
Somewhat, no doubt, a newer beauty tending.
Bafflement upends me, patterns dear
(I did not even know were dear til now!)
Dissolve, and memories hold loyalty,
Just as I hope the future holds for those
Still fresh. Capacities' uncertainty,
Once brash and bounding, now alarms and spooks.
Most times, admittedly, that spook is brief,
A flash, but while it lasts, it frights me quick.
At last, my cognitive hilarity
Recovers, and the sense returns, from out
Its migrainous nebulity and bleach;
My breathlessness, so strangled in my chest,
Gives way to breadth of breath and poetry.
I stumble — but I always was a fool;
I ought to jester in my doddering.
My simpleton comes clear from genius haze.

blood pressure

My upset changes nothing in the world.
It makes my life be miserable and vain.
If other people hold the worst of views,
Deplorable, my anger will not stop them.
And the good that I might do is less
When blood pressure impedes my happiness.

be my ecstasy

Then be my ecstasy, O future ones,
Completing me in joy, if I cannot
Before I go enjoy with you, though I
Would long to do so; take these raptures close
And sing with me: I shall be in the tune.

dilation's drops

Van Gogh my vision with dilation's drops;
The world is pleasant blur and curious,
The trees but swabs of verdant color, sky
A stretched expanse of aqua-white, the fleurs
But rainbow dalliance of cotton tufts,
And people, pleasant bobbing things that stir.
I stroll through color smear in soft of edge,
Alike some underwater creature in
Delicious slow of wet ballet, and drift;
I'm seaweed in the subtle tide and flow.
I'm in some tunneling arcade of hues,
Half-human, half-exotic, all alive.

pastry-frosting canopies of flair
image from a dream

Stone womb, its walls about, bazaar, the fluff
Of pastry-frosting canopies of flair
In parachute wind-undulation over,
Subtle cool of shadows hid from sun.

in Jubilee is your palladium

Moses.
Allow us now reflect on testaments
Of this our Exodus, proven at Sinai
In the rumbling smoke and flame. There you
Affirmed the rule of law and gave your hand
To that great constitution hammered out
By me upon the mountain with our God,
Known first and foremost by his burning hate
Of slavery and foul oppression! We
Were strangers in the land, exploited, used,
Abused, subjected to low bigotries
And levied to their treasuries of war
Against our will. He heard our plaintive cries,
Inspiring us to leave our servitude,
And seek our milk and honey. There it lies!
Across the Jordan, yonder plains. But more
Right here where justice speaks within our breasts.
For there is where the promised land finds deed
And title. Should we ever lose that law,
Not tittle nor iota but the root,
The essence, centered in our history
Of pain and terrible estrangement, all
The heritage that lies before your eyes
In meadow pastures green and hilly acres
Promising of peace and fruitfulness
Would but evaporate, give it some time.
Respect in full for what labor may yield —
Is that not what our own Creator lays
As lessons for us all, when we behold
The fruit of these his labors in this world
What crafted gem of iridescent beauty?
Work is worthy of its honored grace,
Whomever might be smith, if foreigners.
That principle of high regard to us
Was long denied; our labors went despised!
Yet they would have us honor their own smiths
Who craft the idols of our slavery,
Their despotism, claiming such as gods!
Divine? Who put their hand and law upon
Oppression in approval, give them yield
Enough of incense? They may talk their talk —
Indeed, the Pharaoh claims of lineage

Of service to the people be they low
Or widows, orphans, poor, and this is right,
With beauty in the words — but where were words
When we were slaving under spit like dogs? —
They do not walk the walk. And so we walked,
Across broad wildernesses, to this site
Of disciplines and preparations. Art,
May it the beauty of the innerscape
Reveal the laborstrengths endowed to us
With life by that great hand through whom all art
Discovers beauty — and yet I would see
What revelation of the gorgeousness
Of God, which is aught nothing more than justice
In its equity and mercy, may
Live in how it may treat the lowliest:
Let therein beauty's own sincerity
Be judged; let there morality of gods
Be put upon the highest scales to see!
The life is in the hands and what they work;
We cannot honor life where we shun work.
To everyone the duty of respect;
To everyone the honor of our love;
To all the obligation to give back;
To each their due, as God who loves the poor
Allots entitlements of righteousness.
Let these then be your rule and you'll be free.
You'll prosper in melissan streams of cream.
Seek what the God who freed you longs to teach,
And govern your behavior by that right,
Resisting every wrong that comes your way,
Within or from without — and it comes more
The powerful from priests, who wreck the right,
Perverting it while calling on its name,
Adjusting visions of divinity
To power, backing them by abject fear,
And hiring artists' caricature,
However beautiful, of this corrupt
Abomination of the right and true,
So in allurement, it may lead astray;
So in their wonderment, their liberty
Concesses to exorbitant demands
Of once-trustees now arrogant new lords.
Analogy is dangerous, betrays
The different to the similar, and tricks
The mind with subtleties whose imagery

Seduces one from sheer haecceities
Of wonder everything by hand of God
By right is, making such subject to reign;
Therefore, let not the likeness made by hand
Of anything seduce you from your path.
Let God who is the heart of Exodus,
Our Liberation, go deliberate
On which the sacred shibboleths are real,
And represent the heavens' angels; which
Are falsehoods propping up the pride of kings.
But knowing archons wish your work of hands,
And through the cultivated fears of priests
Would have you sacrifice to avatars
What you might freely share in mercy's works,
Why heed? For artistry is gift if it
May liberate, but useless as a scam
Impressing on the mind supposed worths
Of slavery! Keep you afar, I beg!
Mistaking not that this our edifice,
Yes even this, to such idolatry
In time may surely be turned too: beware!
Perhaps if you enshrine beyond all taint
Shabbat, each week, sign of that Great Shabbat
God mandated for us each fifty years,
You may stay free of all that peril, for
There is no slavery where reigns Shabbat!
But let it reign and not be but observed,
Until its holy principles pervade
The all of life in all its everywhere,
And there, the rarely spoken Eden peeks,
With promise of return, if you will heed.
This law has such a final aim in mind,
And towards such restorations tends its way,
Imperfectly and yet indelibly.
For he who festively invests his work
With rest of psalm and contemplation, finds
A unity beyond all servitude,
And in that union, this nation abides.
Free then the debts and take off locks and chains —
A clean slate every half a century,
No matter what one pledged. If it cannot
Be nudged or nagged in such a time repayed,
Forget it! Such an obligation vowed
Was foolishness and never could be kept!
Just let it go! No wergild ought to last

The whole of life or even half of it,
Forbid beyond to chain the legs of kids!
If every other law you disobey
(I beg you not!), see then you heed this one,
And all wrongs will be righted, that is sure;
But if you keep in firm obedience
The letter of the each, but to neglect
Abandon this the values of Shabbat,
Why friends and countrymen, all will be lost.
In Jubilee is your palladium.

the bullies and the bootlickers have won

Invasion of the Bodysnatchers here.
Watch brainwashed masses don red caps of woe.
"He's really helping us, he is!" At last
The stupid people have a champion.
Watch losers justify his crudity,
Ignore his prejudiced catastrophe,
Applaud his bullying as mastery,
And celebrate his rank profanity.
Whitewash it all with paranoid folklore
Some idiots who thought selves clever wrote.
Watch Antichrist pull churches to his will,
Watch faith abandoned to a fantasy,
Watch sensibility scorned as elite,
Watch facts ignored as optional to choose.
Watch values overturned but overnight.
Watch people laugh at children torn from kin.
Watch cruelty take smuggest supremacy.
Watch party line trump their morality.
They're proud of it; kindness is tyranny
To them, they're sick of their humanity.
The bullies and the bootlickers have won.

the rapists and the torturers have crowns

The rapists and the torturers have crowns
And wield the scepter now, and that's why we
The victims weep, and in our shock, hide out.

gorgeous things of awe

Someday what beauty I can channel through
Will so suffuse me, I'll deserve that look
People reserve for gorgeous things of awe,
And all attention I desire will
Be showered on me, and I'll bathe in tears
Of long-awaited joy and thankfulness.

I've earned such irresponsibility

Forlorn, come rescue me, I'm lost, proclaims
That hidden weeping boy of old in me.
I'm trapped, they've kidnapped me, they've threatened me,
They've hurt me, they have frightened me, they've touched
Where I would keep my simple purity.
Come show a friendly face. They all are mean,
They yell, they say confusing things, they flash
Their lights and cameras, they make us pose,
And force on us their dominance and filth.
Come show some eyes that vow the word escape,
That love and take me out of this lost place,
This wreckage where I weep but hopeful wait.
So long I've waited, long and ridiculed,
And disbelieved, I cower here and crouch,
And shiver, like a cornered animal.
Someday this Oliver will be redeemed.
Someday I'll melt into a world of play,
Nothing but play, abandon, sheerest joy,

An ecstasy beyond imprisoned self,
Where all is fellowship and glad delight
In endless adoration ageless youth
(Let them be old but let them be as young)
Know in their hearts for comrades unforesworn.
I've earned such irresponsibility.
I've paid my dues in coins redeemed with tears.
I'm ready for my happiness and love.
I'm ready for my fans — no critics, only
Fans and playmates, giving back to me
The pure devotion I gave through my verse.
Let laughter and communion be penance
For all I've suffered silently these years.

everyone is happy when you grin
for Elizabeth of Night

Your lips are more infectious than my own,
For mine but peddle sores, while yours spread smiles
Whenever you may show those pearly whites,
So everyone is happy when you grin.

today feels like a Messianic day

Today feels like a Messianic day,
Hope fragrant in the breeze for renaissance,
For militancy of our Nellie joy
In giggles and severity of Tim
Curry in platforms, and the play of May.
Today's a Robin Hoodish holiday,
A festival of possibility,
A day when fond utopia seems close,
Where harvests promise interlingual feasts
Of many lands and many peoples one.
Today's a day of high ideals held high,
Held proud, held unnegotiable, held strong.
Today's a day of kibbutzim and cream,

Isaiah's Zion sighing happily,
With children playing in the meadowgrass,
And every opposite in synthesis,
The King of David giving Hegel festschrift:
Neither gender neither hierarchy
Nor nationality, and earth and heaven
Joined in hieros gamos, come, partake
The wedding feast, the bridal chamber's joy!
Today once more such dreams seem obvious,
Seem evangelical and merry, poised
On gleeful epidemic, imminent,
The kairos opened out right here and now.
Excitement in anticipation as
For festivals that soon approach consumes
Deliciously my palate, and my skin
Is tongue against the ice cream of the world.
I levitate in cobalt/white Chagall,
My fumes consumed in licking Hebrew flames
That dance my aspirations to the sky.
In dusty archives of kibbutz, old zines
Of leftist heresies and hopes leap up
Into papier-mâché piñatas formed
Midair in breeze, and puppet-dance the streets
In guise of venerable old Marxist saints,
The resurrection of the dead at last.
I see their apparitions in my mind
And smile : today's a Messianic day!

that empty field I loved

That open, empty field where wheat still grew
Untended, thought but barren by such eyes
For whom commercial space alone is real,
Was better to me fallow, gone to seed,
Than teeming with the denizens of cash,
Infested with a plague of little stores.
I look upon that buzzing, bustling hive,
And see instead that empty field I loved.

but baby, stay
for Elizabeth of Night

Sometimes she goes — it's but for work — but I
Am pining as she leaves — that beautiful,
Fresh face — I need to look upon those eyes
Just one more time — just one more time — again —
Another kiss, another squeeze — you please
Me with your tossing hair — O keep it here —
My eyes are hypnotized with candy drip
Of nectar spill your eyes drop onto mine —
Come let me put that smile on your face
With eloquence of this my diving tongue
Again, before you go — I know you're late,
But baby, stay — I need you — don't you need
Just one more gush, just one more fragrant burst,
My fingers paws upon each every stretch
Of coastline wettened flesh your body peals?
Put blossoms of your pleasure in my face —
They cannot pay enough to go away
From this, now can they? Look at me, I'm cold :
No covering for this unclothéd flesh.
And yet your body's warm, could take my chill,
Yet make me shiver all the same, my dear!
You call that boss — let him know *I'm* the boss
Of these your raptures — and this job's not done!
They pay in cash — I'll pay in bills of moans,
And babe, my wallet's stuffed and longs to give
You all the cash in sighs you'll ever need!
Just stay another minute — just an hour —
Just a day — O baby stay forever!

Let quietude have reign

Let now the storm that hath us wracked begone,
We having weathered withering and angst,
And held the ramparts in the days of siege!
Let quietude its dulcet melodies
Have reign; let comfort now our madness soften,
Lulling all our scathed and sorrowed nerves.
Let us take pride in faith of steadfastness,

When all the sinews ached against the strain,
And patience drew its final spools to fray
Yet held the line if by a single thread!
Let mares and terrors of the night leave off,
Evaporating in the days of Spring,
Soon vaguer spooks of memory, then naught.
Let confidence collect from pledges earned,
From our remarkable restraints and reins
With which we set our fears in tight corset,
And kept our course through trials of our doubt.
Let strain give way to new tranquility,
And ease wherein our loves hold highest sway.
Put down the riled standards of our wrath,
Stand down, removing armories and blades,
Cease forthwith with all quarreling and strife,
Investing better trust in better peace.
Let feminine caresses soothe the heart
Still howling in its anguishes just past,
Reminding that the danger is now passed.
Come now, surrender to the fluencies
Of verdant life beyond the castle's cares,
In meadows where the children carefree play.
There gambol in the sun and grass a lad
Or lass again some lackadaisical
Moments, remembering the joys of youth,
And what it means to smile from one's heart,
No hint of peril anywhere about.
Recall your heritage of happiness,
Once granted as a grace now earned with pay.
And welcome love back to its native throne!

bubblegum yonis from Saturn's rings

I saw a goddess chewing bubblegum,
And blowing yonis bubble-mirth Chagall
From silver-stranded sand of Saturn's rings.
These dew-draped soft camellias of love
Pulsed pageant in procession out to ends
Beyond the seeing, every way, and lit
Like pointellated cream with twinkles' touch.

Each mobile womb in wandering seemed birth
A thousand million infant suns of gold,
Which stretched and yawned and spittle cast out globes
That cooled to marble blue menageries
That twirled about them in a majesty.
She winked, and wonder in my breast awoke,
A spiced pastrami sandwich in my hands,
With indigestion stirring up my thoughts!

I've lost the subtlety of struggle's good

I have forgotten in the fight my friends.
In the division and the fray I've lapsed,
My foes and my familiars come confused,
And I have lashed out everywhere to hold
The fortress, but have emptied it of love
In my fierce melees. Seeking to do right,
Strapping the armor on with discipline
To do my part for good, I've gone astray
And come apart, so my life is attack.
I've lost the subtlety of struggle's good,
Become a creature of my raging wrath,
Impatient with the prevalence of sin,
Consumed with such frustration at the state
Of morals, I have thrashed against the walls,
And thrown my head against unmoving stone.
Besides, I should not think in terms of foes,
As tempting as it is, as insolent
And stubborn in hardheartedness some are,
For it is mental war I fight for love,
Grappling with power's principalities,
To disputate to exorcise archons.
If then the lust of domination I
Give into with the demons' ire, how
Have I then exorcised where I myself
Seem too possessed? I must recover peace,
And practice triage in the culture's wreck,
Where all the foolishness we've let slip by,
And all the toppling of morals loosed

From bearings come into critical mass.
I must not strike out everywhere but choose
My battles, and consolidate the fort,
So it is well-equipped with strength of love.
The storm strikes as it will; I cannot slash
The thunder and the sleet to drive it off.
I must affirm what principles have weight,
And let the many cards fall as they may.
It is my fault, my very ignorance
Of how to wage with high decorum turns
In contest that's responsible for this.
The part that hates bullies raises a row
In the defense of underdogs, but I
Get scalded by the flames within my fire.
Let that be more light, lesser the burn.

they will play you virtuoso

This creature, soft and wet within, with furs,
Deep-felt emotions in a membranous
Papoose of nerves and senses, how
I love this beast, and how I hate to see
Its deep heart be manipulated, played,
And made naught but a pawn by demagogues!
I cherish this mammalian embrace
Of vital passions — I've no cold disdain,
But warmly mourn to see made marionette
What ought be free but all too easily
Is led astray by Machiavellians!
They calculate how you'll react and vote,
Provoking you with chosen stimuli
To eke response that serves their interests well.
You put the full piano of your heart
Out there, and they will play you virtuoso,
Touching every chord you long to sing.
Don't let skinnerians turn what is best
About you — your big heart — against yourself,
Against your larger interests for their gain,
By promising a petty gain for you.
Respect the mammal in you more than that!

love that loves delight

If there's no fun in your salvation, nope.
If there's no dance or playfulness there, nope.
If there's no cultivation of delight,
A little mischief, twinkle in the eye,
A space for solitude and company,
Festivity and song, then sorry, let
The whole world char in flames, I will not budge.
If what you offer is morosity,
Is masochism, I don't care how much
You save, how many cared for : not for me!
I dream of mutuality, of love
That loves delight, that cultivates light charm,
And through its sense of fabulous, heals all.

feather freak of fond oblivion

Too much in this dull lump of flesh for me;
I want to be naked, to be a bird,
To soar, to be adored a feather freak
Of fond oblivion in fluid sky!
I want to meet, and be transformed and held
In beauty the anonymous beholds
In me, a strutting, flitting thing of frills
And thrilling flight! Too much solidity!
Let me, pearled vapor in a flushing breeze,
Be fragrance of delight in sudden rush!
This flesh once seemed a French croissant so light,
A petty pastry full of buoyancy,
Translucent to the spirit, I could float
Through years adrift, hot air balloon in swish
Of heaven's whims in blur of colorsway!
I was no obstacle to me, but let
The sift of self and all-surrounding stuff
And wonder of the many souls perform
Its alchemy yet unimpeded by
My clumsy weight — not pounds but ponderings
Too heavy — spirit moved, and flesh but danced

In imitation, all Nijinsky: leaps!
This matter little gravity held down,
But like an astronaut upon the moon,
But bounded to the call of holy whim!
I never beat the walls with running head,
I never tripped over my very self,
I never hoped in wells of deep despair,
I never languished in a poverty
Of faith — and now my wishes flagrant lie
(For memory corrects my drifts with facts).
I ever saw quotidian details
As prison bars — let me live as a blur,
A vagary in joy's uplifting vague!
I wanted to extend menageries
Of thrilled endearment, where my piques impressed,
And in the wizardry of poetry,
A magic moment bonded hearts' delight —
Then I could fade and slink away to caves
Of wondrous shadows, like a sparkling fog,
Lesser anatomy than blushing mist,
Once more adorable in being shy,
In sinking into reticence again,
A hollow in the caverns seeking out
The sonar of the fays in faint heartbeats
Of sudden awe, or gusts of quiet calm;
And in pleroma of the nothingness,
The stillness still electric, finding lusts
Of sheer abandonment, and symphonies
Of breath never suspected! There I felt
The mischief sylphs, in all their playful love,
Twinkling, devoid of any seriousness,
But presence in the frolicking of air,
Winking at me, and blowing little puffs
Of powdered gold, from which came subtle hints
Of humble genius, simple secrets masqued
In choreography of sparkling eyes!
Therein a Scorpio sits in his spring,
His caverned aquifers beneath the frost
Of Winter-whipped ice cream the earth above,
And in laboratories of the deep,
Concocts in bubbling brews of steam his verse.
Once finished, yellowed manuscript in hand,
Just freshly inked with blueberry and peach,
He runs upstairs, outdoors, in rush and haste,
Excited, little matter time of day,

Or night, and like a Paul Revere on steed,
Calls all — right now — to wonderment and dream:
"The reveries are coming! Reveries
Are coming! Reveries are here, right now!"
Expecting for a crowd to gather 'bout,
And hush in expectation of my gifts —
A pause, a moment of suspense — and then —
I launch my divertissements of joy —
We ride a wild ride of spectacle
And gasped surprise together — stunned applause;
I bow, now blushing, quickly drinking in
The knowing moment of a magic made,
And gladness in their eyes that says success —
And even adoration — but withdraw,
As quickly as I can, to solitudes
Of Perrier or kisses, bubbles lip
To lip in loving nonchalance of sighs,
My exhibitionist exhausted, come
My fonder introvert, and let caress,
Or pages' soft caresses, vellum-smooth,
Be language of the evening! Some go
To gyms — I spurn such philistine excess
In silly regimen (to each their own!);
It's running from my self but drift to drift
Where I work out and stretch my muscle-play!
Escape is flavor of ebullience,
And effervescence is existence : let
This body be but bottle for champagne!
The spirit comes in bubbles; I would drink
That foam, and let it tickle sweetened lips!
Let bones be fluted wingspan, letting air,
Aerodynamic, sift and lift right through —
Or if this frame must be a marble block,
Then heavens, let Bernini blow his breath
Through stone, and whittle weight to brachiate
Away of leafy tracework, ramified
And almost ivory in lightness left!
I am an aviary wish on wing,
A delicate exotic feathered through
With precious colors, preening involute
But peeking, seeking knowing, loving smirks.
But now embarrassed at lavish display,
My moody rationality returned
From flagrancy of trance, I petal-fold,
And Zantedeschia my wings about,

O'Keefe-withdrawing into curtained cups
Of Yoni-crepes and draperies of flair,
With eucharist of gratitude for you.

the ecstasy of we

Ashamed. Somehow I've given privacy,
Too tired in its nauseam, a lift
Of glamor, in secret celebrity
I pose. Where is the ecstasy of we?
Have I public affairs and fetes betrayed,
In my withdrawal from the present funk,
The rotting stench of avarice and hate?
Has all the shock of sheer stupidity
And storming bigotry with all its noise,
Intending domination of the sphere
Of public discourse, bullying the fair,
And shoving out the sensitive and smart,
So ogres may in trampling delight
Their drunken wreck of festivals portend —
Forgotten me of that robust uplift
A truly forward-moving forum lends?
Where stomping, adolescent orcs are gone,
Dispersed to monster truck arenas, where
They may the clouds of dust engnash, and preen
Their belching bluster in bravado's sewers,
Far away, while those who wish to plan
Something a grander species of elan,
For everyone, may gather in to talk,
And in such talking, dream, and with their hearts
In stance of listening, hash out and share
The public business, boldly moving forth
In confidence, love of diversity
Where clash is fertile opportunity
To grow, and not a meathead plundering
Of reason! Ah, that large and public space!
That tall gazebo in the central park,
Where brass bands gather, and the orators
Delight their disputations' audience!
Where flame has sole intent to spread its light,
And difference is delight of moving on
Towards progress! Have I lost that luscious sight?

For banishment is what the zeitgeist guides,
Discretion and its valor well renowned.
For only fools made into heroes, heroes
Mocked as fools, inhabit ravaged space
Of capitols and bandwidth now the trash
Of Augean stables! Bah! This rubbish plied
From mumbling mouths' latrines is not discourse!
Botero's philistines in bloated rage,
Dull Dixie-Pakleds in a steroid rush,
The politics of meth and incel wrath,
This is! The privileged zeks, their life sold out
For General Motors' treason far away
To other lands, now stew in cesspools' reek
Of ripe resentment, oozing, wounded, gashed
And inarticulate but stomping feet!
Aim sights, raise bullseyes, let the primal scream
Find scapegoats : please give us an enemy,
Within, without, or both; with gratitude,
But give the cry, we charge — we'll own the libs,
We'll scowl at language we don't understand,
We'll sneer at well-developed souls as fags,
We'll act like bulls in temper tantrum snort
And stomp, and beat down anyone like us,
Beaten by life distorted in the hands
Of avarice — but we will praise the boss!
Our only dream ever the lottery.
Grandfathers' dreams of union gusto gone,
We'll birdbath in the aftergold of filth
And think it blessing, here's messiah come!
Charged up, mislearned in lies and petulance
Conspiracied to make some hollow sense
Of baffled bruises... O my countrymen!
You've turned the forum into rodeo,
Roman Arenas where the lions prowl,
And those whose name you've stolen cower proud,
The socialists you put upon the cross,
Who speak to you through murk of Bible verse
You praise as you discard! Your buried needs
I pity! But your routes to them are wrong!
Nothing but our catastrophe lies where
You seek! A bitter victory or two,
In melancholy you must overcome
With gloating rage, proves Pyrrhic all too soon!
You rumble and you tumble but fall down.
Take this Cassandra's speech as strophes sweet

And savor! Chimpanzees beating on cans
Never built up a nation! And you look,
Please no offense, ridiculous, good mates!
Cease now deliria and rampages.
Come to the table, where the public speaks.
Put down your guns, discard conspiracies,
Militias of new rationality
Await! Your bitterness cannot evoke
What we all need, a ripened renaissance!
Come back! The Koolaid may be syrup sweet,
But put it down. Your sober fellows wait.
How painfully in anguish we do wait!

we all must have gone mad

When all the tribe surrounds me, I feel safe,
Secure: I sink into an absent mind
And float amidst the company. But when
All go back to their separate homes, I'm sad.
I read of other countries where the folks
All live in compounds, little branchings off
Circling a courtyard, each behind some brush,
Some privacy, some company, but all
Together. All this money spent on rent
For separate homes and separate lives with us
Goes towards the common lot; and children play,
With many aunts and uncles all about
To watch, and everyone is nestled in
Amongst the rest: now that's the way to live!
This institutionalized loneliness
We celebrate with pride is mad to me,
And deeply saddening. Give me a cell,
A little hovel with my honey hid
Behind the bushes, near my rest of kin
And family friends, that's privacy enough
For me! Let me be nooked and I feel safe.
When everyone's around the dinner meal,
And afterwards a little bit, that's such
The all of life and heart, the very best,
But then they each go back, and all is glum,
Too quiet, thoughts too loud, the atmosphere
Too empty, Stoic, full of sufferance.

This individuality we prize
Is often more a burden than a gift,
A cold and isolating vacuum, less
A plerum full of solitude and grace.
That quality I best achieve amidst
The nestling. The best days of my life:
A tiny flat, the mattresses strewn out
Amongst the room, my family sprawled there
In various arrangements, close and snug,
A little reading light while they all sleep,
Then sleeping while they socialize by day.
There's nothing like it, nothing. Most don't know,
I think, in our society, this bliss.
We've made a frigid life for all of us;
I don't know why. It makes me very sad.
I think somewhere we all must have gone mad.

I lost somewhere the essence of my fun

I lost somewhere the essence of my fun;
I'm searching for it, groping in the dark.
I used to laugh, and carefree let the world
Do what it willed. But then it beat me down.
I want to heal, but often don't know how.
I do not understand what I'm to do,
The lessons of this time, how I'm to grow,
Or how to get my hands on leverage
To meet my challenges. Confusion reigns.
Often a time comes clear after it's done,
And all one can do is but muddle through,
Until one learns the ropes through fumbling.
My injured dignity rebels and balks,
Repeating I deserve much more than this,
That somehow it should all have come together
By this point — but life no guarantees
Ensures — I'm scared I've lost the gamble now,
My faith in vain — the confidence that I
Invested in another kind of life —
That living it on credit would at last

Earn dividends, and folk, seeing its worth,
Would gather, coalesce, and crystallize
The fondest of the heart's intrepid joys!
Please say that wasn't but a foolishness.
My gut and bronchials feel burned and scarred;
An anger thunders, lumbering in me.
My impulses do not align with me;
I thrash inside, a stubborn tackling
That, inarticulate, would run and roar.
I need a slam pit but I am too old
(My chiropractor would be needed then).
I had some wisdom and some inner sense
Of what the shapes to come, and how to surf,
If roughly but with confidence — yet now,
Some years of overwhelm have taken toll.
Go-get-em legs teeter like young giraffes,
And all my maps seem lost or useless now.
Prayer has a shared component to be sure —
But what that is, I'm sadly ignorant.
I must go back and find abandoned fun.
I think the loving self I want to be
Depends on it. On love depends my life.

some angel holds my feet before the line

Some thin line, all too thin, too thin, too thin
Between myself and those I'm prone to judge :
Some angel holds my feet before the line.

my most authentic me

If piety to Helter Skelter days,
Those years opened a window for a peek,
A time of revelation: my young self,
My most authentic me, who had been crushed
And smothered, now came out to play at last!
I was exuberant and vulnerable,

True to my whimsicality, no matter
What! Impeccable in my pursuit
Of impulse and its own integrity;
And petulant at times, but childlike
And brilliant : renaissance in dalliance
Of pure puer! Whoever knew me then,
Knew me at mine own genuine and core;
Whoever loved me, loved the very soul,
For heart was pulsing wet upon my sleeve.
Such windows may come only once in life;
Those who were witnesses, a precious lot,
Who saw a star in Bethlehem's night sky.
(A child was born!) If I revere my peers
From those remarkable and magic days,
Why yes, the Goth scene of the 90s was
More fabulous than can be wondered at,
But more the magic : pure naïveté,
And militant : the weight of gravitas
And dull adulthood I sloughed with contempt,
And that is wisdom! Nothing more the wise!
We were the living mockery of all
Who pledged themselves to daylight! We were freaks
In flagrancy, and that was gaiety!
We were approximate monogamists,
Carefree, careless, devoted, troubled, free,
The votaries of whimsy : in that, true.
True to ourselves, we thus were true to all.
My webbed and silken fingers on the floor,
Crawling and howling like coyote, leaps
And boundings, ruffled shirts and shadows, barks,
Given to motion with abandon, trance,
The ecstasy of letting go of all!
But more the quick, fidelity to self,
Letting my utter need for play rule all —
Accepting nothing less! No counterfeits!
My fist against the grownup world of wreck,
That twisting wreckage of a childhood dream.
Ephemeral are miracles, they fade,
And thus, lacking the permanence of things
In their quotidian banality,
Require piety if one stays true.
What better true than true to one's own child?
There piety may speak to each and all.

guard the gates of childhood

I had to guard the gates of childhood,
And let no adult in to spoil the play.
They have dispelling, wilting fingers pledged
To sanctimonious nonsense that kills them,
Guts them from within, and makes them sad.
I had to be a militant against,
And hold the fortress (early plundered) firm
But yet a few more precious years of hope.
It sounds feckless, but it was desperate
And real. The stakes were high. And really, where
Is adulthood devoid of thralldom's drag?
We are not free. The landlords run the earth,
If land or credit. Without being free,
How shall we happy maturity
Achieve? Not the success of but a few,
But genuine fruition of true growth!
Unsacrificed, our youth, which ripens well,
Which in its turning, stays true as it turns,
Becoming seasoned, but with growing bliss.
That outcome is the rarest spectacle.
Resentment rules this land as nothing else :
Indictment of the travesty of age,
A sullen resume of broken dreams.
We rage, and hardly know the why, and cry;
Our hopes we traded for the counterfeits
Of cash. What choice? The rent had to be paid.
Pay rent or revolution, that's the choice
I've always pressed, and we chose sterner rent.
For more realistic fellows realized
Revolt's course could be grim at times, but weigh
Them now upon the scales : the compromise
Has been more stern as it demanded soul
In payment. I know we must make our deals —
I have a piety towards Moses, but
In Exodus precisely, not as thralls,
Even if fleshpots are the tastier.
It's artificial to hold open gates
Of childhood — they soon will rightly close,
For we must grow, and take our challenges
And gambles — but the house is stacked against us.

in sobriety is liberty

We don't want to be told to be sober.
Yet in sobriety is liberty.
Oh, I can understand escape's fond need;
My friends, often my anguish will demand
Escape! Maturity's a burden, let
Us speak the truth as it may stand of now.
We've yet to ripen our maturity.
It's not yet civilized but all too raw
And full of rape. But only sober heads
Can grow, can hold the course, can ripen fruit.

every day of their lives

The total insecurity I feel
Living under a bigoted regime
No reasoned argument can get rid of,
Where those in power listen not to sense,
Black people live with everyday of their lives.
The fear we feel right in our deepest guts,
We liberals who work for hopeful change,
In terror at what tyrants might do next,
The total helplessness without control,
Is what the Black Lives Matter movement asked
For us to listen to, for everyday,
To drive a car or even walk the streets,
To pull a cellphone out in hotel halls,
Or even peacefully be in one's home,
Could be the last, at whim or fear of law.
This terrorist regime from which we've been
Exempted by our privilege, now comes
Upon us : liberals are the enemy.
Now we may fear the bigots as they have,
Our countrymen, who raised alarms in vain,
Not just now, but so many times of shame.
We've now been forced to solidarity
Some of us, not enough, chose earlier.

We see and feel the world as they've been forced.
And life has not been life, but running scared
And frantic underneath a calm facade.
Whenever this may pass, let's not forget
The desperation fellows have endured,
The strength of character with which they've lived,
The unbelievable patience they've shown
(Three years, and most of us are falling apart),
And learn from experts in our midst the ways
To still sing strong, to dance, to laugh with joy
When nothing is a certainty about,
And those who dominate refuse to hear.
If we wish to be great, let's be a We
At last, at last, a We, not us and them.

it wasn't theoretical

If people don't agree with me, I'm doomed,
They'll win, they'll gloat, we'll never overcome
These tyrants — and I'm terrified they've turned
My fellows with their lies and bodysnatched
Us — that's the word, what happened to me young.
Do not believe, do not believe their lies!
Hold on, hold onto the truth no matter what
Confusion they may throw into our ears!
No wonder I can be intolerant
When guts say it is time to now resist —
For no platoon without its unity
Can stand — and that's how desperate it is
For me. The very ones who reigned before
Now hold the reins. It breaks me down to tears.
Why can't you see? Why can't you see? I cry.
If people will not see the light at all,
What hope is there? I'm trapped, and no one hears.
Please get me out. Just get me out of here!
To feel that no one listens, no one cares,
Is madness. That's why I am such a jerk
When it comes to the weighty things of law
And justice, mercy, despotism — yes.
It wasn't theoretical for me.
I had to hold belief beyond the pain.
I had to cancel out their many lies,

And still, with all my little might, a half
Got through to terrify. We who've been locked
In secrecy against our will, we need
To know we'll be believed, that when the chips
Are down, our fellows hold our hands and rise
To throw off all who'd chain the vulnerable.

a boy's shalom

She slips the confines of her silky blouse
And pulls my face towards her bosom's dint,
And gently slaps her creamy mammaries
Against my gasping cheeks, and cries their name.
O ecstasy! O freedom's breath! O peace
Beyond the understanding! O serene
Security! This is an act of love.
Not of arousal, more a boy's shalom
In generosity a woman's flesh
Bestows upon the innocent at dawn.

escape this ponderous self

Oh could I, could I, fade into this morn?
Just lose the overwhelming weight of mind
To birdsong, and evaporate in cool
Of swishing breezes, gentle on the dawn?
This dawn has more a right than me to thrive.
I could escape this ponderous self and dive
In dissolution into its qualities,
The gold, white washed cerulean above,
The rhythms of the passing aeroplanes
And barking dogs, the trembling of the pines.
If oil fast unfurling on the wind
Were Moses as a phantom avatar
Who beckons in the desert dunes to wells
Of fresh oases, this my Exodus
From cluttered structure of metallic rust
Of jagged thought and oozing wounded care
Could be carefree annihilation-bliss

Unburdening my soul of baggages
And lame-dragged rubbish, dropped to open arms
To rooster-glistered polish of the dawn.

times are good

Your hand upon the thickness in my pants
Still growing as you squeeze, in viscous night
Through drowsiness and lazy happiness.
I feel your hand smiling aroused and warm
And warming me in comfort : times are good.

slosh you

Come, sleepy fuck, the brain turned down with lights,
Let me grab adipose and pull you tight,
To slosh you, dim-flourescently from glint
Of moon, upon my firm and hot intent,
The breath allegro then vivace - ah -
I grasp your animal and slip my beast
Between, and in a dumb affinity
Where flesh reveals its truth beyond the mind,
I love you as nocturnal mammals may,
With urgency and votary aplomb,
Giving you everything my instinct may,
Its full array of liquidine esprit
And gusto, whence collapsing on your thighs
And melting in your belly and your breasts.
Come hold me close, the skin our only skeins.

ten thousand steps

If then ten thousand steps I must ascend
To reach that precipice from which I fell,
From where the stars are meadowflower seas

And clouds are flaming cotton candy tufts,
From which the eagles lift wingspans to flight,
That marble columned balcony above,
However long it takes, I must ascend.
From here, deep in the dank of basements dim,
Where light descends a most impoverished pall,
The way up feels impossible at best.
How many steps, how many stairs, how long
The stairwell winding up, how many years?
These questions taunt, yet there the stairwell lies.
I must not dwell upon my tumbling fall,
From whence the maple kisses of the fays,
In veils of lumen-lingerie by breeze,
Was lost to me, and darkness swallowed up
The optics of my moods, for here I am,
And here, withholding from the stairs, I stay.
Each rung, good foot, however many left,
Is one step higher than the lowest pit,
However far from lights celestial
Above — and mind, cease now to calculate
The calendars we shall, traversing, flip —
Step on, my feet, though weary — though we dwell
Midway in dreariness and pause to sigh,
Let such our melodrama energies
Provide for further steppings! Ivory,
Which glims the spiral harpsichord I play
With nimble feet in elevatio,
Be smooth beneath my soles and guide the way
Towards Alma-Tadema's balcony
Of Silver Favourites in heights above.
Once more I'll feed the fish with tangerines
And cinnamon, with menthol melodies
Quicksilver lips deliver breathily,
And leap alike a skimming stone on ripples
Air with my outstretching spirit bird
By bird across the buoyant buoys of sky!
No more this blackstrap melancholy glut
In viscous shadows where there is no hope,
And loneliness is suffocating, thick
As flour in a silo, where my good
Has drowning been in me, as I reach up
Astringently in envy, all in vain,
My fears tormenting I'm more beast than beauty
Here, my ecstasy all strangled, shut —
No more of this! Good feet, though tired, rise!

You may be lead and saturnine in weight,
The drag of thousand sandbags tied to legs,
But work, I beg you, past our sluggardry!
Release the poundage of your weeping mopes,
That dwell upon the numbers left to us,
That sigh a river were it breath in flow
For what we lost, for what we've suffered long —
Let go the gravity of vanities
That but delays us in our purgatine
Ascent! Enough! Let stair be legionnaire
Of vast millennia of rungs, we climb!
Let years be steps in curlicue of mist,
Still we ascend! Let obfuscating fog
Be stair without the sight of what may be,
Above, below, with fear of tumbling down,
We elevate! We must! It is our life!
Dwell not too long, a little, on such tongues
Of butterflies who feed us Chardonnay
Above in sips ambrosial, or soft hands
Of passing angels feminine in grace,
Caressing as they glide to psalmodies,
Or kisses of the star-maidens in sail,
Who breathless render reverie in sighs
As siren-skiing heaven's slopes of mist!
To think of such may weigh us down with wist,
Nostalgic nippings jackal-like that tear —
Although a little glimpse, admittedly,
In tiny doses, may pass time away
More pleasantly upon this crucible
Of rungs we rise with burdened thighs of steel!
However we must climb, we must persist!
Between the smoke below and heaven's mists!

classrooms of the creekbed

Stuffed hidden in the hollow of a tree,
Where hillocks roll into the meadow grass
Down by the reeds along the riverside,
Some old and yellowed pages marked with ink
Stood ready at the draw for trembling hands
To surreptitiously withdraw and creep
Onto a raft masted to bulrushes;

There gathered in their twos and threes, they gasped
By willows' edges learning how to read.
These classrooms of the creek bed, secret schools
Of sallow sand, forbidden lecture halls
Of whispers where the mallards play and dip,
Drew cedar-skinned and scented seekers chained
In servitude who knew that literacy,
Deep in their hearts, was liberty and life.
And so, endangering that very life,
They slipped off into shadows on some excuse,
Perhaps a half an hour at a time
An easy couple Sundays of a moon,
And to the purling of the river waves,
And quacking of the ducks, and heron's call,
By whistling sweet of gentle, warding winds,
They learned the glyphs that murmured syllables,
Deciphering the majesties in print.
Perhaps that wrinkled folio contained
King James in Christ's Shakespearean accent,
Or Jefferson's best masterpiece of old,
Or if lucky, but dangerous the more,
The Liberator, penned by Garrison
And Douglas, alphabets of firebrands!
And were those middle fingers fondling
Sharp twigs to copy runes in river sand
Then let them wash away to hide their tracks,
Raised high, if hidden by the cattail hay,
Towards what lazy, greedy men presumed
To call selves masters? I would think so, yes.
There free and easy corncob pipesmoke breathed
With leisure's laughter stolen on the sly,
A snickering, a smile, and new pride.

not man's best friend

Not man's best friends if teeth on heels through swamps,
If bloodhounds in the boons hot on one's tracks,
If interlopers on the barefoot railroad,
Seeking freedom north the Dixon line.
Not soothing sounds what barks announced one's nest
Quickly assembled frightfully in tree,
Nor sniffs near sandstone hollows in the shade

Where one risked bedrooms of the bears to hide.
What quisling lickspittles in hackled fur
To partisan their loyalty to fiends
And brown-nose masters, hound humanity
In desperate searching for its freer self!
No comfort of the cabin, nor the guard
Of sweet gemutlichkeit upon the rugs,
But snarling, unrelenting savages
Of swift pursuit, canine and merciless!
More mastiffs Tartarine and Stygian,
The horrors of a Cerberean stare!
The mocking chuckles of a Fenris wolf!
Bind down that bristling lupus-cur in thongs,
That these my fetters might fall down in flight!

possums

What bristly, scraggly, silver-stranded ones,
These hissing, fang-toothed, snouted minks of night!
These pouched, oft plump and playing-dead cronies
Of midnight bushes, monstrous yet adorable!
These denizens of nibbling trash,
These bald and armadillo tailed goblins
Of snow-strewn straw and gentle, private hearts!
Though rodentine and ragamuffin, still,
They touch my heart with harmless wild will.

a meek messiah bundled babe in flesh

Sail him down the bulrushes, my friends,
A meek messiah bundled babe in flesh
Floats down the Nile to his destiny.
The child will his people set them free.
Let him come into royalty and learn
The masters' syllables, obscure arcana,
And their maps, and in his time, return:

He shall an Exodus across the reeds
Lead out, to where the manna falls as snow,
Or gentle honeydew on drifting leaves
The elves sip as the sweetest breadstuff thin.
He'll take us North across Egyptian lines,
And in the fire of the mountain, forge
A deal with the eternal in such laws
As architect our freedom in our thews.
Whenever we may run from lashes' thongs,
That bulrush babe with limestone tablets haunts
Familiarly in phantomish array,
Encouraging across the swampy fog,
His ghostly fingers beckoning, come forth!
He savors aromatic roasted skin
Braised in the equatorial sun-splay
Of Phaethon's flirting! For he married in
Our Ethiope blood-macrame, and wards
The passages across the no-man's land,
Present with us all ways to liberty.

I will fly in dreams

I'm sleeping in my purple spangled cape
Because it pleases me to drowse-escape
This banal waking weariness with spells
Of costume-fabulosity and bells
Around my ankles — I will fly in dreams,
And flee the silly world of duller schemes.

your crinkling lips

O cast us, salty Yemaya, on waves
Again, the wrinkles of your crinkling lips,
Which whisper soughing in the dribbling sands
And distant mews of circling gulls in flight,
Back to the Motherland, for from your womb
Like fish in nets we were weired up from you!
And speared like salmon in your folds of deep,

And set to dry, flayed, salted on the rack,
Where jackals slaver aft our flavored skin
To morsel us, and sinisterly sip
Our toil's blood! The heartwood of the trees
Which rusty-roasting overlook those cliffs
In whose wide basins adipose you dance,
Were stripped and malice-carved as coffin-arks
To carry us more corpses cross your tears,
Which swelled and stormed to see us kidnapped so!
Return us, Matron of the melodies
Of seals and baritones of walrus hums,
In rhythm of your jiggling bosom's foam
Across to Mauritania again!
We feed the moistness of your tissues, true,
From eyes that brine if sunset or if dawn,
But we shall lay swirled ivory conches brim
With gathered blossoms of the jungle treads,
And tender porcelain in curvature
That hiccups cream in milky dash for you
Each day, if you will find a mercy swill
Within your fathom-folds of bubbling drifts
To cradle us across your belly's dip
To where the soil of our mother's flesh
Lies fresh and flowering and waiting true.
Wise Yemaya, older than all of us,
Compose an aria called our escape.
Let us hear watersnakes and wetland fish
Upstream be whistling your latest tune,
And let us scent your brewing on the breeze!
We beg of you these boons down on our knees!

where Moses has no worth

Am I a nothing, that so easily
Am set aside? Immanuel said man
Is never means alone but ever ends,
The holiest of destinations; Buber
Says I-Thou, and not I-It remains
The right of every human being; I
Am not a thing, am not disposable!
I'm no commodity fetish for you

To favor as a toy when I prove fun,
And put away when inconvenient!
Some say when people cease to please, it's fine
To cut them off, for only inasmuch
As they may serve, may they remain your whim,
The creature of your fancy; I say this
Denies the shadow of the footprints God
Left in each human being! Namaste
Is baseline of righteous morality!
If I deny the God in fellow man,
I am an atheist more sinister
Than simple doubters, even if I hold
Myself a pietist, for I forbid
Shekinah where she touches down in men,
And though my lips speak holiness, my deeds
Deny. Do not treat me a market good,
A saleable, a tool, a manufacture,
Some inanimate utility
Produced when you may deign it pleasable,
Dismissed when difference renders frictional
Relations, hanging on the sufferance
Of caprice! That is tyranny, not friendship.
Thousand memes and mantras can't make right
A narcissistic travesty of soul.
Am I a soul? Or just a service, void
Of substance, nothing on my own, mere sign
Of value to your preferences? I'll see
Not with your lofty words, but with your deeds.
For if you easily may exile me,
I was a foreigner stripped of all rights
(Even the stranger has a call on us) —
A tolerated enemy perhaps!
These days that may be all that anyone
Remains to us, for holy matrimony's
Flimsy as our bitterness may reign,
And friendship is a pleasant sentiment
Between acquaintances, detachable
At moment's notice. Not an enemy
With treaties — those, though distant, would be rights;
More an untouchable, given permit
To serve, and when the service is all done,
Released into mere anonymity,
The sea of our familiar contempt.
We are such operants these days, but dogs
Of Pavlov, stimulus-response circuits

The buttons train impatiently to switch
At superficial lack of satisfaction.
Let me walk nowhere I have no rights,
Where Moses has no worth or deference,
Where all are strangers, and the foreigner
Is less than human. Let me go nowhere
The lawless careless treat the dignity
Of one's humanity, and let me balk
The sentiment of friends where soul is void.
It cannot be assumed these days, for law,
What's left of it, is caveat emptor,
And people are emporiums of use,
Vulgar reduction of the Benthamites.
I shall not be but thing to titillate,
The vibrator of whim's acquaintanceship.
I am a man, a sapient, a soul.
I claim the rights of every child of God.
But tell me that you are agnostic here,
And I shall nod, and be upon my way.

ten summa of the dignity of men

Ten summa of the dignity of men.
These are the principles of soulfulness.
The rights of fellows, enemies or friends.
Corrode but one of them and all will fall.
Refuse to leave contempt each one denies,
And one by one, a kingdom of disdain
Is built. How can we stand with worth without?
If even these degraded empathies
(Which speak of servants, women much the same),
To condescend to lowest fallen men,
Cannot be granted to a masculine
And fellow, what hope for the least of these,
Whom when in sluggish selfishness we rise
One rung to recognize our similars,
Receive implied in this their own demands?
These minima of due respect are least
In the Basileia of Ouranos,
But preparations, not prerequisites,
Not merits but the first of alphabets,
The practice primer of the bottom line

Below which sentiment cannot be love
(But meager love barely above the line).
If more than this is asked of us, and is,
What that we fail even this minimum?
That is a piteous descent indeed,
Where our own inhumanity defines
Our lost humanity. O wretched Fall!
Even his most diminished set of peers,
Chosen for privileges of dominance,
He stays capricious, more a snarling beast,
Friendly to friends who seem his present friends
(Perhaps if mood strikes right), but enemy
To all who cross his pleasure — and his hate,
Most times, is signed in blood of apathy —
Strangers yonder already his small pale,
But left indifferently, unless they vex,
Whence that small veil of rights (before withdrawn
As matter of his course) exposed as null,
In passion of his wrath, which strikes at will.
Divinity met us right where we were,
Incorrigible, man as wolf to man,
Subjected to a lycanthropic State,
Wherein our pettiest of dignities
Fell lower and then lower, ground in dirt,
Forgotten of ourselves, but hazy grasp
Of rights abandoned long ago in dust,
What dust we toiled in, often in chains.
We dreamed of liberty but knew it not,
Knew not its disciplines, by which the soul,
Well tilled, is kept in its fertility.
That simple wish, that cry for dignity,
Even if nebulous in ignorance,
That yearning call for something better, earned
The ear of one whose word creates the same
As liberates, unburned but full of flame,
Who hates the inhumanity of men,
But loves their every inkling, be it spark,
Of some transcendence sought in ethical
Punctilium, which Moses heeded then.
Perhaps on mountaintops was Moses who
Demanded higher, fiery in ideals,
Tempered by more compassionate divine,
Who scried the low extent of this our fall,
And cautioned, no, meet them where they kiss dirt,
For where their lips are, so their soul shall be.

And in such rugged, rough diplomacy,
The best and worst hashed out a working deal,
A humble place to start, a base from which
Further treaties of higher mien might be
Negotiated. Unfortunately,
We falter even here, at lowest rung.
But let the Sabbath its festivity
Work mirth in us to raise us to our joy,
And in that fond shalom, we may succeed
At last in these our few prerequisites.
Let dignity to all be all our law.

better listen to Charles Ives

These armchair moralists, who've never made
A thing in all their lives, go meddling in
Biographies of great creators, there
To seek with little minds salacious dirt,
And find some flaw so to invalidate
Accomplishments they never could manage,
For it takes heart and full humanity
To make a masterpiece, which flawless saints,
Who've never lived a day out of their lives,
Who've never struggled, failed, and struggled more,
Who've always kept within the proper lines,
Never experimented, also never
Made anything truly great, but passed
Their flatline lives in mediocrity!
Who would not sin must be insufferable
And dull. Excitement calls for gambles, risks,
And conflicts. He who wishes some success
Must never be afraid of failure, but
Must keep on failure after failure until
Right. But busybodies, impotent
And shallow, seek what spice they do not have
In others, relishing in secret what
They publicly condemn, and have both ways.
Grow up, you little snotty do-nothings,
And grow a pair: a life cannot be lived
Without mistakes. And if it could, there'd be
An absence of achievement. Learn respect.
A man creates beauty. Must he as well

Be perfect? Think you've got no flaws at all?
You've got some nerve to poke your tabloid nose
In private matters lost long in the past,
To satisfy your saboteur's instinct,
And play the gotcha! game while feigning pose
Of righteousness. You got your rocks off wrecking
Someone else's masterpieces. Play
The saint, but just a parasite at last,
A little leech who gloms and sucks the blood.
It's easy to tear down but to build up
Takes years of training and experience,
Trial and error ; why lay down that work
When you could just destroy and play it safe
While virtue-signaling, you feckless brat?
Your puritanical nonsense offends
Much more than petty sins, as you pretend
As if everyone did not have a youth
Of foolishness where stumbling was the way.
If you find dissonance in artists' lives,
Then youngster, better listen to Charles Ives.

the swelling mediocrity of fools

When heroes flee, and rush the gates in flock
To fly this world, the world has lost at last
Its quality. At first Astrae left,
Good conscience grieving the injustice here;
Now heroes, ever devotees of her,
Follow in her footsteps. What is left?
The swelling mediocrity of fools.

the boy who wished he was a kite

Sometimes in windstorms I would wish to throw
Myself upon the gales, and lose my mind
(But not my senses) as I blew about,
As helpless as a leaf, as hurled thick through
The undercanopies of midnight woods,
No more a person, but an elemental!

Stripped of troubled mind, controlled by drifts
Of air beyond me, not responsible
For anything, but harmless flotsam tossed
Alike a rag doll tumbling through the brakes.
I am the boy who wished he was a kite,
A Chinese lantern swaying on a string,
Who said, "Mommy, to be a boy's too hard!
This weight of thought too cumbersome and sad!
I want to be a light and aery thing,
Whose consciousness is naught but sensing drifts,
The winds this way, the winds that way, the swell
Of breeze in bloated bosom of the sail,
The freedom of the buoy bobbing in sky!
No anguish, no decisions, sole the glimpse
Of levity and motion, no more thought
Than seaweed in the currents of the sea,
This moment living in the sigh of breath,
The next, the inhalation that may come!
A kite feels nothing but simplicity,
Caress of cool or hot breath on the skin,
And carefree as the serendipity
That carries it wherever it may will!"
His mother smiled, tossling his hair,
Amused by clever silliness he showed.
But when she went to work, the boy slipped out,
Strolled into town and found the craftsman's shop
Who made the most exquisite kites of all.
"Make me from silk and balsa wood a kite
Shaped like a little boy like me, and leave
A space right in the middle like a shrine,
Where one might leave an offering, of fleurs,
Or fruit, or ruffled paper spheres. Make this
A delicate pagoda of the sky,
Wherein Taoist Immortals might drift through
Upon their breezy circuits through the clouds!"
The craftsman set at once to build this wonder,
While the boy set out to find the town's
Old pythoness, who plied her mystic trade
Out of a carved and colored vardo draped
In canopies of violet-black velour.
Surrounded by the silver green of birch,
Parked on the shoulder, by the greenwood gates
Whose vine-entwined boughs alike an arch
With hanging clusters of wisteria
Led thick into the leaf-tuxedo coats

Of ancient springs. They said she had converse
With fairies from those nymph-enchanted rills,
And even let them take her on a ride
Out to forbidden moonlit glades four times
A year for secret ecstasies of dance,
And philemati with Aeolian sprites.
She'd know just what to do. He took the steed,
The iron knocker, stallion-shaped, upon
The etched and wood stained door, and knocked two times.
A redhead in her bell-shaped sleeves and tight
Corset invited him in for some tea.
He told her what he dreamed, and she gazed on
Her sparkling sphere of quartz, and saw the way.
"You must go through these thickets to a cave
Deep in the hollows of the leafy woods,
And entering, wind down below where peeks
Alone of dappled sunlight play on walls.
There by the dripping of an unseen stream,
You'll find a silver statue of Diana,
Tarnished long from age and curling vines.
Unwrap the vines, and wash her limbs with pure,
Sweet water from the hidden stream. Then kneel,
And offer all you are to her, your heart.
Stay there in prayer as long as it may take,
Until a moonbeam strikes the statuette,
And then she will appear to manifest
In light and shimmering vapor. She will guide
You on your way." He thanked her, and at once,
Scampered into the greenwood, winding through
The hanging vines, and followed solitudes
Of cool serenity in mellow shade,
Until he reached the dewy lip of stone
That led into the cave, where shy in veils
Of shadows, dipped in alcoves, he found it,
The silver figurine, still tendril-wrapped
In grape clusters, and dingy without gleam.
With nimble lightness to the touch, he stripped
The sinuous form of coiling vines, then dropped
On hands and knees to feel out where the stream
Was flowing. He could hear it. Then he cupped
Its brisk and limpid flow so creamy-clear,
And carried it to bathe the lithely limbs.
One wipe, the silver seemed a starfield dowsed
In gleaming ebony, almost a flesh,
Until her skin was argentine and fresh.

He kneeled. "I offer this my heart to you."
In silence of the limestone's deep shalom,
Devoted, he immersed himself in faith
And innocence of eagerness and peace.
The darkness slumbered in a sapience
Of subtlety about him. Then took hold
A centeredness he'd never known, that tied
Him there magnetic to the cavern floor,
An anchor from his navel to the earth.
Time thickened up like ghee and slowed itself
To savor, pulsar rhythms of the deep,
Until tranquility itself was time,
Beyond hours or days, just smooth content.
As if the sculpture of his fondest wish
Himself, he kneeled in votary aplomb.
He opened eyes and saw a lunary
Light-javelin sail through the cavern dark,
And strike the silver Artemis with burst
Of blinding glow, whence suddenly a flash
Phantomed forth from the figurine in fog
And slowly danced, translucent ivory
With fairy dust, as if beneath the waves,
A regal sway of luminescent limbs
And mystic feminine intelligence.
The presence made for awe in but her gaze,
In ancient eyes of unfathomable love
And mystery inscrutable. Her lips
Of coalescing mist pursed then uttered,
Like zephyrs trembling in the autumn rye,
Combined with humming of cicada buzz,
Yet soft as fallen snow or dripping smooth
Of icicles, and spoke. "What is your wish?"
A tinsel-ribbon swish of fairies flew
Into the cavern, lemniscating her.
"I wish to be a kite, to give up flesh
For silk and balsa billowing in wind,
No cares, only the feel of drifting air."
"Are you entirely certain, young one?
The spell is irrevocable and firm.
Once cast, there is no chance of going back.
Your mother and your aunty and your friends,
You'd never speak with any of them again."
"But I could see them down below and wave,
And feel whatever they might feel, devoid
Of troubles, drifting in my groove of breeze."

"They'll cry and wonder, weeping for you lost."
"Such weeping is the ordinary truth
Of fragile flesh. Such is why I wish none
Of it!" "You're certain of the gravity
Of this your choice?" "I am." "Then very well.
You must give up your heart to me in tears,
So it evaporates from you. I'll grasp
That vapor, gather and compress it down
To emerald, and give your heart back stone.
You must then with all haste carry it back
To where the artisan has sleuthed from craft
A masterpiece of balsa wood and skein,
And in the little shrine, place there your heart,
The emerald. Be certain you don't drop
The crystal: that would be the end of you.
When it is safely lodged within your kite,
Take it with string outside upon a gale,
And sail it, tying then the tether round
A bough outside the forest's edge. As it
Gets higher, elevating higher up,
Your heart within it, child, you will turn
To mist, your flesh returning to my light,
And all awareness will be in the kite."
He stretched his arms and gave his heart up high,
His weeping mighty. Heart was vapored air
That steamed from out his heaving chest of woe!
She gathered then the nebula seeped out,
And pressed it down to sparkling emerald,
Shaped like a heart, and handed it to him.
He bowed, receiving it with grace, and ran
Outside the cave into the woods. A storm
Broke out, the very winds were jostling thugs
In shoving thrust, the stones jutted and bulged
To trip him, and he stumbled, once, then twice —
He ran, and then a third time tumbled forth,
The emerald heart then hurling from his hands —
With horror he feared rocks would shatter it,
And leapt from where he fell to rescue it,
His palms just barely nests before it hit
The stern and unforgiving ground. He upped
And wound his way out of those haunting woods.
He ran right past the witch's caravan,
And quickly into town to take the kite.
The artisan and prophetess both worked
For free, without the need of payment — well,

This is a fairy tale, that's how the town
Worked. Each gave all they had to give, in turn
Receiving what they needed. That's the fairy
Way! Excited, the great artisan
Unveiled a kite alike a boy with wings!
In fact, not any boy, but just like him!
He thanked him very kindly and profuse,
Then ran out to the edge of town to tie
The string up on a heightened bough, then placed
The emerald within the center shrine,
And let the kite out, up and up towards moon.
As it sailed up into the rarer air,
He felt himself more in that tossing sway,
His body wistful-thinning into mist,
Until no boy but string and flying kite.
The crickets' violins play in moonlight.
His mother wept a well of briny tears.
They never found him, thought a hungry wolf
Had gobbled him up whole. But there that kite,
It taunted, looking just like him, with grin
He sometimes got, and she recalled his wish.
"It couldn't be," she thought. "But could it be?"
Five hundred years ago that kite was flown,
And still it flies, they say, and raconteurs,
Who swore they heard the pythoness gossip,
Tell tales of how that emerald heart still beats,
The kite, shaped like the boy, a consciousness
Heard humming neath the full moon blissful tunes.
Thus ends the tale of old as they confess,
Which this wild windstorm makes me better trust.

skulking in our jingoistic caves

So crippled by superiority,
We're troglodytes who think we're number one,
While skulking in our jingoistic caves.
So trained in a distorted lens, we see
The world with disproportionate askew,
And know it not, while we still swagger, to
Chagrin of world which blushes in our place.
We've been lamed by this false perspective, so
Much so, it's years or decades to recover.

keep the curtains closed

Ah, sometimes sleep is more sultry and gorgeous
Than Marilyn or Angeline Jolie
When she, the comforter, wraps her sweet arms
Around me, dancing slow in snow-globe sea
Of fiery stars upon the drowsy deep.
Sometimes there's no celebrity's allure,
No classic star struck rapture, as her bosom
Wrapped gelatinous and smooth around me.
Who is such a fool as to refuse her?
No, this romance is my raison d'etre.
Everything else must play the second fiddle.
Keep the curtains closed some more; I am
In midst of getting a sensual autograph
From she who is the vixen of the world!

nipping at my flowery heels

A little careless, so to be carefree,
Some play upon the motley balance beam,
The puppy nipping at my flowery heels —
I disregard the worries of the world,
And sing perfume of roses on the breeze,
A dharma bum Lebowskiing on slopes
Of Lao Tse serendipity and joy.

grenade within the garden rows

Forswear the priests of Michael Eltera,
Who rhapsody illusion as the way,
And war against reality, in guise
Of faux-enlightenment, and ply their wares
Against the curiosities of youth.
Annihilationists of ordered mind,
Deep order, ancient order ripe and full,
Awakened by floral and faunal phyla,

Cradled in the blossoming of truth,
Developed in examinating all.
They are grenade within the garden rows,
Bulldozer in the forest, shrapnel mines
In wide naïveté's seekings of sooth.
Beware! Reality is nourishing.
Just open heart and all pours in in time,
Slowly, without the haste of venom brews.
It's snakes who offer venom as a gift.
These Machiavellians of balderdash,
These charlatans of hocus pocus marl
Meant to dazzle wide-eyed dupes galore
With humbug of toxicity's delights,
These devastators of cerebral law,
Are liars, all of them, and dangerous fools,
Subscribing to agendas you don't grasp.
Their literature is advertisement, trash,
Junk mail, but bait for little, stupid fish.
Reality is always more the rich
Than any second substitute at hand.
Forswear salesmen of Michael Eltera.
Delusions serve exploiters' need to cheat.
There's nothing cool, nothing at all, about
Derangement; lovely, young Rimbaud was wrong.
Take then the long path through the forest ways;
Avoid the fast lane; short roads run to hell.
The instantaneous is snake oil.
The seasons are the midwives of all good.

the way is careful and conservative

The way is careful and conservative,
Avoiding precipice and recklessness.
If life is precious, we owe it our care.
For world is wide and full of thorns and hurt.
The world eagerly offers crippling,
Which is all real, too real, and wounds can last.
Thrills seem enticing until debts are paid.
The world exacts costs for foolhardiness.

Take special care for all that's valuable.
Do not expose yourself to foolish risks.
It's well and good to play but not to bleed.
Daredevilry but violates the mean.
The theater and literature provide
The fancy with its wild thrills, no cost.
In life take caution as your loving guide.
An exploration carefully pursued,
Off all the beaten tracks, into eccentric
Ways, may edify as nothing else,
Expanding one's horizons : this is good.
But here be reasonable and wary-wise.
Peek yonder lenses picked up in your youth,
But watch your footing: don't lose common sense.
Whatever asks of you to lose your sense,
No matter what it promises, is ill.
Conventionality is wise indeed,
If one knows how to custom tailor it,
Adapting common standards to one's good.
By all means, let a wild walk through weeds
Enlighten you to ragamuffin ways,
If that's your fancy (it is mine, in fact),
And add a colored feather to your hat.
Why not? But keep your eyes about you here,
And trust your inner cautiousness all times.
That's not the same as crippling fear that spooks
One stay in private claustrophobia,
That cowering misnamed the "comfort zone".
Tiptoe a little out your plotted ways,
And render your routine a playful thing,
Full of excursions of awakening.
Listen to many views but trust your gut,
Bewaring instability of mind,
Which often guises self as novelty.
You can't take too much care in what you love.
The mountain peaks offer extraordinary
Views, but be prepared to steady gait
Against the hazards laddered crags may hold,
And never blush to foster safety first.
Hotspurs may mock, but keep your careful course.
Of course, to frolic like a gamboling lamb
Through meadows is a joy, but do not push
Your luck : where serpents roam, look where you step.
If the impetuous disdain your mode,
Allow your cultivated melody

Its true integrity, despite their scoffs.
There's many perils never worth the price.
Investigate afar if curious,
And view the archive as the accidents'
Emporium, where gathered, you may learn
In safety errors all galore and wide.
The best place for a jeopardy's in books.
Think deep on many things but hold the fort.
The wilderness may tolerate some quirks,
Some careful trust, but keep your senses smart,
Enjoying breath but eyes set to alert,
Relaxed but tuned, and moseying in grooves
That offer shelter. Nourish heart with faith,
But sharpen mind with skeptical queries,
Embracing gifts modernity offers
(Fresh liberty from superstitious fears,
Traditions fallowed from oppressiveness),
But cleaving to indigenous heartbeat.
Investigate but keep the rhythm true.
Mores of many peoples may be wise —
Pluck roses, leaving thorns; learn to respect
From referent detachment lore that's good.
Above all, trust your sense of right and wrong,
Freed from your native prejudice and hates,
Clinging to pure ethical clarity,
In all that may to injury allude.
In druthers' own domain of no concern,
Follow gemutlichkeit as you may will,
But keep your promises a minimum,
Conserving options and resilience.
Be trustworthy as much as you need trust.
Airheaded pleasures dally as you wish
If wits are wise, but hold your heartiness
To gusto that avoids such wounds of heart
As your heart shies from. Care is ever love.
You needn't be punctilious all times;
Live in the pleasant blur of your goodwill,
And where appropriate, let your hair down,
But take account the same of needs and ways.
Create a shoulder in your forward path,
To give you room to deviate a bit
Without concern, where you may hop about
And freak a little, injury to none.
Be curious of tangents : they may lead
To opportunities of marvelous

Surprise, but hold your Ariadne's thread
Throughout, to trace your way back to the road.
No need to follow recklessness, for life
Provides overabundantly the same.
To flinch and divagate is easy; hard
But worthy is to hold one's ground steadfast.
Before all else, mulch up your troth to love,
Enriching it devotedly and proved,
For it is worth the price of discipline,
And it rewards rigors with happiness,
Sudden escapes from rue in well-pledged frith.
Whatever you may love deserves attent,
And to your mother, tending you from womb,
Dishonor not her care in being rash,
But nourish all that worth she nourished first,
Returning dividends in hearty love.

see beyond our sights

We need leaders to see beyond our sights,
Not cater to our own shortsightedness;
Provide a vision past myopias.
(Too often, and to tragedy, we spurn
Utopias for our myopias.)
If we must put our shoulder to the wheel
To live the day by day, we need someone
With broader views to warn what's down the road,
Advising sacrifices in the now
To build resources for a better time,
Not panderers who tell us what we want.
That is not leadership nor statesmanship,
But foolish demagoguery and wreck.
Jobs now but oil in the clog of veins
And fire in the rivers is no boon.
Economy without ecology,
Employment without safety rules and rungs
Is not a bargain but a swindle. Yet —
It sure sounds good at first. So we are sold.
A leader paves our way through difficulties,
Never lying of the obstacles,
Not sugaring lazy avoidances,
But guiding through the straits to better seas.

a little bit of beatnik is a boon

A little bit of beatnik is a boon,
But medicine is ever in its dose,
After which it is poisonous and harms.
The dissolute cannot collect one's soul.
Take care to guard your preciousness with might.
The denizens of accidence may brag,
But little flourishes are different
Than wastrelhood. Good thew is good as gold.
There's wisdom in the beach bum's style of life,
But yet precautionaries too; full half
Of wisdom is in knowing how to sort.
I stray too far, with my patrician mien
Of course, towards the hobo-celebrants,
And their ecstatic prudence of leisure,
And yet stupidities of far extremes
Beyond the pale of sense or mastery
I scorn, as any rightfully ought do.
One's scruples are a guide worthy of trust.

broke the dirty spell

Long many years ago, I once believed
That freedom was a sacrament, and sex
Its gift of fertile joy back to the world.
Moreover, since so many sacred things
Had been reversed, mischief could be a path
To retrieve goods too hastily called bad.
This never was an attitude of harm,
But glad escape from sad repression's chains.
All things permitted, therefore we would choose
Benevolent expressions of our joy.
Because we widely could do anything,
And rules did not apply, we lived in love,
Resentment from a holding back nowhere.
For we did not inhibit but we chose,
In freedom, what we would, and thus no wrath
Had chance to lodge itself within our cells.

We smirked. We knew the secret to our mirth,
Expecting magic from our sharings-forth,
For everything was sharing. That's the key.
Erotic play was offered up for all,
If present or if not, to benefit
The circuit of world gaudium and fun.
We lived in ludic expectation; each
New moment, possibility for play.
The world applied only in half to us,
For we were kin of elves between the worlds,
And thus could not be wholly serious
On human matters; stayed reserved to laugh,
And let the folly find its working-out,
While we, fools to the world, enjoyed ourselves.
Our secret, that the world was upside down,
And many crimes were harmless, made us proud,
And gave us strength. A vast conspiracy
Of sprites unseen beneficently wished
Our synergy, which is to say, our luck.
We dared, and found new rules come to the bold,
A sloughing of the older legal skin,
Exchanged for tried and true maturity.
As liberty is holy, it should be
Revered, and used to honor sacredness.
Its gift was a responsibility,
And delegated all (in theory), we
Selected what seemed fertile and seemed best,
Making delight and curiosity
Our thew. Thus every day was fresh and new.
One never knew the magic it might bring.
We could do anything, and therefore didn't.
That was key our mystery revealed.
No longer building up a savings bank
Of envies and of broken wishes, we
Were whole and not divided; thus we chose
The best that was appropriate each time.
Since we had room for folly, we played well,
Indulgences for accidents and flaws
Reducing them to minimum extent.
If what we wished was law, what did we wish?
To celebrate, to share, and feel at one.
One person harmonized, no war within,
Open to full communion with all else.
Our tantra was, in naughtiness we turned
Those energies back towards the good of joy,

Unqlippothed them, and broke the dirty spell,
Restoring to the light the spark once trapped.
In being whole, we found our holiness,
Self-regulating yes and no for good.
This wholeness let us trust ourselves in full,
And trust as this made us to feel complete.

we tend

But every doctor has to realize
The terrible reality that he
Or she, humiliatingly, cannot,
By light of genius or of luck, save all,
And sicknesses slip through our fingers too,
No matter how we may treat them just right —
Sometimes the injury the world inflicts
Is too much — then we have to watch — and tend.
Without the hope of miracle, we tend.
Without the hope of magic cure, we tend.
Without the hubris we're enough, we tend.
We tend, we weep, we mourn, we tend again.

endurance

I'm learning endurance and how to bear the weight.
I hate it, I hate it, I hate it. Enough. Enough.
Am I yet to the top of this high hill,
Where once again I can let go and coast?

groundskeeper of Muses' shrine

Just groundskeeper of now to Muses' shrine,
The janitor, the leafblower, who prunes

The bouganvillas and wisteria.
A Levite of the marble patios,
And fountain-tender. Humbled from my rank,
My robes of hierophancy ripped from me,
My laurels in receivership, my tongue,
A tongue, no more, no oriole of gold
Who nectar-aerosols the altar's air
With fair and frolicsome encomia.
A rake, pushbroom, and pruning shears in hands,
Some modest overalls and leather boots,
A wide-brimmed hat of straw on sweating head,
Some seed in bladder for to scatter corn
Of marigolds and lupines by the paths.
Once more the ground floor, where it all begins.

deliciousness of me

Deliciousness of me in solitude,
The grandeur of my royal sleep amidst
The wind outside, the children playing, hawks
In gyrie: rich, a wealthy plenitude
Of breath communions, slumbering in peace.

my niches

I need my niches and my alcoved nooks,
My hideaways and multiple retreats,
My many people whom I rest amongst,
And find my different moods nestled about.

everywhere may be a school

No fondness such as Wordsworth felt for school —
I ever loved a campus, less a school —
The libraries and gardens, statue-strolls
And arboral fringes, the ancient bricks

Of venerable buildings before one's time —
The public sphere, the social space I loved,
And yet my education was despite,
More often, not because of class per se.
I had to seek out other points of view,
And surf electives carefully to find
Alternatives — I had to sleuth out books
Beyond the pale to find the boundaries
The far horizons sheltered, not the walls
Of a provincial mindset — that took work,
Of research, open eyes for something new,
Initiative, and long devotion — and
There were professors of unusual
And sparkling brilliance in the mix of this;
Impious not to celebrate these stars
In my astronomy, and more a lie
To feign a rugged individualism —
Which I had in part, no doubt of that —
And yet without that ample social space,
That scintillation of the gathered minds,
That intellectual coherency
At times achieved if fleeting, and that work,
That labor like a mother to her child,
Of such anonymous administrators
Silently devoted, whom we loathe
As bureaucrats, and take for granted — just
As often as our mothers — (all of this
Gathered the morphic resonance of mind) —
Without this ambient, public milieu
Embracing hundred different paths of lore
With wide, wide arms — much would have been in vain.
Perhaps within its own periphery,
Its margin-spaces it neglects most times,
Is where the magic happens. That's the point,
I think, of focus — not obsessively
To idolize the center, but to hold
Together all the fertile tangents. There
The body works its secret alchemies.
Those one foot in and one foot out invent,
And unofficially, in common space,
Or thereabouts, craft artistries of awe.
Perhaps the stronger that the center holds,
The more decentralized peripheries
Are free in their resistance to work well,
The tension taut in elasticity

Creative : solid core but with good stretch.
(For that alone, Avakian should be
A household name : that brilliant synthesis
Is world-historical fertility.)
Extension courses, independent study,
Outside groups with access to a room,
This hive of learning swarming all about
A campus may be where its best oft lies.
And where the center its circumference
Incorporates, a fountaintine cycle
Occurs. "The best of governors are so
Subtle, they almost are invisible;
When labors yield their fruit, they step aside,
And people say (with reason), this is ours."
And why so seldomly are crushes sung,
Not of an individual, but groups?
Many a class I've fallen deep in love with —
Not the syllabus but my comrades!
There's love of camaraderie beyond
The couple — and it often is a crush
More lasting, with more loyalty and faith.
There's dormitories of our deepest loves
We pine for all our lives — and flophouses
In dusty old Van Nuys where gather friends
For endless slumber parties, where a school
Of questions blossoms amidst the best of stews.
Many throw selves into the workforce once
Eighteen (often before), but seek their school
In zines, in scenes, wherever they can glean
New views and deeper knowledges and lores,
From libraries, from thrift store bookshelves, talk-shows,
Call-in AM radio or podcasts,
YouTube— and if they with critical
And thorough rigor keep their course with breadth
(Both breadth and depth are seminal), they may,
By hook or crook, rival the colleges.
Can they transcend the accidents of birth,
The narrowness of childhood doctrine,
The temptings native chauvinism brings,
The stereotypes and masks the simple buy?
Can they expand horizons around the world,
Forever learning from humanity
In thousand cultures? Many colleges
Give less. The Wizard of Oz I'll be, and say,
If you this life of curiosity

And scrutiny of all conditionings
Have vigorously pursued, then this degree,
By the authority I self-invest
By fiat of my genius, I bestow
On you — and everywhere may be a school —
If the student knows how to make it so.

working out the thorns

When shrapnel lodges in the human flesh,
It must be tortuously dug and torn out.
A social body crying with its wounds
And injuries to justice must work out
This legacy just as methodically.
It's not the fantasy of wished-for health,
But working out the thorns from out its threads
That brings forth healing. Thus we must have read
To us our history of injuries,
Our catalogue of sins, for there the ghosts,
Seeking some vindication, restless haunt
And stir up further dramas filled with strife.
Still then the ghosts with diligence and work.

still and silent beauty's divinity

If this — if for to pass through this to bliss,
A portal and an altar in this life.
Riffraff distracting us with roughened scrub,
Raw scrapes make frantic heart's naïveté
Forever seeking fresh its pure adore.
Come center me, if but a moment in
A week, this driftwood comes to ordered quartz,
A sculpture of the flotsam miming depths
Of still and silent beauty's divinity.

Bomba-bin-bal

The elfin pools of Bomba-bin-bal, replushed
From falling follicles of silken gush
Which scrub the canyon rock a polish smooth,
Revered since ancient times of primal awe.
The fairy-fluff of feather-petal snow
In shaded dawn ravines of Cottonwood,
Where morning light is gentle blizzard-Zen
In Vincent blur of shadowplay and sky.
Primeval footfall laid abridge in rope
To web emerald chasms Eucalypt
Stretching redgum and creamy rusted bark
To clouds in condescending mist of fog.
The very pockets hidden from your eyes,
In haunts of brush, obscured by effluvia,
Hold secret beauties of such elven bliss,
Awaiting naming for to sanctify.
And then, devotion of the silent heart.
If but a single tree of majesty,
If but a gentle hollow held by frogs,
If but a boulder holding resonance
Of ancient ages in its dwarven breadth,
A renaissance of simple Shinto waits,
The undiscovered sacred in our midst.

Pelosi ripping up the manuscript

Pelosi ripping up the manuscript—
Classic, eternal, poignant, full of poise
And piety to values of the Fathers,
Seething silent with prophetic sting.
That bell shall ring with bliss all of my life.

Spenglerian Cathedrals of the Wode

Elongate fluvium of xylemate
Florescence, in umbellifers of leafy
Crowns, that stretch the kinesthetic eyes
Of reaching heart through shutter-flutter flume
Of light and shadow. Rubbish in its soft
And scattered holiness of foliage
Is lull-refreshed in sprinkling rain of leaves.
Trunkate heartwood robustial in girth
Deepens chest-melodies of baritone
And peaceful solitude. Wist-corridors
That peel the webbed veils of cotyledon
Whorls with sudden breeze open wood naves,
Where ivy drapes rock-dripping shrines of springs.
The tiptoed footfall furry hooves of does —
Alerted ears in gentle quizzical —
Tender in softened crunch dampened mats yield;
Midnight allusion through the fog to stars
Unseen in breathy calls of bough-perched owls;
And distant whisper echoing through fringe
Of buckskinned beech faint squirrel-tailed chattering.
A lean-to draoithe hermitage in vines
Against cold crags abutting simpering brooks.
A phantom-shimmering in sudden beam
Of soft-exploding sun on gladed floors,
With silent elfin presence in the glow.
These forests live in depths only soul knows.

invitation improvising brings

Emergence of initiative from breasts
Of each, inspired in cooperatives
Of fleet revolt (become the paradigm
Of nascent institution), comes forth first
In invitation improvising brings,
Allowing valuation of the gush
Each soul contributes to invest their faith
In synergistic flows of full fruition.

hives of proletarian honey

No aristocracies! Fraternities
And hives of proletarian honey,
Gathered together from a thousand blooms
And dusty looms and humming mills of stone.
A willing intermesh of vigorous
Pursuits, brought forth to crystallize as one
The differential contributions all
May make. No contests of supremacy,
But willful averaging of excellence
In democratic struggle from the heart.
Community in precious votary,
Fidelity in multiple array.
These monasteries of our industry
Refresh in brotherhood creative worlds.
No vying for the highest, but the best,
The best for all and not simply for one,
A fusion in superlative of gifts,
Where all deposits sublate into gold,
The treasury of the collective wealth,
Measured in laughter, children's play, and love.

I shall not trade my liberty in vain

The strength with which it takes to hold back arms
From toppling grocery aisle merchandise,
Kicking and screaming, throwing bricks at glass
In this degraded age of bully-kings
Exhausts me. Logic dictates this is sane,
Proportional to madness all about,
And yet this slumbering electorate,
Yawning through sheer atrocity and filth,
Half-paralysed, half thralled to their strong man,
Dictate revolt, however right, means jail.
I shall not trade my liberty in vain.

Cassandra bound

Dog whistles now are kettledrums and gongs.
If fists could clench more tight, my flesh were pulp!
This age is an impossibly tough gym
Where holding down my temper's tested hard
Each day. Each day cries out, futility!
Each day cries out, monstrosity and fire!
Not Odysseus chained to the masts
To hear the sirens, but Cassandra bound,
To watch slow-motion kindling of Troy.

if sobs were dollars

If sobs were dollars, O my countrymen,
I were as rich as that man you adore.
Each *dulia* you yield, *Et tu, Brute?*
The knife seeks deeper in my shaking flesh.
O roar, O whimper, O my searing tears
That salt the wounds my fellows cruel inflict!
You worship what degrades us and divides.

Marty in the darker '85

I'm Marty in the darker '85,
No Doc and no Delorian to find.
I know deep in my heart, as Guinan does,
This timeline's not the one we're meant to live.
The petty villain, owner of hotels,
Biff Tannen, now presides over the state,
To accolades and cheap confetti. Farce
Is feature, the satirical has fled,
My mockery has face and blocs of votes.
This is phantasmagoria, not truth,
And yet it stares me clammy in the face,
Apocalypse on simmer hailed with cheers.
Dear Doc, you've disappeared. The maw of time

Has swallowed up your countenance and form.
I have not genius to invent machines,
Deus ex machina, we desperate need.
Time-stranded in the dregs of barreled time,
Molassan, drowning in despair's gathered
Coagulate! Dear Doc, but give the sign;
I flee! Give me the gigawatts, I go!
And yet I have no vehicle to leave.
Reform or revolution: only hope.
That is the only time machine of now.

not a penny in the bank

The wells of metaphor left high and dry;
I'm bankrupt, not a penny in the bank.
I've gambled all my words in vainful rage.
What more to say? Hyperbole is dead.
The spiral down has silenced all my screams.

O bugle, blow!

A war where none fight back's a massacre.
At least in war you have a chance to fight!
Shot at, you can shoot back! You don't take it!
You don't worship paralysis as peace.
You don't accept abuse as cost of life.
You don't distort your mind to love the blows.
You trounce humiliation with your fists!
If war is hell, then massacre is worse.
They both are hell, but one's got fighting chance!
When patience is the watchword of defeat,
Perhaps uncertainty of war is best.
Forgive me, O Mahatma; Krishna calls.
The Kauravas are armed upon the field.
Already lances hurl, already boots
Advance and march, already battle taunts
Are thrown about, already weapons gleam
And promise blood! Already we are downed!

They spit on us and kick us with their boots!
Diplomacy has failed! The reins have slipped!
The dogs are loose and run about at will,
Rabid and slavering for righteous blood!
The yoke with which we might have tamed these beasts
Has faltered! Now they gloat, and hurl it off!
Once more the victory of demon kings
Deridingly is claimed throughout the land!
Should proud Arjuna lay down now his bow?
Though we should hate to see the arrows fly,
And blood be pierced, should we allow them reign?
Should we stand here and watch them injure all
Morality and decency and good?
Should we allow the brutes supremacy?
Should we permit the cruel to hold the crown?
Should we just passively resist when boots
Already trample us, and chivalry
Is smudged in filthy mire of latrines?
This is no life, to watch the villains play,
To see malice cavorting in the grass,
To witness falsehood's popularity,
To hear the muffled cries while hard foes laugh!
Arjuna, lift your mighty bow and fight!
When heroes wither from the struggles, foes
Are bold, and take their savage liberties!
Now's not the time to rest! To quivers! Pinch
The feather-fronded arrows on your string!
Take up the conch, and call the righteous troops
To field! No time to waste! O bugle, blow!

the great, abiding works

The monasteries carried on the Word
While armies of barbarians marched by,
While despots took the throne and waged their wars,
While persecution flourished in the land,
And stood their ground while standing well apart.
They gave admonishments for rampant sins,
And kept the words of prophets in their ears.
While ancient libraries were set aflame,
They sat in their scriptoriums and wrote,
Preserving manuscripts and writing more.

While devils danced in parliaments, they sang
The holy psalms of angels every day,
And fed and clothed the poor nobody cared.
The Hutterites, another kind of monk,
Withstood religious inquisitions, fled
To farmlands in remote and distant lands,
And lived communal lives of charity.
While wars exploded all around, they kept
The faith and gave the Gospel amity
In hinterlands where cared each one for all.
While Hitler ravaged shtetls of the Pale,
Lindgren conceived, developed and gave birth
To Pippi Longstockings, while Tolkien wrote
Lord of the Rings, a masterpiece in prose.
While all the world assailed Korea, Lewis
Wrote The Tales of Narnia. While troops
Dropped napalm on the fields of Vietnam,
Harnick and Bock, at the piano, wrote
A Fiddler On The Roof. In hermitage,
The great, abiding works that resurrect
The spirit in despair have all been wrought.
Pull back the camera then from present woe,
From awful folly, from the spectacle
Of imbecile Sieg Heils, and retreat
To forests of the Druid eremites,
To contemplate eternities of love
And wonderment amidst the cruelties
Growing around us; fade back from this time,
This single slice of film, and deepen plumb
Beneath the char and ash to aquifers.

make room for others

I've had my hangovers, from sheer despair —
I've never hit the bottle (save Perrier) —
Emotions can be raucous in this life;
The flesh is weak; the spirit, powerful,
Oft rages through the cells and wreaks its rends.
Then I am hollow with a headache, floored.
Don't let the drunkards sell on you their shtick
That they're the only ones with hangovers,
Who've had it rough. You live enough, you bleed.

And while I lay there feeling wrecked, I've not
The irresponsible abandon drink
Confers experienced; each every trance
I've had to earn, I've had to work for hard,
I've had to labor through the thick of night.
So if my mercy runs a little lean
For sob stories whining out from their cups,
For folk who almost always get a break,
(For everyone has pity on a drunk),
Forgive me: there are many more who don't
Imbibe, and in despair, do not inflict,
But hold on tight to kindness of restraint.
I won't romanticize the wreck of lives
As something glorious. It's not. It's not.
So many of us have it really hard,
But in our tatters, ragged, keep on track.
Oh sure, we stray and sway, but come right back.
There comes a point where to indulge is weak,
Where cry me babies have to stop and think
Of others, not themselves, and buckle up.
The barflies take up too much pity time.
Make room for others who need soothing hands.

there a thousand sins may be redeemed

The world is fucked and jagged, cannibal
And nuts, and every culture is a cult,
Deserving rank contempt and little else—
Except where some exceptionalities
Bring forth a beauty from the soul called love,
And there a thousand sins may be redeemed.

only the future

There is no Shangri-Law found in the past;
Only the future holds hope of such hopes.
The past, where we project, will disappoint.

It's in the heart; and needing it to be,
We mandate it already has been here.
But keep that vague, if you would nurture it.
Too close a lens exposes normal men,
And all the saddening rigmarole of fools.
Perhaps that verdict, though, convinces you,
It is the future holding all our hopes.

a thousand different chains

A thousand variations on a flaw.
Well, whoopteedoo! Culture's diversity?
A thousand different chains of women's will.
A thousand different ways to press down gays.
Who gives a fuck for such diversity?
It's one big trash bin full of patriarchy.
Buh-bye, rubbish : down the bin you go.

to compost soil

The moment you perceive the purity
Of old traditions was already crap,
You'll know their value was to compost soil
For the Messianic Age alone.

my machismo wars on yours

Here's notice : my machismo wars on yours,
To first defeat you, then defeat my own.
My war on men and all they've meant til now
Will never end until it all is done.

our substance is more of love than flesh

Adam.
How then, such delicacies all about
Us, Dearest Eve? Come taste this flower: soft
And smooth, like flavored cheese! Or try this fruit,
Flavor of roast Mignon peppered with sage!
Observe these broad banana leaves, that grow
Cottony tuft and padded fur for us,
A perfect bed for us to lay our heads.
Consider then these vines high in the trees,
How they exude a mist that gently falls,
And keeps the weather temperate and cool.
And when the day has ripened into dusk,
Notice the subtle musk the roses breathe,
That set a tender somnolence in air,
And how the breezes tickling the rills,
Like soughing distant bells that purring chime,
Do seem to lullaby us. Could all this
Have sprung up on its own, or have a cause?
It seems as if were made for us somehow.

Eve.
O Adam, do you not within your heart
Feel brimming there a presence not our own,
A kind of voice without a voice whose words
Are loving feelings, guidances of pulse?
I often feel this "more than me" within.
When I behold the little fireflies
Above in oceanic ebony
Of evening, or when I close my eyes
Upon some cliff, my hair zephyred by breeze,
Or when the tenderness touches me quick
Of some petite and winged bird, or haps
The silence in a den of foliage
Of doe eyes looking back at me, I feel
A part of something so voluminous,
So all-embracing, and so stolid kind,
I cannot help but feel that is our source.

Adam.
Your words speak truth that my suspicions share.

I wonder if we may open our hearts
Somehow we might more clearly hear the words
This presence whispers. Then the mysteries
About us might come clear!

Eve.
Perhaps. Or else
Even mysterious by greater depth
And grandeur more than we have felt might speak.

Adam.
Sometimes I dream. It seems a memory,
So vague and yet so true. I seem to feel
Warm hands about me, gathering me up,
As if from formless mud, and shaping me,
So lovingly and elegantly, smooth
And lithe, with limbs and organs all complete.
And then, while hands still hold me, why, it feels
Some breath breathes into me some vital spark,
And my eyes open. Then I am awake!
It puzzles me. It seems so real, and yet —

Eve.
And I, I too, have reminiscing dream.
As when we blend our loving limbs and flesh,
But more, more intimate, more mixed in breadth,
More merged, two presences in one expanse,
As if I once entirely were one
With you, inside of you, and you in me.
This cannot be a fancy; it has truth
About it resonating everywhere!
I trust it. Yes, I know we once were soul
Of soul as flesh of flesh. And then some hands,
Just as you say, though feeling like the shafts
Of light warm sun through gold dust of the day
Sends down through forest canopies, lift me,
And pull me as an eagerness aroused
Up out of us, now out of you alone,
And I emerge! Resting in ecstasy.
Your marveling, adoring eyes on me.
And then I wake. But Adam, this is true!

Adam.
What hands then, like our own, did shape these hands?
What fingers, larger than our own, did lend

The slenderness and countenance of form
To ours, I wonder? Must that not be like
The two of us when we were merged as one,
Yet more celestial — made from the clouds
Of milk we see dotting the heavens' breadth
When we look up at night? In fact, my love,
Could that perlaceous vertebrae above,
Be backbone of the grandeur of that one
Who shaped us? Could the body of those hands
Be all the heavens in their majesty?

Eve.
And earth as well. Perhaps like us, once joined,
Then lifted up and separate to awe,
The each upon the other, like we do.

Adam.
Then we are made in likes of paradigm
Of some empyreal presence, who plays
Between abysms with sweet eyes of love,
One to the other, and then back again.

Eve.
Our substance then is more of love than flesh,
If such immense infinity of love
Shaped us to be their humble miniatures.

Adam.
Perhaps the stars then are their children, winged
Like birds, and fluttering about their nest,
As we observe the flighty things by Spring
Give forth to young, that in their time, take wing!

Eve.
It is delight to think so, and may be.

Adam.
I must confess, perhaps I recognize
Of now — some calling that I've felt — is that
Voice you have spoken of inside of us!
If I could translate what those feelings speak,
They've said, explore! Know all this world! Behold
The beasts and animals of every kind,
And seek them out to know them intimately,
Giving each kind its name! I've felt that science

In my breast, the holy urge to know
And name, and give the poetry of verse
To genealogy of creatures! Ah,
I sense that one who shaped us wishes us
To wonder, and to that end, to pursue
What knowledges the beings of this world
Enfold within their very way of life and flesh!
We may induct from each and every
Some larger truths, that from the little crumbs
Of clues may form a grander paradigm!
Perhaps there are eternities in each,
That in humility of finite form
And grasping, carve in cracks and folds some glyphs
We might decipher, and from such deep runes,
Discern more of the shape of that which shapes!
If we could draw out from the modest ones
About us what their quality and essence
Is, in time, the larger pattern might
Come clear! But if to wonder, then, to praise...
Perhaps the names we might to every beast
And winged thing and crawling scitterer
Bestow are pearls upon the necklace we
Might garland round the neck of that which loves,
The very strophes of what psalms it worths!
Then all of us are choir in its song.

Eve.
Such good beyond all good ought have a name
Before all others, don't you think, my love?

Adam.
It may be in the course of things we come
To gradually uncover many names,
But you are right, that which is good has worth,
And ought be named, in order to be praised.
It being summum of our bonum, good
Of good and love of love, for now, let us
Simply call it our God, which is to say,
The height and sum of all we know as Good!

Eve.
It vibrates in my breast. This name gives proof
To intuition's deep hypothesis
My faith has always held! It is a truth!

Adam.
Then let us vow, dear Eve, that we will be
The guardians of love's allegiance
Within us and without, the votaries
Of this our God, the greatest height of good
That speaks within our hearts and all about,
In every name we might give to each kind!
There must be purpose here, so let us lend
Our loyalties to listening with depth.
In time, the subtle whisperings come words;
From words, perhaps, more certain testaments.

Eve.
I swear upon it — but I always have.

Adam.
I too avow the measure in my dreams
And all circumferent about our grove!
From marshy depths of lotus-blooming ponds,
To verdant-bearded boughs above our heads;
From shadows of gullied ravines below,
To mountain cliffs where gentle snow
Is frost on peaks from which the heavens beam,
I swear my loyalty and faith to GOD!

Eve.
May He and She forever bless our lives.

secret weapons

The women I used to date were secret weapons,
Dash of sass and spite, and bird held high
To everyone and everything, bright stars
And firecrackers, clawed, and formidable —
Strange and unapologetically
Alternative — we could do anything.
Our play embraced defiant masquerades,
Flashes of kink, whimsical fantasies.
I dated witches, and I loved them all.
I had a mystery I cherished then,
A taste of Sabbat in their mischief eyes,
A space of mutiny, insolent spunk,

Forbidden joy, in flouting of the norm.
A hidden satisfaction and source of pride.
When we but lingerie and fetish gear
Over our leotards and tights attired,
Black eyeliner to eyes and cheeks and lips,
We secretly reserved as Halloween
Each night and every day, and that was pluck.
One saw the Danny Elfman grin in each
Sly smirk and twinkle of the leering eyes.
Life was a spectacle of surrealist play,
Of sudden camp in public space, of spaz,
Life-vitalizing spaz, and being weird
As celebration of the spirit's dance!
Life was an opportunity for masks,
For pranks, for breaking into stores in drag
And starting scenes of quandary and punk,
As quickly disappearing with a laugh!
Life was alive, and radically silly,
A challenge to authority and laws,
But most of all routine — we broke that up!
We broke the ice that ever chokes the fire
If you don't stand up and raise your fist.
To ever put your fist down is to die.

out of a ship

We carved ourselves a home out of a ship
That beached upon the sands; on rolling logs,
We dragged it up the banks and into town.
Once there, we tipped it tilted on its side,
Diagonal and strange, with rooms awry.
We pitched it turpentine and varnish, lit
Incense of aromatic shrubbery
To honor all the hardwood trees whose flesh
Now knotted dressed the decks and laid the planks.
We excavated carpentry within
The middle of the ship, to open out
A fantastic amphitheater expanse,
As tall as broad, majestic-canyonate.
We scoured factory dumpsters for their scrap,
Took hammers to it, pounded sculptuous tweaks,
Adorned the walls with this metal array,

And sawed out windows shaped just like the shards
Our jackboots pounced upon in alleyways
Behind the dusty glass warehouses. By
Collage of jagged glass jigsawed in oak,
We gathered potted plants to catch the sun,
Inviting whores to make us macrame
To hang upon the walls; they lived there free,
Gave up the brothel, some as engineers,
And others electricians. Many whores
Became quite skilled at power-saws and lathes,
And laid foundations we had bulldozed there
From heaps of soil. Digging out the floors
In places, Betties planted junipers
And tall madrones that stretched towards skylights, thus
An atrium of sorts. The gathered clay,
Besides a potting soil for the trees,
Formed buttresses to hold our wobbly ship
In angular impossibility
That tickled us and made our gonads glad.
We scavenged most unlikely junk, and hung
It up as mobiles, placed wood mallets near,
Encouraging the each to gong such chimes
Percussively at opportunity.
We laid down orange carpet, patchworked neat
From Carpeteria's discarded scraps,
And in the living room, a playground grew,
Where children played and adults frolicked, doves
And parrots flew through high aluminum
Looped most artistically. Collecting sacks
Of concrete grannies in the neighborhood
Had set aside from gardens, we began
To build inside a set of monoliths
And brutalist statues, atop which chaps
Might fish in coy-ponds planted down below,
The lotus pads in fragrant taciturn
Upon the surface, sounds of croaking frogs,
With pithy wood and bulk cement about
Absorbing sounds with meditative hush.
Of course, in unexpected places, we
Built everywhere the most astounding lofts,
With ladders, ropes, and bridges across the gaps,
And leading up to odd and alcoved space.
We lived in there, with habitrails and goats
And gunnysacks for near three hundred years,
And never aged for all the sex we had.

We liked good food and made gourmet our lives,
Inventing Velcro so to make a heap
Of cash we gnashed inside our teeth and tore
To make expensive papier-mâché and lay
The planks of dormitories with the splay
Of wallpaper of centerfolds of Grant
And Franklin, pasting up old catalogues
Depicting Paris maids in petticoats
So Ben could play the ladies' man again.
Kool and the Gang was always played within,
On one speaker, John Cage the opposite.
We piped salt water from the beach to us,
And spritzered it against immense of fans,
To turbine brine of breeze in nostrils proud.
We always wore three linen undercoats,
Ensuring frills were always part of our lives.
And that is it. I won't tell you no more.

Goddamn, this pig

     A pig is actually stuck in my ass right now. It ran in there from the barnyard as it was absentmindedly chewing hay and trying to get laid by a sow, and so careless, it fell into my ass while I was sleeping. I wasn't even peeping my eyes were so closed. I sleep without my clothes in case a floozy trouncing by might fancy me and have her filly way with me by boiled chocolate in mugs and whoopie on the dandelions. Goddamn, this pig, its snouts and scratchy hooves protruding from my puckered anus, crap, goddamn! It's hard to walk, it's hard to skip just like a milkmaid in her skirts, I tip and topple, the colossal hog knocking me about and sniffing my hemorrhoids with majestic bad breath! Fuck! I'm a cripple! Crippled by a rectal hog that's chewing chicory right by the road! Hey, hog, I've got to go, what's up? Stop snorting and cavorting, pig, and find a way to pop out of that little puff my nether rose-carnation. Don't you want to fuck, pig? Then find your sow and get your caboose out of my bottom barn, I need that ass for softness on my seat! Dear Lord, a bestial birth! That's right, you squeal, now hear my stern appeal and you vamoose! Can you believe the things I go through?

pissing gently on the ivory

And pissing gently on the ivory
Of Steinway keys, delicious slurping sounds
Of dripping ricochet of wet ammonia.

your awful arms

I hate my arms, distracting from my dolphin
Dives, I flip about without my limbs;
I hate my limbs. I'm inchworm undulation.
Arms are pussies. One should roll about.
You're traitors, you, who use your awful arms.
Your awful, awful, awful, awful arms.

I huddle broken bones in hovels

I'm much diminished from what used to be,
Nijinsky who in leaping cliff to cliff,
Fell headlong, broke and crumpled, all in casts.
I'm crippled now, but limping to my joy.
I've known the sweetest Pixie-sticks elan
And ecstasy, all pink and tart and blue,
The mountain goat suspense in air of glee!
But now I huddle broken bones in hovels,
Crabby, thrashing, bitter, choked for air.
And crying "leave me here to die!", I drag
My gloomy giver-up through trackless paths
And thorns and barrenscapes of weary waste,
Protesting all the time, back towards my home,
Ananda, realm of bliss, the seat of soul.
How many thousand miles yet of road?
I do not know. How could we fall so far
Down mountain heights through bruising boulders' way
To dales below, impaled on pines? Because
We were a daredevil who braved the skies
On tippytoe and drank ambrosial scents
As nutriment! Our Hinayana felled

By boyish pride and virtuoso wings,
Disaster made the Bodhisattva path
A mandatory one, thrown back to dirt
And soil, there to work my karma out
In pain, and endless whining, just like all
The rest! O patience! Once you were a wide
Expanse, but asthma's made you miniature,
A little handkerchief or napkin! Hope
Is humpbacked, but I'll push this sorry Joe
Through marshlands and the alpine desert ways
Back towards the frolic-lands we treasured so.
(I always was a goof! I never was
As smooth and cool as fancy edits time!
And yet I had my moments! Wow, what flights!
And most of all, a peace, now absentee —
Perhaps it's on sabbatical.) For now,
I play the part, the part of me, one kind
And thoughtful, plentifully benevolent
And carefree (truth be told, the former sprout
Almost entirely from latter), light
And cheerful, when inside too oft I'm but
A snarling badger, poised to pounce and rend,
A feisty, nasty thing that's hardly me.
(Hoping I play the part, and it returns,
In all its spontaneity and truth.)
Where is my joy? I have to work it back.
Ah Purgatorio, with sterner grace
Than I am used to, give me still the chance
Though I may groan! And teach me to endure,
I, who long learned to give up on a fluke,
Who must now learn to trek the longer routes,
Or waste away in wastelands that I loathe.
I've always run, but now I must limp back.

the diplomats of night

Upon a time, when life was innocent,
Benevolence and mystery were friends,
And witches were the diplomats of night,
Who made their mystic treaties with all wights,
Like Mother Earth once did in dawn of time.
The crunch of leaf and twig on forest floor

Was in their every step, and scent of pine
And juniper was in their hair, and herbs
Were alphabet of healing teas they used.
They trusted mild remedies as strong,
Continued over time, and venom spurned.
Their ecstasies alone took them to flight,
Where at the Sabbat, they might rise and soar;
They needed no cheap substitutes of dwale.
Care was their second nature, though carefree,
And thought the consequences out to spells,
Ensuring none were harmed, and that was law,
Not trifle to be mocked or set aside.
They didn't take harm as more powerful,
But good was potent, even in small dose.
They had no curiosity for ill,
But only wonder, which took up their time.
Their magic was a way to bring this world
More marvel, possibility, and joy.
They wouldn't have bothered with the cynical
Idea that power needs to win or lose;
For them, a spell was positive in sum.
These witches were more powerful than now,
Precisely for their lack of degradation,
Their disinterest and their roll of eyes
At what degenerates find interesting
In evil. That was low, too low for them.
Instead, identifying self with life,
And all the guardians of nature, low
And high, they sought to turn experience
To celebration in grand synergy!
That was the Wicca I knew in those days,
With strength and innocence of does and deer,
With zen of forest glades within the heart,
With love in sensuality and trust,
A thousand miles from the smallest curse.
That way of deep integrity is now
Utterly ridiculed by dastards; good,
Keep mocking: it will keep it hid and pure.
While fallen fools pursue their greedy lusts
And think their wisdom's in malevolence,
The older pythonesses hold their ground,
Unseen, unheeded, stronger than these thralls
In shameful worship of their lowest urge.
Instead, they love the Master of the Beasts,
And his lumescent Mistress, for they rise

In mastery above all beastliness,
The tantra in their instincts coming clear.
They count serenity a greater strength,
And solitude the power to commune.
When made the butt of jokes for being soft,
For knowing strength of hares in Easter Springs
(Unstoppable, verdant fertility!),
They simply smile demurely, go their way,
Dismissed, and past such veils, they work their good.
Invisible, and happily, they thrive.

currents of the widest breath

Let me this tired self escape again,
O Lord; release me from this prisonage
Of habitude! Too much these neurons run
Alike a fuse! Unwind me from the knots
My life too tight has tied! I need to breathe!
Many a time this life seems suffocate,
And I would run free in the interstice,
And roam, on currents of the widest breath!

an angel of a man

Often I sleep — perhaps a little bite —
And when I wake, for fleeting moments, all
My troubles vanish like a nightmare's flash,
And I'm restored to my integrity,
Factory settings of identity
And joy before the traumas muddled me,
Before the nursery school, before the Don,
Before love's melees left me wrecked in waste.
I think, if this is who I really am,
Beneath the asthma and the hopelessness,
Why could it not come naturally to me,
So effortlessly, just to be myself,
To feel like me, to feel as good as I
Mandate myself to still behave despite?
If only such a reset button were,

I'm sure I were an angel of a man.

soft lily besos
for Elizabeth of Night

Wet roses in the dark — your lips on me,
Soft lily besos on my back and hips —
In dreaminess I feel your hand now slip
A little forward in its reaching, grasps
What panting in my ear portends. Your thirst
Exudes through fingertips, and sensual,
The kisses keep on coming on my back.
I murmur in a sleepy pleasure's groan,
And let your magic have its vixen way.
I know it's you, here in the sultry dark,
For no one else would I let wake my sleep
As this, with tender gropings of the night,
Confirming ever more how much I love you.

just give it time

It takes some time to come to clarity,
Pain shoved down deep beyond our memory.
Sometimes it's years before the tangles thread,
Before the jigsaw pieces can be read.
Before which, mixed confusion reigns in haze,
As different sides struggle way through the maze.
Debate, but at the level of one's nerves,
Half-conscious; new emergences throw curves,
Written in inked anxiety or awe,
Intrigues that leave their hints and clues in craw.
Horrors that yet still fascinate afar,
To draw one in, so reminiscings jar.
Take care, come not too close to this ill groove;
Keep conscience foremost, and it always proves
The better over muddle and its draw.
Not flotsam, but your soul, is your true law.
Keep distance, though you cry, for life is more
Than wounds, and you are more than any sore.

Just give it time; it takes time for to feel.
Just give it time. It takes time. You will heal.

still tiptoe in the willows and sycamores

What venison? What grits of acorn gruel?
What prickly pads fried on the grill? What fruits,
So watermelon-fresca, from the cactus?
Shadow-domes of tule thatched with grass,
Through which the wind and blades of sunlight twirl
In lazy afternoon, above the furs
Of rabbits blanket-twined upon the beds.
How many soft eternities as this
Abide in fragrant rose of sunset still?
Cup ear to asphalt: underneath, the crunch
Of yucca sandals on the oak leaf paths.
The Hahamonga yet inhabit us,
In echo, in the interstitial breath.
Beneath the boulevards are ancient trails.
Stravaig the shade of cool Arroyo paths,
And old eternities thought obsolete
Still tiptoe in the willows and sycamores.

Our Lady of the Petal-Paths

She strips Rosaceae of her petal-flesh,
So wet, so pink-pearlescent, so O'Keefe
In fragrant tenderness, to ruffle-flesh
Her pride of promenades, in all their shapes
And flagrant glory, as they hover-ski
Down Colorado in the cool of morn,
Each dawning of the newborn freshest year.
The meadows wide as far as eyes can see,
Where blooming whorls of precious buds are left
Bald remnants of their ripeness, to enchant
The petal-feather epidermis floats,
Like Carnival extravaganza, wear,

When sauntering the crowded avenues
Beneath arid, austere San Gabriels.
Where once the wild grape, with purple pearls
Necklaced the roughage of the meadow-grass,
And strutted, vining, twining, through the oaks;
Where then the sun's plump lips kissed orange groves,
Whose juice was liquid from the honey-dusk,
And rows and rows of orchards held up skies,
Our Lady of the Petal-Paths now drifts,
Her majesty in campy gaiety
Of January. Fond Ojibwa trills
Of syllables; by any other name!

flirts and champagne socialists

City of Haute Aristocrats and Flirts,
And Champagne Socialists immersed in art;
Town of Bohemians and Aunty Mames
Proud of their Craftsman elegance and pith.
Los Angeles' socialite sister,
Angel of Glamor, tucked into her nook
Of alders and of willows. Rustic Louvre
And coy-pond garden flaneuries and haunts,
She fancies her Mount Wilson a Parnassus,
And, a diva in her Deco's, she
Cavorts theatrical alike a Muse.
Athena nearby tends her votaries
Who gather in lyceums of high tech,
And play their Eulenspiegel crop of pranks,
While Daedalus, propulsing wings to skies,
Gathers his modern tributants and priests.
Call her the Clio of the winged fays
Who flit about the Queen of Yangna's throne;
She knows her heritage, and so proclaims,
La Ciudas de Los Arroyos, ah!

by one's weariness alone

Come reenchant me; neither old nor young
By age, but by one's weariness alone!
When magic crackles still at fingertips,
The elderly are youth, but youth too dulled
By disappointment yet are elderly.
When world has lost its charms, I then am old.
When every cell sparks with vitality,
And every thing's potential jumps at me,
I'm young, I'm fresh, and I believe again.
Winter has stripped my boughs clean of their leaves;
I'm grey and barren. Bring the Spring again!

aloof

Let me be best that I can be : aloof.
I lift up from common concern and angst.
Give me the classical and very best.
Let us remove from base and petty things.
My charm is in my higher reach and grasp.

unfamiliar wakened ones

I would not be a wheel vertiginous
With personalities rotating up
And down into the water, suffocate,
Then up again and gasping, caprice crowned,
But be the circle in entirety,
Not mere roulette but some consistency.
To wake and be inhabited anew
By unfamiliar wakened ones feels off.
It's spastic to have drastic flip flops so.
Let a benevolent consensus rule.

ten-sided dice on fingernails

Paul Lynde and Groucho Marx bantering high
And snappy with Tim Curry in my brain
As I slop peaches off my hairy chest
And whistle nursery rhymes in double time.
Groucho is traipsing in his lengthened tails
And shaking ash, while Paul sneers in his gin
And snickers; Frankenfurter outdoes Mick
In strutting, and the peaches get sweeter.
I lick coconut cream from fingertips,
While Phyllis Diller styles up my hair.
There's nothing serious with wiseacres
About me, and that keeps me glad and sane.
Fruit leather cuffs like Wonder Woman's wrists;
At times I tear them sour with my teeth.
Tim Curry steals the lengthened cigarette
From Phyllis, blowing smoke rings from his lips,
As I wear macrame with thousand eggs
In nooks and crannies, whence they hatch at once,
Hundreds of chicklets flying loose from me;
Paul smirks at feathers everywhere about.
I spin ten-sided dice on fingernails,
Chewing my bubblegum and pop rocks mix.

jackrabbit's slippers

Jackrabbit's slippers on the glockenspiel
Of moon — now hear the ivory chime in tune
With tinkles from his bunny toes — he kicks,
And snow is fur blown loose by gusting wind.
He mallets sky's pearlescent-pewter gong,
And quicksilver is radiate in ripples,
Crashing missiles made of icicles
Exuded from the smiling, smirking teeth
Of lunatic and glowing gonzo moon!
Old rabbit in contraption made of flukes
And spinning wood discarded from a dump
Dons goggles, plunks out ragtime on the keys
Of soft lumescent harpsichord of night;
The notes like fleeing crickets leap out loose,

And fall as punctuation marks to earth.
Mosquitoes ski on frozen glass of lake,
And sip ice cream through soda straws and blush,
Flirtation lively in their buzzing grins;
They munch on popcorn made of salted snow,
And spit out Pellegrino geyser-high
While high-fiving each other's many hands.
A moose bathes clumsily and skinnydips
In lewdity of nudity of moon,
And basks in purling slurps of buttermilk,
While tipsy swaying back and brandy forth.
The zany fin de siecle creature-choir
Charlestons through booty-shaking night,
The mallards and the foxes getting down,
The possums tossing alternate by tails
Along tree branches, swinging seesaw rubes,
While nightingales and cats sing out of tune.
The ants, amphetamined by nippy night,
Form trains and chug along while breathing fog
And giving rides to spiders in tuxedos,
Little skates petite on feet their tracks.
A Clydesdale plays the stand up bass with hooves;
An anteater its snout plays clarinet;
A goose plucks webs strung needle-tree to tree
Alike a banjo with its soft-webbed feet,
And smokes cigars straight from Havana's shores,
While ogling up swan-ladies' lingerie.
They giggle silent bubbles on the lake.
These past times pass the time til smiling ass
Of derrière of dawn cracks through night's pants
Alike a plumber bending down to fix
The frozen pipes of midnight's starry fonts;
When they that golden cleavage rosy-plump
Behold in ripe vulgarity of morn,
Old Heaven's Hare slams down piano case,
And packs his bags, the moon hung over woozy,
All the animals retiring
To early beds, awaiting the next night!
This happens every moon in Canada.
I snuck out once while on the Greyhound bus
To old Quebec, while selling door to door
New vinyl shower-curtains, and I saw
Exactly what I have described right here.
This beast and bird corroboree of eve
Speak French and New York creole drawled out sour,

French and onion dip from yowling mouths.

old Tom Hatten Family Films

A celluloid simulacrum I am
Of old Tom Hatten Family Films for kids,
The matinees and schlocky fairytales,
The Bernard Hermann soundtracks, seven seas
With sailors on adventures, Greek exploits
Of ancient heroes, Pippi Longstockings —
By rights these are more real and relevant
To me than all the business rigmarole
And hype — this is eternal, and is fun.
There's not a thing that I can do out there.
It all is rigged, the tastes are lassoed in,
The doors are closed, it's all a useless fight,
The stakes are claimed. But in the make-believe,
One can do anything! You can explore
The heavens with your sudden sprouting wings,
Or growing gills, peruse the underseas.
You can just snigger with the witty clowns,
And flower with irreverence and laughter,
If you wish — or you can launch a quest
For romance unimpeded by the fickle,
Pure devotion — or find lasting friends,
Who never stray but always keep the faith!
You can find satisfaction in a tale
That cuisinart misnamed the world can't give,
Where all's confusion, and ideals are mocked,
Are spat upon, but in a magic book,
Heroes are true to principles and love!
Or else, they cannot care at all, in fact,
And quip with utter freedom and disdain.
One can converse with animals and birds,
Befriend a beast, become enchanted, sing
A mystic song one never knew before!
How fallow are the fields of reality;
How lush the meadowlands of make believe!

Taoist cowboy

Ride on a cloud by dawn alike a bull,
O Taoist cowboy of the dragon-mists,
And mount that foggy puppy to the skies!
Let's see some chutzpah in your whooped yeehaw.
Your eyes should glower like a rodeo
When you behold the morning heavens, for
Your mind already's lassoed them in ride!

hilltops float in fog

Hilltops float in fog.
City tops atop the clouds.
Morning in a mist.

mosques of goddess modesty

"Yes, you can actually touch them: go ahead!"
Those domes, those soft and creamy domes of love,
Those mosques of goddess modesty and lushness,
Mine to touch, to touch! Heaven is here,
The mysteries are penetrated now,
Forbidden barriers are now allowed!
There is such awe in adolescent lust,
A revelation and a wonderment.
Religion's barely got a chance beside
This tantric temple where divinity
Is manifest in rapture! Self-confirms,
The fingertips to nipples, lips to lips,
An obvious virginity of touch,
A self-renewal of our innocence,
Belying all decrepitude of guilt.
The snools and crabby, shriveled pundits fail
An instant, and their puritanical
Warnings winnow away as so much chaff!
Some new discovery is sacred here,

Is happening, and if your churches fail
To speak this mystery, they all are lies!
Pleasure is speaking spirit plainly here;
Our hands are priests newly ordained by love
And curiosity! Your book is lame,
A cripple, if it cannot see this worth.
And yet it knows, though you would hide from us:
The Song of Songs, that is the song our lips
This very moment rediscover, yes!
Three thousand years distrusting pleasure's call,
The wisdom of its urges, and the worth
Of totemism, all the animal
Unfolds in us! O Aristotle, you
Divided us from all our matrices,
Our blossoming concentric from the mud,
Wherein our wholeness speaks a harmony!
If reason cannot heed the animal,
The vegetable, the mineral, and lead
It up to higher beauties, it is loss,
Not gain! Shall we obey the desiccate,
Or this, fresh moistness underneath our hands?
We are not what divides us but unites,
So logos must be lover of the base,
And contemplate with poetry our all,
So that the field entire of sentience
May resonate within our open soul!
Never speak blasphemies against the course
Of hundred million years of nature's lore,
Denying evolution's sacerdotal
Wisdom! Merlin lives in woods in us,
Beholding Old Cernunnos in his soul,
The Master of the Forest Animals!
The Shepherd of the Beasts, who leads them forth,
Who draws them willingly to higher ground.
Find logos there, O Aristotle, seek!
For us, for now, inchoately, we read
These texts in eyes, in fingertips, in breasts.

the red-tailed hawk is beautifully oblivious

Tear loose the manacles of stimulus-
Response! The media's Skinnerian!
Pull back your soul from this conditioning.
Recontemplate the essence of your life.
The hubbub is confusion, but it claims
Priority. Don't let the outer world
Muddle your inner clarity and worth.
Retune within and find the centered spot
Of gravity within the shifting dance.
Your intuition is more powerful
Than people wired to the switch exchange.
The rats in mazes press for their cocaine
So desperately and so depleted, ah!
Contention is a cuisinart where dreams
Are banished. Where the psyche moves in depths
Cannot be found on internets of woe
And hype. You need a little breath to think;
The latest instant is seductive lie,
Thin and hysterical. It holds no truth.
Electron-flurry on the bobbing waves
That has no touch with deeper currencies
Which generate the larger, slower pulse.
Fear and excitement mingle in a sludge
And slurry. Rushed opinions have no trace
Of episteme. Fall back, and then digest.
Discover world at pace of redwood trees,
And ask the boulders for their wise advice.
The hustle is a superficial fraud,
However sexy it may seem to be.
The woodlands know authentic rhythms best.
The rivers are so slow, and yet they flow.
The red-tailed hawk is beautifully oblivious
To anything dot com, and world
Rides on a snail; slow down to catch its ripplings.
Therein a peace, therein a truth.

Naxalite forests

Some Marxists then withdrew to distant caves,
Enriching their inherited wisdom
With evolution's deeper majesty
The ancient fir trees and the mountains teach.
Interrogating Darwin from the heart
Of Messianic liberty and joy,
They penetrated deeper, finding Karl
In the marl and the secret springs,
And pressing thicker into Naxalite
Forests, they listened to the tribal lore,
And let the fairytales then percolate
Where Maxim Gorky sits within their souls.
These monks, insurgent to their very roots,
Brewed most subversive heresies of wisdom
There in wilderness abandonment,
And tickled Taoist sages to delve more,
And dare the deeper. There they still remain,
Hidden and woodland wizards pledged to Marx.

in the cleft vagina of the soil

Find then an ancient and abandoned well,
Whose shaft goes down where sunlight only peeks.
Build you a ladder down its narrow sides,
And go where cool and shadow teaches lore.
There in the hollow of the earth remain,
And let the hours of the Mother's pulse
Regather psyche from her franticness,
And in the cleft vagina of the soil,
Meditate, and let the dream return.

smooth hexameters upon a scroll

The sky, filled with hot air balloons, that skimmed
The morning fog above the aqua seas,
Was marvelous, indeed impossible;

From baskets, men prepared their fiery tar
To rain flames from above on ships below.
Beneath, the archers on the decks their darts
Let loose in volleys; as the pine turned pitch
With bursting embers, skins stretched out balloon
Were pierced, and baskets pummeled to the waves
And waiting sharks! Witness the spectacle:
The many Icari freefalling lorn,
The maw of sharktoothed brackish bilge, the masts
Now torches, sails but orange skirts of flame
That licked the mocking fog, and battle stern
Between the birds and fishes! Grapples sky
With Triton, Greeks above and Greeks below,
Marines of Daedalus in floating skins,
And Neptune's favored sailors in their skiffs!
Many a brave man fell that day, and not
A few cowards redeemed their honor lost!
They say the sky was rainbow with the skins;
They say the sea was red against the green.
A bard with harp in hand jumped flaming ship,
And strummed as swam against swallowing waves,
His strophes versus briny crests, and dodged
The sharks, and made his way to sandy shores;
Thus this account, from verses almost lost
He sang to seagulls on the coast with tears,
Keeping his fallen comrades yet alive
In recitation, and a wandering scribe,
Still fresh from school with practiced letters, scrawled
His smooth hexameters upon a scroll.
I found the old papyrus in the dunes
Of grassy Crete as I perused the isle.
Here I translate what crumbled in hands
Against two thousand years of salty wind.

Babylon may weep midst of her smoke

I have denied, and now I build my church
In nooks and crannies of the Empire's haunts,
The yeast within the unsuspecting dough,
Opening air pockets to newly breathe.

Little walled paradises of the heart
In shacks and slums and tenements of Rome
And Turkey, Greece, wherever silent waves
Of slaves heard word their Spartacus on cross
Still lives despite, and Easter marches forth
Under the cover of the foliage
Of Spring. I have betrayed, three times in shame
Jesús, stood by as he was carted off,
And caged, to lashes and to thorns, and hung
Far from my hiding place of swollen tears.
To spread the seed my gardener gathered,
Ensuring all of us were not on cross,
To my contumely and chagrin, I fled,
But now I plant that mustard seed about
Wherever I may wander, and is wide.
O peasant flogged, condemned in Pilate's courts,
In whose sweet eyes we saw the face of God,
The Good News of your love's insurgency
Against the legionnaires and Caesar's mint
Sings on, sings on, and you yet live in song!
The rationale behind slaves' chains melts fast
As butter in your sun, and we affirm,
In barn, conventicle, and shanty, life
Now irrepressible, and daunted not!
The secret passes whisper ear to ear;
Messiah, you're alive in these our tales,
And these our limbs, gathered in your great cause,
Are flesh for you, a resurrection true
Through which your insurrection percolates!
I failed you, but I speak the testament,
In corners of the marketplace, by shade
Of bushes, under moonlight, in the caves
Where silent masses awe to hear your word,
Your call that now begins the coming days,
The advent of the times renewed at last!
Surrounded by the armies yet, and seal
Of Nero, maddened idol of a man,
We keep agape's sharp revolt alive
In hymns and tendings from our common purse.
Though we in shadows praise your glory's cause,
Each day the whispers spread, and yeast released.
Some wisdom yonder this our knowing minds
Fills us of sudden on the moment's edge,
A comforter with whom we improvise,
Discovering the future's secret new,

The mystery of you in everything.
The masters pay no heed to roadside weeds,
Whence all the herbage of your vision grows.
We never know, but any time may come
Momentum we have built at last to head.
Then Babylon may weep midst of her smoke.

July, 64 a.d.

There moon glinted on Tiber's looking glass
In summer sweltering of Julius.
The night was broad; the wind nimble and brisk.
By slumbering of tenements, some straw
By brand to kindling came neath shadowed cream
Of running figures stealthy in the dusk
Of dreaming hours' lunacy, a spark
That slowly sinewed serpentine through stalls
Within the Circus, then burst forth as blooms
Of flagrant mustard, flames that licked the wood
Of slums and swallowed them with sudden greed.
The limpid buttermilk of moon was rivaled
High by orange skirts flamenco wild
In the rushing char. The plebeians,
Like bees smoked out from hives, swarmed livid streets,
And ran the shanty corridors in fright,
The sunset-shadow of the dragon overhead.
Dry wood, tinder of usury
The avarice of distant landlords stacked
In careless recklessness, was gulped,
And swelled the belly of the fire wyrm.
The shieling-synagogue of pallet-wood
And hay nearby soon woke, and heretics
Within their midst grabbed tortoise shell and strings,
Singing mocking laments of Babylon,
And cheered the flames as Gullveig's pyre come.
These insurrectionary hymns sung loud,
Triumphantly beneath apocalypse
In florid tangerine of barrios
Aflame, were later sweet librettos choirs
Mused, and written down at last by scribes,
Became the 18th chapter of St. John.
Amidst, the conflagration grew apace;

The proletarians with torches danced,
Deriding landlords' property with spite,
And looters made a carnival in flame.
The idols wept and melted, statues fell,
Lucre and merchandise soon were but ash;
The city, center of the reign of sin,
Returned a cinder-penitent to earth.
The Lares that Aeneas clung from Troy
Ilium's flames by Vestal Virgins' tears
Reclaimed, and all that piety was lost.
Carthage a sister-city found in soot,
Juno her Dido's pyre-spite at last
Bit old Anchises' son and all his kin.
Gomorrah in her embers eye to eye.
Limbs of Messiah soon were set in tines,
Menorah of sad Actaeon, and ripped
By hounds — as if they saw the naked moon
That night bathing in Tiber's midnight streams.
Holy defiance was impious charm
Chanted in ears of Rome: who could be cruel
To smile delight in satire at her burns?
Unpatriotic and inhuman scum!
Salute the flag: kiss bust of emperors
(No knee at ludi, stand, support the troops!).
They would not bow, thought smirks a sacrament.
They nearly leapt at crosses with a glee;
They'd seen the signs; the advent was afoot,
The flames were prophecy; the Christ was near;
To join his cavalry by heaven's gates
Was but an honor. Still serventes sung,
The Scarlet Woman on their tongues, aflame.

today it's Africa

The offensive insolence of Mao Zedong
Was to suggest that intellectuals
Had something they could learn from poor peasants.
The arrogance of mandarins was pricked.
Whoever is the least of these has soul.
We learn from soul; perhaps we only learn
From soul; the rest is but manipulation,
Never wisdom. Mao said that these boors,

These yokels in the outback, were the pride
Of China, to whom all should look to find
Their knowledge. The intelligentsia
Never forgave him for holding up high
The peasantry, for now they rule in spite.
Today it's Africa whom we must heed,
In trained humility of arrogance,
And see where genius for humanity
Is rising from the grassroots in our time.
The backs of those who built the world know best.

nothing makes me superior

Nothing about me makes me superior
To any peoples anywhere on earth.
The gatherer of berries in the woods,
The Guatemalan farmer growing maize,
The gardener of lilies in rural France,
The Chinese peasants planting paddy rice,
The Africans who salvage pickup trucks,
The Tijuana denizen in shacks,
The hillbilly hunting possum down south,
The islander who easily picks fruit —
The fact I drive a car, and have degrees,
And own a smartphone is irrelevant.
I'm human, and on human terms, am one.
Despite my reading broad and wide, they all
Have much to teach me if I will but hear;
And if I won't, that's simply arrogance,
Unearned, unwarranted, empty as fuck.

the better of us sentient swims the sea

The fish deep in the ocean give me hope.
If only they survived, if only they,
Beneath majestic waves, still slipped in depths,
Parading regal bodies sleek and scaled
In iridescent grandeur as they jet

So turbulent and confident through seas,
That'd be enough to satisfy my heart.
These most mysterious but fellow kin.
Their eyes like mine, their vertebrae like mine,
Their bodies fleshy, topped with skin, like mine.
In every way my cousins lost in time.
A planet where they ruled the silent seas
Is most sufficient to my poetry.
Let Charlton strike the sand and damn to hell
Amidst the fallout and Columbia
In ruins by the shore, yet I rejoice
The better of us sentient swims the sea.
That's good enough, that's good enough for me.

a wonderment of animals

I am a wonderment of animals,
No more, no less, a place where they may awe
From out my eyes — as I the pageantry
Of this majestic march of forms through time,
Protean in progressive tangentry,
But contemplate with Owen Wilson's word
Upon my lips! Let Hamlet celebrate
Soliloquys of Man in glorious mien —
But Greeks, wherever you may love the sleek
Adonis flesh of statuesque athletes,
A hundred more exotic anatomies
Of all our cousins time forgot to us
Declare exquisite beauty in their forms!
The shapeliness and Fibonacci flair
Of all their many curves! How self-possessed
In poise, in gait, in movements most diverse!
In instincts, what fidelity to kind;
In feeling, what integrity and heart!
In their sincerity, how like a babe!
In their tenacity to life, how like
A barnacle upon the tide-swilled rocks!
In lineage and provenance, how aged,
How venerable in tenure, in every way,
More settled and more confident than man.
This very frame of bone and blood is loan
I borrowed, with a variance, from them.

Let tens of millions, more, roll back the years,
There is the cleverness of nibbling
In grasses under moonlight: archives, play
That sweet refrain of quiet crunching; years
Accumulate eternities of breath
And slumber in what woods I've never known!
I was not needed, never thought of, dreamed;
They drifted forward, neither ponderment
Nor keen regret at absence of myself.
I am but plagiary of what they were.
These cells, these lips, these ribs, these senses, skin —
I am collage of all the kinks they worked
Out long ago, and passed as plan to me!
There was a time where neither net nor snare
Nor spear nor arrow ever vexed their flesh,
Where they in teeming droves dominion held
As far and wide as any eyes could see.
No manager was ever known, no chart
Of productivity and profits, no
Collector of the tax or rent or debt;
Whatever empty niche was permitless.
They were the undisputed kings and queens.
The sixth day up to noon was quite enough;
They were content, and we, irrelevant.
Yet come, rewind the tape, my body morphs;
I am the mother of the chimpanzee;
Rewind, I am the mother of the apes;
Rewind, I am the mother monkeys nurse.
Rewind, I am the mother of the squirrels.
Rewind, I am the mother of the voles.
Rewind, I am the mother of the birds,
A dinosaur; rewind, the lizards hatch
From me; rewind, I am Tiktaalik, first
On shores, mother of all amphibians;
Rewind, I am the mother of the fish;
Rewind, I'm mother of the vertebrates;
Rewind, I am the mother of the worms;
Rewind, I'm mother of eukaryotes;
Rewind, I'm mother of bacteria;
Rewind, I'm Mother Earth, mother of all.
That's how far back the family extends.
I'm but a little branch, a tiny twig,
Somewhere out here in boondocks chewing chaw.
I am a wonderment of animals.

I am a rainforest

This colony of cells in harmony,
O Plato, don't you owe some reverence?
This maelstrom, this cascade of living things,
Exquisitely in tandem, is it not
A miracle as worthy of your awe
As any wonder the philosophers
Should cultivate? Your twisted city-state's
Priorities have blocked you from this good.
Gymnastics to train military men,
Making the body but a robot — what
Is this but species of contempt? You treat
This gentle flesh the way you do your slaves,
Expecting odd obedience from this
Endearing animal. Your wars and slaves
Have skewed philosophy! The city's sins
Have mangled your ideas, O Babylon,
If Athens by another name! How then
Impiety towards this most holy shrine,
This altar soft and sinuous where *nous*
Is numinous within, the mystery
Within the emerald cavern of the nave?
I am a rain forest, O Socrates!
A mountain woodland fertilized by mist!
I am the physiognomy of life's
Engeyserment upgushing lush through cells,
Verdant geography of earth in skin!
These creatures in community of care,
Organic ecstasies spontaneous,
Expressions of the Gaian mastermind,
Endowment of her gifts of living jewels,
They are not slaves, they are the elders' moot!
The council of the wise ones in my flesh.
I owe them dulia indeed, and thanks.
Their ceaseless service, communist and pure,
Is what opens the opportunity
For psyche to emerge in midst of this,
The fairie of the woodlands crowned in groves
Of self-arising vegetation lush!
Fidelity to *viriditas*, friend!
A city? Fix your eyes. This polity

Could teach your Athens something nutritive
And most instructive! Have you ever seen
A citizenry so unselfish, linked
In every way, so altruistically?
The ministry these holy deacons lend
Deserves your gratitude, forbids disdain!
The puppetry of calisthenics lies,
Spreading the violence of the marionette,
Yanked here, yanked there, whipped this way, that, and pushed
And shoved, straitjacketed into a brace,
All that the readiness of war proceeds!
War here, war there, war everywhere with slaves
Galore as booty to work mines and farms,
And have them silver-spoon you as you mock,
Deriding their good services and gifts!
No wonder then the body you abhor,
If these its cells are helots in your mind.
That unexamined life of slavery
Is most unworthy of your human soul,
Of all the beauty you so fond adore!
The *nous*, my dear aristocrat's a nymph,
Hallowed in breathless *nemeton* of cells!

in fragility

We can be cracked, we can be broken, all
Of us, none are invulnerable: not one.
This life is but a vulnerability.
Resiliency is in fragility.
We are affectable: we must take care.

we are the friend we would be to our soul

Where no control is possible, step back,
Be philosophical. Consider fate
Has cloistered you to give a precious gift:
The opportunity to learn the soul,

That matter most dispersed in busyness.
Sometimes one storms the kingdom with all force,
Sometimes an Exodus withdrawing all.
The way of things expands and then contracts.
Go with the movement, surf what waves may be,
Not those you wish, which are but phantoms' stuff.
To read the season is the half of luck;
To follow its most subtle currencies,
Not obvious to bluster, brings one peace.
We are the friend we would be to our soul,
Says Aristotle, and if we have might
To ponder, let us give it then the time,
For contemplating is the food of soul.
The nous, the meaning-making of our heart,
Reviewing all the chapters in our life,
Restores the native order to the flux,
And gives the naked narrative its worth.
In this biography, we pan for gold.
We sift through all the strata of our lives,
Giving the precedence to sagely dreams,
Which in enigma shelter precious seeds
Of insight; and then those ambitions grown
From who and what we really are inside
(And those alone, no more, our gifts' intent),
And then our knowledges from life and books,
And beauty, and the crowning piece, our loves,
If intimate or charity or both.
That is enough. That makes for gold of soul.
Not through excoriating for our sins,
(Though we must honestly enunciate
Where we still cling to lower rungs, to climb)
But in our loving curiosity
That notices the little things of life.
If life gives you sabbatical, receive,
Drink deeply, make the most of hermitage,
And learn to love your soul with all your life.

strangers sharing tea and thoughts

What is a weed but life itself untamed?

What is a weed but nature undesired?
Weeds challenge us beyond utility.
They ask if we will be with them as friends,
Not servants; strangers sharing tea and thoughts.

favor from her violet hair

Purple petals, light wisteria,
But lavender in cream, left here and there
By sprinkling rain and breeze upon the tiles —
Sign of favor from her violet hair.
I touch my forehead, giving Freya thanks.

I'm Jagger in his supple strut

Peach is the exudation of my arms
This morning — I am flamingo nectarine,
A lithe and winged thing, a flowering
Of sweetest scent, a heartthrob's fleshy zest,
The miracle of me, a vixen sprite
With Jacaranda petals in my hair,
A body shaped for Mercury and mint,
The hint of sculpted chocolate and of cream,
A dreamy luxury, exotic, pure,
Illustrious, with leotard and hose
Of shamrocks and of silk woven from webs,
And truffle-flesh so smooth, with rabbit tufts
Of fur about the fringes — I am sway
Of banners in the breeze painted with Kells —
I am a piper on a grassy knoll,
My knee bent stork upon the other leg,
The pollen of the Spring like Holi dust
About me rainbow neon dragonfly
And swirl — I carry fennel and a cone
Of pine that smells of cedar, and my curves
Are covered smooth of dotted Klimt in pelts
Of fluffy fawn, and red madrone of dawn —
I am a harvest festival in limbs,
A kilt of pumpkin blossoms round my waist,

As sinuous as squash gourds these fine hips —
There's Autumn leaves wherever I may walk,
And moon has ivory lips of light that glow
Upon my blushing, nymph-kissed cheeks — my skin
So baby-soft — I dance with hamadryads
In the spinning blades of storming leaves
Beneath the canopies, the blur of browns
And oranges that fall upon our nose —
And then I'm Jagger in his supple strut,
I kick up foliage and fairy dust,
And linger in the limelight for a time,
Before I preen these plumes so pink and white,
And glide, with peach aroma, into sheets,
There then deliciously slip into sleep.

fuck the human race

Because the bloody scumbags of the earth
Will buy a set of pens for just a buck,
And have the nerve to sell for nine bucks plus,
And no one blinks an eye, well, fuck the human
Race! In any world of sanity,
Such profiteers would be despised and egged
Whenever they might show their face at all.
Instead, they're "enterprising". Fuck this world.

in gratitude and grace

A wretched hate allowed me to survive.
It drove me through the valleys of my fear,
And lashed me yonder my futilities.
When I gave up many a time and felt
Despair at ever gaining back my mind,
My joy, this seething rage pushed me on through,
Refusing no, refusing never, set
On passing all this weak surrender. I
Would still be wallowing for all my good;
It was aggressiveness that got me out.
I would be still in fear's paralysis,

In incapacity, infirmity,
But drive would not allow it, would not bow.
When spirits sank before immensity,
When even hope could simply not pull through,
The fight in me — the FIGHT!! — yet raised its fists
To fisticuff defiantly a world
That seemed to set intimidation's snares,
Refusing sniveling, being a worm!
Was not my gentleness that let me live!
My peace would just as soon have let me rot!
What got me up and shoved me through was spite,
Derision, sheer contempt, if for myself,
In all my fibrillating misery,
Or for a world whose price of peace is soul,
Is dignity, demanding we succumb
And acquiesce, instead accepting war
As more acceptable and dignified!
I fancied I'd fight for the underdog.
(Including thus myself.) At first, I did.
And mainly I did thus. But when I found
The sad extent to which the underdogs
Had taken in the masters' principles,
And pledged allegiance to their ruling lies,
Then I fenced with the masters in their hearts,
And valiantly attempted to cut loose
Their bonds, and shocked, found that they cherished them.
Angered, I whipped myself to passion more,
And tried to grapple with constraining ghosts.
The underdogs did not appreciate,
As you might guess. And now what ought be love
Was but contempt! Hubris, where had been fight!
And yet my engine — hate had thus propelled me —
Still was clash and brannigan. But now,
The anger nurtured in me took on life
All of its own, becoming habit. Now,
What motivation without rage and fire?
Yet that flame, I did perceive, burned me!
No longer wet and weeping, I was dry,
And crisping, almost kindling. Set a match!
And I might blaze! What kind of snarling beast
Within my breast had I fed to such size?
What wolf had I saddled through icy fields
To ride away from my lame helplessness?
I loved that puppy and its fiery glint,
The way it never would accept my no,

Its sheer persistence as it ever ran,
Getting me yonder glaciers' lulling arms
Happy to lullaby my soul to death —
It would not let me sleep, would not allow
Me sit and shake, and cringe before nightmare's
Hallucinations — no, it nudged me on.
There never was more faithful of a hound.
Now though, its roughened bristliness has grown,
Its gulping appetite for meat augments;
It licks its chops within my heart and gloats
On carnage, filling me with images
Of gore that horrify and make me weep.
This savage thing of beauty I have loved!
How may I lovingly now let it go?
When young, it took its pity, formed a bond
With me, a wretched thing in its homeland,
And loyally, beyond its fatherland,
Conveyed me forth. O sweetest, fiercest whelp!
Savior and boon companion! Howls of frost
Now call you home, my friend, now call you back!
Return to your fond habitat and home!
My mark is on you, and you are tattooed
Upon my history — we weep! These tears
Are hot, now steam, they scald us both, you see!
What love named hate have we aroused between us?
Such affection in a mutual
Teeth-baring, ah! You were but youth when found me:
Juvenile ventures called you out!
Yes, we are fond! But now you are in prime!
The tundra and the hunt call out to you!
I cannot keep you here! What kind of friend
Holds back a friend from destiny and home?
I'll know to fight now when I need to fight;
You've taught me that, but I need not fight all,
Not anymore, not all the time, but you —
The hunt allures you! Go to it, my friend!
Follow your hungers! Now I thirst for love,
For gentleness. It is a foreign spice
To you. You look at me. I know. Such love,
Such gentleness you have beyond compare,
Committed even yonder my despair.
I recognize and love that in you, hound.
But you know what I mean. The carnivore
In you tugs at your fur, and you must go.
Not out of my rejection, but my love!

Go now, you beautiful ferocity!
Once home, that savagery transforms to soul,
Mere passion in the joy of habitat!
You'll think on me as fondly as I do
Of you — but you'll be happy then, not caged
In me! You'll thrive back in the snow! Adieu!
I keep a little piece, a souvenir
Of this your rage, a loyal love, in me!
I honor you in gratitude and grace.

ruckus is necessity

There's times that ruckus is necessity,
Where friend must grapple friend for dignity,
Where giving in to what is going on
Is worse than trouble, where surrender rots
The soul and leads the country to abyss.
A little feistiness is medicine,
And yes, I know, the taste is rather foul
When you want sweetness! But a slippery slope
Requires doggedness, not slick and smooth,
Requires nails that dig into the soil.
Giving in to what is wrong is wrong,
Even if it may smile pleasantly.

soul doesn't care

All of this flurry here? Soul doesn't care.
Trenchant hysteria? Soul doesn't care.
Official must's and should's? Soul doesn't care.
The waking world's strict plans? Soul doesn't care.
It's not in consciousness, but in your dreams
That soul speaks forth poetically her needs,
Her deep concerns, and there you see at last,
This world is relevant but to express
Her longings only, nothing more — or less.
Agendas of importance to the state?
The urgencies of time and history?
The stresses that consume our waking life?

Whatever, only as it serves the soul.
When breaking news is adamant, she yawns.
The self-importance of our false control
Reflects so faintly in our inner depths.
The world itself, where its soul is concerned,
Dreams at a deeper, slower pace of peace
And wisdom consciousness can never grasp,
Not ever, with its missionary rage,
Unless it listens, unless it hears and heeds
The silent and symbolic pulse beneath.
If in your dreams the waking world is pale,
Is spurious, you know your soul don't care,
No matter how the demagogues may yell,
No matter how the preachers fulminate,
No matter how the rebels pitch their cause.
She has her own agenda. Listen up.
Your peace and your fulfillment are found there.
She knows your moods, she knows your deepest urge,
She knows the certain ways you fool yourself,
She knows your fads which you assert as truths,
She knows the bluster and the yada-yad.
She rides it out, and speaks her deeper will,
Her wisdom, which we're fools if we neglect.
For party and appearance are but skin;
She is the marrow, blood and bone, of us.

walls of quarantine come down

There is an arc that passes through your life,
The seeming randomness of it, that ties
The many separate chapters, as one goes,
And only markable as one grows old,
Together. Meanings juxtapose and merge,
And period comments on period.
A conversation brews within one's dreams
Between one's many lovers, and they grow
More intimate and comfortable within,
As polyamory reveals its truth
Inside one's heart and brain and dreaming soul,
If nowhere else. One's friends, each in their time,
Step out from haze and introduce themselves.
Part integrates with part, through dialogue;

Familiar walls of quarantine come down,
And one learns to affirm with wide embrace,
Yes, this is what I am; I am this wide,
I am these loves, this gorgeous splay of friends
With all their backgrounds and relations. Still,
It stays a mystery, but some comes clear,
And 'some' is so much that it's good enough.

back in the game

My hope is back in the game and healing up
Its wounds. The outside world is so diseased
With pessimism, faith of most these days.
To stretch one's heart towards brighter days ahead
Is heresy, and goes against the tide.
Leave off the silly pestilence of doom,
Addiction to the gloom, and look around:
The trees still arch their doughty boughs towards sky,
Their greeneries unfolding in ripe splay
To taste the dripping honey of the orb;
The bees the yonis of the herbs caress,
Collecting there their fragrances and dew,
Their colors reveling in breeze-blown skirts;
The bunnies take their salad in the grass,
And roll in knolly meadows, scampering;
The earthworms undulate in loamy clay
And tunnel breathing room for roots in soil;
The breezes, generous, freshness disperse,
And fan manly perfumes of chaparral;
Clouds yet sashay in lazy absent-mind
To cotton-wisp collage the drifting blue;
And yet I still hear children in their play,
Rambunctious, eager, irrepressible.
It seems to me the globe spins ever on,
Each coming season waiting in the wings
For its debut, each personality
Of time with character endowing chance
With loveliness and style; still the arts
Mosaically pursue beauty with woo —
The resurrection marches on apace.
We wound, and heal, and come into our strength,
Resilient and refreshed, learning to leave

Anxiety to self-indulgent types,
Who ever since the world began have screed
Their Chicken Little sky-laments of gloom.
This world is bold and vigorous and new.

decoctions from the sky

Deliciously decoctions from the sky,
Prepared in brewing roots of roiling clouds,
Fall down to nutrify the tuberous
Clayscape beneath the tender skirts of herbs,
And trunks, now glistening with running dew,
Perspiring from limp-hand emerald limbs,
Effulge in upward ecstasies of gush,
As fosses from the featherlands of flight
Shower and splashing bathe their branching tines.
Elation of exulting, lilting frogs,
Eager to sink in mountain-torrent streams
Invigorating in their frigid whirls,
As they, each fond Parisian of ponds,
Elopes to water serenade a maid,
To burgeoning of tadpole Hoi Polloi.
The red-tailed falcon whimpers soft in nest,
Its grandeur sulking, used to sunny skies,
While rabbits, snug in warrens, thankful cheer.
The birds petite in waxy down rest blithe,
The water raining from their tufty coats,
As they but blink, and sometimes drink the drops,
Deep in their labyrinths of branch and thorns.
The lizards raise their scaly brows neath rocks,
Their heads this way then that in ponderment,
As they peruse new puddles in their quaint,
Low-lying stone ramadas cool and flat.
The Spanish tiles put their tap shoes on,
And cabaret the ceilings with their jig;
The rooftops simmer in the rising steam.
A cottage formed of fog cups round the house
In still congeniality; the air,
But wisps of cheesecloth breath before, and dirt,
Inert, once silent, both are now alive;
I hear their organism quivering
Distinctly out the window piping bright.

The scatterwet in heavy spray throws down,
Its perspirant blanket all dampening
The music, una corda, of the plains.
I sit with potted mug and sip hot tea,
Great running rivers of the shedding roof
In prodigality of waterfall,
The canyons round cathedral-like in rain.

nothing but facts

Don't trust what you may hear, trust only facts,
Established, scrutinized, well-vetted facts,
For folklore is a fad and fraud these days,
Degraded from its faded glory-years.
What people propagate with flippant words
Is rustling and flurry, hype and flim.
The facts, the facts alone, nothing but facts.
Rumors inevitably lie through teeth.

no Vandals at our doorsteps

No Vandals at our doorsteps but a virus:
Literature and music, theater
And dance, and even fond athletics — crickets.
Streets as if an atom bomb. Boutiques,
Barbed wired. Epicurean temples,
Ghost towns. Laughter, hubbub, gusto, but howls
Of empty wind. Each Polyphemus to
His dripping cave. Article IV, Clause 1
Of Section 4, the guarantee, and yet,
Total eviction of the public space.
Where Rome once stood, now crows and squirrels carouse.
No Irishmen on mid-March avenues,
No darkened chapels with communion ale
And lager, not a street preacher to be
Found anywhere, not even for to screed
The ending of the world, and yet this was
A kind of eerie emptying. The land
Once known for tar and feathering was still,

Obedient, deserters of the field.
The public abdicated, laid its crown
On barren sidewalks for the Visigoths,
Then fled, in cowering, and took their stand
In cell block homes on thrones of toilet rolls.
The heritage, irrelevant. The rights
Of common cheer and free assembly,
Sacrificed on altars to the germs.
Not one petition for redress of grievance.
No republic without public presence,
Boisterous debate. If but a fright
Allows emergencies to seize the state,
To vacate boulevards and close cafes,
To send the poets home to ruminate,
Sundered from arguments on patios,
The libraries like mortuaries, null.
Trust the authorities, stay in your homes.
O, Pinochet would glee at such a chance.

hovering swarm of rose petals

Once you, upcoming diva of the boards,
Sauntered in hovering swarm of rose petals
(That followed for the honey of your eyes),
And spread your winged perfumes in haughty flight.
What furs the very beasts left when they fled
Your beauty, stunned, draped shoulders' elegance,
And lent the shepherd girl a royalty
She always had within if she'd believe.
What happened? Did the hobgoblin of home
Chain you in dripping cellars, shorn of hope?
I saw a brilliance; I did not lie.
How fares the burying of beauty's dreams?
Awaken, white as snow, from tomb of glass;
If these archaic lips are not the kiss
Arousing you from haze (the kiss is verse,
The kiss of calling from the soul's wise halls),
Find then what prince may charm you to your wits.
Basements befit you not, but theaters.

sunlight once was sparkling caviar

When sunlight once was sparkling caviar
Reflecting in the wettened webs of ponds;
When dusk was spray of fresh kombucha, rich
And deep on shallows of the shadowed hills;
When stars were raindrops of the nebulae,
And comets Phoenix feathertails of skies;
When day was youth and vigorous and clean,
And afternoon still adolescent-strong;
When joys were certainties one could but grasp,
Like ripened fruit to lips of succulence;
When work was frolicking, and frolic, art,
And ease award of meeting challenges;
Back in such days before one uttered hope,
For cheer unmitigated was hope's sire,
Yesterday, and but a month ago,
Before this gloom was mandatory meal,
One could sip beauty from the heart of things,
And happiness from echoes of a smile.
Children trooped as yet through poppy furs,
The tangerined, soft pelt of herbous earth,
And folks were still in awe of birdsongs' lilt.
I do recall such times as yesterday,
For literally they were months ago.
They've turned the volume down on gorgeousness;
The world is dim, and mandatorily;
Who in hysteria has time for charm?
Each dawn is alpha in its prime, but now,
Omega's all that anybody sees.
In dull delusions of the end of time,
They wreak such weight on light and fluffy things,
That these, the effervescent revelers,
Who sip through straws of piccolo sweet breeze,
And render world its flautist psalmodies,
Are isolated, kept on lockdown, trapped.
Meanwhile, not terrified enough, they shoot up
Panic with euphoria, and who
So dares to cross their junkie fantasies,
Their methamphetamine persistency,
Is trounced for heresy of holding hope,
A contraband and substance most controlled.

Amnesia's surfeit velocity
Is raptorous, as few can now recall
The sun-masseuse's fingers on their skin,
The feel of warmth, the blow of mild breeze,
The spa of morning steam from sagebrush fronds.
What if what if what if? they cry en masse,
Portending wreckage they seem most to crave
Even as they appear to spurn, and yet
The treasure of experience they flee!
The memory of when it was ok
Is my reality, and I insist
Upon it, not this gothic attitude
The latest faith and fad; I faithe in Christ,
In resurrection, and unending hope.

a cocktail rare and dizzying

She slips into her copper entourage
Of glistening silk (with which she covers bones),
The air redolent as a dowager,
And each step heels a runway as if ice,
With powdered sugar snowing on ripe lips.
Her epidermis caramelized and smooth,
Her blended tones of pheasant-feathered hues,
Ripe earth, sweet clover hay, and honeydew.
Her varnished leather soft as roebuck suede
Invites wishes of would she let caress?
Her breath, aristocrats' inheritance
Of lavender awakened by the dawn.
Lips like the oranges of mandarins,
No syrup tastes as sweet, no pulp so wet,
She is a cocktail rare and dizzying.
And where those wings (not lips but feathered things)
Touch ground — ah, if it were your skin, you'd melt —
Such earth is flowering with herbs and fleurs
That shiver moist in wind of her descent.
She utters murmured rosaries when wet,
Her skin, rippled bocote, is salivate
With angels' cries — I've heard such chiming bells
When she is mistified in weeping joy;
And she moves like a waterbird in swirl
Of tumbling water as she graceful writhes.

Just silent sound of spray of waterfalls.
She is a paramour of seelie-folk
In selkie-skin who flirts the undulate,
And coyly giggles jovial in folds
Of brine and moonshine on the brandy waves.

disappointment made into a god

Oh Eve, you gave yourself to atheists,
Who pledge to flutterings and naught but flux,
Who make devoted worship of their doubt!
Doubt is not questioning, nor inquiry,
Nor curiosity that tends the soul,
But disappointment made into a god,
An idol of corrosion whom commit
The faithless all their faith! That cannot lead
To fairy inscapes of the natural world,
Once, you remember, native land to you!
You had a gift, the very ponds once spoke
To you in ripples! But the blinder world
Of men would not affirm, and soon their doubt
Aligned with bitterness your heart knew well,
And like a woman scorned, you scorned untrue
The revelations mysteries had lent.
Yet I that pulse you merely spoke to me
Still tend, I know it's there beneath the pain,
The pain these atheists make into shrine.
Of course they are beloved brethren, Eve,
But that does not give blind men eyes to see.
With walking sticks and Talmuds of their Braille,
They bring their gifts — they clean the temple's filth —
And we adore them in their crippled kind,
But such can never be our faithful guides.
Their minds are brilliant, yet their hearts but moan.

friendship of dreams

When I said that I would love to be friends,
For that's how it began, and underneath

The love was friendship, and the friendship, love,
I never knew a twenty-year and more
Adventure would commence : friendship of dreams!
And yet in such sweet sleep as few may joy,
She's been to me, that purple-haired allure,
A messenger of bliss, an avatar,
A deeper friend than ever waking life
Might eke if squeezed to last of living juice!
I spoke the truth, for true Amour makes friends,
Deepens through adoration philia,
And makes of courtesy the deepest pulse
Of high regard and dear sincerity.
In these dreams more of miracle and awe,
Religious, drawing down the violet moon,
I've kept inviolate her marriage vows;
Even in sleep, have always kept it friends,
Have never crossed her wedding to that man.
She's grown into such wisdom in my dreams.
Still full of spontaneity and spunk,
Somehow she has a seelie depth of now;
Her flighty callowness of youth long fled
For rich and matronly updraw of life
Eternal, my Olivia Newton John,
Who guides me, bringing all my dreams alive.
Could this weak stuff, this faithless waking world,
Sustain such Diotima ecstasy?
We know the dim regard this fickle plane,
Senility its hobbled character,
Holds for eternities that touch the soul,
And what contempt for beauty, aged as wine,
It shows, this skittish and erratic zone
So many give so bafflingly their faith!
Sometimes once in a life, the cave's mirage
Lets through a sparkling shaft of upper sun
From what great world of perfect forms beyond
Reflects in mud so turbidly as here.
A little flash, a brief epiphany
This too-distracted mind might easily
Ignore, or tasting, put aside and shrug,
When there was the transmission Destiny
Allotted, but a glowing glimpse of seed,
Which planted, nurtured in the soil of soul,
Might ramify and arborate to tines
Of creamy blossoms, froth of heaven's seas,
A guiding tree, to lead the monkey up

And heavensward. Only such faithful love,
As never leaves the garden and its field,
Can come to know the certainty of forms,
Whose ink this watery papyrus can't
Hold onto long that it soon blurs and fades;
But when your heart, by being touched, has seen
Such light this broken mirror here below
But faintly shows mosaically in shards,
You know, you know. The skeptics are all green,
Just squirted from their mother's womb last week,
Yet silly call their deepening jaundicing
Maturity. Maturity, such fools?
Who random chase the scatter in the flux,
Concluding all is flux, these flighty fools?
They reap such faith as they have faithless sowed,
Mocking at faith, for it would not reveal
To eyes and ears and scorning disbelief
Its mysteries! As if a woman might
Disrobe at once and on callous command!
And if she won't, then she's not real at all?
You shall not woo? Devotion well invest?
You ran after the superficial life,
What struck the eyes, and worshipped surfaces!
You've trained yourself to disbelieve, I see,
And the instruction now has taken well,
Long-scrolled diplomas of your prejudice.
Forgive me if such erudition fails
To deep impress a poet's fondest heart.
But rarely come the planetary shifts,
In whose most fleeting transits may appear
Great clarity in moments but a flash,
But if one notices and cherishes
These soft eurekas whispering through time,
Deeper reality, of precious worth
One drop of which is more than all the gold
This world can hold, may penetrate the mist,
Refracting through the marshy water's skein.
Such merest glimpses hold more truth and weight
Than all the clutter of quotidia,
The oatless chaff most take as evidence.
The ancients knew, and showed such piety
Towards miracle as merits rarity
All more the precious! Who knows who she is
Of now — I wish her well — but what she left
In me has blossomed, taken on new life,

And in that life, she speaks as anima.
If she had stayed, and never left, how might
This young philosopher have seen such light?
That was this life's illuminating trauma,
Birth from treasured womb into a world
Brand new and gleaming through my blur of tears,
Where wonder only gradually awoke.
The sages speak the mysteries their hearts
Intuit, with such metaphors the mind
May muster, but they know not through the mind,
But with the heart. The mind but clarifies
The primal stuff, the glimpse of which the soul
Allows the heart, to whom it does reserve
Its secrets. Mind may then a piety
Perform, suggesting with felicity,
In dialogue, the various views of worth,
And through this, polishing the inner sense,
A soft and almost silent sense, yet strong
And pulsing. Dialectic brushes up
These artifacts from revelations' glimpse,
Alike an archaeologist, who sweeps
The dust away from lost antiquities.
In such delight as ludic peels the veils
From altars in the temples, may the mind
Muse on the mysteries — and only this
Is true philosophy, for wisdom is
The soulful life collected through one's dreams,
Affirmed as deeper knowledge. Who disdains
Intuitive reflection is a fraud,
An eyeflash in pedantic trickery,
Who may impress with catalogues of chaff,
And galleries of butterflies on pins,
But know not how to fly, and cannot soar!
We do not know — alone is that to know,
For wonderment is wisdom's true midwife,
And knowledge is the faithful, playful love
The mind renders the soul through serving heart.
Knowledge is but a mystery we serve
As we explore, once more the dust to shed,
Ecdysis, turning facets of the gem.

her title on the scrip of soul

These shores, these sands, these lands, this broad expanse
Of just-so sunset, trees only like this,
The very angle of the sun on streams,
The way the breeze itself smells — yes, it has a scent —
Have these not claimed us, captivated us,
In every way matriculated us
To these fraternities of hill and dale?
And if the Earth herself has chosen us
Amongst her children in this precious land,
Can any man gainsay? Can swipes of ink?
Can merest leaves that fall in heaps from trees,
If bound voluminous and stamped with seal?
Who has authority surpassing Earth?
She writes her title on the scrip of soul.
No deed in county records. Here, my heart —
Now listen, though she whispers, now she roars!
If she now trembles in the surge and rush
Of gurgling veins, her melody, none else,
There is my deed, that I belong — to her!
And you, a man, but mortal bones and skin?
Who are you that a ticket in your hands
You think entitles you, without a feel
For her, without the intimacy she
Withholds or gives, according to her will,
To claim her? You don't claim her; she claims you.
Show me her signature tattooed on you.
Sing me the songs belonging to each site.
Recite the cemeteries' addresses,
Where ancestors have learned the peace of stone.
Expose cerebral folds where bark has marked you.
These are deeds. Your paper gossamers?
Dandruff of trees, the fluff of cottonwoods.
But bare my soul and read the wedding vows.
Or ask the forests and the marshes — they
Were there, were witnesses. Ask then the ducks,
The dragonflies, the will o'wisps, the cane,
The bulrush. Ask tobacco, ask the rice.
Behold this webbed shrub, its tufts as white
As this my aged hair; behold its bark,
As walnut as my skin, and watch it span
The miles to horizons — this mere bush,
From whom the threads spin out to all your clothes,

Your every bedsheet, pillowcase, your sails
That fleet the seas — the very soft and glow
Of all the comfort that you've ever known,
The blanket from your cradle mama rocked —
This fluffy thistle of the briars hands
Just like mine own have tender tended — it
Was there as witness to my marriage vows!
To Earth! Ask any of them, they will know!
Observe these colonnades, this masonry,
This most exquisite plasterwork, these stairs,
These roads, observe this steepled church, its bell
And belfry — tell me what you see. I see
The hands of these my grandfathers, their sweat,
Their toil — there — hear now as yet their huffs,
Their heaves, within the very marble-stone!
Is that the breeze? I think it whispers — I
Can hear my uncles, cousins, grandmothers,
The aspirations of their muscle-thrusts,
Their life! Intent and hope and wonderment!
Constrained, but bursting at the seams of chains!
If labor is the half of property,
The very pledge and proof John Locke averred,
Are we not half in blessed ownership
Of all the eye beholds? Earth swears it so!

it's tangled through with you and me

This plant, it's tangled through with you and me,
Half brown, half white, all weed; the way it scrapes
The hands like brambles. All our tangles, all
Our liveries, pretensions, fashions, fads,
Beau Brommelies. This cursed plant, this plant
More beautiful than any, delicate
And scrubby, ruddy-red with blood in veins,
This weed that ambles to the skyline just
As men in chains may rankle lined in rows:
This shrubbery is but America
In vegetative effigy and bust!
Our softness and our prickly thistledom.
The dreaminess of clouds on crispy stems.

A scoop of sherbet held on chocolate twigs.
The ocean foam, batted by winds on slender
Tendrils tender in ballet upstretched
With Wenge arms that pray in rustling breeze!
This herbage still crestfallen with the tears
Of sundered, bound beloveds; more the rain
To frothy thickets than the heavens' pour,
For all the twigs were wettened by the brine!
The ruthless, savage sun, the taste of dust,
A bitterness, skin absolutely baked,
The break of lashes on the scarring back —
These legacies this gorgeous thing holds too:
How can it stand? No wonder it must crouch!
The weight of whiteness on its shoulders lames
Its scraggly reaching up to beg what rain
Might drench and pardon it from searing sky!
Yet it flies high as flags may furl in breeze,
Once loosened from its pods. And there its fur,
White snow in billowed wool, ships forth on foam
Alike its looking glass on tossing waves.
It also knows of tenements and slums.
Its sotto voce psalms have keen laments
For looms that claimed the fingers once of maids,
Of Olivers in dusty warehouses,
Of churning belts, storm of tinnitus roar
Of mills, monstrous cacophonies of halls
Where sullen, soot-besprinkled cinder-folk,
In discontent of pennies for their pounds
They made for Barings, fabric-wove the webs
The uptown socialites and dandies wore
As sauntering on boulevards. It knows
The stench of smoke in Manchester and Leigh.
There's Birmingham on either side of seas.
It knows the sighs of both, the hopes and dreams.
Can any disentangle brown from white?
And not be naked? Nor have bed to lay
One's head at night to sleep? We are entwined,
Our limbs in troubled love, hard love, but love.
This plant that clothed Columbian Adam and Eve
Declares it so in testament of limbs!

the walnut

The walnut, elderly, is silvery-white,
Yet olive-brown in youth; its heartwood full
Of chestnut baritone, its blossoms snow
Frozen to fragile glass with satin cream.
Do any of these limbs feel prejudice
The one color for other colored limbs?
They all are one, and self-affirm one flesh.

exit the newspaper

Exit the newspaper and deepen time;
Look out ancestrally with ancient eyes.
This time with all its hypes and fears shall pass,
A simple moment in the full surprise.
We're being poisoned with adrenaline
About such things we never may control.
Step back, withdraw into a larger view.
It's futile to engage in maddened times.
Make good your bold retreat, fill up your stores,
Prepare the paradigm that is to come,
Always outside those watching every tick.
The new is born digesting all the old.
So many fertile, fallow yesterdays,
Abandoned, ready to arouse our wits.
The bear knows when it's time to hibernate.
Ready in winter's gloom the coming Spring.
The most important worries of the time,
Wide hailed and brooded, are irrelevant.
No ancient oak will ever give a damn,
And as for me, I walk the Druid's path.

get on through

The way to get through Donald Trump is sleep.
Just sleep. Just pull the covers up and sleep.
Leave off the circus show; we all are fucked,

So just relax: we've been for quite some time.
Apply the Stoic *apatheia* now.
It worked in Nero's time. It will work now.
I've had it wrong the past three years, I see.
Resistance is not on the schedule now.
If fascists infiltrate, no one seems care.
The task is to survive and get on through.
Mirage like this can never last too long.
I've let some fool and all his cronies wreck
My health. To hell with that! I'll go to sleep.
Just sleep on through this sordid presidency.

the Chattanooga barber

The Chattanooga barber with the crimp,
Who offered an initiation, hair
Made kinky: Jung, go Black! Accept the gift!
Dreaming in Africa, your psyche wields
An offering of opportunity.
The barber is a psychopomp, a guide
Beyond your European boundaries
And crass colonialism: take the leap!
The fracture in your being here is seamed.
But you refused. Superiority
Was more important than becoming whole.
Horus in Tennessee had offered dawn.

disaster this! disaster that!

To push away the paranoid and dour
With a grouchiness they cannot bear
Is my felicity and will of now,
For I don't want to hear it! None of it!
Disaster this! Disaster that! Just shut
Your fucking mouth, I do not want to hear it!
Goddamn Americans, still Puritans
In their apocalyptic, doomsday shit!
Just shut the fuck up, do you hear me, fools?
I will not live in midst of fear or fright;
If that to you is flight, vive escape!

Don't give a fuck! Just shut your fucking trap!
I wish the best to all, now let me be!

aloofness is the savior of my life

Goodwill to all who live and let me live.
Benevolence to all who live on earth.
May they be happy as I wish to be.
May they find joy and even share in mine.
May we vicariously share peace and love.
I live away from hubbub and its pain,
Will not descend into the troubled mind
Of these contemporary times, no way!
I live in blissful contemplation here,
And wish you all the best, as I wish me!
Aloofness is the savior of my life.

corrodes the pitch between the plumes

How is it that we lose our loftiness,
Our wings that will us towards the heavens' heights?
Beauty alone makes feathers meld as one,
Nobility of character and love.
But every ugly word or deed corrodes
The pitch between the plumes, and plummets us
One echelon the lower, one degree
The lesser of that beauty we so need.
Thus Plato, thus the common sense of heart.

there I once was young

The innocence still pulsing in the bruise,
I yet caress the wound to feel its trace

And outline : there I once was young, there world
Was freshness in the opportunity
Of knowing, there the nimble spring of dance
Was still incipient in legs of mine,
My mind expectant of each wondrous wight
I happenstanced to fall upon with joy.
No bunkers salvaged from the shrapnel there
Between, but thinnest, most receptive film
(At most), so every butterfly was in
My aura, every beetle crawled inside
Of me, and every hummingbird zipped through
My wonderspace, ever-gasping delight.
I pause before exquisite sentience
Of this my flesh inquisitive and wise;
There is a creature here to tender love,
A royalty in larva furled as yet,
Intelligently shy but peeking out,
A gala-soul awaiting fond debut.

erastes and eremenos

Erastes is the spirit, *eremenos*
Is the soul, the wooer and the wooed.
You cannot know the soul; only pursue.
Her modesty is coy and curious;
She's wise and leaves her beauty's fading trace
Miragenous-evocative in signs
Of wonder, and the game is to follow,
And ginger-question, intimately soft
And with the tenderest respect and love.
She is not catalogued nor pinned but free
In her enigma: sphinx is her true name,
And mystery with love is what she brings.

giddy Oz

And even now, and even now, the lights
Are flashing, Santa Monica and Highland;
Strobes through penetrating thick of black,

Fog rising through the smoke to balconies,
And linen blouses billowing neath fans,
With twirling skirts, Guy in his wedding dress,
A hundred wannabe LeStats about,
Miss Frankensteins, Shermy in polka dots,
Blonde Ursula with cigarette and gin,
Me crawling on the floor alike a dog,
Soft Cell with silly sirens chauffeuring,
And Jason Lavitt at the turntable.
Right now. My heart is nowhere else. Brainbug.
I'm can-can kicking in my purple tights,
My slut shorts frayed, their jean-threads hung with whips,
Court Jester Mercury above my brows,
Eyeliner blazoning a "Gothic Chef",
White cook's hat on my head above raised brows,
The most enticing vixens anywhere
Surrounding me in haughty gaudiness,
And all I'm thinking of is that Elyse
With violet-wine of hair in San Francisco!
As if she, hallucinate, were right
In front of me, flirtatious, silly, wild;
Once I had a heart; now it is hers,
And so I dance with her in proxy! Boy
Inside of me pledged thoroughly to her,
My bumbling Diotima harlequin!
My crazy, scattered, lost-devoted girl!
My Gothic ragdoll, Renaissance Faire lass
With chopsticks in her hair, a bang slung down,
Those Rolling Stones lips plump, those pearly whites
In ever-bashful smile : there I am.
This body, divagating, has arrived
Wherever it may be, this inky blur
Of modern, sheer irrelevance — but there
My dear puer, heart throbbing's, in his prime,
If yesterday, or all ten thousand days
Since last night I was there upon the floor!
That was the cruciality, the very
Pinnacle, the cliff from which I leaped —
And now in free fall still, I yet may soar!
Flash-forward from that night — it's all a dream,
As unreal then as now, and yet so real,
The senses were intensity itself!
Now in the Castro, where we both belong,
In artifice and lace; because we don't
Belong, we do — the incongruity

Is truth, the heart less shy with makeup on,
For everything about our souls is queer,
Is witchcraft, crescent moon and kinky kicks,
An elegance wrapped rose absurdity
In tissue blown wet breeze and salt to skies,
Where buckwheat rust of ruddy steel gates fog
Across the cold and Orca bay! And all
Is unbelievable, is giddy Oz,
Queen Anne and livid-lavender, tall steps
And sudden hills — I got to Kansas City
On a Fridey, and by Saturday,
I'd learned a thing or two — an L.A. hick
In citadels and cynosures of art
And culture — this is Athens, this is Paris
Mark Twain wrote Pacific on the shores,
The elfintown chalet of Harvey Milk,
The Ferlinghetti candy cane cafe.
Where Beatniks snapped and Gary Snyder dipped
A quill in inkwells for to calligraph
The Tao Te Ching — but most of all, where love
That dares of now to speak its name, redeems
The lilac frills of Wilde's noble thrills.
For gay men in their own delightful hood
Are somewhat of a womb, if masculine
And pretty, and their sensibility
Converted me, Damascus on the hill
Above the fog — my Christ is Attis, she,
My Cybele — she stripped this modern flesh
Of all its chaff and left me elfin glow,
Reborn, geography of Castro streets
(Psychometry and style) in my heart.
Forever, I am there. I walk with glitz,
That is but streaming, celebrating heart,
And hardly stand the straight's normality.
It lacks the funk, it lacks the needed bounce,
It lacks the scintillating irony,
It lacks the feminine and masculine
Unhinged in each, it lacks the giggling spaz,
Without which joy is exiled and chained.
Nine worlds beneath the tree I do recall.
I call to mind corsets and platform shoes;
I call to mind black lipstick, lingerie
As uniform, velour dresses I wore
To class; I call to mind the Faeries here
And everywhere; I call Vanir, whose spells

Gardner-distribute their fertilities,
The Lord and Lady, and I kiss the Earth,
Their mother. While I stroll the esplanades,
My Toni Apricot, anonymous,
Is here, clandestine to my slinky eyes,
But we will meet at the Mumia March
Four years as hence; no doubt, he styles up
The place, bell-bottom sauntering, with grace.
It's all encyclopedia of soul,
These moments set to burn so brightly bold,
No longer lined in time, but juxtaposed,
A waveform simultaneous and pure.
It has not passed. It's present here and now,
For history's the substrate of our dreams,
And most vice-versively. I wrote such spells
By living them, by daring; now they swish
In cursive in the grimoire of my life.
I but need to recall, and they come clear,
My Ariels! O sylfan sprites, evoke
What elegances those times did portend,
And make their flavor new the recipe
Of now, so all that cultured promise lives.
I see the periwinkle hair at dawn.

I brought up beauty from the toiling deep

(The truth is I would not go back there for
A million dollars! Those were mines of ores
I delved in coal and polished into glass,
Astounding work of dwarves. But I am dwarf,
A grounded wight of weighty stone and root.
I brought up beauty from the toiling deep,
I earned my heritage and laurels then
I rest upon, and worthily, of now.
Today may be more placid, steeped in calm,
But let me say, adventure is a bitch.
Only recalled does it seem glamorous.
Contemporaneously, it is tough
And dirty, pocked with thousand holes of doubt,
Despairing, full of heartbreak, messy, shrill,

A shitstorm, crazy — with a little thrill.
If you get out alive, you peel that thrill
From all the ample bullshit, — and you run.
Come sit with me by fireplace and scan
My scrapbooks — dear — but I ain't going back!)

cheating scars the heart

It's true, alas, that cheating scars the heart.
I know that well, my injuries still throb.
You can survive, but there's a lessening
Of that fond joy that only comes from trust,
And one's jouissance in sexiness is lost.
Flirtation, once unalloyed purity
Of sheer delight, now takes a taint and stain,
The sting still lingering. You get on through,
Of course, but it may sadden you, and spoil
Some of life's pure cream to curdling.
One's freshest, truest love sends sexiness;
At first one feels a glee and stirring thrill,
But then the commentary rears its head,
The doubts — was this for me alone, or else—?
Such poisonings of sweetness are a shame.
I take the sugar, let the bitterness,
Which has no place, subside, good as I may,
But sigh. It's true that cheating scars the heart.
I'm grizzled, got my battle scars, I'm tough,
I'm strong as steel, I'm tough as nails, I've seen
It all and made it back to love — somewhat.
I'm there, but some of zestiness I had
Has fled. I'm more no-nonsense now, a shame,
For silliness is much of sexiness.
I'm adamant in my vanilla stance.
The less shenanigans, the best for me.
Excitement is anxiety for me.
Let's keep it calm. O cheating scars the heart!

someone else has all her eyes

You suddenly aren't anywhere at all,
Save hither-thither in your flurriness.
You're space-walking, no solid ground to foot.
You're puzzled and you're pulsing in your pangs.
The atoms in your body are now doubts,
You are but gas, a vapor, little worth
And notice — someone else has all her eyes.
You're sideshow, freak, an appetizer, fluff,
A laughingstock, a has-been, stripped of rank
And dignity, a little clown, a shrug,
A second thought, the last place in command,
The so-so coat on hanger in the closet,
Gathering dust, your one-time glitz is dull,
The spotlight now has shifted. You are dark
And trembling. No due process, no real rights
But whim, and favor more capricious than
Endearing. Shock-depedestalled from throne,
One's crown on sale on eBay, bid who comes,
One's scepter wilting, royal robe in fade,
Usurped without a trial, fast impeached
Without the courtesy of notice, robbed
Of role and gravitas, a foreigner
Without a title, sans a passport, fleeced,
An empty category, shambles, ash.
Now pick yourself up from your bootstraps, bub,
And summon dignity from wounded roots.
Your healing factor will in time kick in,
But calluses and scars will be your skin.

drinking in the accolades at last

What I intend to do is but to stand
Upon a stage, and doing nothing, bow,
Receiving hours of long-earned applause
In limelight and in cheers of thankful glow,
For years and years of thankless work and toil,
Drinking in the accolades at last.

my liturgy of this your bust
for Elizabeth of Night

These contours and these flavorous sinews
My tongue, the servant of my heart, knows well;
I've not forgotten nectarine of this
Your juicy curves, and the exquisite taste
Of you — my liturgy of this your bust,
In Aphroditê's hyperdulia,
With rain and forest waterfalls of scent,
My lips but silent hymns upon your skin,
Is clear — and yet my dear, tease on these eyes —
They never can rehearse enough your flesh,
Your wild feline fur and arcuate
Meandering of skin so serpentine
And simmering like a summer's humid night!
Oh, no, refrain again the chorus these
Delightful, jiggling things enjoy to sing!
I sing along! A harmony begins!
The beauty that the eyes alight upon,
Wise Diotima says, wakes up the heart
To joys once dormant in its breast. My dear,
You are the other side of dormancy,
The soaring of that falconeer called love,
Who yonder takes the eyes to fonder things,
Frugivorous enticement leading forth
To adoration lifting up the wings!
Each time these eyes alight on you, they love.

just know they'll flee

It is humiliating to need help.
So if you help someone, just know they'll flee,
Eventually. You bear the pain they dread.
Remember, you are not immortal, son;
While providence yields daily needs to flesh,
You are not limitless. You must conserve.
Abundance means enough and little more,
Not everything, and being mortal, you
Have not the resources divinity

May call upon. Therefore be wary-wise
In portioning your love as stewards are
Who guard a trust. If you invest, be sure
The stores can bear the loss what risks may come.
Be generous, indeed, not foolhardy.
A little excess is a pleasure-touch,
And charity is ever laudable,
But profligacy bankrupting your spirit
Leaves you drained, with little else to give.
Give not to those who know not what they ask,
No sense of measure in distraught demands,
But give as portion pleads its kindness come.
Know that the cup alone suffices need;
You need not give a bushel, short of stores.
A pint of uncooked rice yields two good meals.
That leads them on their way to getting fed.
If with such food, so much the more with soul.

the testament of Spring

And suddenly, the orange blossom bliss
Of April's future dreaming of its fruit
Comes clear on clarion of streaming air,
Aroma-river running fresh to nose,
The season celebrating in its scent.
Alive, and palpably alive, I breathe.
The earth turns on in tumbling roll through space,
And coyly turns its face away or towards
The sun, according to its flirty moods,
And seasons inch the months towards their turn.
This fragrance is the testament of Spring.

the sins of heroes

Now is the time. Now we digest the sins
Of heroes, idols, those on pedestals,
To test our strength, test our humanity,
Test our maturity, test our aplomb.
Will we turn over those we hoped were saints

When we discover they were flawed like us?
Sometimes as flawed as they were no doubt great,
And being great, thus being great in flaws.
Will we accuse alone? Can we forgive?
What kind of strength does it take to forgive?
And have it not be letting off the hook?
How do we struggle with the heroes' flaws?
How do we count our tears and add their worth
To what disquieting and weighty scales
We balance long-admired, precious deeds?
This beast we are wrestles with angels, ai!
We all are chimeras and centaur-folk,
With hooves and hairy breeches underneath,
And seraphimic sculpted form above.
The one who reaches highest often strains
From swampy depths where all one's sin is plain,
And hell of being broken is enough
To steel one for the strenuous ascent,
From whose forbidding heights the ones below
Presume a guiltlessness never quite true.
For good's not good enough for us; we want
The perfect. We demand heroes be saints.
Our calculus naive: else we deny,
Or we disparage. How do we digest
A hero who's ninety percent ideal —
Amazingly ideal, profoundly so —
But ten percent — and maybe long ago —
Some nasty, beastly thing the closet hides?
Does that but swallow up the awesome good?
Does good remain in balance, with a taint?
Do we applaud but cringe as we applaud?
Do we add scars and blemishes to busts?
May those hurt by our heroes add their scrawls
In etch upon their statues' posing limbs,
As footnotes hagiographers forgot?
Imagine : Mao gave Stalin a passing grade!
No honors student, not a B, a C!
Yet still a C! Assigning seventy
Percent correct, thirty percent in flaw!
Courageous and astonishing! For we
Forget, the Moonies of the Cold War press,
That Stalin was a hero to the millions,
Leader of the global working class!
To give messiah but a passing grade!
Yet in that time, his statues were torn down.

Khrushchev declared he was a monstrous sort.
Our tabloid-slobbering lips remember that!
The father's flawed! How can we now believe?
Mao weighed it out. Now that's maturity.
Refusing monsters, refusing idols, too.
He held the black coal in his weighing hands.
He felt the pain, he faced the monstrous angst.
And in his other hand, he held the jewels,
Behold, found buried in the very coal!
The breast that feeds us still feeds us as well
If it at times is dry and can't give milk.
All bad? All good? Let's say : it's still a breast.
The answers still elude me, still I weep.
May we like Rashi calligraph in swirls
About the holy texts our notes — of doubt?
Can we dare say King David killed that man?
Can we observe that Abraham pimped Sarah?
Can we note in margins Israel
Cheated his very brother for his birthright?
Heroes may need their stigmata marks,
The gashes in the marble where leaks blood,
Accusing blood, and yet the statue stands.
Hold to the fire, holding high our loves.

my body once anemone

I feel, and in profundity thereof,
My dignity presides in sentience.
With thought, without, I sense, and circulate
My feelings through my flesh and sensings out
Into surroundings. O, my body once
Anemone, once jelly in the waves,
Diaphanous with tentacles, once fish
That swim scholastic through the jelly deep,
Once tadpole in the estuary shores,
Wet clammy gleaming coat hopping on sand
And lily pads, once serpent slithering
Through fragrant greenery and jungle niche,
Once humble and nocturnal shrew in twigs,
Once frittering macaque on rushing boughs,
Once kindly stateliness of silverback
In deep behemoth fur-ballet through leaves,

Once now this hominid so curious
And odd! Still mollusk lips! Still hands of fins
My fish-before-me's handed down to me!
Still senses sharp-sensate and colorful
With keenness when I once was nighttime shrew!
Still soft magnificence of primate flesh,
Enfolding jungle memories in me!
Throughout, this pulsing lunar consciousness,
This cell-to-cell communion of the self,
In its ecstatic enveloping of
The ambient and radiant expanse,
This near orchestral movement murmuring
Within my pulse and breath, the modesty
Of subtle genius in proprioceptive
Effervesce midst streamings through my flesh,
These feelings, ah! I've followed them throughout,
I've surfed their moonlit froth from tide to tide
Through brachiating, cousinate divides,
And all along, the elemental touch,
Precursing deep emotion, stirred within!
This moist koinonia that knows itself
As moving colony of tissue-scape
Foretells in inner rumblings some hope
Its breath portends as it aspires out,
The antecedent gossamer of love.
Asleep, awake, the alternating trace
Of noticings and sighs, faint histories
That coalesce, neural corroborees
That share vestigial secrets, whispering
In goosebump dialects and slithering tongues
Dryadic genealogy of me
Through dendral thickets ancient in descent!
I feel, and eons feel as well through me.

sociopaths to our own soul

Are we but sociopaths to our own soul?
Schizoid and fickle, eager to dismiss,
Disparage, promise and abandon, spurn,
Preoccupied, promiscuous with all
The dazzle of external thrills and trysts?
Are feelings absent, loyalty bereft,

Our conscience lackadaisical at best
When it concerns our soul? Those letters sweet
She missive-sends devotedly each night,
Those poetries and narratives she weaves,
Do we disdain, discard, diminish, kick?
Do we these treaties tendered genuine
And welcoming, our scribbles mocking scrawl,
American against indigenous,
The ink yet fresh but treacherous at birth?
What faithless wreckage we must seem to her!
What idiot that dotes upon false gold,
Surrounded by her gilded treasuries!
Abusing her at every opportune,
Offhandedly, then slandering to boot!
Philandering, then giving black and blue.
If she may fit in nightmare, or give threat
Of leaving, O the promises spill out!
The next day we're with mistresses again.

speak cryptic and we love you

He lacks obscurity, he baffles not
With blurred enigmas, too upfront.
He doesn't tickle us with riddlings.
He leads us not into the dark of woods,
Abandoning us to the peep of moon,
The howls of wolves, the chill, the hackled skin,
The iridescent dew in dawn-touched webs,
And say to us, you find your own way out!
How can a clarity be poetry?
Speak cryptic and we love you, you are wise;
Speak sense, we sneer, you are sophomoric sot!

somatic moseying through time

I am the pleasure of this witnessing
Of inhalation, exhalation, pulse,
The flow of Qi through my meridians,
The shifting feel of temperature on skin,

The ambient acoustic rippling,
The shadow rousal of images in flame
And flicker, rhythmic come and go and fade.
I am the one who's privileged to be here,
In this somatic moseying through time,
Relaxed in primal twilight of the night,
Content, and simply feeling all my life.

riddle through their mouth

Moral dilemmas you can't comprehend,
Which puzzle you and trouble you by night,
Are dear gymnastics of the conscient soul.
To struggle out the borderlines that burn,
But yield no simple remedies or fix,
No matter how one turns them —which most wish
To turn aside and leave in shaded shrug —
Is just the school our evolution needs.
We make our children riddle through their math,
Enigma into algorithmic nous,
That in their technical capacities,
They thrive (with any luck), and yet we leave
Them flailing infants of morality.
We hand the toddler matches then we pray.
I hear atomic djinn warn, "Best catch up!
I've fellows following, already lit
Their fuses; here is powderkeg, O man,
Your magnified propensities released,
Ready to make a slave of all of you,
Unless your conscience has the muscle-strength
To match!" Already infidelities
To that small voice like whisper on the wind
Was most notorious, before this burst
Of Daedalus amongst us everywhere.
We'd best work calisthenics of the soul
To build up character and train our minds
In I-Thou empathy and dignity,
Responsibility in aching through
The weighing of the difficult from good.
Just where frustration comes, where hands throw up,
Where you'd as rather leave it in the blur,
Keep going, pioneer: there's your good work.

an animal at risk

Not quite so easy as you would pretend,
When grey to greyer blurs the black and white,
Where certainty to ambiguity
May fade, and one is left in moral knots.
If one is noble almost through one's life,
And yet a serious transgression comes
To light, from long ago and shaded haunts,
Some shame or weighty harm against great good,
What then? Demotion to the lowest rank?
Conversion of the saint to lowest scum?
What if a criminal, inveterate
And cruel, renders a benefice so strong,
Its aid and use are undeniable?
Do we promote him in our moral minds?
Does good digest the bad, or bad the good?
Does love but nourish hate, or hate feed love?
Which is the greater fish? Suppose a lout,
A hooligan who's harmed in his own time
Too many souls, perhaps has snuffed their life —
Say some astonishing new alchemy
Authentically transforms their conscience,
And they turn a new leaf most genuine
And hereonin — their life is changed for good —
How do we then propitiate what ghosts
Are ambient around the dried, stained blood?
How do we jury out the Furies' claims?
And living victims, memory still fresh,
If yesterday or decades past in wounds,
Shall we then elevate to offices
Their perpetrators? What shall they think then?
What fair promotion can good mercy work?
What medal-stripping may true justice wreak?
If justice sets aside all clemency,
If mercy lightly relegates what's fair,
Is judgment true? And if a life — a life!! —
Has spark primordial of the Elohim,
However it may hibernate and hide,
What trepidation must we hold to judge?
Herein is vessel of the juvenile
Divine, the brood and caviar in yolk
Of faint, potential Christs (however frail

Of now) — how can we handle these effects
Of foreign embassies divinity
Has left amidst us? Do we have the right?
But can we yet avoid the weighty claim
Of justice clamoring against our ears?
We have two hands; we are the scale between;
We cannot shirk the duty — we must weigh,
Best as we can, and it may teeter long,
A fragile feather flagellating fine,
The subtle settlement in riddled blur,
Yet we must read the enigmatic glyphs,
Take pains, stretch out our empathies and angst,
And set divergent claims in their aplomb.
We're judged by how we judge; that is due weight,
The terrifying implicate we owe.
The judgment we must render to ourselves
Each time our duty obligates us judge
Should make each shudder. Scrutiny is cruel
To everyone. What skeletons you shrugged
In shadows tucked away — ah, no big deal —
Your pangs well buried — everyone has some —
We are the creatures that chagrin has shaped —
Come blindingly into embarrassed light.
(Perhaps you thought yourself a paladin,
And then some witness from the past comes forth,
Not your best moment, that you set aside
And shrugged, "nobody's perfect": here's the face
You never faced, the eyes you would not see.)
Exposed and tender, privacy laid bare,
One's fair repute an animal at risk,
A vulnerable extension of ourselves,
The self that others infant hold in hands,
The love we hope our tribe will keep intact,
In peril, all the archives of good work
On swordpoint — of a single file found!
What human cannot fear to tread such ground?
We stumble, like when we first learned to walk,
Yet we cannot still toddle through our life,
But must at last come up onto our feet,
Where only braggarts boast — the wise are cowed.

settled bureaucrat of life

We need some rules to set the thresholds firm,
And yet thresholds require judgement calls!
A line is good, and yet particulars
Often up close may blur that very line.
The threshold you must keep, but lines are guides.
Wet tissue of the context qualifies
Our generalities, and lines may inch
This way or that, where thresholds really lay.
It's juvenile to think in absolutes.
Case study brings humility to light.
The principles stay true, but in the case,
Apply themselves diversely all along.
A set of rules alone is not enough.
Without abandoning one's precious trusts,
One must learn how to improvise and surf —
The waves, though patterned, do not follow rules —
They rise and crash and turn about at will.
Sometimes the heart must set aside the rules,
When love and conscience light a higher law,
With trivia's effluvium dismissed.
Many a thing has low priority,
And doesn't matter if it deviates.
Obsessive rank and order lose their point.
You're on your own recognizance by law,
You get to wing it in your lonesome life.
Wisdom is not conformity to rules,
But virtuoso skill in using them,
The how and when and how much, where and why.
That takes a lifetime to assimilate,
And even sages still are but old fools.
How much the easier if we could click
A checklist mindlessly, robotically,
A rigid, settled bureaucrat of life.
Perhaps that falls short of humanity.

bric-a-brac of rumble-tumblement

Encubbiment in barrios and haunts,
The alleyness of fuddlehoods and nests.
High furrows where the shadows gather noon.
The bric-a-brac of rumble-tumblement,
The shanty-shamble rambling of roads.
Jongleurement of brick and stone and wood,
The arms of walls, embrace of Wabencraft.
I lost myself in shuffling rabblement,
Dividing strings of saunterers through lanes;
The pocketscape of neighborhoods was mask,
A glorious mask, the hijab I had need
To shy away my modesty from eyes.
There life was subtle blend and not distinct,
An ecstasy of simmering, mobile merge,
Relief of ample tangents given stone,
Escapes mere whim could slip through and explore.
No cameras, no satellites, no planes,
But dim bazaars with broad-strung canopies;
I was invisible, and thus alive!
No numbers, papers, ISP, or cards,
I was the beauty of a shiftiness,
Quicksilver in the bodied press of flesh.
The boroughs were a blissful gobblement
Of unwelcome identity. My face
Became the sound of me, my inner feel,
What intimacy I might share inside
An alcove in a narrow aisle. Cheese
Was everywhere, odiferous with stank
And local flavor; birds were self-policed,
Gregarious on sudden wing and perch.
You could branch off some side street, where a right-
Angle were never found, but stragglement
Of polygonic miscellany, ah!
The dialects and curses to be heard,
The sawdust pizzerias, barbershops,
Poolhalls and shadowed cushion-booths of pubs,
The statuaries, bougainvillea-crawling
Wicker chapels hid in brick ravines,
With candles, Rastafarians, and Jews.
The huddled feel of monuments and halls,

Gothic and thicket-mimicking, the joy
Of rickety and madcap sprawl
Confined in close astringency of walls.
Magicians, monkeygrinders, fortune tellers,
Cabbage stalls and tempeh breweries,
Caricaturists with their easels, wives
Babushkad in their bustling eagerness,
A coin to kiss and dunk a wench for fun.
I fall in love with every passing face,
Its shapely ugliness and eyes of spunk,
The whole menagerie of characters.
There's smell of wine and chocolate, baked croissants
And bacon, incense, garbage, brothel funk,
Wet dogs and peacocks, squealing alley-pigs
And strumpet hackle-cats screeching their yawns.
There's endless racks of draperies and clothes
To crouch and run through, hide and disappear.
There's grease and candywax, there's cobbled stone,
There's mocking crows on wooden posts askew,
There's men in overalls with pockets full
Of steaming fish that flop about in schools,
There's maids with lemonade and boys with frogs,
And children kicking cans, and dilettantes
Unfolding bedsheets in the billowed breeze
To watch delighted as they ripple forth,
And gallop through the pathways cackling,
Ecstatic cloth a finger kite of winds.
I follow them and shadow in the folds,
Coming upon a slender fiddler, hand
Outstretched; I give him five and sullied coins.
I buy a pigeon from a vendor, let
It go, and whisper charms to soar as prayers.
Jouissance is being there and yet nowhere.

trained the ladybugs

I've trained the ladybugs into my hair
As acrobats and pets. They swing at will,
And rope the forehead canyon walls, and flee
Upon a wing just as they will. They knit
My hair into a dew rag, trampoline
From bounce to bounce, tobogganing my scalp.

They infiltrate the forest of my head
And make me silly to the little girls
Who pass me on their scooters while they chew
Their bubblegum and listen to Brittney Spears
(Whom if I were to rail, O then the tears
To "leave Brittney alone!"; I shall not tread).
My ladybugs make gardens in my locks,
A trapeze orchard filled with their sweet play.

the unfinished cathedral

The unfinished cathedral in the clay,
The mere foundation, over which was built
A hovel roofed with straw, where one has lived,
And thought that was the sole inheritance.
Neglected stones are cause of so much pain.

mist by some oasis font

That I the sun might hold in leather palms,
And blow a wish across the orange sands,
As blue to purple darkens in the dusk,
My longing for the gold and guile guise
Of she with Sheba's signature on skin!
Palm-date confections dipped in camel cream
And honey I will bring, and petal-weaves
Of irises and roses as a veil,
From which her soft and soulful, hardwood eyes
Might blink at me behind her curling locks,
And there in mist by some oasis font,
The fog might modesty make of our lips,
And what their mysteries in sheer of night.
Some nymph within the womb murmured the songs
Of soft her lips so full to me yet babe
In amniotic dreaming — so fulfill,
Beyond prenatal odes, those charities,
So wet and plush, of kisses, gift to me.
Skin is but oil, and her eyes are flame;
Love is then nebula with plasma gleam

Electric in the witches' tide by moon,
And hands are paws in fury's testament
On goosebumped vellum marked with kisses' ink.
Her beauties might exhaust my mines of gold
And silver syllables; then let these eyes,
Adoring, say the rest, of her allure.
The distance only fonds devotion more.

imitate flamingos

Let me my limbs elongate towards the light,
And imitate flamingos in their flight.
The golden laurels in my tossing hair;
My glistening skin more handsome almost bare.
The laughing fellows light on nimble feet,
In festive tunics; gusto is complete.
The choral round, the tambourine in hand;
The double aulos buzzing by the sands.
The ships at dock, their linen sails like moon;
The feast by shores we offer to Neptune.
Gymnastic sinews free as tossing breeze;
The body made divine rests into ease.

an amazing kingdom on its way

Jesus.
What ails her?

Husband.
She cries out by night in angst.
It's every night, and wakes up wicked sore.
She cannot do her chores; she but reclines
And stares, while gurgling.

Jesus.
What is her name?

Husband.
It's Hannah.

Jesus.
Hannah, it is Jesus, child.
Tell me what it is that ails your soul.

Hannah.
I ache! Confusion in my breast! I weep!

Jesus.
Ok, ok. Now listen to my voice.
I'll take you on a gentle mental ride.
Just feel my hand, and trust this tenderness.
You once, child of Eve, lived in the Garden.
Love is but a womb wherein the soul
May be reborn again from Eden's stead.
Let us go back then. Will you go?

Hannah.
I go.

Jesus.
Clear now your mind, and take the path through fog,
Backwards, and back, and still back even more.
Just let imagination drift, and soar,
Back-seeking, through the tangled web of life,
Until your heart pangs and it stops you there.

Hannah.
I follow, Lord. I feel a depth of peace.
I'm moving through the water.

Jesus.
Good.

Hannah.
Yes, yes!

Jesus.
Who were you prior to your woundedness?

Hannah.
I was a fish! I swam through salty seas!
I sought my mate with desperate thrust in depths,
And scoured caverns of the coral, but —

Jesus.
What is it? Speak the wound that silences.

Hannah.
Alas, there is a shark! Of sudden, oh!
A struggle, teeth, blood in the brine, I fade —
That wounded hope to find my mate is lost!
O lingering in skeleton on sands
Beneath the waves!

Jesus.
It sits in you as yet!
Hold now that lonely, aching hope, and bring
Your warm humanity to its cold blood!
Take up the hope, and promise it your faith,
That you shall lead it to the Kingdom's steps!

Hannah.
I will! I will! I will!

Jesus.
Now deeper still.
Before the fish, say now where roves the soul,
What yearning spools you Eden-bound and back,
To where our Source called you by name of light
Out of the waters of the brooded deep.

Hannah.
I'm still, I'm grounded, feeding on the light.
So slowly I stretch out my craggy limbs
And spread hands more bouquets of greenery!
I drift so gently in the tender breeze!
My toes elongate into dampened soil.
I bear fruit. I only long to feed,
To let the sunlight in my heartwood breast
Ripen as nourishment for all who need,
And I'm content, my roots in rich enough,
My canopy of leaves in happiness.

Jesus.
Come back here whenever you need to heal.
Here is your key into the Kingdom, this
Your passport. You are born once more from first!

Hannah.
Oh Lord! I feel it! And the ache is gone.

Jesus.
(To Husband)
She is now healed. See to it that you love
Her in this vulnerability and truth.
Here is the woman you have pledged to care,
Pristine. Add no more wounds, and live in peace.
This is a taste. A little taste, but true,
Of an amazing kingdom on its way
Of now and yet still coming. Be on hand.
You might as yet have opportunity
To share in building it. Remember this.

Hannah.
Oh Lord, our gratitude!

Husband.
Oh Lord, our thanks!

Jesus.
Thanks be to God. Give him your thanks of faith.
Show him what this has meant in times to come.
And now, beloveds, I am called out hence.
I leave this house in peace and newer faith.

such an evil bitch

She's such an evil bitch, that Kellyanne
Conway, I think that many men would like
To fuck her, out of sheer perversity,
To shut that lying mouth and make her moan.
I don't assert that's something to be proud of,
But I think I know the loins of men.

we have the right to never bow

Culture is never sacred, but a tool,

A tool that if it turns against ourselves,
The makers, we may righteously discard.
That right is called the Second Commandment.
We have the right to never bow ourselves.

life as my defiant fist

And if you ask me how long I'll have rage
Against the ones that did the hideous
To me, the answer is, forever, bub!
They met their match when they set to abuse
This one. I nodded and I kept my mum,
And buried it, but I remembered it,
Ready to bring it out and come out swinging.
All my life is one prolonged revenge
Against those dominating sociopaths.
My spite is life as my defiant fist,
Raised ever in the air, and joy uncaged —
A freedom unimpeded by their paws,
A rapture in my soaring wings of flight!

a simple, pious sip

My tongue hangs out — I reach — I grasp — if air
Could squeeze itself alike a fruit and lend
The water held within its vapor— come,
Condense upon this too-parched, desperate tongue!
O nymphs, who lounge on thrones in eddy pools
That splash the coursing wander-work of stones
Down mountainsides with fern lending its shade
To cool the ripe and icy rivulets,
Lend me but droplets from your wealthy stash,
Your banks that overflow! All that I ask
Is drink, a simple, pious sip, some moist
Refreshment! Kneeling here's a supplicant,
His hands outstretched, his mouth but dust and sand,
The castoff from the desert winds so dry —
He's desiccated like a mummy, skin
But lizard scales, a tongue once juicy lush

With succulence now leather flaking off
In sun devoid of clemency and rue.
I know you revel in the white cascades,
And play in plenty of the aerosol,
Slick creatures of smooth eloquence of spray!
These streams are gardens in your tending hands,
Who ripen crystals in the translucent surge,
Each droplet like a grape, a berry of
The icy flows you hoe with fingertips
Of loving grace! Could I but glean the edge,
The merest corners of your rushing vineyards,
Scooping scrap from useless undergrowth,
But perspiration from your ivory arms,
Nothing but dew on petal-cups of rose,
I'd ever be your loyal votary!
I stoop beneath my dignity to beg,
And shall discover even more of crouch,
If you some pure and purling alms might lend
These hands made bowl in mendicant assay.
I but ask billionaires for not a dime,
Mere pennies, pocket change, beneath your note,
But shake of hair, but drip from naked limbs,
But pearls that rest and fall from smiling lips,
But exudation of a sudden gasp,
But imprint from a kiss on satyr skin.

in Notre Dames of sun-swept forest floors

Even the fauns and fairies come to fawn
Upon Messiah's Springtime rising, for,
The winter's shards melting away in streams,
The daffodils in newer sprouts of grass
Caparisoned in gowns of living sun,
Portend when everything will be reborn,
When He shall join the Is and Ought at last,
And never shall that seam be let to fray.
The mist of milk-asperging Seelie folk,
In shyness of their regal elegance,
Shall mushroom-minuet with humankind
In Notre Dames of sun-swept forest floors,

While gamboling lambs teach wolves their deeper souls,
That essence prior to predation's dawn,
And lack, filled up from every corner come,
Steps off its petty throne, when Jesus comes.
This April's day of merry foolery,
We dress-rehearse for that full day to come.
He waits, expectant like a mirthful groom,
For us, the bride, to ready this wardrobe,
To dress this world in draperies of love,
And show, becoming love's totality
(As much as this now fragile world may tend),
The King of Love may come into his world,
And marry in a wedding that shall last.
This day those nuptials we foresee and woo.

our reveries have truth

We lean upon the digests we receive,
That in veracity they represent
Compression of the best that could be found.
For on these nourishments we feed our souls
With such impressions it loves contemplate,
And turn around from every angle's gleam.
The psyche loves this shadow-cinema,
This feeling through the ambient milieu.
And if the digests brim with piety
Towards those ancient rarities they claim,
Our reveries in twilight states have truth.

impressions

The mind but echoes back the cavern walls
The news, to where the anima, by springs
In shadows, meditates, and draws upon
Impressions, both precise and vague, as fluff,
To spin into what yarns she loves to weave.
These are our truths, though they run fictional.
The mind supplies materials from world.
What it finds relevant, she may but shrug;

What it finds flimsy, she may count as jewels.

how far will we allow this Faust?

Philis.
I'm only saying men must have a hedge,
A limit yonder which they dare not stray.
Our hubris long has left our symmetries.
We lost proportion in the forward march.

Petros.
How soon should we have then abandoned pluck?
When we began to stand upon our feet?
When rocks might chip and flake to make new tools?
When lightning strikes suggested to us fire?
When thus we made more foods edible?
Perhaps observing fibers in the plants,
And imitating spiders, weaving webs,
To dress out skeins for coverings and tents,
Perhaps this went too far? Or when we learned
The habits of the animals about us,
And the types and kinds of flowering plants?
Was that when we surpassed the bounds of sense?
For surely all of this at least is found
In all the simplest people we have met!

Philis.
Still yet there must be bounds or we may sin.

Petros.
If these, the simple, were not curious,
With roving minds that longed to see and know,
And more to try these smart, intrepid hands,
In endless tinkerings, indeed, in play,
In joying in a gamboling with world,
How then might live such hominids so frail?
Right from the first, they thumbed their nose at "no",
Whatever "no" the world might bring to them.
What choice? To fold? To go back in the trees?
Eliminate our curiosity,

I'll grant you'd have a different beast, not man.
But grant that interest we've ever craved,
How would you then restrain our restlessness,
Our fervent seeking, and our mimesis
Of everything, that in its time, our mind
Improves upon? To learn, to dare, to try —
Are these not essence of humanity?

Philis.
Your catalogue excludes the very best,
Our heritage of rich, mammalian
Emotion, with its tenderness and care.
And yet what innovation can compare
With maternality, the nurturing
Of young, the bringing into gentleness,
The seeds of love and family and tribe?
Without the heart, how ruthless is the mind!
I fear an ape who ever seems to war
On other apes, but ingenuity
Now funds a treacherous and terrible
Arms race! We must tame that fierce denizen
Of Mars, and bend his mind to charity,
To empathy, to softness, yes! I say
Humanity's a feminizing path,
Domestication of the warrior,
Bringing him home and laying down his arms.
The intellect may be a sociopath,
And all too easily! It gathers facts,
And generates conclusions without heart.
How dangerous this raw capacity,
This callow calculator! If you want
To know the key invention of our kind,
It is the nest! Creation of the home!
I know! How juvenile one may dismiss,
Put on a rugged individualist
Costume, and macho out the mountain man!
But, really! Without home, what is the road,
But desert, schizoid sand, and emptiness?

Petros.
Is this your sage rede to Ponce de Leon?
Balboa? Francis Drake? Or Buzz Aldrin?
A home may be a nice place to return,
But life is in the never-ending search!

Philis.
Return! Yes, that's the word! We must return.

Petros.
You atavists who wish to turn back time!

Philis.
I didn't say that. I said to return.
So readily you denigrate the worth
Of what endows the journey with its heart.
Odysseus! Odysseus! Without
Penelope, where would that wretch be now?
But drift in salt and swill! But mindlessness
Held in Calypso's arms! But swine beneath
The rafters of Circe's estate and isle!
Home is destination and return.
Without a home, a voyager is lost,
Just facts in terrible bewilderment.
So sing your romance of the voyages,
But keep in mind what you would most neglect.
Home's where the heart is? Homeless without heart!

Petros.
So where are we supposed to thus return?

Philis.
To who we are. To some humility!

Petros.
Humility? That worthless value Zeus
Hurled with his lightning at Asclepius?
Whose crime was daring to discover cures?
For horrible diseases? Should we bow
To them? And make those illnesses our gods?

Philis.
Observe your fond contempt, how you degrade
This proudest virtue, giving us the worst
Example you could find! Humility,
However, is serenity, is peace,
Is grounding in the earth of this our flesh.
And yonder that, a caution most profound
For child-species playing with a match.

Petros.

Without that match-play, would you have cooked food?
A toasty fireplace in wintertime?

Philis.
A time may come when we may go too far.
I'd say already that has come to pass.
Atomic bombs and biowarfare? Phones
That monitor our every move and snitch
On us? How far will we allow this Faust?
We ought restrain his puppeteering
Impulse to control, control, control!
Take notice how invasive tools have come.
That's only the beginning! Privacy
Is yesterday, vestigial and frail!
The implants, scans, and probings yet to come
Will rip to final shreds our Bill of Rights!
This isn't paranoia, but the facts!
Intrusiveness in color of the search —
Perhaps that's all the search amounted to!
A theocratic technics, promising
Empowerment of demons yet in man!
Each tool but magnifies the reach of ghouls,
Hands them a knife to etch upon our hearts!
No no, don't start! Don't ask me to believe
That in the end, the better use will win,
The worse shall yield! You have no solid grasp
On how we might control control itself!
There's no one at the helm! The tools revolt
And have their way and wreak their blinder will!
Idolatry is rampant; we must bow
To technological altars and priests,
Who totally uncritically approve
Whatever new device the psychopaths
May dream! Do not insult my keener mind!
Already I know what you seek to say!
"Science itself is critical." Bullshit!
Not morally! Since when has it restrained
Itself from any new ability?
And ever asked itself what was the cost?
No, we must sacrifice for research sake,
Enduring every deviate advance
Some technocrat decides will be our bonds!
Meanwhile if we object, along will come
Some technic Pollyanna to convince
It's all for good — we should submit — at last

The best will win, it's just a little shock
For now — and how can anyone object
To choice? Well, no one asked my choice! No one
Consulted me about a hundred toys
That now have spread throughout society!

Petros.
What would you have? An Amish lifestyle?

Philis.
Perhaps!

Petros.
Oh posh!

Philis.
Don't shake your head!

Petros.
Come on!
You want some stagnant, artificial past?

Philis.
Just wait a minute! Some is rational!

Petros.
Is rational? The Amish?

Philis.
Hear me out.
They have a process to sort out these things.
Do you? Do we? At least they offer choice!

Petros.
Offering choice? They ban technology!

Philis.
Not all!

Petros.
You want to live a hundred years
Ago? You want to ride in buggies? No,
You don't. I know you don't. Face up to facts.

Philis.
The process. They have one. You don't. We don't.
They give a choice to the community.
They watch an innovation, how the young
On runabout experiment. They look
At how it changes things, how it affects
Conviviality and face to face.
They value that more than a newer tool.
As well they should! They've got priorities!
They get a vote! They get a chance to speak
On how it makes them feel! Yes, makes them feel!

Petros.
So now inventors must submit ideas
Before emotional democracies?
Be vetoed by a feeling?

Philis.
Well, why not?
There's some who aren't so snide about the worth
Of feelings! Councils have capacity
To bring together not just minds but hearts!
To gather intuition, moot it out.
To give wisdom at last authority.
To let the people speak, and hear them out.
Do they approve how this is changing things?

Petros.
And let them censor ingenuity?
Oh no, no no! A hundred times and more,
No no! Let Galileo stand before
The Inquisition, where he can bow knee,
And cringe and beg for their permission?

Philis.
It pains for you to think he might submit,
Might humble self before the people he
Intends to change. You'd rather have it be
Against their will. Technology above
The legislature! Let no one debate!
At least the Amish give space for debate.
We might not like the verdicts that they reach.
But they at least have some way to speak out.

Petros.
We live in the most open society!
If people want to grumble on the new,
The forums ring with such complaints!

Philis.
And then?
Then what? Dismissed. Completely ridiculed.
There, there. You shake your head and laugh at them.
Senility. Just grumbling dinosaurs.
It's adolescence put in charge of life .
Revenge upon the old, now obsolete.
The choice is not an individual's.
Be real! A new tool spreads throughout the land.
And everywhere it touches, it commands.

Petros.
Perhaps the one who first crafted the bow
Ought come before the tribal council, kneel,
And wait for them to give a good report?

Philis.
You don't seem to approve democracy.
If people have no power over life,
If they are relegated to the small
Decisions, in the aftermath of change
They had no chance to veto, what is that
But impotence? The Congress has the right
To vote for war or peace, but must not speak
On matters that sweep through a nation like
A cannonball, a firestorm, a war?

Petros.
You take hyperbole to newer heights.
Demand. That is the vote the market gives.
Your yay or nay is in your pocketbook.

Philis.
An atomocracy! A vote for each,
But none for all. So we are ruled by fads?
So trends decide the changes of our lives?

Petros.
It's better than bureaucracies and star
Chambers! How many years must we all wait

Some crystalline and genius thing of new
That could renew our lives, restore our health
To pass inspection? Would you censor Bach?
Require Beethoven to gain consent
Before his symphonies allowed to play?
Should newer beauties have to pass a test?

Philis.
If beauty, no. If horror, yes. Suppose
The biolab had had to pass a test,
And that Fort Dietrich failed. I'd call that good!
Designing new diseases for the world?
That's madness! What if we had had the choice
Between extensive railways, or our cars?
Whole towns and cities would be different!

Petros.
That's choice! A car is liberty at will!

Philis.
For each. For all, it's a dictatorship
Of roads, and they get the priority
Of funding, permits, reach into our lives.
Now look. You think you can purchase a nuke?
Of course not. National security.
So if some things go through the Pentagon,
Some patents are prohibited or seized,
Why not democratize security?
Are we the people mindless to our needs?
Do we not know our own security?

Petros.
Inventors must receive a plebiscite?

Philis.
Of sorts, perhaps.

Petros.
Are old inventions grandfathered in this?
Just new inventions? How far back do you
Extend this licensing? The radio?
The telegraph? The telephone? Should we
Convene a hearing — interrupting all,
Put life on hold — for every little thing?
And then? You'll have to turn your dishwasher

In to the authorities? Or confiscate
Their televisions? Sorry, Washington
Decided you can't handle that! How far?

Philis.
If you mean to reduce this all to farce —

Petros.
You mean it's not already farce and more?
Let me provide you with a bag. You see
Those cats? Now round them up and put them back!
What's next, Kaczynski? Should we follow him?

Philis.
You say Kaczynski, I say Oppenheimer.
Who marauded more? What beauty then?
Ask Hiroshima's citizens their vote.

Petros.
Unfortunate.

Philis.
Unfortunate?

Petros.
A loss.
Unfortunate. But how can you forfend?
Suppress our very nature to reach out
And know? To try something that none have tried?
Without that spirit of the bold, what's left?
Destruction gone perhaps, but broken souls.
Can we forget? Can we look up at stars,
And say, oh well, it could have been? We who
Touched feet upon the glowing dust of moon?
We'll turn our backs and say it's not for us?

Philis.
Perhaps that could be fresh maturity.
To ask the heart permission first, endure
Her sharp interrogations — with the pace
That councils take — and then vow to abide.
Perhaps she's merciful more than you know,
Delighting in the new that's beautiful,
And yet insisting on forbidding ill.
Is that so hard? Can you not bow to law?

Petros.
I see our eyes cannot find level ground.
I tire of these bindings on my mind.

Philis.
I tire of these handcuffs on my heart.

Petros.
I go in peace.

Philis.
If it were so, I too.

my sighs have fled like butterflies

I would be moved, and yet my heart is still.
In doldrums, it still beats, but trots along,
While I would dream of happy galloping.
I ought be more than stone, an idle rock
The years have sculpted into shape of man,
And yet as dumb as idols in a shrine.
I would be touched, and yet my skin is numb.
I should feel goosebumps in their follicles
Shiver to virginal receive the palm
A goddess in late adolescence grants.
And yet I'm leather stripped of feeling nerves.
The gasp has left this gossamer of skin.
My sighs have fled like butterflies in breeze.
I pass the days in stupor of a null.
I would be moved, and yet my heart is still.

the hamadryad anima

I praise Creation in my idleness,
This bedded body, closed eyes, centered, calm.
The marvel of self-intimacy's flow,
The thoughts and images autonomous,
The cycling feelings gushing and profound!

This most organic bioregion, ah!
This loyal, loving panoply of cells!
Praise then the artist through its artistry,
Beginning here, this pristine wilderness
I co-inhabit; from the Source it comes,
And like all things thereof, is very good.
Praise then the hamadryad anima,
Who tends this lichen-covered forest tree
With love, and dreams her spells with images
As banquets of perception for her cells,
The nectar of the pollen senses grasped,
The nutriment of lullabies, the kiss
Of fellow-feelingness, caress of flesh
With liquid sweet impressions of the night,
Mystic epistles of significance
Through which the tissues share in purpose; this
Gives meaning to their workings, and they go on.
She bathes above, asperging in her spray
All those below, a sweet ambrosial fosse
That runs and trickles through the textured flesh,
Distributing the gatherment she lifts
Beneath to grasp. And here is order, grain
Within the living wood, fresh sap still green,
A strange and wondrous symmetry, in midst
Of vital mess, no lined geometry
Of squares and angles, but the analog
Of spiral waterfalls of light by night
That Fibonacci-fold and hold forth stars.
Here Zoe, animal by anima
(Assembled bones and beating blood in rush
Of scintillating touch, which deeply moves,
And motivated by such loving breath,
Creeps through the undergrowth, and finds its way!),
Fawn-gentle rests in simmering of cells,
Zhuangzaic in simplicity and grace,
As shambling as the litter lush of woods.
Shabbat here nightly works her miracles,
Her wu-wei gardening of wisdom's crops.
She rests, and yet all happens beautifully;
She takes recline, and dream is explicate.
She dwells in sheer shalom, and world's relaxed.
In her embrace is when is said it's good.
Six days of midwifing his paramour,
Then one whole day but resting in her arms,
But gazing on the spectacle of birth.

This body is such birth-stuff that they dreamed.

giving it one eye

When media its Eye of Sauron turns
On someone, every headline will bombard,
1000 plagiarisms, little else:
Observe. Attention is bombardment, news,
Harassment. All conform to the same party
Line, a paraphrase or two. This tool
Is not a light shone in the darkness, but
A laser, concentrating, burning up.
It makes a mob by giving it one eye.

the enemies of reason

The use of music as suspense to drive
Irrationality in what should be
Reporting of the truth is prevalent
And troubling. Revival of the old
Orality with visual to boot
Has let the enemies of reason in
Again, against Plato's express advice.
Logic, not rhetoric, should rule the news.

we must assemble

No, public life *is* life, the very life
Of being human, our most basic right!
To rob that strips us of our politics,
The face-to-face engagements hashing out
Our differences convivially. No,
It strips humanity of dignity
To ban the gatherings that make us men.
We have the right to laugh together, play
Together, sing together, eat and drink

And dance together: this is thriving life!
It's cowardly to just submit to bans,
Consenting to hysteria and fear,
Without substantial protest. This is weak.
The lack of faith breeds mere obedience,
As none offer alternatives to Rome.
No higher power than the saeculum,
No God but Babylon, the intellect
A flunky to the state of science, robbed
Of staying power, piety, and faith.
Believing that they follow reason, but
Messiah is the Logos, who reveals
Alternatives to chronos. All the news
Is bad except for Gospel news: the time
Is now, is here, we must assemble, meet
To bring the Body of Messiah close.
You can't forbid the holy Eucharist!
And if you did, observe this pendant cross,
Its declaration of defiant will
To Empire and to laws of slavery!
We aren't bound by any law but love.
We owe to no one anything but love.
The sole authorities with delegate
Approval from above are those who serve,
Who serve Messiah's cause and fellow men,
Who never prove a source of fear to good,
Who never break commandments set by God,
And these the governments of men have none.
Ecclesia is not negotiable.
It is the essence of our worship rights.
We are to be contagious, with our love.

ill words have no worth

I spoke ill words, but ill words have no worth,
Though they have weight beyond their little worth.
But anger is a frail and petty thing,
Which it knows well, which is why it must roar,
Hoping its volume makes up for no depth.
Intensities are surface things, that slide
Away as time moves on, but friendship stays,
If it was love, for softer things have depth.

The heart in reverie remembers love.
My words were froth in crashing tides that fades,
But friendship was the ocean blue and deep.

to labyrinth within

This opportunity to labyrinth
Within, and fully plumb each tunnel's depths
In solitudes is so delicious: watch
The inner figures uppen 'hind the eyes,
Water-ballet of retinal elan —
The shadow-theatre of reverie,
The Balinese reflective-pantomime
Obscure of meanings — this temptation lush,
This keen seduction — but I have no choice!
The sweet excuse! The needed quarantine,
You see — and thus the monastery runs,
Like Julie Andrews, to green vales and mounts!
Great marble Parthenons of numinous
Expanse of me and me alone! To be
The snakelike drift of fragrant incense smoke
That seeks the ceilings — all that magnitude
Of dream and musing — shallow pathway pools
Of water — shafts of sunlight colandered
Columnal — Alexandrias of parchment
Tickling me with scholiast allure!
To tend the feminine moodscape of she
Who dwells me, soft Minerva of my flesh,
The animate librarian of life,
The honeyed queen of this my tissued hive!
To celebrate nuptials with sleep alone,
Luxuriating in this honeymoon,
This owing no one anything at all
Sabbatical, where I can give my all
Devotedly to whim's serenity,
Therein to honor sophianic shrines.
To make a gala out of hermitage!
To dress the sacerdotal living flames,
Accoutrements of altars polished well,
The nave's long halls and alcoves swept and waxed!
An introvert symposium, a sweet
Eleusis of the soul! And thus enticed,

Beautiful itch divine I craving scratch.
Yet solemnly, emptied agora weeps
With dignity, and waits solicitude,
Her gallerias, vaginal arcades
Of grey and blue Carrara in neglect,
Her plazas void of plush cupidity,
The click and clack gregarious of soles
In laughter silent, votive hubbub hushed.
A too-neglected goddess perils us;
It is the theme many a myth well known.
Her court of royal carnival lays bare,
Her festive invitation of the Hoi
Polloi stands jilted in the marketplace.
Her fêtes and gaieties, with which she wooes
The numina of multitudes in throng,
The genius of the gathered demes, are wronged.
So while I maenad-frolic in my soul,
The anima mundi needs love as well.

nothing but drifting mind

I hear the howling winds outside the glass,
This brittle membrane of translucency.
The room is dark. The bed and blankets warm.
Nothing but drifting mind following sound.
Friend to the just-so happenstance about,
Sufficiency of senses is enough.
This feast brought to my door, but lying down.

surely I withdraw

Who gives a fuck is such a lovely place,
A space to live one's life in coziness.
The people never listen anyway.
The exhortations fall upon the deaf.
I can't control, but surely I withdraw.

she weaned me off my gothic craze

At last she weaned me off my gothic craze.
No more indelible allure or draw.
Disgust and numbness, and the memory
It once enticed me. But the fucked up souls
Who filled these awesome costumes in were sick,
Were broken — nothing left to offer me.
She cared so much what people in the scene —
How little I — thought of her; thought that gang
Of addicts with pretentious airs were friends.
Took six and twenty years, but finally,
The spell was broken — all of that a fraud.
A beautiful aesthetic, marred by fools.

surrender is the best of paths for men

After all the betrayals, comes the peace,
Beautiful apatheia filling me
With satisfaction: all that drama fades.
Defeat can be a very calming place
If one divests one's fight from vain pursuits.
She loves me or she doesn't; friendship stands
A better proposition overall.
Then love is will not whimsy, care not angst,
Companionship not struggling in the dark.
Surrender is the best of paths for men.

fuck rock and roll

I hate the spectacle — the giant mobs —
The smell of beer and piss ubiquitous—
The amplifiers much too loud — the sad

Concern for looking cool, for being liked
By idiots who don't deserve the time
Of day — the slimesters and the scenesters — lame.
I hate the dime a dozen bands, the rank
Conformity in rebel guise of hip,
The rampant adolescent attitudes,
The urge to imitate the immature,
As if the callow merited such worth.
Fuck rock and roll. Fuck it and all its clubs.

Lucretius, ah!

A dance of particles, of musical
Notation clashing in a slow ballet,
A streaming tide of blending fronts, which form
Cascades of growing chords! Lucretius, ah!
Composer of the symphonies of time!
Assemblages of subtle senses sift,
The substrata of Debussyan drift,
Pythagorean quantum harmonies
Numerical in Arirang form storms
Of energetic mathematics — oh,
The beauty of nonsensical ascent!
The protozoan elegance beneath
This all phenomenal expanse of eyes!
Atomic poetries not understood
But grasped in ecstasy, whose forms of verse
And assonance alliterate the world
With iridescence! Beauty underneath
Epiphenomena familiar,
Poseidon's oceanic melodies
In nimble salt-spray soft-Coltranic spurts
Of dissonance and polyrhythmic groove!
There is an ambient Monet in things,
A blur domain inherent in the stuff,
But sharpening of shifting colorfields!
What dreams may infiltrate this vast milieu,
Unconscious in its simmering melange?
What physics underlie psychologies!
Are we but resolutions of this blur?
Lucretius, nature's sweet Kandinsky! We
Are swimmers in the avalanche of chords,

Configuring in spontaneity
Contingent law whose grandeur grows apace!
We are such simpletons in face of this,
Such feather-Pierrots in pantaloons,
But bubbling babbleries in boiling time!
If none of this makes sense, rejoice, my friends!
Gorgeous complexity has struck a chord!

frozen glide over the lake

Gelidic glass of smooth and glowing chill,
The gleam of frozen glide over the lake:
The polish of the breath of stooping sky.
What glim of glace in flour-sprinkled flakes!
What winter waxed grandeur from crystal kiss
Of heaven's blue holography that blows —
Such cool and minty glint of eglantine-
Skinned water-gel in undulating sleep!
One slips so easily on frigid slopes!
Eloping with the languid nereids,
Who charmed in ice-enchantment slow to still,
The stealing zephyrs celebrate with zest!

crystal carousel of molecules

This molten stew the soul holds in suspense,
That longs to melt, and join the elements,
Symphonic anima arranges up
In crystal carousel of molecules
That minuet with perfect elven grace!
She sings what would disperse with quiet charm
That stills the restless flurry riverine
To placid flow and frolic, festive waltz
Of effervescent fellows' harmonies,
And gathers grumbling loners to the choir.
Salt Lake City Tabernacle, this!

this bold capacity to understand

How dare you? How do you have gall to spit
On this most precious gift, the human mind?
How dare you, sir! This bold capacity
To understand, and through that, figure out
Solutions to our problems? Spit on that?
The ingenuity creative hands
May spin, as mind and fingers interchange
Their thoughts? And insight linked to insight, passed
Through generations, growing ever strong?
You'd spit on that? You'd say to learn is vain?
You'd throw paideia down the gutter, gut
The project of improving through the growth
Of mind and heart? You'd squander that? For real?
I think you haven't thought this through at all.
If the inventiveness of us is wrong,
Right on its face, pure menace, nothing good,
Fold up your bags, the human race is done.
But we are not, and do not have to be.
Put mind to the complexity of test,
And let us see the mettle of our souls.

whipped cream of dreams

This delicacy of closed eyes is rich,
So much so that I wonder to myself
Why anybody wakes. This is the life!
The conscious life of mere events is dull;
The body is a flavor when asleep.
It is dessert, a pastry in the flesh,
Whipped cream of dreams, a powdered glace of grace.

a trail of apples with a single bite

Gourmet of pure beginnings, pastry cream,
A little nibble of the inner bread,
Then onto newer cream, leave off the bun,

Move on; the middles are too difficult.
The bloom and blush of giggled dawns of love,
The flutter and flirtation and the glow,
The levity and ecstasy, intrigue
Of mystery and curiosity —
The best — now interrupt, and onward sail —
Onto unknown, fresh orchards — for new fruit,
A trail of apples with a single bite.

fireworks in lockdown storage

I'm such ambition in frustrated grasp,
Such striving lost in backwaters of time.
Already I'm defeated, yet refuse
Surrender — that refusal is my life!
My honor is insulted in this world,
The gifts I bring repeatedly rebuffed,
Achievement rendered marginal and void
By envious and apathetic souls.
Why should a single man have his awards,
While I remain the decades long deprived?
It isn't ego that I wish revered;
I haven't struggled through the years for that.
It's worth. I dedicated all to worth,
In faith of recognition and good use.
I didn't sprout these fruits for their neglect!
To be upstaged by pushier ingrates,
Who, less to offer, more aggressive sell
Their twaddle, their obnoxiousness the key
That opens every lock of all the rungs!
I've thought that worth was worthy of some grace,
That gift alone without the blowing horn
Sufficient! Why should overbearing pricks
Rule everything in bellicosity?
It makes no sense. It isn't fair at all.
And don't you dare — you shut that filthy mouth —
Don't dare to tell me life is never fair.
If those were given to me as the terms,
From get-go, I would kamikaze self —
A life devoid of justice is no life!
Yet as it stands, my life has been a kind
Of gentle kamikaze, bonsai soft

And yet insistent. I indict this land
The vile antichrist of antichrists,
Apostate to its core, a lying smile
On its cheating face, that calls the name,
While slipping daggers in the neighbor's back,
Or resting criminal in apathy.
What enemies needs Christ with friends as these?
The worst ascend the highest on the backs
Of all the best, who they insult with joy.
My patience frays; my dreams are fireworks
In lockdown storage; O, storm the Bastile!

the problem is the liberals

In fact, the problem is the liberals,
And always has been, in their brokering
Of discontent, to shore their class rule up.
They're weak and hypocritical and cave
At every opportunity, no balls.
And blaming Trump won't bring your courage back.
Excuses and excuses — but they hate,
And always have, the radicals much more.
They'll pinch their nose and bed conservatives
A hundred times a day before they'll pledge
To someone genuinely holding change,
And when they do, it's sloganeering lies
As pressure tactics, no sincerity.
Their petty little bandaids on the wounds
Have no intention of rescinding hurt,
Or ever ending stepping on the poor,
Just stepping lightly to assuage their guilt.
"Excuse me, sir, do please keep carrying."
Conservatives are rude, but they're polite.
The natives holding carriages on backs,
You think they care that one's superior
In courtesy? Get off my fucking back!
Now now, let's not be rash, or get extreme!
We need a kinder, gentler piggyback.
Perhaps some better wages, benefits?
A health plan? There you go, now pick me up.
But wait — you didn't come through. Your promises
Are watered down and weak — What can we do?

It's compromise, that's how it works; besides,
These right wing brutes won't let us do our job!
And surely you don't want to carry them?
We'll give you little treats — see how we care?
Ahem — now let us take the stage and weep —
My artificial tears, please — O, the plight!
O terrible and terrible indeed!
O shame and shame and endless guilt for all!
Hairshirts and flagels! Ah, the awful brutes!
How did I do? Not bad, eh? Job is done,
Clap-clap, a humble bow and accolades.
Don't you feel better now to carry me?
Your every issue I conveyed with angst! —
— But where are the results? — Now patience, boy,
We must have patience. That's the way of things. —
And thus the Pharisees throughout all time.

fingers in Kidron's waters

Let fingers mingle in Kidron's waters,
To feel the dust of images once crushed,
To pan for gold Josiah laid to waste.
O waters, let these hands survey the silt
In which the sculptures that the mothers made
To honor the Shekinah rest in rubble;
Fishes eat the Asherah's remains.
Kidron has holy fishes, Levite swans,
O herons nest in twigs once monuments,
The pride of artisans and worshippers.
The nereids thereat are plentiful.
Forbid the nations of the nymphs and fauns,
And banish phantoms, still they shall abound.
Still dance in dreaming minds the Seelie folk,
If legal or illegal. Murderers
Of priests and seers are nidings if are kings.
Kidron still holds the memories in waves.

too far the jungle law still lingers

My friend, staring me in the looking glass,
You're not as yet, alas, fully human;
You're on your way, but still the savage ranks
Too high in you. Too far the jungle law
Still lingers. Too much inhumanity
Oppression and its history weighs down
The wisdom in awareness with the scars
Of sore divisions in you. Brotherhood
As yet is crippled, weak, and faltering.
Too far the cesspool of society,
Its vulturage of offal of the friend,
Made other in the margins or beneath,
Has percolated down into your bones.
The praxis of Messiah is your crutch,
Not second nature yet; fraternity
Is muddled in the bubble privilege
Surrounds you with. The scaffolding of Christ
Is all you have to bring humanity
Closer to you : pursue, pursue, pursue!
As yet, your essence is a P.O.W.,
In labor camps, in Trails of Tears,
In fields of cotton crimsoned with the lash,
Lost in the siphonage of human blood,
Exiled to where we do not welcome in.
I do not yet see everyone in you.
I see a most deformed particular,
Bleached of the color of his fellow men,
Who even in his dreams is monotone
And sheltered. You've allowed too much your time
To imprint you, and let inertia bleed
Your solidarity. Messiah comes
In color of the other too dismissed,
Completing where the partial you distorts.
Where you should have Elijah's chair set out,
Too long you've let dominion have his seat.
Too comfortable to ask the demon out,
You've let the arrogance of being man
Against women, against the colonies,
Have welcome, even meager, in your house.
It's true you've raised a little peep against,
A limp protest, then let him have his way,
Elijah left outside a homeless wretch

For lack of throne in your infested home.
Too much the vermin of idolatry
You've given leave to fester in your heart.
You've learned to but inure what you shouldst oust.
I love you, and the lovely lives in you,
Beauty in struggle with an ugliness
From creeping pestilence noxious and proud
About you everywhere in heritage;
Erect your colonnades to lift this weight!
Raise up the walls, relieving gravity
Of vast millennia of hurt from heart,
Still gasping in the rubble left in you.
Lift up the burden crushing her the soul;
Create an open nave cleared of the dust,
A gallery where she may find her own,
And welcome in her fellow aliens
(For she is strange, and much too long estranged).
Then light from the clerestory may shine
In you, and bring humanity's own seed
(Messiah) flourishing within your heart.
The archives are still mired with gore and smut.
The records that you play were pressed 'midst hate.
You sampled broken shards, corrupt gestalts.
The library is filled with rodent dung,
The corners of the books half chewed for nests.
You've acquiesced to all this sullying.
You need to renovate your Muses' shrine,
To sweep the halls as Lenin swept the earth,
Escorting archons to their compost pile,
To putrefy in their gehinnom's lap.

invested in a single drop of good

I have no time for vain, pearl-clutching games
Of moral gotcha, puritanical
Amusements of resentful, petty minds,
Pretending shock that no one is a saint,
Just waiting, shit in fist, to hurl it forth,
And bask in Pharisaical conceit,
One-up-man-ship in guise of righteousness.
My ethics, militant and adamant,
Are human, granting dignity to face

One stern confronts with fury, hoping for
The best in all, while calling out the worst.
Invested in a single drop of good
Against the rampant ravages of sin,
If only chance of bringing to the fold,
Ecdysis from the age's vile roles.

divided from our neighbors

Our faces pressed into a foreign mold,
Divided from our neighbors right and left,
Inviting not, but Othering our kith,
Until beneath our notice, we have caved
Beneath discomfort bred for us against.

the reason many rouse themselves at dawn

My smooth gluteal crack is melonesque,
Mouth-watered envy, admiration's gasp,
The reason many rouse themselves at dawn,
A succulent epiphany of flesh,
A sculptor's masterpiece, the coveting
Of birds and passersby, an ivory cure
For women's longing, as they pine at night.
The swish of this my dish soft porcelain
Astonishes, yet brings the masses rest,
That things of beauty yet still touch this world.

yet you do

You live through all the things you most had feared.
What you believed you couldn't withstand, you do.
You're stronger than the weakness that forebodes.

There's resources of vast millennia
Within, you hardly know, right there to tap.
You thought, I can't survive, and yet you do.

one never gets credit

If I got paid for all the work I do
While shitting, I would be a wealthy man.
One never gets credit for all that work.

a Sidhe in shimmering

With apparitious blur and hint of light
(A single hypodermic of the moon
On lambent gel of pearl-dewed shadow-skin),
A Sidhe in shimmering from out the woods
Whisked in the webbery of gold-green leaves,
Each step a zephyr-kiss of phantom toes
On rustling litter of the turkey-feathered floor,
And breathed some spectacle of fond-soft sound,
What iridescence of adoring ears
Made marble nave of oaken galleries,
To where some well millennia had sunk
In limestone with calligraphy of lichen
Stood suspended in the inhaled gasp
Of forestry's beloved hush of wind.
Translucent lace veined cellophane on wings,
She slipped a teardrop captured cold in time,
A crystal pendant scintilling with gleam,
From off a sun-forged necklace molten gold,
And kneeling, whispered silent ripple-hymns
On goosebumped skin of water resting deep,
The old but polished stone about the lip
A woodland altar, and her offering
Ghost fingers flicked as quartz fell into fords
Beneath the earth, and satisfied, she rose,
Turning with glance of such mischief-allure,
And sweat-evaporated soft to fog,
The mist about the hidden fountain thick.

Munhumutapa

Nine feet in silken ribbon threaded gold
Behind their headdresses alike the beams
Of heaven on the rippling skein of sea,
As they, with practiced dignity, advanced
In saunter through Munhumutapa halls,
Fine damask gold-rose satin on their robes,
Brocade against mahogany of skin.

raindrop-fall as mist on me
for Elizabeth of Night

This glaze of peachy pulp that coats my bones
Is leathered cream, Oil of Olay, a silken
Membrane breathing mysteries of touch
Your fingers raindrop-fall as mist on me,
Each spray a feathery weave of baby's breath,
Your kisses prairie gentian with dew
On delicate petals, purple-bruise and rouge,
Your breath the silent rolling fog of dawn.

these chants
for Dead Can Dance

The thinnest gossamer of elfin breath
In harpstring of the springy boughs' leaf-flakes
By midnight's lunar Mass — the dripping pulse
Of percolating streams down mountain stones —
The coo of cavern zephyrs swift on ponds
In play of shadow-shift against what light
The lichen-speckled branches colander —
The will o'wisp of wicker-bulrush marsh —
The veil of angels in subliminal
Recall of waking reverie — these chants.

from floe to floe on icy seas

A single step ahead of tragedy,
With chaos at one's heels and all about,
Is every Renaissance philosopher.
What can one do but dance ahead the flames?
One improvises in the groping dark,
Uncertain how it all may coalesce,
And doubting, bitingly, at yawning gaps,
Yet nimble taps the boards with sole of jig.
It ever is adventure somewhat mad,
A kooky lack of practicality
That blesses everything the poet does.
We leap from floe to floe on icy seas.

Monica

Long patient did you minister your wounds
Of pride, and seek for infidelities
Some salve, but much abused, hope was the balm
Alone. How fiercely did you contradict
The happenstance of brutal accident
This careless world abides as everyday,
When you, deep in the grotto of your heart,
There at the very springs, where sunlight breaks
Through ivy on the polished altar, prayed
Alternatives, and put the "should" above
The reckless "is", imagining the best
Above the worst as commonplace and rude.
More polished was your faith, defiant, firm
Against the vulgar crudity of things.
You sculpted every day the rougher stone
To chip away at sin, and ugliness
Peel back from stubborn rock, to carve the face
You knew was underneath disdainful sneer.
Instead, a countenance of fulgent light
You summoned, and as thoughts are fleeting wisps
Dispersing and evaporating, you
Kept steady this more perfect face in heart,
Until instead of gossamer that fades
Alike the cobwebs, nay, indeed was stone,

The image statuesque of whom you loved.
In an eternal glow you saw the soul —
Like you, so long neglected, shut inside
A cloister, while the body grasped at whores,
Mere trivia of sensate luxury,
Dispersing self in anything at all —
And pulled her back to who she might have been —
And even further, back to Eden's glades,
In whose most hallowed alcoves she alone
Might find the meaning of her longings' breath,
Their dignity and context — so you kept
Your eye a single looking glass, where vice
Might never spy nor cloud the reverie,
But in your mind, unalloyed might the ore
Its molten gold most unsuspected find.
What else is prayer but this, to shed the skein
Algae'd with pondscum from the filth of marsh
In which we thrash, the membrane underneath,
Still pulsing with fresh yearning love, revealed,
As young as was before was clammy caked
In passing mire? You were laundering,
Pressed cloth on river stones, and beat wet rags
To wring them of their running streams of soot —
Your heart ate honey, locust bread, by banks
Of this the Jordan of your inner haunts.
You kept your purity of vision real
Against the unreality of time,
As it careens in fickle backs-and-forth
Along its sultry river banks, so lost
In error and sheerest neglect and woe.
What was your prayer but mighty summoning,
Goetia of exiled potentia,
The images of light the Elohim
Had lain so gently in the subtle soul
They are but apparitious in the din
And glare of clashing things' cacophony?
You kept the songline throughward dissonance;
In meditation in cellarous heart,
Preserved the melody fragmented by
Distraction, so insistent, if but whisper,
It abided all irrelevance.
You made the miners' mastery your own,
And tunneled deep to echo-lands beneath,
Where noise of maelstrom up above was dim,
So that the silent majesty you brought

Might resonate through years in marble halls.
The soul that should have been received, received
By you, and sheltered in its banishment,
Until such time your most beloveds woke
From dizzy stupors then reclaiming her.
She had a refuge in your shrine of prayer,
An architecture worldly types oft scoff
As nothing-stuff — but in those precincts, she
Found sanctuary — for you never flinched
In your belief, that disobeyed the laws
Of zeitgeist — that a better world was nigh,
If hearts might seize on it — indeed, on hand,
If still a phantom yet was rapid dawn —
In night's retarding, you saw Eos glim!
Still yet these mountains of your Berber name
Rest dormant in the city's midst and wait
Our soulless emptiness to reach its pang,
At long last introspective, calling out
The name of Anima your African
Foothills and heights keep hidden in your depths.
O Womb of Augustine, awaken us!

you are here when you are not
for Elizabeth of Night

Your lips are feathered animals with wings
That flit and flap to visit me by night.
Your lips are phantoms that in ghostly kiss
But rouse my longing for the whole of you,
And sweetly taunt me terrible with lust.
Ah, that those thoughtful words you utter breathed
Two centimeters from my yearning tongue!
I'd sip those words and savor that fine tongue
That whispered them to me while eyes adored,
And trace the semiotics of response
With fingers in soft cursive of caress.
How can your presence and your absence blend
So far that you are here when you are not?
The wick you lit still candles through the wax
Of this my flesh, which seems to melt with you.
The reverie of our adventures lives,
Just as the echo of your laughter rings

Resoundingly in me without surcease.
All measures which display distance now lie,
For though the miles stretch, you are right here,
And every absent moment is but sweet
Anticipation of your flesh on me,
As even now your spirit here abides.

second Baudelaire in mystic robes

That pantheist, for whom all things were God,
Who threw himself from ceremony to
Fresh ceremony, with enthusiasm —
Mystic of the every mask of God —
No boundaries — O how I envy him!
In elegance and robes, and circled round
With Hebrew names, the incense thick in air,
The candles all about — promiscuous,
Given to every spirit, whom he saw
As mirror — if a shard — of Elohim —
Exploring every nuance in his soul —
Voyant of each mythology and race —
No mountain higher than he would ascend —
That rock star prior to the rock star's age —
Flamboyant, equal opportunity
Lover, if queer — a dilettante whose taste
Was epicurean, voracious, wide —
A wicked sense of humor — widely read —
An underrated poet rapt in verse —
A denizen of sultriness and spice —
The author of a dozen tomes arcane —
However flawed, however full of sin,
Shortsightedness and selfishness and lust —
I can't help loving him, despite it all —
He simply was too bright — too full of spunk
And gumption — underneath it all, a new,
Ecstatic Dionysus for our time —
Puer aeternitatus veiled as man —
A worshiper of wonderment and awe —
A tragic, tragic life, that didn't pan out
The way he'd hoped — the way that he deserved

For all that genius scattered everywhere,
With disappointment all about, what loss,
Despair — his campy love of scandal, air
Of Rabelais and willful libertines —
His vision of an age more sensual
And sybarite! — and for his shadow-side —
Flirtation with the fascists, sacrifices
Full of gore, and things best left unsaid —
I must condemn — and yet what Anakin
Within that shroud and cloak of Nuit's stars —
What vast potential — ever straining forth
For more — what curiosity and wit —
What hubris — what sad junky hooked and trapped —
What second Baudelaire in mystic's robes —
If you would place him in the triangle,
I still must have converse with this fine soul.

this vast collage

The impressionistic knowledge base of folk:
A headline here, a snippet there, a slice
Of life, a synthesis of what's been said,
And what from this they think is typical —
This vast collage, papier-mâché, melange,
Collectively has wisdom in its heart,
If not misled by tabloidism's slants.
We piece and patch together this our world
From bricolage, and make a general sense.
It's in particulars that wisdom grows,
Case studies: when the jury meets the men
It must acquit or else condemn, it kneels
Before the hallowed gravitas of this
Its onus, and their principles are put
To test and task by the complexities
Of lived reality — and here, where they
Know well the difficulties of a life,
They're often better than a learned judge —
Though he has knowledge more precise than theirs,
They have experience, which they can trust,
And hunches wiser than the adages.

demammals us of sense

We've lost our senses, lost in the abstract:
Our animality, our body-sense,
Is often our salvation, for it draws
Us close in presence and affection's warmth.
We feel the other close to this our skin,
Their breath, the way their body moves, their eyes.
But the new electronic quarantine
Of cyberspace *demammals* us of sense.
We lose our minds when we're so out of touch.

libido dominandi

He's parched, on hands and knees, his eyes half-glazed,
Half-crazed, he pants, his thirsty tongue wags out,
Mouth full of grass, with burs in naked fur,
He raves, his sorrow raging in his breast,
His emptiness consumes him. Gilgamesh.
He lost it. In his mad craze to control,
He desecrated hallowed, sacred groves,
Refused the heedings of the Goddess Love,
And lost his very soul, his Enkidu,
His wild self, and now on feral fours,
He licks the dirt and growls alike the beasts,
But has no joy without his counterpart,
The paths of immortality now shut.
He thought he were a kind of god himself;
He sought to sink his tentacles through all,
Manipulate and puppeteer the world,
Forgetting that the world is full of gods,
And soul is intermingled with the whole
(Thus Aristotle wrote that Thales said),
Whence everything resists single control.
Only in dialogue is harmony
Achievable, for nymphs and fauns abound,
If seen or not, for soul pervades the all.
He thought to raise himself above the high,
But found like dust to dust, he was but man.
In hubris, his *libīdō dominandī*

Gave offense to the divinities,
Who thrust him in the clay and knocked him down.
He worships now the emptiness itself,
And thinks that wisdom in his wretchedness.

forbid ye not the Dionysia

Forbid ye not the Dionysia,
I beg of you, on hands and knees implore!
If bodies fail to lend themselves to nymphs,
To let the satyrs speak, and sylphs profess,
These vales where Monica runs through will weep!
These ceremonies keep the soul alive.
The world abides in them! Do not foreclose
The wamkish, where the spirits dance the folk!
The land shall hunger, and the countryside
Shall thirst to mingle with the flesh again,
To rise ecstatic through our moving limbs,
Receiving audience to witness them!
O willows must tangle with costumed ones,
And oaks and walnuts be the colonnades
For festive ceremonies of the grape!
These are essential, vital facts of life.

the canyon holds the vulva of the town

The balm of May is on the walnut leaves;
The mustard simmers in the fragrant sun.
The oats, content in tickling of wind,
Rattle their sough, and elder flowers palm
A mirror to the sun. The land is clean;
Its greenery is fresh. The purple sage
Sprouts dainty bugles from its many pods,
And hillsides lounge their curves in velvet chaise
Of fluffy chaparral. Through wicker mesh
Of willow brush, and verdant flags of reeds,
Peeks Robin in a flash and hint of hood,

The feathered fellows jubilant in tunes;
The whisper of the Stratford Bard in breath
Between the alders, aerosol'd with scent,
With echo of the naiads by the stream.
White lurid naked limbs of sycamore
Bathe brothel in green pubic-sheltered creeks,
And stretch their sultry Aphrodite tines
Towards canopies of linen-billowed blue.
The rust of raptors cuts the winged air,
Their plaintive cry in rippling clarion.
Give ear, and eyes, excite your color mirth,
And drink liqueurs of tinctured, textured hues!
In bosom of the lowland lap, the gates
Of Seventh Rays, swirled with their spiral steel,
Toupeed with sprays of snow-white lips in bloom,
Stands sheltering the gnomes and dragonflies,
The archives of the wizards yet arcane.
The shaggy peakside shocks of Lincoln green
Entwine flirtatiously the jutting stone,
While oaks lean in, conspiring their limbs
Across the road a garlanded arcade,
And fireweed makes candy of the slopes,
Pastel if neon pink. The ancient ones
Cavort serenely in the gullies' gills,
Unphased, untouched, irrelevant of men.
Now snowflake-flits the adolescent moth
In fickle steal-me-kisses from the fleurs,
While long nosed giant dwarves above look down.
Beltane is advertised for all to see
In blazing lightning strikes of beaming sun,
Which ziggle from her fiery fingertips!
The canyon holds the vulva of the town
In moist and alcoved cups of loving arms,
Preserving uterine its mysteries.

the lurid spa of afternoon

The fennel furry fringes green the edge
Of highway serpent paths, and poison oak
More further in guards well the sacred groves.
The Spring has garmented the slopes in gowns
Of flowery velours and copper green.

She dips her limestone toes in cooling baths
That lap upon her briny, and she sinks
Into the lurid spa of afternoon.

becomes new rhyme

Antony.
Your face so fierce it ravages these eyes
Alike a tiger — thirstingly for you,
Your eyes but make me pant — you knock me down
With beauty from unearthly wellsprings — I
Am stupor, little more, in sight of you —
You change my breath — its little feet recede
Like waters from the sands suddenly shy,
Then too allured, the tide must hurry back —
I'm rush of gust on sails in gale of you!
Your smile peels my calluses from skin,
Crustaceous years roll back to fresher days,
When heart was membrane love did play upon —
You are a string quartet that shivers me —
These goosebumps are the currency you trade.
Your face is serenade alone — your grin,
The mischief of an open kiwi fruit
In sour-sweet of succulence and juice.
I am some shepherd boy with sylphan wings
In frolic along the mandala of you,
My piping reed the tune of you in me.
In the illuminated manuscript
Of you, gold letters edged on stunning bronze,
I am some cap-and-bells in gloss aside
The discourse of your gorgeous curvatures
Some scribe in cursive inked so long ago.
I'm exiled from my smooth decorum when
You look at me, or I at you — I'm lost,
Utterly in sudden bewilderment —
The wind has taken this my stolen breath,
And given it to you — if you inhale,
You take me in — I'm wafting on your lips —
I'm in your moist and cavernous acclaim —
I'm ecstasy itself in your embrace
Of but the air — what air you took from me
In simply gazing! You're the tiger's mate,

Who stalks me in the forest dark by dream.
I was a solid thing; in you, I melt.
Once man, now puddle, but a consciousness
So aching and acute of beauty thine.
A life of prose in you becomes new rhyme.

giggling in their leaves

The sweat of summer Jack drips down the tines
Of woodland bridesmaids giggling in their leaves;
His smirk is fertilizing pluck of lust,
The burst of pollen on the blushing breeze.

hobo hum by phantom night

A hiker slipped from these steep cliffs ago,
A hundred years or so, knapsack on back,
Ecstatic scaling of the sheerest heights —
And fell abyss in melancholy shock
To beauty of it all, and met his fate.
He'd made these hills his herbal hermitage,
And plied his teas to those who ventured close
To where he timbered shed upon a knoll.
They always saw him wandering about,
And some still say they do, in ghostly blue,
And humble hobo hum by phantom night.

such shape as will bewitch the heart

Holofernes.
She's likely more a djinn, ephemeral
And spiteful in her beauty — species of
A gorgeous reptile, cold blood and aloof,

Unworldly, creature casting out a trance —
A dazzler of the deserts, gilded gleam
On sifting sands. A torn-out vellum page
From grimoires — this her face, a stolen spell,
Her body but a charm, and amulets
Her eyes! A Picatrix unrolled in flesh,
A scroll of Aphroditic glyphs in sex,
A flighty flight-risk burglaring one's heart.
Don't lift the lid on this the bottle's brim.
Once aerosol'd in recels' scented cloud,
She takes such shape as will bewitch the heart.

Melusine.
My heart's not fickle; it is shimmering,
Alike the serpent's scales, in back and forth
Of shifting light; I'm loyal through the all
Of fond allegiances that come on me.
I'm not a slut; I am betrothed to each.
Apostasy to every boundary line,
Loyal as yet to all the nations' lands,
I'm bigamy again and yet again.
Catch if you can — you can't — into such fonts
As are my purling haunts I slip — I dive
And melt while diving — then I am but splash!

the temples Theodosius forbade

Making hollow shells of monuments,
Mere walls and pillars, ruins of an age,
The temples Theodosius forbade.

perfect stillness of a moment's breath

Cool lulling of the motive air through panes,
Caressing by the world in gentleness,
The perfect stillness of a moment's breath.

this suite that lilts my ears

The biplane gyres on the whispering loft;
The distant buzz leaf-blowers hum on breeze;
The river-rushing restless breath of wind;
All swirling in this suite that lilts my ears.

let me be crying swan

Let me self-pity beautifully, friends —
Let me be crying swan — in pink of dusk —
That tilts its neck as if to drink the milk —
Carafed by crescent-cutting moon — in sky,
And keen its plaintive Turkish loonings' — rasp
For mate who fled the highways of the breeze!
This ache! This ache! This ache that grips my gut,
This melancholy howling pain within,
This richest sadness — scraping my insides,
How may I sing it, serenade my soul
Its evanescent longing for itself,
Its precious essence — weeping —in my trunk
For some sweet worship sorrowing its worth?
Be melodrama, my intestine grief —
Libretto forlorn diva soliloquys —
Cry rhythm — cake-sliced breath so sweet — of verse,
And stretch your palm to pet the billows' fur!
Silk-captivate the spirit audience
With this your child klezmer melodies —
Press back of palm against your knitted brows,
And make your grief the sweetest aria!
I hear you simpering in me, my pain,
My pouting gut; release those sobs, and sing!

buxom moaning murmurings

Those lips release the flowing, molten ore
Of air, a silver alloy mixed with gold,

Which cools metallic-smooth in ears of awe.
She ushers smooth the forge's white-hot flow
Through lips of liquid candy-cane, that mint
The flavor of the steaming orange melt,
As it, now icicle in air, is rush
Of lunar ivory-argentine, so curved
And shapely, buxom moaning murmurings
That woo the flutterings high in the breast.

she dines with Petrarch in the attic space

A jilted bride who ran to railroad tracks,
And threw the petals of her day's bouquet,
Forlorn and one-by-one, as she looked on
Receding distant steam of chugging train.
No note, no reason why, but empty space
Upon the waiting carpet, family
And friends assembled in the chapel's round —
The sole goodbye the chug of fleeing wheels.
She sits, white-lily lace in tracery,
On dirt, mascara moist that runs to rouge,
With only riddles for her absent vows.
Enigma plucks her lute a plaintive tune.
She's wedded now to loss, which has more faith
Than men — she weeps to summon sleep by night —
She sips a foaming latte in the dark,
And ponders in her cloister scholar's thoughts.
A hammock in the attic, incense fog
Against the windowed moon in sepia,
With cobwebs' cracks upon its snowflake glass,
A stack of hardbound books on either side.
A scrapbook's textured folio on stand,
An inkwell and a quill, with Autumn leaves
And glue, and ribbons, traces of her pen
In cursive odes, with dribbling stains and drops,
The scent of roasted dust and spice of must.
Her cats curl round and fluffy purr her limbs,
As she adjusts her spectacles and reads.
The night's too long to mourn, for Artemis
Has work for harvesters with ivory scythes

The midnight bumper crops of philosophy.
Her melancholy brewed to roasted brim
Has freed her — now she's almost glad he left,
Her lovers multiple in serenade
Of discourse : Aristotle, Plato, Proust —
Her sorrow, musted, cellared, now Merlot,
And Dionysus is a kind mentor
To her — but simple sips amidst the leaves
Of weighty tomes. She writes her masterpiece,
A dissertation on good riddance, grins
A wicked satisfaction, knowing verse
Shall prick the weeping eyes of many pricks
For years to come, who never shall her have,
As envy grips them — and in laurels' loft,
She dines with Petrarch in the attic space.

a silent snake

The lemon-maple marvel of those fronds,
Frosted white fuzz with fur, the scent alive
Upon my fingertips — and Everlasting!
Cup the feathery cornsilk tendril-tips
Of green-blue sagebrush on my palms so sweet —
And suddenly behind me, slithering out
Mown grass, a silent snake! I step back fast,
Now looking round alert and everywhere —
Three feet perhaps between us, but the snake
Unphased, slow paced, and curious, its tongue
Wisping the air as if to lick it clean —
So smooth, so certain, liquid in its gait —
A rhythm of the earth's deep thumping pulse,
Tai Qi but limbless, royal nonchalance,
A simple spasm, and the serpentine
Movements but glide like melting ice on rock,
And glisten in the straw. Adrenaline,
Cold and electric, lightning strikes through nerves,
And yet a fascination miracles
My breath epiphany: this wondrous beast.
I calculate the distances, the time
To bound across the field, how if it strikes,
The measure of my leaping if I will —
But this indigenous inhabitant,

Native and grounded to the very earth,
Is unconcerned, if quizzical of me.
It grooves in furrows of a deeper time,
No rush or flurry in its fleshy bones,
Modernity but gossip lost in breeze.
Inching along, coagulate intent,
I take a closer — cautious — step to see,
Beholding this professor of the grass,
This druid of the rocks passing to me
Its lessons in its cadency and stride,
Quicksilver slow composure — I am awed.
And then — how slowly they are quick — it slips
Over the rocks, and round about the hill
Into the labyrinth of grassy slopes —
Is gone — and I, in tonic of my fright,
Invigorated by its discourse smooth.

doe-eyes to human-eyes

You were a deer who slipped out of my life —
A gentle, wild miracle of grace
I met within a speckled forest glade.
Time slowed, we swung into a minuet
In broken glow of peeking sun, and stared,
Doe-eyes to human-eyes, as we skipped round
A nymphic fountain of the leafy haunt.
It was eternal — until time broke through,
And spooked your shyness — then you ran away.

that's the shit that man can be to man

The old man found a vacant lot of weeds,
And fitted bamboo poles and willow rods
Out of a wagon that he rolled along
Into a line of post holes. Then he wove
Some wattle from the shrubs about the lot
Through all the posts about the rectangle,

Until he'd made a basket most profound,
An elevated nest with crannied nooks
To hold his many — "Sir, can you come here?"
He turned around. There was a puzzled cop.
"What are you doing, sir?" "What does it look
Like? I am building something!" "Sir, is this
Your property?" The old man sighed, and wiped
The sweat from brow. "I haven't any such.
I'm just a poor old man." "You cannot build
On property that's not your own, old man."
Then he harrumphed into a tizzy. "Look!
I haven't got a thing! But I will build
My library!" "Your library?" "That's right!
I've got about ten thousand books or more,
No place to store them but in little chests
I've buried in the ground about and such.
No more! This gallery's a beauty; I
Will treat her like a woman and build her house!"
"But sir," the cop both pitying and irked,
"If this is not your land, you cannot build."
"Should I abandon them? And make them feel
Like whores, like harlots of my lusting eyes?
No, sonny, they are going to have a home!
You see this hive? I've built it honeycomb
As home for them, my many vellum queens!
In here, they'll buzz about, the honey of
My mind, and I'll relax and simply read!
Ain't bothering nobody! Do you see
A single person using this old lot?
Neither do I! And not for twenty years.
It's time was put to some good use, I say.
I've wandered round these parts for forty years,
I've lived in wagons, sheds, and treehouses.
I've grown my food in secret garden plots
Behind the shrubs and bushes, by tall trees :
Potatoes and tomatoes, beans and corn.
I've cooked in coffee cans above a flame,
And used a rock to hammer old tin cans
Into my silverware. I never asked
A handout in my life! Took care myself!
But I've kept busy all these many years
In books, in books, I tell you, sonny, eh?
I've spread a little bleach on newspapers
And made myself some handsome folios.
On them I taught myself calligraphy,

And sir, I've written symphonies and verse.
Those very volumes hang in ziplock bags
From pine tree boughs to keep them safe and sound!
Well, that's ridiculous! They need a home!
And this is it! I'll cart my sculptures here,
My painted cans on broken branches, plant
Them right here, yes, I will. And then who comes,
Whomever! They are welcome to come in
And read. Relax and read. You'd rather have
An empty lot? I'll build a garden for
The kids! They'll come! I'll tell them stories, feed
Them stews, and let them borrow Dr. Seuss!
I've got a lot of those! They're really good!
You know, I had a son. He went to war."
A crack broke in his brittle voice. He wiped
The moistness from his eyes. "Never came back.
I've seen such sorrows that I hope you'll not
Behold if you live to a hundred years!
Come here, now look inside! And don't you mind
My foolish tears! Now look at all these nooks!
You see this basketwork? My Pa taught me
The knack. In every woven pocket, there
Will be a book! I'll fill this place with plush
And ample pillows! Fit for kings, I say!"
The cop called in for reinforcements, cuffed
The man, and dragged him off to jail, then set
The whole elaborate structure into flames,
For that's the shit that man can be to man.

the wonder of the stubbornness

The wonder of the stubbornness!
The grace of creatures so entrenched!
The beauty of resistance, ah!
Security in solid things!
That simple ones persist in self,
Rejecting overwhelmingness,
The gift of each insisting each,
Worth of particularity,
The loveliness of my own niche,
And every other niche beside,
Is guarantee of liveliness,

And solid ground to walk upon.

plaintive sermons to the bears and sheep

Go to, with mission of converting all —
Convert the minerals, the vegetables,
The animals — convert the badgers, skunks,
The hawks, the worms, the rattle snakes and ants,
The bees, the flowers — make them change their ways!
Convince them that their ways of life are wrong!
Persuade them your way is the only way!
Dissolve them in universality!
Annihilate them if you will, them all,
To lead them back to God's infinity,
Erasing finitude and somethingness;
Make nothing of the everything about.
Good luck! Permit me, please, the comedy —
I need such mirth and humor — to observe
Your plaintive sermons to the bears and sheep,
Your dissertations to the eagles, tracts
Left out for rabbits, pitched appeals to rats —
To leave behind their modes of life as wrong!
To live as you do, only as you do,
Attacking badgerness and eagleness,
Assaulting rabbitness and rattleness,
Assailing sparrowness and possumness!
For God was wrong to make the many things,
To forge the many ways with many names!
It pleased him not! He could not find it good!
You go correct that error! Make them see!
Dress them in little suits and coats and ties.
Make tea for them. Explain to them the rent,
Discuss necessity of doing work,
Of paying bills and taxes — this, the best
Of all conceivable existences!
Go out, observe how God may bless your task,
Your narcissistic mission to convert,
Then come and count your conquests to my ears.
Give me the score. Then sit with me and laugh.

the only life for me

My clammy hands, cool to the touch and webbed,
Oft suction cup the mossy tines of twigs.
I teeter over rheoll rapids wet,
Then leap, and make the splash embrace of mate,
And gurgle in the whirlpools with my pals.
We croak a round of willow jamborees,
Each rhythmic rise and fall like pattering
Of gently rushing rill around our flesh.
We bring the rustic melodies of creeks
To alder-spray of winged redolence
Of breeze, and bathe our smooth and naked skins
Luxuriant in perfumes sycamores
Generously exude. Our little ones,
But lately free of sacs and membranes, dash
Whipped tails ecstatically in squirm, and squirt
Through divagating currents pulled in thrills,
Oblivious and silly to the fish
That dash, a tad annoyed, throughout their gangs.
It's glistening gravel tumbled smooth caress
By chilled and feathery flows, and wild romps
In swirling frolickings of dashing drops
That doldrum-roll and rapid undulate,
As one, as happy as can be, bobs up
And down, sometimes the sunlight through the cracks
Of leaf-mesh up above flashing on face,
As sparkles hopscotch on the humid skein
So serpentine and certain of the creek.
It's shore and shallows, lounge and lyric leaps —
This is the life! The only life for me!

shuts me from the holy of holies

What happiness is rare of rarities,
A sunshine for she touches me so quick;
And all more precious for her rarity
With which she veils her mystery in shroud,
And shuts me from the holy of the holies —
Yet if every other year she comes,

And in the twilight but gives me a glance,
Even in dream, then all is glow again.

why I wake and dream

She's more than color, more than flavor, more
Than fragrance to my wonder-sense, which she
Awakens: she is why I wake and dream.
She once was linked like shadow to a girl,
A silly poppet who is now grown up,
But she has taken wing, eternally,
And keeps me company with spritely cheer.
Who's more the echo? She, or that sad girl?
She was a mother in a way to this
Elusive Grace of Aphrodite's train,
Who's spun off cartwheels on her very own,
And visits me at will throughout the years.
I poured so much of me into her lap,
She carries all those heirlooms of my youth
That I bestowed upon the silly girl,
And how that ragamuffin made me feel,
Delicious, special, melancholy, weird,
And magical, my shepherd-girl a'fled.
Now every song that Elfman sings is hers,
If Halloween or Yuletide fantasies,
But this, the spectral echo's much more kind.

the old man who had strangled sons

An old man strangling his younger sons
Upon the altar of his aging years.
"I am more precious than you all!" he cried.
"I am the treasure for which you must lose
Your life." They plead through rasping gasps for life.
The senex makes a bargain. "If I let
You live, you must surrender all your joy.
Give up your festivals, and live alone.

Go incubate yourselves, so I may live,
And I will let you go." They soon agreed,
And sadly shuffled off to darkened caves.
He squeezed the blood out of their hourglass.
The sand ran down and through how many times.
The sons were lean and starving in their haunts.
They had no active lives, no company,
No sense of purpose, just their barest life,
But pulse in veins without significance.
At least their selfish father was alive.
For several years they squelched themselves and pined,
And then he bit the dust as all will do,
Delayed or not, but everybody hated
Him, the old man who had strangled sons.
And that's what they engraved on his tombstone.

if masters did not contradict, no gain

Because he speaks against my liking, I
Shall hearken, and my faith shall rise to meet.
Who shall dispute against me earns an ear.
I read across myself and find the prize,
So all the difficult may come and teach.
If masters did not contradict, no gain.
Great for my mill all who oppose my thought;
Wisdom is found in weighing heresies,
And finding where the wrong comes into right.

ode to a mosquito

I ought to simply end your delicate,
Flirtatious life, little mosquito — but
The dainty way you swim so airily
Through swirling fairy cantrips of the soft
And buoyant breath-expanses charms me some.
I think I'd join your sheer irreverence
Ephemeral sailing to the ceiling's heights,

Then guiling in my gyres as you do.
To me, you're ruffian and thief of blood;
To you, you're Hermes, swift diminutive
On fennel-feather wings; I am but free
And ample snack for lads who love to fly,
And never worry where their drink may come!
My vexing friend, you follow Christ with faith
Perverse, yet Matthew 6 you carry out
Much more devoutly than my kind! How can
My hatred melt when I think life is fun
For you, but fun and flight with little sips
Of swindled blood? My hand ought come to crush —
And yet my silly pity hinders it,
You gallop on the air ballet so smooth!

surging in the vital jazz

The people are a hydra — I am one
Head rising surging in the vital jazz;
Lop off a head, another one shall rise —
We resurrect in mutual embrace.

so very woman at the well

Closed eyes — already breathless — lost in sweep
Of my flamboyance — art is on my mind
Yet as I sleep — then through the fog, she comes...
Already she is... so so so so so so ...
She is a magic carpet, hovering
Me on the air, invisible ... she is
So numinous — her body is of awe —
She has enchantment in her depth of eyes —
I'm votary — it's instantaneous —
When she appears — when she may deign to come —
In dream — the beauty of her apparition ...
Here — she's here — an evanescent touch —
She dwells alone here in my heart these years,
These many years — the Tinker Belle the girl,
The caterpillar, left to grow her wings,

Her Wendy things — while I am foiled green
On hose about my limbs, still flying — free —
Yet who believes — who anymore believes —
The fairytale so long ago it seems —
Sometimes in weariness at this dull age,
I sigh — forgotten of its mysteries,
To which I have been privy, let it be
Two dozen years ago — magic is real:
I've tasted it, I've touched it, I have loved
Its very body as a woman: real.
Some deity descends within a rose —
But sniff the air — that fragrance is your proof —
Your heart unfolds the evidence — you sing
A different timbre, and your melody
More true — you harmonize with things of Spring —
Rare miracles still walk the earth, this day
Of haze and secularity — but veil.
Peel back the misting lingerie and see,
Some secrets of the heart abide. This Waste
Of Eliot is superfice, a mere
Blindfold for fools, a bluff for simpletons,
A riddle those demanding more unfold.
Call it impossible, and it shall be.
Epiphany, if whimsical, is here —
You must be votary of simplest whim
To find — give over to your moving moods —
The moving ones; leave stagnant sludge behind —
A Quest — a knight must have a quest, although
The goal is but excuse to get you out —
The reason is the divagating path
You stumble on, so easy to dismiss —
You have places to go — this backwoods road,
Barely a stepping place the brambles grow
So thick, the wild roses bend and form
A twisted canopy of fragrant thorns —
Trust curious feet — that tangent from the way,
Enchantment beckons. When you feel it, more
And more the magic, real, unfolds its web —
And takes you on its capers, madcap romps
You can't believe, absurdity and fluff,
But trouble and its scent, yet saving grace.
Exactly what you didn't ask for, yet
Exactly what you did — God is surprise,
The Earth holds secrets, ancient ways still hum
Intelligently in hormones of awe.

She came to me, astonishing and pure —
I am a vesicle of gratitude
When she alights on vapor as I sleep,
She's so... so very woman at the well,
The laughing bright, the ghostly white, the sight
Of sunlight through the fog, and beauty's might,
The sculptor in the darkest night, a wight
Of dulcimers and windchimes, pastries light
That melt upon the tongue — she powder comes
And leaves her trace upon these murmuring lips.
It's true, it's real, if only in a flash,
A window in between the passing spheres,
A rolling transit, through the colored stain
Of glass down in a mossy grotto — let
It be a season, and it lasts a life.
Let Aspergers doubt everything — it's true.

a woman in her all

That God appoints his avatars, just look —
A man's a prophet every hundred years,
A woman, every moment. Not a priest
But was a shepherdess, who knows the ways
Between the ways. Sterility is such
A manly thing; fertility is such
The woman in her all — and God is smart,
Outside the institution, in the midst
Of mischief — ripe material to save.

in severalty of orgy

That someone, somewhere, lies on sheets, with skin
On skin in barest trace of breathless touch,
And juices flow, and heaven's on their lips,
A birthday suit of angel wings — if not
Myself, then someone — this saves me — my hope
Is everyone in severalty of orgy,
Simultaneous gustophany,
The happiness in appetite of gush.

It's not me, now, but that is little angst.
In time, it shall be lover boy again.

in software's slits

To Marvin Minsky, executioner —
Your silly little algorithms fail.
They're weak, pathetic, soulless bits of code.
They cannot fathom mind. They are but sin
In binary, your demons set machine,
Your sick molesting hands in software's slits.
If your abominations win the earth,
The less intelligent at last prevail,
You pencil-necked, Poindextered devil's toy.

leches bite the dust

A funeral is such happiness and light,
Exquisite freedom to those touched too soon,
Who get to see that leches bite the dust,
And in real life, the vampires don't come back.

doldrum on

I shall not heed the nightmares of the herd,
Nor give assent to intimated doom.
I don't believe in mass projected ends,
Nor hearken to the panics of the age.
Life's difficulties doldrum on in waves,
As readily as opportunities,
The which, the more creative, dominate.
Though husks be dry, the roots find hidden springs.
The world is fresh, and ever shall be so.

we all must lick the curb

All pleasure must be justified and paid.
If anybody anywhere is down
For any reason, pleasure is unjust.
For pleasure is a privilege, no right.
It must be strictly rationed and restrained.
To think that joy's a birthright: shame on you.
Adjust yourself to the unhappiness
Of those around you : that must be your share.
How dare you feel no guilt in feeling joy?
You're too entitled if you would enjoy.
Whoever's treated worst must be our mark,
That high, no further. It is not that they
Should be assisted on a higher path;
No no, we all must crawl and lick the curb.
To thrill in life is irresponsible.

tirades on tap

O inner grump, O inner grump, come to
Me, speak, and show yourself, what kind of wight
You are. I think you're wrinkled, green, and squat.
You wear a tartaned tweed of itchy wool,
A cap upon your scraggly hair, you limp
And grumble, pointing your old finger out
To scold, and point out all that's wrong about.
So much is wrong! You've got tirades on tap!
You want to rant, and folks to say, yes sir,
And maybe even then still just as pissed,
If not a little satisfied at last.
You've lived inside a log a hundred years.
Inside, you've studied at your library
So long you're wise, but nobody will hear.
For fifty years, nothing but their neglect.
You're irritated, crabby, over that.
You'll sit and smoke your pipe in rocking chair,
Flipping through illustrations from your tomes,
Allowing them to cinemate your mind
With dreams of alchemy and theurgy.
You've sworn the world off from depths of despair,

But don't get you — I understand — started.
I get it, yes I do. Your hermitage
Makes sense to me. I too am all fed up.
I'm tired of the melodramas, screeds
On how the world will end — get off from me,
Satanas! I've no time for such bollocks.
We need a lecture hall, my little friend.
One in the forest, with a fireplace.
A Bardic university perhaps.
Where only those who make some sense attend.
I see a twinkle in your doubting eye,
You're smiling against your reigning mood.
You want to scold, to snap and fuss and teach,
And still the accolades — a little bit.
You've had a little taste of utopia :
No one will ever disagree with you,
But hold you high. And when that go too far,
In praising you, you'll scold them then for that,
But glow a little before retiring
Back to your little wet and hollow log.

I am forever we

To render outer worlds irrelevant
And find devotions in one's very heart;
The psyche has so many loves; it squirms
In protoplasmic adorations, fond
And fond and fond, for fickle Cupid still
Infatuates, for commonality
He embassies within us, making hard
The monolithic tendency we choose,
Crossfertilizing it more curious
To make fond friends but deep and everywhere.
Once touched with innocence, and always touched;
Now in my dreams I am forever we,
And Eros is a justice with a charge:
To sculpt and work the clay we have received,
To sort votary gifts on temple grounds,
(Our heart is ever such a shrine and fane)
And render worse the better more to find
Its inner jewels. Biography becomes
Less accident, essential, as it's claimed,

And plumbed; it renders up mythology
That's lived us in our troubles and our raves,
That's called to us from our obsessions; yea,
Eros tends us from petty things to heirlooms,
Opens up our stubborn nut, expands
Our loves to taste Anima Mundi's trace
Throughout our divagations. Cupid says,
You have no choice, but I alone shall choose,
Confuse, befuddle, so to serve you up
A richer palate : every love's a course,
A teacher, whose complexity shall learn
You something vital: these are all my tasks.

a we without the me is but a scam

The awful, ugly word of sacrifice:
The call to martyrdom that drains the life,
Crafted by every priest since kingdom come
To squelch the servant class, and force their hand
Against themselves: service, no liberty.
How dare you think yourself worthy of rights?
No no, in selfishness is some new thing,
A saving grace; I thank divinity
But more and more the masses shall demand it!
If the earth be crushed, much better be
Than that the soul be quelched for sacrifice!
They used to burn us in their Druid cage;
Our blood was needed for their harvests' yield.
It's for your country, it's for God, for love:
Forever have these sent the soldiers forth;
Forever has submission of the slaves
Been justified by these "nobilities"
Replete with mud and blood as bonds and gags.
Thank heavens masses said, it's now our time!
A we without the me is but a scam!
Leave off nobilities: without my choice,
Without my liberty, society
Is prison, but an archon's labor camp,
Dress it up as you will! If service asks
My bondage, it is bondage that is asked.

Easy enough to say all life has cost,
When others set the price, and I've no say,
But when the coin is happiness itself,
Who then but I may budget from my purse?
When I am free, my generosity
Is full, but place me in your bonds of gold,
However gleaming, and you make a slave
Where stood a willing minister of grace.
Without a self, there's no self to be shared.
A self is shared, not given, or it's lost.
This immolation women have been urged
Forever: kind to others, cruel to self.
Suttee sums up the service bondage asks,
Call it devotion, call it kindness, call
It anything you like : it's all for shit.
Uprise ye Dalits, take up your selfishness!
Uprise ye women, mandate your own needs!
I shan't surrender my provisioning
To any who don't love my liberty,
For they don't understand my deepest needs,
And those who'd sell themselves at cheapest price
I shan't appoint the brokers of my life.
Let's put to death the word of sacrifice,
Replacing it with liberty of choice.

a bard has duties to the warriors

In that intense machinery of ice,
I'd be naught but a snowflake, soon to melt
At nothing but a beam of twinkling sun,
While they would hold together no matter what.
How can I then help but admire them?
It might be true I have not what it takes
To be a Soviet, yet nonetheless,
A bard has duties to the warriors
To praise where bravery has won some turf
For justice, for the people, for the dream.
I stand attention with my firm salute.

Sophia

She comes at first a strange, exotic fay,
A wisdom you don't come on everyday,
A guest who gently knocks upon your door,
A quiet voice that speaks of something more.
So different, she might spook — but she is kind.
She calls you to a different frame of mind.
Where you've been trapped, she comes to lend a hand,
To loose you from the bonds of your own land.
She speaks a truth so deep yet thought a lark
By those in power who would make their mark.
Some understanding simmering from below
Arises when she comes and when she goes.
Her voice is clarion, and often fall
As she recedes old Jericho's high walls,
For wisdom from the very earth and soil
Awakens in the marginals who toil,
And enspirited, they start to rise,
New confidence as they attain new eyes,
Which she has given when she came as guest.
She leaves to them to settle all the rest.
Yet comes to advocate when called to court,
An eloquence that comes from out the heart.
She speaks of justice, mercy, and of love,
Before she flies away, a water dove.

the hope of liberty

The protests are the hope of liberty,
The human spirit as of yet uncrushed,
The witness that restrains the despots' will.
The frightened cower in conformity,
And strike out at the disobedience
Born out of freedom's courage, but the gut
Is often wiser than the frightened mind,
And understands greater priority
Of precious rights over just being safe.
Our freedom is the greatest thing we have.

the angel in the animal

The soul needs more reflective time alone
To find perspective on pondered events.
The instantaneous but overwhelms,
Imposing brutal prematurity.
Speed is the enemy of wisdom's pace,
Which needs a garden and its compost pile.
Only traditional mores long thought
And contemplated by our critical
Array with requisite humanities
Is adequate to meet a rushing time,
Which must, even as is, be slowed somewhat.
Best to abey, and find some grotto's haunt
In backwoods scrub, and keep one's rifle greased.
Raccoons and foxes keep their fierceness rough,
And find a way to thrive in margins' brush.
Trust then the angel in the animal,
Foregoing Erisychthon's company.
The blind spot in the hero brings him down.
Remorse, throughout, and in advance, the cure.
Hungers the soul in reactivity,
Emotions caught in knee jerk back and forth.
It must digest, and take its time to feed.
Religion is our fate to animals.
We make our prayers through what we do to them.
In vivisection is the cry of soul,
The mind, inanimate to pity, made
A despot desperate to impose control,
And that will come too soon to bite us back,
Homo homini lupus, tragic fate.
Venationes and the cross are peers.
What we to them, we to ourselves in time.
The mind, lost of its senses and its heart,
Is our most dangerous dilemma now.
The schizoids seek to datify the world,
And cage us in autistic dungeon pits,
To thrash and cry the animal within;
Technique itself grown to a sociopath.
Dissect and reconfigure at one's whim,
All of the world the toy of billionaires,
Who wreck, and think their mayhem something bold.
The antichrists have robbed utopia,
And turned its engines all against the soul,

Bedlam philanthropists but maniacs.
My animal but howls and whimpers, spooked,
And leaps about the shadows of its cage.
Calm down, my mammal, let us dream and think,
The old way, with the slowness of our heart,
And find in meditative ways our plumb.

a dark ages would heal

Evil has doubled down, and made its own
The tools good hoped to make anew this life.
It takes technique and twists it to its ends,
So progress is a travesty itself,
Whereby we have empowered all our ill.
We've handed shadow weapons to prevail.
The tinkerers have let themselves be bought.
My piety is to Neanderthals,
The oldest strata in our human soul.
My mind shall serve in tenderness that heart,
And raise its sword against the schizoid sword,
The butcher, who would organ-harvest all,
And make chimeras to its ill's delight.
The worst has taken hold of genius, ai!
And scopophiliacs have closed their grasp,
And slaver to panopticon the world.
Frantic menageries within mourn now
For habitats replaced by sterile zoos.
I panic, for I need to run more free,
I need a world where wilderness is law.
The Amish way may be Messiah's way,
Slow gardening to put down deeper roots,
And in the slow, to overtake the fast.
The tortoise is the herald of the Christ.
Trust not the djinn who promises your wish.
In that unthinking haste we'll be undone.
Faust is a maniac. Put him in chains,
And let him ponder in a cellar damp
Remorse he desperate needs to save his soul.
Sometimes I think a Dark Ages would heal.
Give us five hundred years to contemplate,
And catch our breath, and let our hubris rot.

we aren't streams of data

Megalomania, I diagnose :
Moronic grandiosities of whim.
This is the sickness of these rapid times.
Each mind would make itself a petty god;
The idols are the archons' *narcisisse*.
We are not streams of data. We are souls.
The bureaucrats confuse their indices
For human beings. We are not receipts.
Ambition is a perilous ally —
Watch it at every moment : treacherous.
It smiles, then it tries to take the helm.

Torquemadas lurk in every age

The memories of being hunted down
Too many times dimly linger within.
So many heretics, so many pyres,
Ancestors who weep within our souls.
Who say, go on, go on despite it all.
I find their heirlooms, delicate and laced,
Inside my history. They rooted down
In backwoods, where their alchemies could rest,
And find a rhythm in rurality.
So many fleeings, so many refugees.
My heart is heavy with humanity's
Cold inhumanity to fellow folk.
It's in my sudden tempers and sharp tongue.
It's in curmudgeonry that makes me gnome.
It's in my melancholy and my hopes.
The Inquisition's found so many names.
It finds a way to justify itself.
A wolf inside a fleece of holiness.
If we demanded warrants, asked for writs,
It was to keep Dominicans at bay.
Frustration is palladium of rights,
For Torquemadas lurk in every age.

the hillbillies' instincts

The instincts of the hillbillies are right,
If their ideas are somewhat always off,
And if they carry barrels of the tar
Of history they've never quite resolved.
America has always been a stew,
A jambalaya. There our rights reside.

we've lost a man

This man, this was a man, we've lost a man.
George Floyd, a human being, American,
One of our own, a precious citizen.
Once more, the gendarme in its arrogance
Has executed on our very streets,
Usurping judge and jury, against the law,
One of our very own. And all the names
Would make a litany in horror's halls.
A slave was one the law saw not of worth,
Whose life itself was nothing. Have we passed
Yet our Thirteenth Amendment, or does it
Stand interrupted? In its second clause,
It authorizes any law it takes
To wipe the badges and the incidents
Of slavery, to make sure no one is
A citizen of second class. If lives
Themselves don't matter, cops have nullified
Our constitution: that is mutiny.
Dismantle the departments, tear them down,
Rebuild from scratch, remove the KKK
(Which evidence has shown is moled throughout):
Whatever it may take to make this right.
And make a statue of George Floyd in bronze,
And one for all the many names like him,
And plant them on the very precinct lawns.
A man, this was a man, our fellow man.

Russian roulette for Black people

America is a Russian roulette
For Black people, and every time they're killed,
It could be one of our beloved friends.
When for the color of your skin you're killed,
It could be anybody. That's no rule
Of law, no justice, and no hint of peace.

honor bonds of youth

We fall away, for we explode and drift
Off into tangents, never turning back,
Neglecting to retie our ribbons strong
To our illustrious Maypole of yore,
To reaffirm, to reconvene, to find
The common ground explorings-out neglect,
And honor bonds of youth that never die.

cast me out of court

When I my head lay on the pillow, I
Then think of you, and when I do, I call
You Evey, out of sweetness, for you're dear
To me, though you have cast me out of court.

inhibited by narrow minds

I leave behind whoever doesn't get me
In my growth, if they obstruct my path.

I love, but don't allow the blossoming
To be inhibited by narrow minds.
It's fellow travelers upon the quest,
Or those at taverns on the varied way,
Who keep my company and stay my friends.
And I come back, returning to my loves,
Reunions and sabbaticals of joy,
But then commence again the ever quest.

burning every bridge

I'm going for broke, and burning every bridge:
Whoever wants to swim with me through ash,
Let's go! It's gone too far, the world's off edge,
The craziness is everywhere and round,
So I shall lunge my fiery screeds of angst
Against injustice, and if it inflames,
Disco Inferno, baby! Let it roll!

let your care be where it wants to be

Find where you care by letting go of care;
Just let your care be where it wants to be,
And maybe nowhere, floating free in bliss.
You've got to, and you must, you should, you ought—
Well maybe not — perhaps you needn't care.
Perhaps the world does fine without your care.
Perhaps the animals and birds care less.
Perhaps they never fret outside their nests,
Give not a single worry to the news.
The news is Springtime, or a hoard of nuts.
The news is breeze so fresh upon the face.
The news is drinking up this life they have,
Enchanting apathy towards all the rest.
To be, to simply feel, to love, to live.

a more ambitious prick

Whoever claims to know, they may not know.
It's likely that they've got it wrong somewhere.
These priests are based on lost shenanigans,
Some brilliant pioneer left in the dust
And slandered by a more ambitious prick,
And now the truth's a buried footnote few
Remember. And the stronger they assert,
Well, maybe they don't know as well they might.
One thing's for sure : when they want you to live
By what they peddle, likely it's control
They want, not benefice. Just look around:
There's probably some dissenting voice about,
Whom they abhor as heretic for sure,
Who offers something far more interesting,
And truth is never a democracy.
Give half an ear at most, and never more,
Remembering the ages lived their lives
Just fine without the expertise of priests.
As usual, the hillbillies are right.
And Jesus too : just improvise through life,
You should be fine : that's how the most have lived.
And let dissent humble what claims the truth.

never really cared

I've never worshipped private property.
I've never really cared when it goes down.
It's just not of importance to my soul.

into betweenity

Too much am I with I; that I could melt
Into betweenity, and be amidst
The great affections of the living crowd!
Yet what is solitude but being full,

Not empty, with an inner multitude?
Being alone can be a gravy, rich
With flavor, thick and wholesome, nourishing.
But then a tavern might have solitude
In all its hubbub if one might there melt,
And absentmindedly, just drift between
The conversations, bliss oblivious.
No more to steer but let the sail have sway;
To loose the rudder and give up to winds.
To say, I trust, and let that carry one
With reverie amidst where flies the flock.

precious sacraments

The slut in me is such a friendly thing,
A harmless fellow, meaning no one harm.
A chap with ample curiosities
Who simply dreams of strangers' soft embrace.
And yet the superficialities
Of such leads nowhere to connections' depths;
A shallowness and shallowness collide.
Few really have that special spark I love,
And many soon reveal their biases,
Their stubborn bigotries that shan't repent.
Therefore, my little friend, abey, and hold
Your fantasies as precious sacraments.

like cobwebs' dust

Sometimes I sob. The Soviets are gone.
We live in ruins. Modern cities rest
On graveyards. O the sagas of the bold
Have passed! The messianic edifice
Has fallen! We are lost in hopelessness
We call sophistication. Time has slowed,
And yet quotidia is rushing by.
The testaments are tombstones no one reads.
The children do not hope for futures now.
The gloom of armageddon seems the news.

The lack of faith is laziness in charge.
We do not anymore wish to believe.
This moment's spell is self-indulgent fluff
A rising tide casts off like cobwebs' dust.
The people burn down bourgeois monuments,
Their fists in air: where there's oppression, there's
Resistance, so said Mao, and so it is.

in midst of blackest pitch no light at all

The world is on a cross, and we await
Its Easter. Everywhere the dawn seems far;
The archons rule the night with cruel revenge.
The great redemption that we hoped lies stretched
With bloody nails through wrists on upright wood.
A hundred thousand sprouts of green each Spring,
And yet the Winter rolls around each year.
We build the Kingdom up so patiently,
Yet our fond Notre Dames fall down too soon.
The haters' malice moles its way with spite,
If from without or from within; we creep,
Not leap, towards that dear millennium,
Our feet upon a treadmill. Good Friday
Reigns as an age that won't release its grip.
We fools still sing the matins in the dark,
To herald sunrise that we know will come;
In midst of blackest pitch no light at all
But pinpoints, we show wild confidence
Unmerited by what surrounds our song,
And still believe. The world shall be renewed.
The forecasts of the final day are skewed;
The plans of emperors are pocked with flaws,
And we through tribulations plant the seeds.

the little bunker bitch

The bitch is frightened of Americans.

The little bitch, the little bunker bitch.
Tin plated dictator is cowering scared,
The little bitch, the little bunker bitch.
That piece of shit's scared of Americans.
The little bitch, the little bunker bitch.
Scared of the common people of our land.
The little bitch, the little bunker bitch.
He has to pull out all his little tanks,
The little bitch, the little bunker bitch.
Cuz bunker bitch is crapping his old pants.
The little bitch, the little bunker bitch.

hope at last goes viral

The arc of Thomas Parker is a rainbow,
Sign of peace and new prosperity.
Its long hyperbola is shortened whence
Our tzedekah unflinches and stays firm.
Hold now to right; give up no path to wrong.
See through the Pentecost to everyone,
So that it seethes a fire through the land,
And hope at last goes viral in our time.
Each act of justice is a grappling hook
With which we tug the further end more near.
Now let ropes of koinonia pull close
And drag the needed love to us at last.

woven in our very fibers

How often I don't want to live at all;
How often hope seems to have run its course.
How often it is hard to simply breathe.
How often endless sleep just seems like peace.
But then we cannot shirk the duties fate
Has woven in our very fibers, nor
Fail those who lean upon the life we share,
And so we must refuse the denouement,
Pick up our bootstraps, shake the dust, and live,
Believing against all that marks despair.

my soul alone suffice

If I could roll myself up like a rose,
And ruffle in my folds away from pain,
I'd vegetate electric in my beauty,
Dreaming not of anything but love.
I'd recollect fond personalities
I've cherished who have vacated my life,
Yet in my love of them, they'd be right there,
More present in my adoration than
If they were here before my grateful eyes.
Parnassus would be right within my heart,
My muses, magical, around that font,
For love is ever spell for which we yearn.
But my fond innocence has injured me.
Where I desired silk, sandpaper rules;
Brillo instead of velvet; everywhere
But rough and bruises where my faith was tried.
I was a ballet dancer 'neath the sea
Attempting graceful pirouettes with sharks.
My earnestness simply no match at all
For all the jaggedness encircling me.
I had a pulsing skin of gelatin
Surrounded by the scrapes of coral reefs.
I leapt so light, as if my flesh were cloth,
Soft linen in the currents billowing,
But these raw membranes, sensitive and fresh,
Abraded in the rough-textured terrain.
I loved with all the purity a child
Gives, but rebuff's been the coin I'm paid.
Let me but origami this my heart,
And scroll Rosaceae all my petals pinched,
And rollick in the morning dew, eyes closed.
If they but came to me, my priestesses
And priests of Charites while I revered
In reverie, my soul alone suffice.

heaven's dulcimer to ears

It's not the unattainable I want;
Perhaps attainable if I worked hard —
Now that would stretch me, make my talents reach
For higher heights, and make the colors glow.
If never easy, it were possible;
I could be secret source of pure delight.
I could be heaven's dulcimer to ears.
I could be eye's enchantment of a dream.
I could be hidden squeal in deepest folds,
The tingle in the sudden rush of awe.
What heights would I not scale to be as such?

right wing, left wing

Let me this ruffled wing of feathered fronds
Unscroll from my right side of majesty,
And let me raise these ivory-lument plumes
From my left side; both glorious and soft,
Both weathered by the wind yet beautiful,
Yet neither soars without the other one.
Right wing, left wing: together they uplift.
Together they may hold so swift the sky.
Coordinated, they may sip the air
Of stratospheres; coordinated, sail
The scarlet cobwebs of the flaming dusk.
Apart, they flail the useless spasm, vain;
Apart, they simply fibrillate and fail.
United as a single wave, they skim
The sculpted breath of heaven's buoyancy,
And lift me up above the narrow sights.
Broad view, wide heart, wise intellect, deep soul,
And spirit in its flight that ever seeks.

now burn it down

The fire is the friend of liberty.

Now burn it down. Now burn the whole thing down.
The fire's comrade to equality.
Now burn it down. Now burn the whole thing down.
Let all the architecture in the land
Fall down to ash and level all our fates.
Now burn it down. Now burn the whole thing down.
Let everyone live in pavilions.
Now burn it down. Now burn the whole thing down.
No yachts, no mansions, penthouses, estates.
Now burn it down. Now burn the whole thing down.
No monuments declaring men as gods.
Now burn it down. Now burn the whole thing down.
The fire can restore humility.
Now burn it down. Now burn the whole thing down.
I baptize you with tongues of living flame.
Now burn it down. Now burn the whole thing down.
Wherever rank injustice reigns, bring flames!
Now burn it down. Now burn the whole thing down.
Where arrogance has gotten upper hand:
Now burn it down. Now burn the whole thing down.
If '64 in Harlem streets of woe,
Now burn it down. Now burn the whole thing down.
If '67 summer in Detroit,
Now burn it down. Now burn the whole thing down.
If '68's despair at loss of King,
Now burn it down. Now burn the whole thing down.
If '92, another beaten King,
Now burn it down. Now burn the whole thing down.
If 2020, enough is quite enough,
Now burn it down. Now burn the whole thing down.
Let these my ears hear that old sweet refrain,
Now burn it down. Now burn the whole thing down.
Not local neighborhoods, but everywhere,
Now burn it down. Now burn the whole thing down.
Let retribution for the crimes resound,
Now burn it down. Now burn the whole thing down.
Cry rage at life insulted far too long,
Now burn it down. Now burn the whole thing down.
They've had their time to right the glaring wrongs,
Now burn it down. Now burn the whole thing down.
Make crucible of old Columbia's crown,
Now burn it down. Now burn the whole thing down.
Reduce their luxuries to singing ash,
Now burn it down. Now burn the whole thing down.
Correcting had no real priority,

Now burn it down. Now burn the whole thing down.
And let the fire be their discipline,
Now burn it down. Now burn the whole thing down.
They'll have nowhere to live or work again,
Now burn it down. Now burn the whole thing down.
Until their love extends to everyone,
Now burn it down. Now burn the whole thing down.
And all are equal under warmth of sun.
Now burn it down. Now burn the whole thing down.
Now burn it down. Now burn the whole thing down.
Now burn it down. Now burn the whole thing down.

wet as yet from womb

Imagine no within and no without.
The vulnerability so soft we see
As quarantined inside, poured everywhere,
And every interaction fresh and raw,
Dancing upon one's membranes, so without,
Within, these have no referent at all.
Those first of days, totality and truth
In utter trust and fond sincerity,
Where, in exquisite sensitivity,
Our nature, wet as yet from womb, was good,
Unstained, unjaded by a thousand blows.
The merest coo was poetry and psalm;
The nursery a vast cathedral gemmed
By elven artisans enhancing awe;
A trip outdoors swaddled in arms of love
Was *mikvah* in the Garden: holy trees,
What emerald webs, what jewelry of green,
Vast blue above of awe one sipped and breathed,
A squirrel was miracle mercurial
In handsome ruddy robes of regal fur.
And everyone we met, some holy priest,
Some face of sacred relic, some sprung joy,
Assigned the precious senate of our saints,
Enrolled at once in precincts of our heart.
Friendship — to babble lovingly — so swift,
So unconditional, so open, free,
With undiminished troth, one's life a gush
Of all untrammeled authenticity

And warmth. Why, if one cried, the world was tears!
If wonder lit upon one's eyes or skin —
But every other moment — never was
A Moses more enrapt with burning bush
Than this tremendum, all religion but
A distant echo of this marvel-play
That splashed through us as ocean waves of wish!
Not but an anything was less than dear.
If tickled, laughter was the universe,
The smiling face above, a deity:
The innocence of first idolatry!
For all translucent with theophany.
And what we felt in arms, such full embrace
Of total love, no later sliver ranks
A thousandth in its greatest passion throes
Or sweetest trance infatuate and dumb.
If then the former centuries knew grief
Ruthless in loss of early child — ah,
Crestfallen broken cemeteries' rue —
Perhaps such souls in fact were quite content
To simply savor those the best of years,
To sip the delicacy, purest cream,
And go — forsaking all the calluses
To come, uninterested in treachery
And disappointment, hardening and loss —
No no, strawberries and sweet buttermilk
Of purest youth sufficed to feed their soul —
Then back to heaven, home again at last!
Someday, the yearning we all keep in trust
In some deep treasury within, for that
Original security and faith
To be the state adults restore anew
On stronger stones and firm foundations, will
Touch ground, and life will be a wonderment!
Retire, poets, painters, harpists, then —
Your arts were but the trace of prophecies,
The vague alluring blur of what's to come!

the dojo of the ocean

I guess the lobster live the truest lives.
Hard crusted shells but soft and fresh within,

So pink and succulent and sensitive,
Protected in their cavern grown about.
They surf in gliding current-skim the sands
Beneath, and click their silent, crawling limbs
To trawl the bottom shores for nutriment,
Drifting in beingness and lush content.
What zazen sitting hundred years could crown
The dojo of the ocean? : gaze in eyes —
A Bodhisattva robed in hard-shelled red
Stares back, primeval innocence of sea,
An ancience, an aeons-consciousness
Of mud and salt in gold solution gleam.

the classic ages living in their bones

The century plant sends up its towering stalk
An efflorescence of its essence, once
Each several decades, grandeur in its bloom
And beaming height : intimidating thrust
And blossom-crown, a stunning monument.
Yet everything it brings to higher pitch
In its expression is contained within
The humble, just-so-happens plant itself.
So human cultures give a ripening
In majesty and imposition, then
Melt back into humility and grace,
The classic ages living in their bones.
So look at Africa, diaspora
Of Egypt; Guatemala, Mayan maize
Returned to husky campesino fields.

beauty involute in holiness

There's scoundrels who would love it to convert
Vaginas into public access routes,
The pawing property of anyone,
Quotidian, a surface habitat

For passing snacks of pleasure, nothing much,
A fast food joint, an anywhere for free,
A colonized convenience for all.
No sense of privacy or specialness.
No shyness at the altar. Sacrilege
Emporium, no rarity or sense
Of pricelessness, of precious inwardness,
Of beauty involute in holiness,
The sacred trickling deerpath to this world.
No awe before the greatest miracle.
Vending machine for foam and spastic spew,
With intermingling naught but shake of hands,
A casual terrain of calluses.
A quick discard in kingdom of the numb.
And they themselves, these men, do desecrate
Their own wonders, their curious quick beasts,
Their monoliths in sweet floral burlesque,
And render them too commonplace and rude.
What could be majesties, what doors of gold
To beauties so exquisite in their gasps,
They all transfigure everything inside,
Is tossed for instants' insignificance!
The temple grounds the artisans designed
With deities in mind their glorious pools
And sputter-fluff of fountain feather-spray
Reduced to plumbing and vulgarity.
They call this free; I call it poverty.

a little grace

Sex could be hamburgers, a shack of snacks
And still be holy-ordinary, if
Regard and playfulness and friendliness
Reserve a special moment for some prayer,
A little grace before the deli dish.

fall to the ground

Debates are over: people in the streets

Are taking down Confederates themselves.
The hemming and the hawing now are done.
The statues of despots fall to the ground.

the modern Minneapolis Bastille

The station gloriously burst in flames:
The modern Minneapolis Bastille.
A burning bush, a stark epiphany,
A holy apparition, as the folk
Burn down the archons' idols: Babylon
In smoke! Now tongues of flame speak liberty!
Oppression comes to ash! From ash, new soil.

spoiler eager for the chance to wreck

The fretting somnolence of pessimism,
All consumed by zeitgeist's narrow fog,
Myopic in its gloom, devoid of faith,
Completely unimaginative and dull,
A hangover disguised as philosophy,
Believer of the worst and worshipper
Thereof, delighted by disaster, thrilled;
Its sole libido how things might go wrong,
And sexless otherwise; lost in the fret
Of small concerns and time scales, out of whack
With ratio and proportions of history.
An utter failure, drab and impotent,
A spoiler eager for the chance to wreck;
An old man, ever old and senile.

epitome of Romans 13

By all means, serve your higher angels, those
Whose righteousness is your exemplary,
Who serve in all they do the Exodus,
Who cannot but love good, admonish bad,
For we are lower than these seraphim,
And must accede their tutelage of light.
To such, our offerings of gratitude
Are asked with full surrender of our heart,
But as for men, the only thing owed them
Is love, and love alone, for no mere man,
Even a criminal who breaks the law,
Is worthy of idolatry or scot.
Who would in hubris of his heinous deeds
Defy divinity whose name is love
Is not subordinate to love, and not
Thereby ordained; it is to cherubim
Alone we must in adoration heed
(And not in *latria*, but *dulia*).

proverbs from the sinews of their gut

Such love we hold for our antiquities,
Even the sounds of our archaic words
Are heirlooms to our ears, the heritage
Passed down from prudent ancestors of old,
Whom in their imperfections yet had grit,
Endowing gumption in sagacious saws.
There is a drum that resonates in us,
First fashioned and then beat the eons past.
We listen to the echoes still in roots.
Those roots are worts, our precious, healing herbs.
There's much unlaw in any set of laws,
That must be righted. That's the way of things :
The crankiness of passing moods oft prints
Itself a blemish on the ancient law,
And yet in spite of all of that, it holds,
The law that speaks the people's ways, in main.

The main thrust has a wholeness good for folk,
If details in new times must be reformed.
O hear them raise of old their deepest voice —
Hear baritone, hear plaintive common drone —
Hear wisdom in the pasturage and dell —
Hear cartwright, tumbler, cowmaid, hunter, smith —
Hear proverbs from the sinews of their gut,
The cries of thigh muscles down to the feet,
The trust in marl and the rooted earth,
The call of those who took to springs their prayers,
Who held good faith towards mountains and towards trees,
Who had a pithy feel for verdant things,
Who felt awe under stars and in the woods —
Hear now, hear now, hear now their ancient voice,
Present in words you struggle forth to speak,
In longings from this body they too shared,
In snarls and in tangled knots of pain,
In lovely pleasures they too most esteemed.
Hear them — they call to you — they lived a life —
Each one learned what he could and lived a life —
The choir lived a hundred thousand lives,
A multitude of sorrows and of joys,
Of hopes, successes, disappointments, loves,
Great loves, enduring, dirty, holy loves,
Loves throbbing in the breach and drinking deep,
Loves aching in the wounds and healing up —
The least of you is in this little life
(Of nature most important to your thoughts);
The greater part of you is deeper yet,
Is in the ostinato under things.
They are the pillars holding up this roof
You are — beneath you is a hall of many moots,
A cavern with a dripping well where weirds
Of old still simmer, all those earthy quirks
Of character and destiny survive.
There is a bottom ground to all your hopes,
The hosts who own the house in which you live,
The common testators of this your trust.
Antiquities give feel for dronings old,
Which still adhere in hint and in the trace.

the sabbath is for man

If then you say, we cannot change our ways,
Our old traditions are too venerable;
A shame if they offend the poor oppressed,
But these our narratives and images
Are sacred to us, I will say to you,
Precisely that is your idolatry,
To treat as sacred that which has oppressed.
Cleanse then the badges and the incidents
Of slavery from out your images
And stories, taking feelings of the low
As valuable, and changing thus your ways.
As difficult as it may be to change,
To wash the baby carefully to cleanse,
And toss the bath water, it has its worth.
Traditions can be baptized, wrung of filth.
The love of neighbor trumps old pieties.
The sabbath is for man, not man for it.

shalom

Come port, sharp swill, that missiles sheets of brine!
Come starboard, lifted bilge that leaps the decks!
The sudden darkening of shrouding fogs,
The kettledrum of thunder beating round,
The lightning's jagged lances hazard hurl!
Watch mast in wild wobble to and fro;
Observe the hillocks lift the craft aloft,
Then drop in gaping maw of sharp-toothed sea!
The heavy, saturated sails stiff-whip,
And ripping in the gales, rain forth their spray!
The sailors holler woe and curses throw
From gritting grimaces their rough-hewed fright,
Their burning hands strain at the struggling rope
To turn rebelling linen back to course!
"Not possible! This is the doom of us!"
"The marshy ghouls lodged in the silty deep
Arouse, and angered at our trespass, shriek,
And shake the vessel like a petallage
Of blossoms in a towering typhoon!"

"Aye, it's the briny Sheol- shibboleths!
Their rotting fingertips beneath reach out
To rend us and descend us to their lairs!
The putrefying brides jilted and tossed
A heathen sacrifice now seek new mates!
We'll each be husband to a smiling corpse!"
"Awaken now the teacher!" "Hold that jute!
Pull steady, lads!" "Some howling nephilim
With strength of hundred hands in maddened winds
Resists! What is a man against a fiend?"
"Go batten down the hatches!" "Nay, descend,
Waken the rabbi!" "Still he sleeps? But how?"
One slips beneath, tossed here now there, and sees
Serenity in sleeping flesh of peace,
Pure glow, rejuvenating innocence.
Gently he nudges. "Rabbi, wake! The winds
Have taken us to trial of the waves!
The hellion-magistrate, in blackened robes,
Slams down his ruthless gavel of the gales,
His cackling legionnaires in leaping grey,
The jury, mock us, as they take the helm!"
"Calm down, calm down, what is the trouble here?"
"The course was smooth when we set out at first,
But then, the breezes, sinister from cliffs,
Alighted raptor from the mounts, and seized
With tossing talons this our wretched skiff!
The closer to the other side we sail,
The very waters rise to mutiny!
The Beezelbubs they feed with children's blood
Extend their ghostly limbs throughout the sea
To warn us back, and screeching, terrify
Us from our course! "Go back! Go back!" the pack
Of grey hounds howled, we seemed to hear them cry!
The drowned souls of the heathen dread us come!
Ill winds, which are pollutions of their sins,
Threaten with admonition, "Turn ye back!"
We must return! The other side is death!"
"Now cease your superstition, I will come.
Some little wind, your fancies darken you?
I felt the pulse and throb here where I lay;
It was exhilarating! I could feel
Mother Shekinah rocking me to sleep.
She holds us all in loving hands of trust.
I've told you all so many times. If now,
She strikes a mood to bounce us on her knee,

And tickle us her infants with her breath,
Have spirit, man! Is but a gaiety."
"Come quick! Or else to splinters and to shards
We'll soon be wrecked, and exiles on the sea!
Finned monsters then will have us for their prey!"
With squint of irk bemused, the rabbi rose,
And shook his head in humor, stepping up
Onto the deck. Behold the miserable!
The sea-dogs soaked and sullen, pale with fright!
The bosom of the bending boards in heave,
The swallowing by shadowed crests and troughs,
The javelins of fire catapult,
While sheets of bronze are malleted with clubs!
The rabbi, robed in gentle-threaded white,
Raised hands and closed his eyes to soulful feel
The moment. Murmuring, he seemed in prayer,
An ecstasy. In confidence, he hummed,
And seemed to join his droning to the winds.
His peaceful countenance stunned them the more
Than all the wrack about, and mesmerized,
They near forgot in daze the raging storm.
How long? Time seemed to still, as if they stood
The silence in the cyclone. It might fret,
But suddenly, an equanimity,
As in the sanctuary, settled in.
The seconds melted into minutes now;
The worried minutes sighed and gained their ease.
He stood and welcomed what the wind might give,
His arms in wide embrace, and with command
So captivating, trust so broad and thick,
They were amazed; and if they tossed, he grinned,
And hummed the more, and if the lightning flashed,
He quivered in a rapture. Gravitas
In sheer abysm, peace was conquering
The livid terror battering the mast,
And then he whispered, "Silence now thy lips!
Shalom!", and opened eyes. "The sea has heard our peace,
And follows suit." Behold! Serenity
Peeled back the blackened crepe, and calm restored
The gentleness of waves to lyric lull,
The crinkles on a sunlit liquid glass.
Now cormorants their happy gossip cawed,
Now shores abroad slipped naked from their rags,
Now sea was sibilance and simple hiss.
He turned, ironic frown with glinting grin.

"Whence now this unbecoming cowardice?
How slips your faith so easily away?
Allow your trust to billow from your bosoms;
Any sudden storms will soon subside.
We who hold hopes in trust for all the world
To find its ballast once again, cannot
Just shake like leaves in Autumn quiverings!
In prayer, O little leafs, recall the tree.
Bring close to mind the boughs, and then the trunk,
And then the canopies webbing the stars,
Descending down to solid roots in earth.
Did you not read how Wisdom is a tree?
Then if you fibrillate in tinkling breeze,
O little leafs, recall the larger tree,
Of which you are beloved foliage.
A lake will do as lakes will do. Keep you
Your mind upon the mission. Shores abroad
Await the news we bring! Now the whole earth
Cries out in groaning neath the Roman yoke;
The ghouls you fear are princes with their staves,
And yet the poor of every land abound.
Let us fulfill the vow to Abraham,
And be a blessing to the nations round.
The Gentiles know this Gospel in their blood,
Their marrow cries for it! If then consumed
In superstitions — as you all still seem
Yourselves — or hateful ancient prejudice —
Too much alike ourselves, we who divine
Ghouls in the waves — our fears — as we approach.
Now let such nonsense deliquesce and fade.
The life of equity is imminent;
Green sap even as now returns to husks.
Such joyous news is nutriment, we've seen,
Amongst our people, and will be with them.
Come now! Let courage navigate our paths!"
Astonished sailors, humbled, mind their sails,
The ship a polishing of silvered glass.

ease and oil

What wild crimes would I be driven to
If I lived fully all my unlived life?

How many women would I chase and stalk,
To worship at their well the magic drink?
To stalk them, for it seems when one does long,
The other runs. To yearn is certain doom
Of possibility. I'd run away
And join the theatre, live in a troupe.
I'd frequent playgrounds in the midst of night.
(I have! I often do!) I'd camp outside
The literary agencies until
They'd represent me, spreading news of me
Afar and near — and not for ego's sake,
But recognition of the work, the work!
The sacred work! To recognize its worth!
The ladies would invite me to salons,
Where I'd be featured, and my beauty cooed
By oohs and aahs. New muses would allure,
And whip me frenzily to newer heights.
No more would eloquence be fervent task,
But ease and oil, buttermilk and cream.

smoke screen

The death counts are nothing but sabotage,
A smoke screen used to cover over good.
The moment anyone begins such crap,
Talk of the gulags or the executions,
They're dishonest, fundamentally
Dishonest, and it's nothing but a gotcha.
You choose to engage in either way,
You've lost. Defend or minimize the loss,
You're in denial or a monster; cop
To all the accusations, you must now
Capitulate, admitting all was wrong.
The fundamental good in Stalin's term —
And anyone who can't see that is *blind* —
The mass empowerment of rising up,
The people by their bootstraps lifting up
Each other: all of that was *very real*,
Important and significant and *true*.
It's for that very reason tears are shed
So copiously by the crocodiles:
To make sure no one sees benevolence.

But something's missing in the tragedy
They scribble etchingly over the truth.
(And I will cry with you by tragic tombs
And hold your hand to mourn a little while;
Soon the sackcloth wearies. We move on.)
Don't label me a Stalinist; I'm just
A man with eyes intact who sees what's *there*.
Whatever else was tragic, that was *there*,
And of the two, the triumph is more true.
A nation learning ego skills at last,
Cooperatively, those right at the base,
And building, building, building by their hands.
So cut the crap. You're ignorant and vain.
Gird up your loins and penetrate the fog,
Beyond the tragic patina to truth,
The deeper truth. Not so to glorify
The image of the villain, but the folk.
A miracle, and everyone agreed.
They didn't call him Uncle Joe for naught
Back then, and all around the working world,
But they have managed to spray paint in blood,
So all of that is but forgotten now.
There's precious baby in that bathwater,
That no one's telling you about at all.
At all. I won't defend the cartoon mask
Cold Warriors so lovingly designed,
Replete with blood and mustache. We agree,
We hate that fellow. Meanwhile, getting back
To business, there's stories not yet told.
A million dozen stories more, the gore
Obscures. There's grateful lives there in those graves.
They'd speak, if you would listen. I have, hm?
I've felt them, deeply felt them in the tomb.
They say, their stories aren't being told.
The joy of new capacity in limbs,
The whirring, buzzing, stirring nation proud,
The sheer excitement in the midst of pain,
The sudden opportunities at hand,
Denied for long millennia of tears,
Utopia at last its feet on ground,
And being there, more gritty, full of coal,
Imperfect, birth pangs throbbing mightily,
The labor long, but in the amniotic
Blood, more real; the lowest, finally,
Given a chance, a rough and scrappy chance,

Unguaranteed but genuine, and all
Together in astounding unity
The world has seldom seen! There's charcoal smears
Around the portrait, but a purpose found
Is greater than the sacrifice it asks!
A sense that anything was possible,
That all the obstacles could be surpassed,
That older limits were but starting points,
That futures from the ground were being built!
It all was difficult and torturous
And totally exhilarating. There's
The core of it. A revolution is
Apocalypse, whose fires are the forge
From which the partisans struggle to yank
Out fortunes and their possibilities.
It's new life from appalling atrocity,
And hardly could be otherwise, in fact.
No Exodus without the pestilence.
The whirlwind comes regardless. Will you build
From what it wrecks? Or tutter from the armchair?
Shadows in the caverns murmur truths.

seanced with the proletariat

I've seanced with the proletariat,
Reached back my mind to hear their hidden thoughts,
To scry the Union of the Soviets,
And found beneath the chronicles of woe,
Astonishing and subterranean
Triumphant diaries from whispered souls.
These tabernacle choirs of the deep
Lend strength to me in trying times with spells
Of great sobriety and healing truth.
They told me I was Peter ere the crow,
But afterwards would build them up a church.
"Are you the one defending floods of blood?"
Not me, not me, I never knew of such.
"Aren't you complicit with the crucified?
I never knew him, never met that man!
"Have you not spoken up on their behalf?"
Oh no, of course, with you I do becry!
So is confirmed my foul apostasy.

Yet I shall heed Porciuncula's call.

a limestone rabbinate

Vigor! Fountain spray of foundry sparks!
The sounds of beaten anvils struck with lust!
Muscle and iron, grit and lofty aims!
A sooty gusto rising with its tools.
Devils and gravel, coal and kobold umph,
The conquest of the mountain! Altar stones
And sculpted boulders, reverence for the hands,
Dolmens and canvas, bunks and barrack grounds.
Kabouters of the mines with charcoal hearts,
Their chunky bones of jagged rough-hewn ores,
Their leathered skin with fibrous meat a'flex,
Who dance in falling rain of snow-white ash,
And sip long pipes of clay to gaze through smoke,
And catch a glimpse of times still yet to come.
The spirit of the slam pit, flesh on flesh,
Collision as a miracle of love,
Rough camaraderie, now organized
A jointed body, efficacious skill
In pride and plan, with careful strategists
Leading the folkmoots' hiving gumption, craft
And mastery! A gospel in the slag,
In welding tools and mallets, tracts of steel
And amber revelations, visions etched
In petrifiéd wood, eurekas felt
In handling new machines, revival camps
In burlap: mettle, fiber, fortitude.
Abrasive reveries of pebble tunes,
Guffaws of vulgar raptures ripe with hope,
Hope succulent and fresh upon the boughs.
A crowd of fellows who see in one's heart,
And recognize the yearning talent there,
And lend a hand to help and bring it out,
In councils of coordinate elan.
And everywhere the coal-smudged Levites, raised
Atop their rickety wood platforms, speech
And fire from their livid clarity,
Ensuring this granite evangelum
Is carried vein and percolate through breath,

Thumping their tomes, a limestone rabbinate.
The cinder-paupers heretofore tossed out
And lost, in alleyways of tenements
In squalid rags, despised as nobodies,
Cold apathy, ain't that a bloody shame,
Forgotten, spat upon, and ridiculed,
Now masters in their land given a chance —
And be it tough and tumbling with hard knocks,
The leper-colony of poverty
Was worse — let's make the best of it, ol' lads!
Raise up morale, who were but fading embers,
Boot on face, abandoned to their fates,
However ragged in the shambling task
Of now, a better lot for all by far!
A chance! However criminal in sin,
However hopeless, ugly from the start,
The beautifuls deride in cruel contempt,
But now, be it obscure, an earnest chance!
A wager in the chain of linking arms.
Be it a fool's errand doomed yet to fail,
Yet we will make it happen nonetheless!
And let it slip to ruins, we succeed,
Laying the groundwork for the generations
Come, despite derisions. Let them write
Their horrible caricatures and screeds,
Pour splashing blood upon our sooty face,
Attempt snuff out our craftwork and our calm —
Well, we put Nazis cursed into their graves:
We overcome, with monuments of soul
That even rusting in the forest swathes
Bespeak an age of glory come to plebs.
Such undermemories are ever felt.
The very rocks are testimonials.

assert astonishing taboos

Let all the grandmothers and grandfathers,
Who unionized the loggers' camps and mines,
Who proudly marched the streets in their red flags,
That generation ripe with radicals,
Silenced alone by being set in graves,
Now speak again! For they would be a storm,

A thunder on the earth, as they once were!
They'd bring the jalapeño flavor back
To tepid generations gone too bland,
Assert astonishing taboos now lost,
Arouse to combats without compromise
Against the bosses and their hired chiefs!
I hear them echo in this crop of youth!
Their Aramaic letters in the flames
That fly as banners through the city streets
These early weeks of June. They cry no more!
Their children, calmed by affluence they won,
Embarrassed, cowed into conformity,
Maniacally attached to property,
Demure, but now the grandchildren arise!
And in their hearts, the melee of their sires,
Who never hesitated go on strike,
Who fisticuffed with scabs and thought that right,
Who had a rough morality more pure
For dirty hands, and quibbled not the scrapes
Oft consequent to fresh creative tasks!
They ever kept their eye upon the ball,
And worried little of the means at hand;
They did whatever it might take to win
The people's cause! And let the preachers weep
Over their cavils! Vigor was their name;
They raised the fist and meant it. They had fight
Etched on their souls, and struggled all their lives
Against the status quo with gusto! How
Disgusted they have bitter wept in tombs
At offspring so obedient and duped,
So caught up in the empire's fantasies,
Deluded and demobilized and plump.
They had the Suffragettes' and Wobblies' soul,
The dogged scrappers for a better cause
Within their breast : John Brown and Garrison,
Ida T. Wells and Cyril Briggs, Dubois,
William Z. Foster, Anna Louise Strong,
Ol' Eugene Debs and Carl Sandburg , Emma
Goldman, Whitman, and Sojourner Truth.
No one got anywhere by being nice,
By being calm, by staying cool, but flames
Raised on a riling brand! Don't stupefy
Our ancestors as grannies knitting quilts
And darning socks, and ever nodding heads;
The pavements were their holy ground, the stead

Of their revivals : never did they ask,
But they demanded. And they organized.
They knew the tight-knit discipline as well,
The chainlinked arms of marching side by side.
They were not doddering infants drinking milk
From talking heads, but sailor-mouthed rebels.
It's their old voices now we most need hear.
Their manifestos and their soapboxes.
They'd teach us moral courage we have lost.

slow geology of generations

There's deeper depositions of the stone,
More solid layers, covered over now,
But inching towards the bedrock of our lives.
The slow geology of generations
Settles rhythmically down into law,
The baritone and drone beneath our souls.
Some ranks are tepid in their scattered silt,
While other rungs were more volcanic slag,
And full of ash and fire. That's endowed
Within the earth. The very roots partake.

you strike a bully back, you win the fight

The generations absent of a chance
Would take an earnest chance if given it,
Even if haphazard adventures writ
In sweat and scabs. They were not pacified.
That infiltrating, cunning saboteur,
Mahatma Gandhi, had not yet his claws
And tentacles wrapped round the people's heart
To strangle them, by making moral waifs
Of them, mere quibbling ninnies caviling
Their pearls, lest anybody come to harm.
Such luxuries befit the privileged,
Who get to shake their heads from safe parlors,

And tut at scrappers aiming for the chance.
"Let us make sure we bow our heads to rules,
And tip our caps to gentlemen and kings,
And beg! How fiercely we will kneel and beg!
And call this groveling our courage proved!
We raise the fist — but in sweet-flowered lace,
Perfumed and pink, with feathers in its webs,
Our placards ruffled crepe (recycled, pure),
Demands honeyed polite to not offend;
Allow us vigil — better that we shame
Than change things, but we are so very kind!
A single feeling hurt we do abhor!"
Absurd and puritanical theatrics.
Move aside. There's rank and file come
To take their chance — and they don't give a damn
If nitpickers of virtue may approve.
They know the greater sin than risking sin
Is letting sin's ascendancy stand tall.
"Two wrongs don't make a right." That isn't true.
You strike a bully back, you win the fight.
I'm sorry you will see a bloody nose.
He had it coming. That's how you stand up.
That's how our rights are won, by fighting back.
And if we make a mess, we'll clean it up.

whisked away

But all my soul sometimes I think in this,
This song by Michael Jackson: all my past,
My hopes, my teenage yearnings, all my love.
This album is the thriller of my life.
Michael, Michael, composer of my dreams,
How could you? How could you? You were the one,
Our idol, we believed in, who brought us
Together, all of us : how much my soul
Rides on these dance moves and these rhythmic tunes.
You've etched yourself indelibly on me,
But Michael, precious ones you scarred, you scarred.
Yours is the score of my youth; what of theirs?
And yours? I know that too was whisked away,
As awfully as you whisked theirs away.
This knot — of what you were, and what you were,

Has made me try to say just beat it, but
Your songs arise returning from my breast.

neither tasted nor betrayed

The delicacy of her fingertips
Mere millimeters from my very own:
My heart were crepe and petal in her breath.
Her lips were but a lunge and plunge from mine.
Eternity suspended rapturously.
Curled up so close. She wanted this as well.
Her flesh the wine-red mother of the must,
Her eyes the symphonies of Oregon grapes.
I couldn't, yet was helpless not to; inched
But breath and silk beside voluptuous
Of all of her; her body, trance to me.
My who wished with religious wish her who
To touch; the very who of her, her heart
As fragile as my own, and as exposed;
I was express of plum in yard of her.
My pulse as veiny pulp and Muscatel.
My yearning was but reach before my hands;
Suspense was eons in the instant; sigh
Was endless skin evaporate of me.
These flowers nature now would intertwine,
But let release occur, a law alone
Between, no barriers at all but law,
What vapor, what a flimsy, silken thing,
A terrible and tissue-thin tyrant.
But ought between me and my deepest dream;
The crystal pitcher at my cup's smooth lip,
As ready ripe to pour as in my hopes.
Come water, O refreshing splash, O spell,
Rejuvenate me with your wettened wish,
Fulfillment all but at the very urge,
Asking naught but acceptance, but a choice —
And ethics there a sword above my head,
Sadistic, asking of me loyalty,
When tendrils of a vegetative bliss
As petal-soft as myrtle were prepared,
As if by Mother Earth herself for me —
Here's everything you ever chanted asked —

How can you spurn and scorn it brought at last?
The cold stone statue of the cruel law
Its Damocles above me; can and can't,
Must not and must. Would loyal ask me pine
When quench of years' long thirst was at the brink?
One must then sacrifice; why be it me?
Why must I lay down this, this sacrament
So frail and so chiffon of offered fleurs,
This nothing but a beauty, not a sin!
This brandy to my lips too dust and parched?
If I abstain, is but mundanity
And blip — nothing is added to the store —
Is never noticed and has no reward —
And yet I cringe and weep forever! Spell
Fulfilled but I reject! Will fate then hear
Single request again, if with my surge
Of constant fervency I ever asked,
But now, the dish before my very mouth,
Destiny, chef, presenting, garnishes
And sculpted fruit upon the porcelain,
I cavil? That were low and mean. You sailed
Across the galaxies to knit two stars
Together — but — I have a caveat?? —
While you in labors I can't understand
Turned heavens and the earth to bring my wish,
I have committed in the knowing-not,
Presuming never was the answer — now
A plusher plate you offer — and my hand
Will rudely push aside this paradise
Conveyed but breath and inches from my face?
I am an ingrate! Honor asks too much!
Has honor no exception for a gift?
Will it abase me to spit on divine,
Miraculous endowments? My restraint
Were ordinary price of her restraint,
Of her respect I hold so very high,
And reasoned, decent, gentle, loving-kind.
But now, but this, the cost exorbitant —
Refuse refulgent, priceless pearls of light,
Send back a fairy-missive sent by saints
(It seems to me for laboring my wish)
Because it is untimely, came too late?
How is such frosting on my cake askew?
How is such honeyed snow that flakes upon my tongue
A foul offense? This poetry and plum?

I ask but custard ordered long ago.
How long my taste buds have but shrank and dreamt
Of levity of pudding, satisfied
And innocent! How can an innocence,
For being but untimely, be a crime?
(It is not crime but injury I fear;
The law is gossamer but love too dear
To even think to wound; I cannot cause
Such eyes I cherish to gush forth with tears;
For but a moment's ecstasy, such pain?
She who adores me as I do adore?
I cannot fast from little cream for her?
Me, who oft fasts from many different sweets?
That were offense! — But that's entire point!
I were as starving — sweet deprived of me
So long — now it's my tears — what would she choose,
Salt water from her eyes on silver scale,
My portion of the sea on other scale?
And if this tragedy I do collapse,
My ecstasy and yet her agony —
Perhaps not ever known if either way —
By staying in abeyance, will it boon?
She'll never see her altar's sacrifice!
My gift of everything will seem the air,
A nothing, nothing registered at all!
In texture of the everyday, is fine,
Is wholesome worth and worthy, but a sylph,
An angel has appeared to bring my wish!
Would I not take the wound if it were her,
If an untimely angel brought her dream,
And cringing, weeping, yet through clenching teeth
Be happy for her? If for some mundane
And ordinary lust, what stupid crime.
But if a merman from the waves would kiss —
I wouldn't wish it no — but if her wish?
I were a denizen of jealous swamps,
A marshy heart with mossy strands and scum!
Why were a wish brought with dilemma's fist?)
All of these thoughts more swiftly fraught than spoke
An instant from the lips I crush upon.
My eyes are closed to savor this suspense;
I do not move, if closer or if far.
Keep this, this priceless tantalizing taunt,
Dessert so close the scent may almost taste.
If taste forbidden, let its scent allure —

O let me live in such alluringness!
The questions frangify, cobwebs in light —
A noise, and I awaken from the dream.
The waking grey awakens me from grief
So technicolor, such exquisite grief
It were an appetizer to the gods.
A sigh; I've neither tasted, nor betrayed.

thick like butter

The sunlight's breath on goosebumped breast exposed —
I open arms embracing twilight's cusp,
Last glory of the blaze of day on hill,
The cypresses like torches of the ridge.
The wild oats are livid in the light,
The amber air intoxicating, thick
Like butter. Summer night is simmering.
Day sizzles in the pan of cooling dark.

to funk the summer eve

That horn again through Eucalyptus-sifted
Night, click-clacking on the distant tracks.
Boulders off-gassing heat from daylight's sun.
The pine and oaks hold firm yet sway in dusk,
The rusty bruise of deepening black. A skunk
Upon the whiff to funk the summer eve.
And for a moment, everything is good;
Anxiety takes rest; the world heaves sigh.

I often shower but to weep alone

I often shower but to weep alone.
Yet not alone, for choir of my tears:
The roar, the thundering that meets my sobs
With overwhelming rain, that washes pain

Away. My feelings so intense at times,
I drown them in the water's ecstasy,
And wonder in bewilderment at world.

the greater sin

Dereliction is the greater sin;
Neglect, the hateful, prime unneighboring.
To nobody a somebody is hate
Beneath contempt; refusing fellowship
A cold erasure. We must break the bread
With all the neighborhoods in every town.
It's showing interest that shows neighbors love.

yet I rise

I am a wreck that walks, a shrapnel-flesh
That hobbles in dilapidated limp,
Collage of crude prosthetics rudely patched,
An amputee of melees. History
Is hump upon my burdened, broken back.
My injuries have made me Frankenstein,
A remnant of my fresh original.
I stagger like a man who's half a corpse
Through minefields, half-remembering the light
Of beauty, hope a torn meniscus, smoke
Surrounding me, the fireworks of bombs
In echo burst about me, yet I walk,
Half-walk, I lumber forward, yet I walk.
Belief a fragment yet an heirloom of
Its glory, I still keep the ember here
In swinging thurible aside my hip,
And blow a'times to orange it to life
And taste its recels billow on my face.
A ragged flag more torn than whole still holds
Its colors in its stains, and to the grip,
Still reassures, reminding in its rip
Bygone unfurling flapping in the breeze.
The scraps, though wretched souvenirs, are seeds,

The heirloom seeds of gardens yet to come.
And though I stumble in unsteady flesh,
Half-broken bones, and ache that marinates
The disappointed years, I shall those seeds
Yet carry over ruins that I walk!
The shards of beauty's memories may cut
My clenching palm, but though they bleed, in time,
When reassembled, shall a looking glass
(Howbe pique assiette) magnificent
Reflect new lamps of light in old discards.
We carry Eden's reminiscing trace
Though we may amble through the nightmare's ash.
I shall not be unfaithful though I fall.
My gait is stubborn rising to my feet
After the every tumble, difficult
And sputtering and cursing, yet I rise.

he had the tune

They ask me, what kind of self-hating Jew
Are you that you adore that Ezra Pound?
Well, I'm an Irish Jew, for one, a kind
Of rabbi-leprechaun, Hasidic Druid.
Look, we're all a mess of shambling stew.
We're putzes rising to our betterment.
Pound was a schmuck, but still he had the tune.
He was a baffled crank, but still he sang.
It's yet a new thing, beauty, young and soft
And fragile, very rare, appearing where
We least expect it, then it vanishes.
We can't afford as yet to raise our nose,
But be surprised and grateful when it comes.
The lotus in the sewage treatment plant.

every fruit

My heart is like a bird, and every beauty
Cages me within their wonderment,
So that I fly about within in joy

And dazzlement, all twittering with song.
I'm absolutely captured, and I'm stunned.
I'm drunk on every fruit the orchard grows,
Transported by the every garden rose.
The loveliness is everywhere about.

high and dry

Anchises.
Is it my fault I'm smitten by your smile?
Or shall I be blamed for falling fast
And long for eyes and curves so beautiful?
I'm but a victim of your stunning spell.
It can't be helped. You're doing nothing wrong.
It all is right, too right, so very right,
Yet wrong the way it leaves me high and dry.

unnoticed were my fruits

I made the sun to rise in me
And thought it would be majesty.
I hoped the trumpets then would blow,
But no one seemed to even know.
My tears refreshed the roots.

I yearned somehow to stir the tribe
With elevated, striving vibe.
Aspiring to ascend to clouds,
I was not noticed by the crowds.
Unnoticed were my fruits.

One cannot save oneself through work.
One's light is pinpoint in the murk.
No matter how noble you seem,
That will not render you redeemed.
We cannot earn reputes.

slithering reptilian

My vanity could compensate my loss
(The bounce and fullness of my sheening hair,
The beauty in whose mirror I beheld
Something transcendent to my low esteem),
But now these crow's feet and this coming grey
Deprive me of the joys requiting pain.
I could assuage the ugliness within
Through playful vanity, a soulful flirt
In mirror's dalliance, and thus invoke
The diva in my dreams — now that was balm,
That soothes the burns the world has wreaked on me,
Distracting from my sheer irrelevance
Through make-believe of wonder and applause.
Sometimes I feel a creature mean and low,
Some slow and slithering reptilian,
His creeping belly to the hugging earth,
Alone and frightened, seeking for a cave,
Some cool alleviation from the heat,
To pant in shadows yet enjoy the sun
Outside my limestone dolmen, there to lick
My wounds, forgetting all in twilight's shade.
Sometimes that lizard (if that's what it is)
Feels so rejected, sad, a savage thing,
An animal of thrash and hissing teeth,
Too long insulted with too many wounds.
It is a leper, oozing terribly
With sores, incapable of shrugging off
Resentments that now permeate its guts.
It cries! It shrieks! It wants to tear apart,
It yearns alone for lashings-out with tears.
It would love roses but its eyes are dust,
Encrusted with its weeping these long years.
No matter how I may urge it forgive,
This older atavist knows not the how
Of such — the wretched thing but seeks to hide
Or snarl — it has reached its limit point,
Perhaps a hundred moons or so ago.
Can such a hazy being dazed in fog,
Still creeping unevolved upon the earth,
Conceive of letting go and starting fresh?
It has no memory of mammal genes
For it still yet to come: softness eludes.

How may I help it with its shrieking sores?
It might be such a lovely thing indeed,
Mercurial wonder of desert dunes.
Could I give it the gift of listening?
But quiet my escapes to hear it hiss?
If I then followed it where it may lair,
And breathed in hollow shadows next to it,
Might it relax into its basal sighs?
Perhaps escaping with my vanity
Offends it? O I should relax as well.

come, vandals!

A

The new iconoclasm rocks!
Shaking foundations with its shocks!
Toppling the despots carved in stone!
Knocking them from their public throne.

Shaking the archons to the dust;
Where they were iron, leaving rust.
The never-heroes fall to ground;
We never wanted them around!

B

The rock was taunt but now it's grain.
Our hammers turn it into rain.
It powders then it's gone at last.
The vandals now correct the past.

A

A warning to the governments,
Their idols and their monuments :
If we such granite turn to flour,
It might soon be your last hour!

CHORUS

Come, vandals, bring salvation near!

Upset the tyrants; make them fear!
Come, vandals, knock the towers down!
And turn this nightmare upside down!

Come, vandals, quake, and shake the blues!
Make them retreat! Let them now lose!
Come, vandals, speak the underground!
Silent too long, our voice is found!

A

We might be cure for your disease.
If rock tumbles, well, flesh is easy!
All this vandalism's good.
The people speak, as well they should.

If votes are null, why mallets talk!
We burst the chains and break the locks.
We don't ask you to give us leave.
Instead, we give you no reprieve.

B

The culture you thought for all time
Is but a ruin now: sublime!
Insult the people long enough
And they will fire back, but rough.

A

The history you have idolized,
The people, rising, vandalize.
Now there's a certain plebiscite!
A mandate at the rebels' fight.

CHORUS

BRIDGE

This tearing down but builds me up!
Refreshing juice from rebels' cups!
This knocking over brings me mirth!

Beginnings of a rebel earth!

The air is clear and clean at last!
The people move, and they move fast!
But storm the streets, and weeks work years
Of what had gotten jammed in gears!

A

You thought the public space your own?
The people will decide alone.
Call them the rabble if you please.
They'll still bring statues to their knees.

You haven't listened; now they speak.
With hammers they lay their critique.
You've kept them down but said this stands.
They've taken it out of your hands.

B

You thought you could but occupy?
The mob declares: now say goodbye!
The ones your statues mocked for years
Now posse up and take arrears.

CHORUS

they outlaw this my heart

It aches each time I think of you, it aches,
Your absence — O it aches, that you're not here —
Each time I think on it, I think I die
A little — so it feels — it aches so much.
To shun me is to hurt me to the thick.
My every fear comes true — why is it so?
Why do the ones I love abandon me?
My pantheon has fled. I worshipped them.
I called them to my mind when I was sad.
My bank was full, so any check I wrote
Was good — I did not need to write the check.
My bank is short on funds — benevolence —

They do not wish me well! It aches me so!
Why does it ache like this? Why do they hate
Me so? Why do they hate the one who loved
Them so? It wasn't supposed to be this way.
The world's awry. The loves that should have held
Have broken. And the little boy within
Doesn't believe me anymore when I
Give word that I'll protect. I've not the force
Or power, for the world has gone astray.
As people age, they're supposed to then mature,
And life gets better in the golden years.
I ache through life. I limp upon my wounds.
I haven't figured out a better way.
I am an amputee. My limbs have fled.
My loves that I could call upon are gone.
It doesn't count how good your heart may be.
It doesn't matter how you love at all.
A broken world. I sudden wake from sleep —
Their aching absence palpable and cruel.
I am so hatable, so hatable.
I must be, for they outlaw this my heart.

two thousand years ago

They hurled the same contempt on us as well,
The Romans, calling us barbarians
And spearchuckers because we lived in woods.
The forests frighten city folk like them.
Our fierceness, for we wore wolf's heads and furs,
Alarmed them, and they set their sights to slave us,
Sent us to arenas, spat on us,
Declaimed their high superiority.
We know that deep humiliation too.
And now, how it is salt on Roman wounds
To see our own descendants do the same
To you, to witness Rome within their blood,
And double the offense done to ourselves.
Take you across the seas to foreign lands,
Forbidding you your languages and thews,
Coercing you to build their newer wealth,
Then hating you with burning apathy.
We too got angry and we stormed their towns.

They called us Vandals too (that was our name,
In fact, although it didn't mean that we
Were wreckers — it was far more beautiful.
The Romans twist the beauties that can't grasp,
They always do.) We built our roofs with thatch,
And walls with mud, as your ancestors did.
We loved our wizards and our storytellers.
We were proud, and held our heads up high,
Even defiantly, in face of Rome,
As often you do. Not so different,
Our peoples. Had we visited, how much
In common we would find ourselves to be!
And yet I rue our issue seems to pale,
Forgets the elk and panther in their blood,
Can't hear the pulse of rivers nor the winds,
Is tone-deaf to the animals and trees.
Alas, no wonder they oft brush your worth
Aside; somehow you kept your drums and tales.
The beat and thump your ancestors lived by
Still lives in you. They do not recognize
Our image faintly in a blur in you,
Or worse, perhaps they do, and thus they shun.
They brainwashed our descendants, told them we
Burned in their hells, and they would have to leave
Us, O! Within their blood we've wept these years,
And howled into our shields that they might hear.
Your ancestors and us are much the same,
And pleasingly, both different as well.
We know your lives matter. We knew it too.
How pleased we've been to see your rhythms wake
The hips of our descendants to their zest,
Frozen too long by fears of cityfolk.
Allow us speak a prophecy of frith.
These trials and these storms at last shall pass,
If coming generations share the feast,
Break bread, share laughter over bubbling cups,
Tell tales that speak biographies of heart,
Refind integrity of animals
Within the soul, in time, a brotherhood
You can't envision just as yet shall gel,
And future generations will scratch heads,
And wonder at the fuss. Give it some time.
We speak to you two thousand years ago.
We come in peace, and swear that on our spears.

Oscar to Bosie

My heart is crepe you fold into a bud,
And when I think you might be thinking of me,
I become curvaceous pewter shaped
Long-lipped, cream saucière, and feeling drips
From me like gravy. You are such a dish
One licks one's fingers, just to savor more,
And you are every chef's most consummate
Desire: delicate, delicious, soft,
And flavorful, the crown of their gourmet.
But when you turn away your shunning eyes,
I am chagrin as shy as sheltered doves,
And all my succulence withdraws in wilt
Within me, petals pulled back, purling dew
Of subtle brine, and I am enervate
As all ennui, and cannot lift a limb.
But say these wings are half-plucked of their tuft,
You could instruct me fly with single glance;
A smile sends me ceiling through the sky!
You must belong some pinch of falling frost,
For when you may approach me, I am shiver.
Call my name, I shudder: I am yours.

stern rebuttals

This is no time to ask us to be kind.
This is a time to fight the power back,
For stern rebuttals, strong rebukes, for scolds,
For getting in the face of what is wrong,
To sting and scald deplorables to silence,
Fisticuffs in words to intimidate
Intimidators back under their rock.
In neofascist times, you must be tough.
It's time to peel politeness from the crap,
And call the sewer sewage with firm words.
To recommend one must be ever kind
To bullies is reactionary shit.
For every shout, you shout back louder still.

For every macho threat, you double down.
You give no quarter, nor make comfortable,
But let them know they're not welcome at all.
And hurt their feelings as much as possible,
To humble them, pull down their hateful pride.
Don't talk to me of kindness in this time.
You're nothing but a Neville Chamberlain,
Capitulating to the worst of men,
And quoting Gandhi, Jesus, anyone
Who'll back your cowardice with noble words,
So you can make the evil feel at home.
For what you fear is conflict. But it's here.

John Brown is in my breast

I'm swallowing the fire and the smoke;
I rumble in my belly, and the forge
Is fired in my soul, where molten ore
Runs groove white-hot to foundry molds of worth,
The archetypes of prophets in my flesh.
I've got the bluster in my breath of coals;
My nostrils snort; John Brown is in my breast;
Isaiah rants atop a mountain peak,
While Jeremiah charts apocalypse,
Whose flames renew the greenery of hills.
My dukes are raised for verbal fisticuffs;
I fight for flocks of gamboling, loving lambs
With representatives of roving wolves.
There's blacksmith in the sooty glow of brain.
My hammer's raised; it knocks heads just as well
As anvils. If they would abuse the mind,
That most penultimate of nature's gifts,
To justify the wolfen hierarchies,
They had not reckoned locust-eating John
In furs with honey on his smoking lips
Barring the Jordan from their wicked path,
His hands on hips, reading the riot act,
And like the staff slammed down at Khazad-dûm,
Announcing like the thunder not to pass!
I take the professoriate of coals,
And thump the liberating tomes with zest,
A scrapping badger for the ways of right,

Against the cretins of the gremlin age.
That whosoever should intelligence
Betray to archons with their lust to rule,
Shall find their ranks and badges stripped of them,
By one well-tempered in the battlegrounds
Of archives, who has bit his mettle down
Upon the stacks, and they are libraries.
Such volumes, reassembled in their troops
To form a mighty army for the good,
I am the general of, which I direct
Guerilla in the weedy plains of mind
Against assuming fools who think they're wise
While bullying about: they meet my storm.
I'm not naive to think that being kind
Will placate ignorance and prejudice,
But know a little knock about does good
To bruise the egos of the arrogant.
Meanwhile I bow my head in modesty
To practice equity and mind my place,
While shoveling the billets in the forge.

a little less than best

I was the same, perhaps a better, man
When I knew less : less arrogant, more kind.
So if I was a better form of me
When what I knew was much more vague and sparse
(Or rather, not as focused — general),
What is the worth of knowing more at all?
I got on fine before, and happily.
What lacked in accuracy gained in mirth,
And frankly, general schemas work just fine.
A rubric is sufficient in its blur.
Detail distracts unless it shifts the gist.
How often knowledge makes one take on airs!
What difference does it make when all is done?
If folk are mainly good, a little less
Than best is negligible; if folk are wrong,
And harmfully, what will correction do?
Will they reform on being told they're wrong?
I think I mainly fight to let the worst
Know they'll be challenged when they intimidate,

And throwing round their weight gets them knocked down.
If knowledge loses track of heart, it fails.

just pinch your nose and eat

The choices we are given in this land!
"What flavor would you like your excreta?"
"Oh, I'd like bubblegum pistachio."
"Flavor my bovine excreta with mint!"
"I'd like a double fudge with walnuts please!"
"Can I have something else than excreta?"
Sharp pause, and "WHAT??!!" "What are you saying, man?"
"We give you all this choice, you still complain?"
"Well, I —" he hesitates. "I'm grateful for
The flavors, but I'd like another choice
Of what gets scooped into my ice cream cone."
"That's what we've got, pal! Learn to live with it!
Be reasonable! Just pinch your nose and eat!"

Aphrodite knows no color walls

Is not love evidence division lies?
For Aphrodite knows no color walls.
She cannot be controlled or quarantined.
A nation's boundaries are naught to her.
Alliances and politics balk not
Her sweeping hand of generosity.
Apartheid hath no strength o'er her domain;
She draws together close those kept apart,
And brings her tenderness to trauma's wounds.
Love educates the fool to understand,
Where ignorance or arrogance held sway.
Love rouses all the highest in our soul,
So we can be the best for whom we love.
Love integrates, and sutures what is torn.
She bridges old divides with new allures.
She makes for curiosity and care
Where apathy once reigned, for love transforms.
Love has a universal range and scope.

She crosses every ocean, every shore.
Taxonomies of men are laughingstock
To her; what matters is the beautiful.
She never knew a caste she could respect.
Love knows the smell of flowers, sight of lips,
The sounds of pleasure's sighs, hold loyalty
Above the silly flags of passing states,
For while they come and go, the human heart
Has lasting sway over allegiance.
The rules of separation she revokes;
She has no care for pettiness as that.
Love undermines the hierarchies and walls.
She crosses no-man's-lands and breaches gates.
Who would forbid, she sets them free to love.
No fence barring variety can stand.
She doctors our divides with loving hands.

the sacred temple grounds

And with his whips, he persecutes the rich,
And makes for them to flee, and where they set
Their banks and monuments, he knocks them down,
Restoring public life to cleanliness.
He has no honor for their property.
He doesn't ask permission to disrupt.
He's not polite when spilling all their gold,
Or chasing off their oxen and their sheep.
He doesn't give them notice in advance.
Buying and selling aren't holy acts,
And desecrate the sacred temple grounds.

fear is political

Fear is political. The phobia
Of fellow citizens when one is Black
Deprives our fellows of their civil rights,
Dehumanizing those who act on fear.
Fear is political. The media
Are culpable in shaping images

Of terror that condition some to fear
Their brothers just for being who they are,
Associating color of the skin
With criminality. They should be sued,
Class action suit, intention to reduce
To citizens of second class, which is
No citizen at all, but one despised,
And hounded, ever subject to arrest
Or death for simply being who one is.
Fear is political. Who calls the cops
From prejudicial fright, from fear of skin,
That calls up phantoms of their shadow self,
Assaults with deadly weapon fellow men.
Fear is political. Your heart is stone.
You've locked your doors and shut conscience's gates
To children of our mother 'neath our feet,
Sequestering from their fraternity,
And listening to slander's whisper-wisps,
And heeding innuendo over right,
Have shrunk in paranoia and in fright.
Fear is political. You're troglodytes,
Who cower in your caves and watch the news,
Then swagger in the grocery aisles proud,
Ready to pull the trigger any time.
Fear is political, and it must stop.

or you will have it shut

It's true — I do not wish to hear from you
Your filth — I try to fill my soul with wealth!
But hate — it puts me in an ugly state!
Your dreck — inside of me makes me a wreck.
The gist — of innuendo like a fist
That slams — and whispers slanders as it damns.
Your words — are nothing more than bigot's turds.
You nag — with vitriol, but need a gag.
Throw out — what you have written, without doubt.
You're worth — the greatest censor on this earth.
You shut — your mouth or you will have it shut.
I feel — throw out the key with no appeal.
We should — for words like this jail you for good.
I'm fine — I do endorse Antifa's line.

One needs — the beauty that the spirit feeds.
But you? — you're nothing but a low yahoo.
You will — for everyone to feel as ill.
You're slime — and wish to wipe on others grime
That comes — from out your dirty, soulless gums.
Shut up — I will not drink your poison cup.
You zip — or we will sew your wretched lips.

peacocks now reclaim philosophy

Affirm profusion and extravagance!
Because more desiccated souls complain,
That's more the reason to make fountains lush!
Utility is but futility.
Let peacocks now reclaim philosophy.
If Solomon wears Joseph's varied robe,
Which is but blush before the petal-craft
Of Primavera's iridescent gown,
Then life must have exuberance and zest.
The poor need beauty not austerity.
Cathedrals make their life more glamorous,
And theater fills them with majesties,
Lest they suffer impoverished fantasies.
An inner richness rendered manifest
Is charity, for art is better alms,
And hopeless ones need gardens for the heart.
The monuments still need their patronage,
So beggars have a promenade to stroll.

the mystic merchant

Travel with me across the many lands!
Where silks and spices run with caravans.
Adventure brings its luxuries and jewels,
For yonder every country's yonder rules,
And in between one finds exotic gems,
Exotic foods, and most exotic femmes!
And what one country thinks as commonplace,
Another finds extraordinary grace,

And miracles are worth some extra gold,
For I risk life when I venture so bold
Across the deserts and the mountainsides,
A solitary, without other guides.
There's robber bands as you have never known.
There's old abandoned campsites filled with bones,
Unlucky fellows, victims of the sword.
Surely you may this modest price afford!
For after all, this treasure comes afar!
Packed on a mule I rode beneath the stars.
The many lands make many different things.
You never know just what a new one brings.
What one makes cheap, another buys more dear;
Vice-versa, soon prosperity is near!
I wisely choose what I think best will sell,
And lug it over heaven's way or hell.
The humble profit that I humbly ask
Is certainly the value for my task.
Will you go out to search the foreign lands,
Endangering yourself at many hands?
Of course you won't! That's why I'm here, my friend!
A friendly merchant. Now look you attend:
These shapely fruits are only found abroad.
These spicy herbs? That make a meal applaud?
They're also from those strange lands past the hills.
Exorbitant? It just covers my bills!
Now no more silly talk. Let's make a deal.
I'm flexible, and since you do appeal,
I'll tell you what : I'll throw in there a pearl
Once given to me by a mermaid girl,
When I walked by a sailors' wharf of wood,
And this delightful one, right where she stood,
Began to juggle gems from neath the sea,
And for a kiss, rendered a pearl to me.
Her lips were pearls! And so this pearl reminds
Me of those lovely escapades in brine!
But for the price I charge, I'll part with it,
If you buy seven fruits without a fit.
Yet for a little more, you'll have this spice.
It makes a royal feast of even rice!
Perhaps you'd like as well this soft, smooth silk,
Lunescent-white as if made from moon's milk.
They weave it top their camels in the dunes,
Embroidering Arabian in runes,
Those mystic women shrouded in their veils.

Now let us put it on my trusty scales.
That's not too much! It's worth the labor cost.
It's worth the dreams that nights of toil lost.
So what if I live in a kind of trance,
Enjoying all this rich extravagance?
I'm bringing you the world right on a plate!
I'm offering encounters with strange fates!
Behind this varied merchandise I hawk,
Are people. Oh, if you could hear them talk!
Their tongues are odd! Their clothes even more strange!
It's wondrous folk you meet out on the range.
A story in my every item here.
And you could house this tale inside your lair,
But for a petty price, that's all I charge.
And at your fingertips, the world at large!
Just think what all your friends will say to you,
When they discover all of this is true!
You'll be the talk of every town about!
It isn't every man who earns that clout!
But you'll have something no one else enjoys.
They'll envy you so much they'll raise their voice!
The women always love a man with style,
And you can have them all for little guile.
So shall we call this deal a bargain, pal?
Let's shake on it and say it's fair not foul!
Enjoy, and adios, I pack my bags
On my old trusty mule for her to drag!
I'll be this way next Spring, so you come back!
I'll happily supply what you may lack.

your sweet vagina's made of subtle lace

Your sweet vagina's made of subtle lace,
And silk-embroidered roses at its sides.
The pelts of minks adorn its pouting lips,
And fragrance of the alder tree exudes
From every pore, refreshingly, like nymphs
By fountainsides who spray their chic perfumes.
A moist and spongy macaroon lies hid
In satin coverts where the honeydew

Is nectar of reward eagerly sought.

Neapolitan at heart

We all are Neapolitan at heart;
Our flavors blend a bit where they abut.
We are pastel and soft with varied tastes,
And we inhabit mutually this life,
Encradled in each other, nurseried
Where innocence has met its sadness, hope
Its challenges, and flavor its desire
To be blended at its edges' lips.
And our lips, if by touch or word or breath,
To blend. The flavors stay distinct in zones,
Yet there commingle where they run along
Their epidermal sweetness thick and smooth.
We are the ice cream of each other's eyes,
Where prejudice resents this sweet delight
It feels the same yet won't allow itself.
Come, chocolat, and come, pistachio,
You come, vanilla, and you, strawberry,
Enjoy each other, Mardi Gras your mouths,
Make merry in the sensuality
Of bodies' rhythms! Well beneath what minds
May gasp and fibrillate in venoms' steep.
The ripened red was first; the green-blue sea
Brought forth vanilla in its eager time,
With theobromine dragged against its will,
Yet inconceivable that frosted dew
Of cream and honey ever might suffice
Without its stimulating flavor-styles!
We are opportunity to taste
Our subtle savors' rich, diverse palates.
Now let us let our joys be in command.

the Dresden of the everyday

I'm searching for an anchor anywhere —
My past is crumbling with its monuments —

The landmarks that I loved or hated, yet
Which oriented memory in space
Come down, come down, the old before the new.
All of the framework that I've lived within,
It disappears, and often with the loss
Of friends and loved ones, who might mark the joys
And struggles with me, physiognomy
Alone sustains my heirloom memories.
In desperation at this frightful loss,
That on and on and on and onward drives,
The demolition mandate of our time,
The Dresden of the everyday, I cry,
"Not one more thing! Please don't take one more thing!"
Therein my life was lived, therein my loves —
How many now are vanished bitterness,
A sweetness exiled to my lonesomeness —
Inhered within their settings, I could go
And lean over the bridge we leaned against,
The stone and concrete whispering the kiss —
The masonry remembers — and the stream
Down in the chasm winking sparklet-gold,
And widowed to a poignancy locked up
In loss, the fond materials would soothe,
And pitying my tears, would comfort me
With testament that yes, it was right here!
Except the bridge is gone of now for good,
Its granite taken, and the landscape stripped.
The sycamore I danced beneath with her,
The statue where she first confessed her love,
The tracks where once, with giggling, we chased,
Are gone, are gone, are gone — they all are gone.
Until it feels some cruel conspiracy
To rob the elders of their heirloom dreams,
And strip them of their precious poignancies.
It's progress, so we say, but it is loss.
Something of who we are is in the stone,
The asphalt and the xylem, lime and steel,
The petals strewn autonomous in fields.
The movie theater where I first saw
The Wrath of Khan — now why was that not made
A temple? For you see, these are our shrines.
Therein the nymphs and fauns of longingness
Were subtle legends in their priceless haunts,
And one could simply silent visit them,
And soak emotions in their redolence,

A misting of the eyes that felt alive.
The solid slips to liquid then to gas;
Labors and craft, the great achievements, fade.
Even the mockeries we ridiculed,
The ugliness we railed against, is gone.
How kindly they endured our keen contempt,
And stood defiant, letting us rebel.
Now how I miss even those homely ones.
So when you come to me and say, tear down,
I know that many things deserve that fate,
And yet I hesitate, for what remains?
But promise me the beauties be preserved,
I shall applaud injustices torn down.
Say to me, these your bearings have some weight,
And piety for wondrous rarities,
The essence of such times as won't return,
Shall find a lasting honor in our hearts,
Why then, I suddenly find I can breathe!
Then we can scold Manifest Destiny.
What is Mount Rushmore to me really? But
A landmark, but a common welcoming
Of common feeling — yet it is a stain,
A gashing wound, salt in Lakota eyes,
Spit on the vellum's sacred treaty rights —
You're right. The Grandfathers in granite peaks,
Before the dynamite, were sacred shrines.
The land is aching with the drowning loss.
The wound is everywhere — the ghosts do wail —
I hear them in my pleas. We've done this thing,
We've done this terrible and awful thing.
We've tried to build our beauties on our sins,
And that unwhole foundation can't abide.
500 years we've swept away the shame.
It is our only lasting monument.
It stands when all the other ones are felled.
And so we live in rubble, cinderlands
The wretched recels meager eke to skies,
And crows choke on our smoking excrement.
The frogs in tar but bubble down and die.
And beauty's such a fragile, helpless femme;
So she, my damsel in distress, declares:
Two thousand years of spitting on the nymphs,
Millennia of shadow thrown on them,
The reckless bigotry against the fays.
But there's no delicacy in that pride

That pompously asserts its dominance,
And captures art, imposing grandiose
Insults in stone, to force victims to cringe.
I never saw Confederate I loved.
Let then such marble be a quarry field
For newer sculptors' freshest masterpiece.
I shall not cry but rather celebrate.
But then if Gandhi or if Jefferson?
My feet now falter. What if you could find
That Michelangelo or Donatello
Had committed some egregious crime?
Do Neptune and his Neriads come down?
The Medici's were never known as saints.
Must what they patronized now say goodbye?
I feel a fondness for the ages' arts;
It anchors me that beauty's set in stone,
That cities value what the vandals hate,
That brutal men are made to bow to craft.
It's taking so much out of me these times.
The Rio de Janeiro's library
In flames, the Buddhist statues pulverized
By Taliban extremists, landmarks wrecked,
The smoke at Notre Dame, graffiti tagged
Across those 30's murals made with love.
The answer's no, nothing is sacred, no.
I cannot live this sacrilegious life.

deliver me to sages' feet

The more I'm saddened, all I more withdraw.
Just let me read Talmudic tracts and Grimm's.
The ashes from the fires of our times
But make me weep as I scoop them in hands.
Away, away, to other times and climes.
Let me at Heschel's feet become a scribe.
Let me with Hillman toast the Renaissance.
Let me with Elfman cheer in Halloween.
All theater and dance are in rescind.
The festivals are canceled. I'm in grief.
My body longs for the surround of throngs.
Divisiveness of despots does its work:
We all are at each other's throats, not theirs.

There is no president, but Fear is King.
And no one listens anymore at all.
It's utter melancholy by decree.
No no, deliver me to sages' feet,
And let me there eat grapes and lemonade,
Dip avocado into goddess sauce,
Discover jewels in new exegesis,
That reads against the grain and finds the hints
Of treasures long forgotten in the texts,
Salvation histories between the lines.
Unearth the traces of utopias
Despotic pragmatists have not erased,
Or else the disappointed deemed unjust.
Cancel the cancel culture. Keep the bran,
The texture, leaving Weber bread for fools.

disciplines of delicacy

But make the breath alone your nutriment,
And life becomes translucent levity,
The flesh the whisper of the subtle winds,
The spirit on a raft that rides moonlight,
A foggy ocean liquidine of light.
Let wafer to the tongue with berry juice,
And scent of celery, and live upon
Bamboo arched over streaming forest brooks,
To meditate upon the washing rocks,
And watch the evanescence in its flow.
Snug in the alpine study of the light,
In hermitage where song is spirit's web,
Until one's skin is gossamer and frond,
The folds of water's vaporing in air,
The thinnest citrus slice of sunlit wing.
Be then but caterpillar's coming out,
A moment in the wet of new-birthed flight,
A thousand fleeting lives accordioned
On swarm, again, and yet in bliss again,
But heaven in the theater of awe,
A witness, and no more, to miracle,
Ananda-breath in nectar, yet no pain,
Until one's flesh is wonder, nothing else.
Bones porous and of helium, so light,

One rises in the dawn a kiss of mist
Against the bathing blue of bosom sky,
The clouds one's footpaths, and the birds one's kin.
And practicing such lucid rarity,
One's shadow sheds, and fleet are feet on air,
One's nature more resembling the stars,
As light and bright, to take one's heaven's haven.
Body naught but sentiment and lilt,
Reflection in stained glass, and glittering gold
Of dawn running its liquid fingers down
Metallic cylinders of aisle rail
Somewhere in anywhere cathedral, touched
By poignant drift, the simple flow of femme,
One's beating blood but quicksilver of grace.
These are the disciplines of delicacy
Hominids aspiring to elves
Shinto in snow-alpine cool elevate,
What Japanese foliage the mind may know,
Accustoming oneself to sunlight's tides,
The substance of the spirit, as one's home.

a glimpse of Halloween

Sometimes throughout the year, I'll get a glimpse
Of Halloween, an evanescent glimpse,
As if it stole in for reconnaissance
Then slipped away — and then I feel such joy!
As if the greatest moment of the year
Came by to reassure me, I will come!
That is the season I live life around!

because of these, I stayed
for Jade

We could do anything we wanted! There
Was freedom and defiance in our love!
We holed up from the rest of everything,
And lived in joyous thumbing of our nose
At any rule beyond our quirkiness.

Our whimsicality was our own law.
We stayed up and we slept in as we wished.
We fucked and slobbered juice just as we wished.
We ate like petty kings just as we wished.
And in the all of that, we loved the world,
Not as an obligate but on the side,
Good will in perfect liberty and love.
That freedom felt so good it made it worth
Whatever breaches of the law and knots,
Whatever hassles. Where we chose to live,
Was always Sherwood Forest, Ingle's Wood.
Conventionality was not our rule.
Anything whatever the fuck we wished,
And usually was lazy, sex and books
And beach and sleep, we did just that, no more.
Oh yes, we fought a lot. Oh God, we fought.
It was a hell in paradise for sure.
It was a firebrand that burned the gut.
It was a windstorm in the sacred church.
And yet I knew she always had my back
When it came to my talents and my mind,
My weird proclivities and love of show
And costume — maybe little else, but these.
And these were so damn valuable, I stayed,
Through all abuse and hurricane, I stayed,
Because of these, these precious spirit gifts.

a meal is blessing by itself

Migliore.
We ever must be purely excellent
As masterwork the candidate to arts
Presents with trembling pride to his own guild.
Not just the best, but very exudation
Of the cream itself, the sweetest drop,
The finest rarity of rarities,
The utter shock at beauty this profound.
And if we falter, we are such as scum
That lines the marsh and stains the lotuses.
To be a single rung beneath the top
Is worse than being at the bottom rung.
It is one's honor's end, the insult's apogee,

The lingering denouement of dwindling hope.
It is the mirror cursing at the face,
The name bowing its head, equivalent
In every fine particular to shame.
We should be polished glass, the moon's disgrace
That it could not be smooth upon the lake
In wintertide of ice gleaming as us.
We should be graceful as would captivate
A heart of stone and melt it down in awe.
We should be rapture in the birdsong's hush
When something swift and royal passes by,
The envy of majestic, subtle things,
The taunting edge of the impossible .
Where doubt shrouds on capacity, we leap,
Surpassing, handing limits back their ass,
And shrug as we look back it could be more.
Enough is an anathema, a curse,
Salt on the wound of our achievement's ache.
Better self-replicates in exponents,
Each one an ante on the one just past.

Bastevole.
That demon nipping, whipping at your heels
I exorcised long decades in the past.
Tranquility is in obscurity,
In letting rhythms of the bones set pace,
And trusting blood's organic calendar.
Come what each fruit as it may yield itself,
Some small, some large, some bitter, sour, bland,
Or sweet. Each ripens in its native time,
And every one is perfect as the rest.

Migliore.
That may suffice for yokels past their prime,
To dodder in their gardens of retreat.
Such words console impoverished heirs of sloth,
Not those who still contrive nobility
Steeply attainable at costly price,
Yet if achieved, a sale second to none.
Less than new laurels every year's disgrace,
Utter abasement worthy of the weak.

Bastevole.
So testifies the fiend to drive you on.
He hardly can persuade save in such threats.
Only a loser heeds such hokum, right?
That's what he says? I've been around the block.
I know his mischief and shenanigans.
I know the petty malice of his shtick,
The vaudeville melodrama of his rage.
That leech is nothing but a gutter punk,
A wino with his get-rich quickly schemes,
That lead to bankruptcy but vow the world.
You could instead have happiness and peace.
Just step a little off his beaten path.

Migliore.
And be a lesser than my excellence?
That cringing day of fools will never come!

Bastevole.
It's excess you revere, not excellence!
You take yourself too far, then you collapse,
And snipe yourself for failing when you fall!
That is the foolishness! You mustn't think
That every moment must be all the best.
Absurd! Insulting to the good of good,
The ordinary good, which will suffice.
It will suffice! Gourmet is excellent,
Why not? And yet a simple hamburger,
Some fries, a shake will do — is good and fine.
A luxury dessert is beautiful.
Those who prepare it ought to have their praise.
But one can't live on cheesecake by itself,
As heavenly as we all know it is!
You're like the foolish farmer, who destroyed
His crop when it was not the very best,
And starved but for his noble few of fruits.
The seasons vary with their varied crops.
An excellence is good surprise, but good
Is good enough! And you're but immature
If you have not progressed to see this truth.

Migliore.
Such truths of mediocrity are lies
To those who may aspire higher up.
To those who aim beneath Olympic grade,
Your rustic idylls may retain a charm,
But do not help to train the sterner stuff.

Bastevole.
Well then! Let's take Olympic level feats!
I do not envy, for the good or bad,
Those who, through dedicated toil, win
The highest gold, yet is once in a life!
Once in a life! A taste of nectar! Then?
What then? What can compare with such a peak?
You've climbed Mount Everest, so what is next?
If all your worth is in surpassing, how
Will you advance when that is it? What then?
To wallow in your glories past from then?
To shrivel, caught in single history,
No worth but when the demon gives you praise?
Should they then say, no no, I want no good,
Because it's not a noble, priceless good?
To waste away on caviar alone!
Abhorring fine things for they don't excel!

Migliore.
But when you've tasted such a singular,
Exquisite flavor as brings heaven down
To earth, how can the lows give you a high?

Bastevole.
If heavens stay beneath, where are the skies?
Even a bird who skims the sky's delights,
The heights where lightest snow finds its own home,
The undercream where stars lay down their feet,
Their slippers slipped, and wading toes in clouds,
Must then at last from voyages of prayer,
Where wing and wing against the wind are hymn,
Come down, and utter birdsong liturgies
In humbler nests nearer the humble earth.
The daemon terrorizing you has dealt
You potent drugs to keep you on its path!

He keeps you high sufficiently at first.
Then when it falters (for life must have breath!),
It's your fault, your fault, your fault, am I right?
You're punished when you're angel-less but man,
As if to be human were something low!
Welcome the bran, the wholesome grains of life!
The doughty texture which gives frosting root!
The cream may crown the cake, but cake it needs!
A glutton hobgobbling his honeypot,
And snarling at approach of any less
Is some strange denizen of swamps, not skies.
You give homage to father of the skies
In reaching towards them. What of Mother Earth?
A farmer likes dessert, after the meal.
Sugar is sweet, but it is not a meal.
I have no angst against the highest sweet,
But it has left its cavities in you!
You fester in such caves where worthlessness
Torments you, blinding you to your own worth.
Be good, and know that good is good enough.
The greatest work is everyday's good meal.
Confectionaries have their honored place.
But learn a meal is blessing by itself.

a simple puppy dog

Keats.
What is a poet but a crushaholic,
Falling ever easily in love?
With everything, with everyone, with life,
Infatuated at the drop of a hat,
Impressed and dazzled by a beauty's wink.
A poet ever is a lover boy,
Enchanted, helpless, thrall of he or she
Who strikes the eye and strikes harder the heart!
Airhead, transported, lost at sea one glance,
A simple puppy dog, a sense of fun,
A weirdo sensibility, a goof
And a romantic, and a tender child.

she is Oshun

She is envy personified in flesh,
The emulation ever maid would wish.
Even the name of beauty weeps beneath
The rank she holds, too unattainable.
In ecstasy each woman sees herself.
If one could shape emotion to a face,
As lovely as her regal countenance.
Each man believes she is a goddess come,
And being true, she never disappoints.
Never possessed, remaining out of reach,
Yet imminent wherever love is brim.
Her cheeks shellac on suar carved to curve,
With Shea dew exuding from her limbs
Deep cinder-bronze smoothed sensuous on skin.
Gold scales alike a snake adorn her breasts.
She's oil in the air that undulates
In sun alike the rivers where she wades.
She is Oshun. She is the name of love.

this poem now shall hold her

for Elizabeth of Night

She sat outside and took the wind to face,
To smell the fragrance that it carried forth,
And waved at the conductors on those trains
That passed — and there some sliver of your heart
Is folded in the landscape — there's your mom,
Beloved, beautiful, your aching heart —
You choke up as you tell me, for you miss
Her as the baby chick the fluffy hen
Who folded her within her wings so warm.
And now that house, where this fond memory sits,
The land that holds the phantom-cherishing
Of she you love with all your bursting heart,
Is being sold — O say no more goodbyes!
O landscape, hold her, cradle her, keep close! —
But when you cry, your tears are on my cheek,
Your weeping nuzzle on my loving chest,
My arms embrace you and the memory.

Where once your sister's cozy house held her,
An evanescence of eternity,
This poem now shall hold her in our arms.

reflecting foliage

The sunlight tracing circles on my eyes
As I lay sleeping, sparkles and bright swirls,
In shifting patterns as the shadows shift,
Reflecting foliage moving in the wind.

the brimstone in the human heart

To stare into the barrel at its dregs,
The sewage at the bottom of our souls
(The violating lecheries and crimes),
And still believe in human nature, how?
The sticky tar of sin around the sides,
The stench, the brimstone in the human heart,
The sulfur of our inhumanity,
The asphalt of our melancholic guilt,
Can't be denied by those with open eyes.
With such as these, what hope utopia?
Who dares speak high ideals knowing of this?
What sparks of light remain in filth-smirched coal?
This is the Hades of our human world,
Inhuman world, infernal kingdom, damned,
The hell amongst us, devils in our midst,
Demonic rulerships, obscenities,
The hierarchies of horror and of ache.
Messiah came into this effluent,
The offscum inundate of history,
To baptize our ordure and scrub the muck.
Sin is an ambience of excrement
In which we breathe, and it conditions us,
It chokes our aspirations and our hopes,
Diminishes our possibilities.

He came to diagnose, to name the root,
Proclaiming lucre as the origin.
In deprivations incubate our worsts.
The mold and damp of spirit ground to dirt
Festers in our resentments felonies.
What grime grows in the cubbyholes therein?
But sunshine brings the answer to us: light
And exultation, sharing everything,
A heart of joy in militancy's faith,
That penetrates the cynical domain,
And sees the hidden lamps where there is coal.

unanswered letters

Reality is crueler than beauty.
Unanswered letters. Longings never met.

I lived inside the angels' minuet

What lignin then too thickens xylem mine,
That I am glued and flotsamed from my sense
That once was overwhelming beauty filled?
Bring on that spell that wipes the dust of ash
From glass once clarity that held in palms
Of quartz the golden dew of noontide's light!
I was a creature easy mesmerized,
And lived in mental architecture grace
Alone hath made -- in whispers made of verse
Were columns built to limestone canopies,
Whose traceries looked soft to eyes to touch!
I lived such wealth of feeling, money weeps
Its poverty before my palaces,
The billionaires but beggars at my doors.
Mood was a piccolo whose notes I breath'd
Arpeggio, and I was sylph of swoon
Within the currents of my metered tongue!
I lived in trace of encore of those days
When choirs sang the living earth from light
Into its verdant blooming from the night!

Come, tender shoot, come, stem, come, foliage,
Come, lengthened pinnate pattern writ in green,
Come, blossom of the crepe with folded pinch
That then to curtsey-billow in the sun
But opens to a fragrance named of love!
Come, rind of juicened pulp that bursts too sweet
It wilds the tartened tongue to spinning wow!
I was a mime who mimicked this bright week,
When all new things were newly sung to life.
I lived inside the angels' minuet,
In ballrooms made of gold and silken fog.
I had such bliss in nonchalance of charm,
The mayhem and the maelstrom came to dance,
And found their lost gestalts in sheer of joy,
So that a time, in letting go their ire,
They found, ephemeral, their harmony!
If you had come upon me in that poise,
Your heart would know nothing at all but play,
Leaping Baryshnikov from hymn to hymn,
And that fond spell extended every day!
The mind is all the paintbrush that we need;
But wish and will, and what the heart perceives,
The landscape sparkles, though banal eyes dim!
At best, this world is raw material,
To work up into something sensual
And orderly with energies of heaven!
I would live my life in such ballet.

fetalize your newborn eyes

If storms were letters, rivers cursive glyphs,
The space amidst the ink the blowing breath,
My tongue then were the quill of that jet stream
The djinn in abjad run 'long vellum fields!
These words would be the wombs to birth you fresh,
And in recital, never leave that youth,
Like Idunn's apples peeling back your age.
I'd fetalize your newborn eyes anew,
First touch of weblike light through crystal haze
On membranes soft and vulnerable and wet,
That breath, the first to take, would widen lids.
Time were more viscous, yet one's steps more light.

I'd chant, and you were but a reverie
Clothed in those cobwebs wrapped about your bones.
Perception were a mikveh every hour,
Objects cherubim -- the world would bleed
With lambence -- hush and awe were everything.
You were a skinnydipping youth in beds
Of kelp-sway, swimming lushly towards the sun.
My phonemes were my fingertips of fay,
Awakening with single touch your joy.
I've soaked this alphabet in marinade,
And opened every pore to savory.
I've kneaded every hum and poignant breath,
That when I speak, the panoply of Gaia
Spills in amniotic pageantry,
Like Noah's beasts in bounding from the ark!
And there the rainbow o'er the freshened land,
The running labyrinths in which to hide,
To leap, to divagate into the world,
The zoophilia of bliss reblissed
In foliage renewed, to say this day
Is fresher than any has ever been!

Mephistopheles of silicon

The science fiction that I never chose,
That never was put on the ballot box,
But billionaires may fancy in their schemes,
Approaches. All the Renaissance now weeps;
Petrarch upon the mountaintop sheds tears;
Ficino fits in sobs; Bernini moans;
And Botticelli's Primavera pales.
Humanity they loved beyond their breasts
Now stands upon dissection tables nude,
With probes and interface to violate
And desecrate integrity of soul.
To butcher, stab, to interfere and carve,
To rape the nerves, expropriate the mind,
And digitize delusional the heart.
An eerie Serlingesque dystopia,
Deroddenberried, cyber-Tartaran,
With denizens in grey, conformities
Determined in advance by technocrats.

I'd rather die than have the Earth so ruled.
The anima itself at precipice,
That even Machiavelli hesitates
Before vulgar manipulation's plans.
A cold, metallic future drained of blood,
Where flesh is someone's property again,
Stamped with an ISBN microchip,
And this fine soma's masterpiece the Greeks
Admired, molecule-enslaved and -stamped,
Surveyed, a creature of the contract's ink,
Cold Mephistopheles of silicon
Infernal with sadistic mockery;
Domestication of the animal
We once so freely were, and all our joy,
The cyber-simulation of cocaine.
A life of rape by nanites and control
Beyond its sanity, the misery
Of all our savage fantasies empowered:
Arms-race of enhanced capacities,
Bionic inequalities gone mad,
The wealthy now a race of lording borg.
As if a legion diabolical
Set out to make this world a living hell.
This is Guantanamo of Microsoft,
Domain of Camerons and Mengeles.
O rise O human spirit, rise again!
Rise up refusing travesty's control!
Leave off from Yaldabaoth: he has gone mad!
Reach out collective hands and take the helm
From oligarchs and geeks, and turn the ship
Back on a course that fits humanity.
The Renaissance is counting on our pluck.

to Eleanor of Aquitaine

Henry II.
For me, you are the fond embodiment
Of that enchanting, mystic-lilting tongue
Your country speaks; for love of you, I love
The history entire of your land,
And it is but the physiognomy
Of you, writ large; it marinates in you,

And I have but to sniff, and there your scent
Is redolent in customs, costumes, forms,
And landscapes, for you animate them all.
Alas, in absence of your company,
That Martinelli spritz so apple-sweet,
(Alluding to fond orchards' pollen-pomme),
Your culture is the other avenue,
The lost, forgotten alley, into you,
And there, in swirling tea leaves in the cup,
Do I scry you in coalesce and dance?
I do. It is an heirloom left at tombs,
A kerchief that I take to cheek too fond,
And fondle in the brittle melancholy,
Breathing all your fragrance in its breeze.
It's palpable where absence of you reigns,
And every speaker of your subtle tongue
Is but ventriloquist, wherein I hear
The hypnos of your logos in my heart,
Religious in its gist of fog and mist,
That would enswirl me in a living swoon.
Through dearness of their anonymity,
Those throng-soirées of cities overseas,
I may again the Eucharist of you
Feel light dissolve upon my raptured tongue,
And be a creature fleshed in nought but bliss.

this Machiavelli of the comedy

The petulant amusements of that lad,
The son of Venus! What an idle child!
That author in original of soaps,
Forlorn and lost and crossed, forbidden loves!
That genius of the melodrama's stage,
The spirit-confidant of Ovid's verse,
The jaundiced patron of the tabloid rags!
He lounges in his smirking laziness,
In shelter of the shades of antler woods,
While palming currants to his ample lips,
And lightly paws his bow with nonchalance,
To weigh his jolly caprice in his mind.
Until his wandering eye finds its delight,
Alighting on some poor old picaresque

Who wanders in his sloven misery,
About to unbeknownst cross on some maid,
Or wife or widow -- all that matters not,
The more incongruent, the better, no? --
And makes her in her slattern normalcy
Appear a queen just lately born from light,
The wonder of the world, while then her eye
He sets upon some scorning scoundrel, far
Beneath her dignity, who'll scowl at her,
And now, the game is off! Let revels start!
This Machiavelli of the comedy
Sits back, and sips this pageant of his mirth,
Admiring absurdity in play!
O how he'll long, and how she shall abey,
And how that other he shall turn her down
(After, of course, tasting his lechery).
Until these capers coalesce their fools
Into a stunning jocularity,
Mere dolor to their yearning hearts of woe --
We are the sad absurdities we love --
And all the slapstick complications build,
(Annoyances in earnest to our wills)
Up to a climax of frustrated moans!
Brows palmed, the clutching of the eager heart,
The wish to die, if one can't merge with her,
Or him, the nunneries of loneliness,
The pinings in the monastery towers,
Desperate antics in the marketplace,
Foolish confessions all to no avail,
The verse in vain, the chocolate a waste,
The haughtiness of scorn, the hopeless prayers,
The fleshy escapades of sudden shame,
The fever of their longing but a lark,
The memory of what was fantasy,
Wrapped in petty banality, a glance,
A whisper taken out of context, hopes
Solidified into delusional
Array, recalled as history and charm,
The blusterings and idiocies, rants
And tantrums, jealousies and envious rage,
Pathetic and incessant tears in cups
Before bemused, incredulous close friends --
The spectacle of mockery and rue!
And then, perhaps that he will go away,
She pities him a single stolen kiss,

That lingers in his fevered mind all time
(In rocking chair, he tells his grandchildren),
Which only lights the powderkeg again.
The rich diverse etcetera of this
Is afternoon's guffaw on Cupid's lips.
Then listless, he might yawn, and take a nap
(His mother's incantations smoothly glide
In bliss without his interfering schemes).
But then the mischief set on lonely hearts
Awakes again, and some new victim strolls
Within his grin of adolescent gaze.

in thickets of Topanga

It was a destiny, the theater,
For me, my inroads into poetry,
Wherein I found the language for my love;
And all that rich emotional expanse,
Compressed in smothered me, found its domain,
Where I could stretch, and give this heart its gym.
It was a mystery salvational
And kind, a blossom buxom nursery
Of fleurs and romance, myths and rhapsodies,
A hall of mirrors wherein characters
Galore could stare me back into my face,
Revealing hidden aspects of my soul.
Awhile I pondered in my pining brine,
The bafflement of keenest love just snatched
Still palpable, I made my fond return
To those fine boards, where I had hope to find
Some form or fame that might eternalize
The peerless charm I met within her eyes,
O eyes of elfin, fond Francesca, fay
Of wonder, woman of enchantment's sway.
Like salmon, instinct rushing home to seas,
I blindly in my faith sought out the Bard,
But lately schooled by Ezra Pound in verse
Of Languedoc, and all that heritage
Summed up in Dante and in Petrarch's rhymes --
For I had need of poignancy in poise,
The lasting evidence of miracle,
The trace of angel blood in crystal cups,

The hologram of faerie in the glass.
But ten years marks this mountaineering road,
Where I in desperation scaled the heights,
The poet of the Globe my trusty guide,
And there the eglantines and edelweiss
Of meter gathered on the mountaintops,
A novice in the classic forms of lilt.
It was new species of a breathless awe,
An invite into labyrinths of wist
The ollaves of the mist once taught in woods.
I could have walked on rainbow's precipice,
I had such bliss, I had such reminisce
In innovative form of all was dear.
In thickets of Topanga found my school,
Wherein the hidden lore of troubadours
Could open doors of love antique for me,
Wherein, preserved in amber, there still beat
Medieval hearts, alive yet in the words,
Still pounding in those lockets made of sound,
The romance fresh a thousand years and late,
The talisman that did the lady true,
A shock of fairy hair on scrapbook page.
I had to make antiquity of this,
To frame the shard of lost eternity
I once knew in a kiss and gentle eyes,
So it might be a relic of that spell,
And feed the hungry in intriguing tale.

hollow to my hungry lips

For is to be what is, intolerable!
If all is lacking in its brimmingness,
And nothing but its barren seemingness,
The world is hollow to my hungry lips.

currency of fire

Because police are never brought to heel,
For loyal service unto property,

But ever are acquitted of their crimes,
Therefore, be it enacted that the streets
Shall prove their trial courts, and riots pay
Their commutations in the currency
Of fire and of broken blocks of brick.

right from wrong

Make right against wrong the bedrock of your life,
Your very backbone, marrow, and your blood.
Trust in it in all things, and never budge,
For knowledge or for anything at all.
If all else darkens, let that be your light,
And let no glib-tongued sophist turn you wrong.
It's easy to mix up the mind with spin.
In days to come, many heroes will fall,
For led astray by schemes or by foul lusts,
They ceased to trust the right they knew inside.
It may be difficult to tow the line,
But tow the line when it comes to these things.
Where wrong is not, experiment at will:
Try many things, explore, and find your path.
But right from wrong will help you in the dark.
By scent alone you can find your way back.
How hard the burden when a hero falls.
A gut-punch to the stomach, nights of shock.
But hold your course, surrender not your faith.
The map is in your conscience, through and through.
There's no excitement worth defiling that.
Authentic heroes often are unknown.
They humbly do what's right when all have strayed.

gaslighting is the norm

We all are being mind-fucked every day.
The media are psyop transmitters.
Mass brainwashing is going down right now.
Laugh as you will as goalposts shift and change.
Gaslighting is the norm. We're being groomed

To fully trust the counterfactual
And doubt ourselves. We're being trained in fear.
Manipulation's at an all time high.

champagne brooded on seas

Upon each fingertip she sprouts a rose,
And tiptoes on the marshy lotuses
Gracility across a glassy lake.
She sets her snares in soul so it allures,
Touched numinous by fond divinity,
Recurrent awe that captivates and charms.
Wherever she may walk, and she but glides,
Her blossom-entourage accompanies
The wisdom of her mischief-strolls through hearts,
Where she plants longings strange and wonderful,
At odds with planned intent, full of surprise.
These ladies of the musky rose of dusk
Make slow and magical and full of bloom
Wherever their smooth pirouettes may brush,
And everything serene falls into place,
A lightened touch that covers all in lace,
A delicate epiphany of charm.
Shook ale makes froth; the ocean lagers forth
Its snowflake caviar of fizzing foam;
She hails from such champagne brooded on seas.
She is the crackling spritzer bubbling
Amongst cavorting swordfish and fresh trout.
She rises on a shell to sheer *en pointe*,
And teeters on the tide while combing hair.
Her arms are apparitious wings on wind;
She waves, and linen bell-sleeves scoop the air;
It seems she has a thousand arms; she skates
With lilting limbs that circle to *en garde*.
Her ludic levity of heartfelt joy
Melts even hardened hearts, and in her play,
She captures with a web of mystery
Who would voyeur through stealthy strew of brush,
And drag one's jaw in innocence on grass.
She has no angst against the wagging tongue,
But leads it to higher profundity.
Eternally she's polished smooth desire,

Sculpting animal delights to arts
Of shapely gasps, that open miracles
In fond eurekas — sense and order grasped
In smart arrangements of fragility,
That vaporize the brute to sheer perfume.
There in aroma's overwhelm of mist,
To sniff ambrosial revelatios
Of the celestials: a wistful hint,
The gist that is the answer to a prayer.
And she is off; pursuit lies in her clues.
Her flesh is in such clues that sweetly wink.

my soul is Scottish

Let me remain flirtatious in my winks.
I do not ever want to be pinned down.
My soul is Scottish; fog is natural.
My substance is in stealth and pithy hints.
I slip aside commitments, which seem cruel.
My fickleness has rhythm, and is thus
Dependable. I occupy a range;
Within those wide parameters I am:
More specificity is tyranny!
To drift is my delight. I live to roam.
To be "around", somewhere, vicinity,
Approximate, a ballpark — there I am.
Just let me divagate a little bit,
Embracing my circumference of whim,
And then you have me, without having me.
Make bonds elastic, gossamer, and light,
For chains but lose me. Charm is better glue.
It draws my turbulence back from the chase.
What do I chase? Allurement's purity,
Distilled in essence most elusively.
Allow me this, and you may have my love.

you always might be wrong

Admit you're wrong again and yet again.

That way lies freedom and integrity.
Be ready to be wrong. Investigate.
Sure, have your rant if need be, then review.
Where were there places where *they* had it right?
Where in your stubbornness were *you* quite wrong?
How much of what *they* said had relevance
Your pride could not admit? Now choose the truth.
Let no identity except with truth
Guide you, and then you can accept its way
Against your blusterings. You may be right,
And it is right to fight for what is right,
But then again, you always might be wrong,
And often truth is somewhere in between.
Some piece the other side brought forward sticks.
Don't fight it! If it sticks, concede it! Learn!
The better person will admit he's wrong.

you really don't know half

Believe me, if you're white, the *chances* are
You don't know *shit* — you don't know even *half*
Of all the racist muck in history.
However erudite you think yourself,
You don't know half, you really don't know half.
The likelihood is your degree is void
When it comes down to this. Just zip your lips,
You are a novice of naïveté,
And need to listen. Sit yourself in class.
Learning's chagrin will bring humility.
It's even worse than you ever believed.

gossiping inside a burning house

The inhumanity of man to man
Is what is meant by sin, and nothing else.
It has nothing at all to do with sex,
Unless dehumanizing is involved.
Caviling peccadilloes is a sin
When weighty matters suffer for such ilk.

The weight of evil still burdens the world.
The deeply held hatreds, the cruelties,
The damaging of children in their youth,
Inhuman degradation, poverty,
Misogyny, a dozen bigotries.
That's sin. Pearl-clutching tabloid fantasies
Of all the dirt the other may possess
Is useless, vulgar busybodying.
It's harmful for it weighs these things all wrong.
It's tattle-taling while the world is burned.
It's gossiping inside a burning house.
Put out the fires: that's the task at hand.

poetry is truth

The headliners hog all the public space
With their divisions and their vile hates.
It's competition, war of all on all.
That's not the world at all. It's just a show,
A weak attention-seeking game of fools.
Don't let the newspapers define your life,
Or social media divide your friends.
Mark Zuckerberg is enemy of all.
The world is just a psyop for these creeps.
Use your imagination. Get away.
It's but annihilation on those paths.
The world of beauty is the truer world.
The news but lies, but poetry is truth.

oblivion is best

Sleep is obliteration, and I love it.
Fuck this life. Oblivion is best.
This world is maelstrom's hurricane of hate.
It all is war, and everything is wrong.
No matter what you do or don't, you're damned.
I'm just as horrible as anyone.
Just let me run away and hide inside.
There's too much pain around. It's all too much.

I'm frantic, and I just want me some rest.
Sleep is obliteration, and I love it.

carnation is salvation

Carnation is salvation. All my folds
Are frills of petals round my centerfold.
My breadth is ruffles regal about my bud.
They make me beautiful and plush with worth.

let's get out of here

The denizens of hell held them a moot.
"Who has it worst of all in this old hell?"
They fought and fought and tore themselves apart.
Then one of them said, "Let's get out of here!"
They lynched that one the worst and left him dead.

walking wounds

O, tossed trauma to trauma! Battered hard,
A blind and groping beast of frantic fear!
From shock to awe and back to shock again,
Events but knocks and blows and baffling wounds,
That now the many of us are but wound!
We're walking wounds, who startle at each fright,
Beleaguered animals in corners, shrunk
In terror, snarling, ready to lash out.
You are the enemy! You've come for us!
They're everywhere! We've got to fight them off!
Nothing makes sense! We're weeping in the dark!
We're sobbing! No one cares for us at all!
Assimilate one terrible event,
Five more are rushing, nipping at its heels!
Four years of this! Divided! polarized!
Adults in form but children underneath.

We've got to clique to save our little selves!
Exclude whoever's not wholly on board!
No time for ambiguity in war.
Do not confuse us with your strange dissent.
A thousand different things impinge on us.
The things we took for granted are now lost.
The anchor's gone, the ship is lost at sea!
The tempest shakes us! And the lightning strikes!
The coral claws and scrapes the outer hull!
The decks are drenched with bilge. The sails are torn.
The captain's raving mad and senile, drunk,
Hurling vituperations to the winds!
O screech! O howl! O spirits tossed as us!
The waves tilt right, we hurl against the walls;
The waves tilt left, collide against their walls!
The lanterns are extinguished. Darkness reigns,
But glint of sliver's gleam through timbers' cracks!
Wear the insignia that shows we're safe,
That you are one of us, and not of them!
Our fists are raised! But more to block our face
From blows that cease not morning to the night!
Our intellects inscribe our fear in ink;
The battered mind is broken and forlorn.
We search so desperately for any sense.
Give us a crumb, and we'll make meal of it!
When will the coast be clear, and we return
To something sane, imperfect though it be?
Let's hide, we've got to hide! But let us know.

to the heart of me!
For Elizabeth of Night

You've loved me in the dark and through the fear.
You've laughed like sunlight when the days were dim.
Believed in me when I was nought but wreck.
Stayed by my side when I was lost and sad.
You've kept me near your heart when it's been cold.
You've let me love you when you were forlorn.
Some light lit up in me when I saw you!
Somehow I kept together those four months,
When separated, we were on our own,
But sweetness, honey mine, never alone.

You were beside me here in bed each night.
Your arm across my chest as I did sleep.
When I despaired, I doubled down with you;
When you were insecure, I gave my love.
You soothed me in the doubts of those dark days,
When no one knew how long we would be bound.
In turn, I tried to be strong as you need,
And Herculean, lift our hopes back up,
When as you say, it all was just a mess.
But we were clarity and light in love,
Though broad confusion wreaked its thunderings.
Our hearts never faltered a single time!
And you loved me indelibly as I
Was loyal — to the heart of me! — to you.
We've been through terror and through loneliness.
We've been the pawns chessmasters knocked about.
We've fumbled in the dark. Nothing was clear,
Except our love. We got on through, and shall.
No one can say when all of this will pass,
But one way or another, we will love
Through separation and togetherness!
And find a way back in each other's arms!
I ought to fall and kiss your blessed feet,
And rise, columnar, kissing legs to hips,
And higher, rising on your belly up
To thirst-quenchers, and kiss their lovely tips,
And nibbling licks like roses on your neck,
Rising to kiss your forehead, cheeks, and lips,
Then look you in the eyes, say I love you.
My bosom-friend, my paramour and true.

let it begin in me

I've been a sponge for the collective mind,
A whore possessed by spirits in the air.
A medium for all the fears and doubts,
Despairing hopes, and melancholic fits.
The goblins rived me with their bigotries;
The hatreds flooded me from every side.
I struggled in the shadow's wettened clay,
Six feet beneath the earth, in cloistered marsh.
The nation reared its raucous, howling ghosts;

The many battlefields screeched forth their angst.
Betrayals, loyalties that never died,
Desperate, keen aspirations towards a time
Better than what they knew, better than them!
They gave their all in blood and dirt and bone,
That sins they knew too well might be redeemed.
These remnants one who got on high evoked,
Ripping with reckless hand Pandora's box,
Have borrowed me, and ripped their way through me!
That history storms in my breast and cries.
Put it to rest! Put it to rest at last!
So many tired, weeping ghosts out here.
The ghosts of dozen tribes still echo forth:
Collisions of the peoples, bruise and wound,
Misunderstanding, treaties torn by lust,
Algonquin and Ojibwa, Creek and Cree,
Lakota and Shoshone and Dine;
The Chinese on the open railroad tracks,
The broken hearts in cotton fields down South,
The Delta blues, Johnny come marching home,
Impoverished Swedish, Minnesotan snow,
The Irish in the Appalachian coal,
Sonoran spines bent over picking fruit.
The senseless prejudice, the secret loves,
Suppressed redemptions striving for the light,
The patriotic loyalty towards home,
Home of the lakes, the mountains, groves and plains!
A thousand festivals of thousand folk.
It's all stirred up, and I'm hardly myself,
A fool seized by our epileptic past,
That fibrillates in me, and wars within.
Let there be peace! Let it begin in me!

a cantrip in a carousel of stars

Etherium and not quotidia —
I would but coast and undulate on air —
I would incarnate little wisps and gusts
That blow through leafy hollows, lips on bark
To bless green sap, the fellows of the wood —
Listen to whisper-presences in leaves
And sunlight-waterfalls that break to glades,

And gossip of the latest wizard spells.
Lighter than straw, and leaping legs outstretched
In ivy-woven hose that kicks the sky,
I would be daze in skin of web and breath,
A cantrip in a carousel of stars.
I would be powdered snow against blue lips,
A dalliance of bubble-skein and breeze,
The nonchalant flirtation of the gnats
In tease and aspiration, wings a'flit.
I'd be pricelessly strange, the yearned-for quirk,
The touch of practiced levity and lure,
The treasure of fanciful grammarye.
I could dine on the zephyrs' assonance,
And make the heaven's clouds my candy webs;
Hors d'ouerve the sugar-mist of fairy breath,
And sample the buffet of sylphan verse.
This body's not the meat of gravity,
But collagen of purrs and ivory,
The essence of a feather's ample fluff,
A flesh distilled from nothing else but fun.
I'm strange composite of the thousandth wish,
The substance of the children's Christmas dreams,
The lads and lasses' bonhomie towards fays.

so much I have to marshal

Roulette of sleep and personality:
Where on my spinning wheel wake I today?
For all of them are not in harmony,
And their divergent moods severely jar.
Whom yesterday was devotee of love,
Today is skeptical and eremite.
And I must be the one to smooth them out,
And ride conflicting moods over their bumps,
A heavy labor for consistency,
Dissenters hollering beneath the mask.
It tires me. These urgencies are strong,
They're fiery, and demand their loyalties.
To hold such partisans who'd rather split
Together takes its toll in toiling sighs.
I throw myself behind one surging thrust;
The next day, that's passé, and new thrusts urge.

The wind opens my library at will,
And where I land, the wind alone may know.
My library's diverse, and whim is strong.
So much I have to marshal all alone.

perhaps an elemental

I wish I could be nowhere — free and clear
Of anguish, thought, or any lasting care.
Perhaps an elemental, vague and rare,
The feeling of a breath, but little else.
No controversies, no considerations.
Bliss. The blessings of a nothingness.
To vanish, letting life subsist as such,
Simplicity. The absence of an ego.
Everything but me, there beauty thrives.
I am an interference in the midst.
Let go of "me", and I am free to breathe.

to wild air

If I could, I would raise my arms and soar,
A hurl off of a cliff to wild air,
And be the wings upon the wind I'd be,
That freedom, nothing else, and disappear
Into the oceanic weather's pulsing breath.

you orthinate my seeking soul

O sky, you are so gracious and so dear,
So wide-embracing and invitingful!
You make a falcon of me, crimson wings
With turkey feathers autumn in their hue,
That sift, soft brushes, drifts of seeping wind
Across smooth, oily surfaces of lofting pulse!
These pinions made of plasma of the dusk

And falling rust beat on the musk of fleurs
That flurry through the fragrance-tides of breeze!
You hold me, sky, so tenderly yet firm;
Your fastness is my freedom! I am held
On loving buoyancies, and skim the brim
Of warm expanses bellying my trim.
You ornithate my seeking soul's own shape
So that I sweep your skein in yearning prayer
That dons abysms as the depths of faith.
Sky, keep me in your all-massaging sea
Caressing and encircling the earth,
And feel the substance of your nothingness
As grace. You are the courtesy of breath.

yet I got a ride

The day the eagle swept me from the ground,
I was a'scampering from bush to bush
In madcap leaps and sampling the greens.
That day it comes to everybody, so
They say, if rattlesnake or eagle or
The owl, ominous, perched on pine tree bough.
It comes to everybody — yet I got a ride.
That day I got to see all of the sky!
Though clutched in claws and talons, I was free —
As ne'er the ground could ever be for me —
The oddest ecstasy amidst my fear.
This was the final moment, beautiful
And clear — I saw a hundred rabbit-miles,
Five hills over, trees were little heads
Of lettuce, oceans were the waving weeds;
The crows magnificent in mocking flight,
The sparrows little wisps in zipping flit.
I'd never seen such vistas! Higher yet
The craftsman of my soon oblivion
Took us on wings into the deeper blue :
I felt some denizen of canopies
Of fine, cerulean silks, with arabesques
Of cursive clouds, and every coming breeze
Had different personality and wit,
Caressing me amidst my sullen fright.
I saw what seemed a little drinking hole,

Yet was as large as mountains underneath us —
That must have been some big drinking hole
I never saw! The mountains could bathe there.
I missed of sudden with a rush my fields,
My nibbling roots, my fellow fondest hares —
Those afternoons I took for granted, O!
Delicious eveningtides, the herbage fresh
On lips in cool of shadows' lavenders!
The snuggle-bundles of our common fur
In burrows' midnight fantasies so soft!
The comfort of those cuddles with my kin!
Alas, alas! No more! I see the sun!
More drunk on ale and spilling self about,
It sloshes light and sweat about up here,
A monarch of the upper oven skies!
This is the end! Too beautiful for me!
I was a scampering thing, but now I fly!
Becoming in my renderment what wings
Will still expanse the meadows of the winds.
Farewell to fur, to intimacy's fluff;
Farewell to carrots flavorful and sharp;
Farewell to mazes in the wild straw:
I loved to run your courses, and to hide,
So still, but breathing soft, within your nest;
Farewell the evening and the break of day;
Farewell the sky once canopy, now sea
That swallows me: I fold into your blues.

let's get to work

The wondrous fantasy of being done!
The work is finished! Such a fine voila!
The stew is cooked! The jambalaya is done!
No toil in the fields of fallen pain,
No drowning for to swim in shadow's marsh,
No laundry caked with blood and filth to clean,
Is needed: thus the game that we pretend.
Postracial? There are generations yet
Of laundry to be done: let's get to work.

swindled from our feet

The taste for liberty is dead, my friends.
It's ridiculed and mocked as privilege,
And then derided as entitlement.
When fear is in command, conformity
Is mandatory, and no sacrifice
Is good enough: just immolate yourself,
Lay down your rights, and every one of them.
You selfish, selfish lout for wanting rights!
To give up months of public, social life
All for the common good is insufficient.
Bow. Get down and bow. Abandon all,
Salute hysteria, relinquish mind.
You are not free, but live on sufferance.
Be grateful you're allowed to live at all.
If anybody ever had it bad,
To ask for more is utter privilege.
Thus liberty is swindled from our feet.

a love affair with public space

I have a love affair with public space,
Now interrupted by hysteria.
My fast evaporating world, alas,
I shall shore up in faithful histories,
So heirlooms given up at bargain price,
And ripped for dice amongst the Roman mob,
Shall have some memory to give them place.
There once were restaurants and gatherings;
There once were caverns which served beverages
To crowds in dim and shadowed pungent light.
There once was lively wit's vitality,
Where all gregarious propensities
Within the soul could find in hubbub joy.
There once was gusto where robustness thrived.
There once were street scenes where the peasants danced
And gamed to uninhibited delight.
There once were skating rinks and music halls.
There once were theaters and amusement parks.

And these were the cathedrals of the folk,
The jolly shrines of our togetherness,
The fanes of concord and exuberance,
The wellsprings of democracy and hope.
But now the avenues that Whitman praised,
The wharfs where buzzing musclework of men
Found song, with criers bellowing out "Fish!",
The bubble-sea of bright balloons in tow
At cotton candy carnivals with toys
Abounding for the winning, and the sports
Where hotdogs mustard-slathered filled the stands
Are empty, and my rendezvous are gone,
A newer type of Puritan in charge.
The forums have been purged, the fond boutiques
Forbidden, liberty a dirty word.
The lovely anonymity of life,
With flashing face and laughter in the round,
Embrace of unknown fellows in surround,
Is banished, and austerity is boss.
A winter without end has been imposed.
I shiver in the frigid reign of frost.
And anyone who yearns to have this back,
Who suffers in this deprivation's loss,
Who speaks of courage, freedom, and our rights
Traditional to social animals,
Is pilloried as selfish by a mob
Not even gathered but by distant poll,
A mob of separated paranoids.
A frightened despot-band who claim they care
When they don't care at all about the soul,
Dismissing human need at will,
And endlessly, in rank conformity,
And sheer hypocrisy and bankruptcy,
Who'll sign their blood over to Devil's writ
For safety, the new idol of the time.
An idol that has closed the churches' doors,
Declaring temples an anathema,
Forbidding congregation by the law,
Or color of its usurpated theft.
To give your rights for merest right of life
Has ever been the writ of slavery.

assholes are our saviors now

How strange, the assholes are our saviors now;
They never will give up their liberty,
And may God bless them! While the liberals
Wish gloating death on who will not conform,
And call that caring. I find that most strange.
Is there a way to care for freedom too?
Is freedom such a bankrupt state of things,
It can afford no avenue of care,
That only tyranny may render aid?
Tend to imagination, fellow-friends.
Have better faith in liberty than that.

denizens of grey who hate all joy

A happy wedding made the virus spread,
The San Francisco Chronicle informs,
Its ninnie-finger wagging in its prose.
The moral of the story is: beware,
For happiness is dangerous these days.
Those who indulge are worse than criminals.
They're horrible people to be condemned.
I note they didn't mention any deaths.
Nor was there talk of any suffering.
But testing positive alone is sin.
The level of resentment any fun,
But any fun at all arouses, shocks.
To want to live your life is now a crime.
Because it's quantity not quality
Of life that's now supreme: how Catholic!
How right to life! And how sectarian.
These denizens of grey who hate all joy.

a truce for Carnival and Lent

I sought an alchemy of opposites:
To mate Calvin and Dionysus, ah!

To make a truce for Carnival and Lent.
I went beyond the single partisans;
I fell in love with all, and sought their child
Of hybridity! A single flower
Makes no garden, but a hundred fleurs
Might stop the heart an instant for to gasp.
When they told me I had to choose, I chose:
I chose the both of rabid contraries,
And all their most unlikely issue: that
Was gold to me! And much the better choice.
Extremes are wonderful, yet seldom serve
The wholeness of phenomena or soul.
They are fantastic stimulants to goad
Us, lazy in complacency; as such,
Important medicines — and yet a cure
May be a poison at a higher dose.
What is a city but an elohim
Of contrasts, angels on the every side
Of any issue? Such is glorious!
Let us have music of polyphony!

down to the very bone

I've lived five lives, down to the very bone.
I'm so exhausted. How can I stand up?
I think that long ago my soul ran off.
I've been trying to woo her back to me,
And yet I'm spent that I don't feel myself.
Sometimes a hollow shell that longs and yearns,
Or otherwise feels but a den of sin,
An awful thing who needs live to repent.

chapel of the moonlit-webbed sky

I am in fingers of the weather's angels,
Held by tenuous and stellar trails,
The trace of subtle light by mystic night.

I leap, and clouds cat-cradle me aloft.
I'm nothing but the leap — all else is fled —
My worries flee within the sudden thrill —
I'm total trust in giving of my flesh
To nothingness, the substance of a breath!
The winged ones made of electric light
Extend their gossamers of threaded silk,
Suspending me midair in ecstasy —
My body is a liturgy of flight.
I've lost whatever still is ponderous;
This flesh, champagne of helium and frost.
I plunge, and there I strip myself of sin,
A sinless luminance who's naught but plunge,
Who's wish in wind, and weightless sacrament
In chapel of the moonlight-webbed sky.

feathers pink and haughty

If you could see me as I truly am,
You'd see me thatched in scales of feathers pink
And haughty, grand, my dignity in fluff
And bubbles, sauntering like a collage
Of nature's colors, like an ancient chief,
Adorned with the accoutrements of birds
And serpents, such a synthesis of dream,
Surreal in majesty, and deeply touched
By all the beauty of this sudden world.
You might guffaw, and call it artifice,
A cultivar of houses made of glass
(Clerestories where special flowers grow).
Why can't I be a common weed like all?
How dare one take time to develop style?
It's too late, my friends, the deed is done.
I am effete, and deeply proud of it.
If that offends, oh well, let it offend.

lucky skits of children

If I could switch my molecules to fun,

So that my very substance was delight,
The sediment of troubled sin released,
Relieving me and leaving me in joy,
I would! I'd make the laughter cartilage,
My hopes my breath, the gushing forth of love
My blood, solidity of fond embrace
My bones, transmuting everything to light,
The weightless body of an angel's flight.
That would be resurrection to be yearned!
My essence but the comedy of birds
And lucky skits of children lost in play.

they'd look like this

Perhaps there's no religion but ballet;
The rest are fraudulent idolatries.
The ballerinas are our priestesses,
Who preach not, but they demonstrate the flight
Of lofty angels beauteous in air.
The eye becomes a medium of heart,
In which they show the steps of loveliness,
The effortless abandon of the soul,
Self-giving to its levitation's boon.
These are the ways that elves traverse the fields
And meadows: here we see their subtle trace
In movement; here we see their pantomime,
Their only tongue, a language made of gestures,
But the signatures of yearnings' shapes
In grace of style. So we learn the ways
Of sylphs and seraphim, for whom the ground
Is bounce of fog to further fund their flight.
If flowers could find speed and grow for us
Before our eyes, they'd look like this, we know.

lurid blue of sky voyeur

I am a slug most sensual and nude,
Ecstatically embracing Eucalypti,
As I creep and slink the naked boughs,

Ascending up and towards their red-gum crowns,
In exhibition of the lurid blue
Of sky voyeur, and tingling at the height,
I merge my flesh on bark, and taste the thrill
Of vistas far away down in the dales.

from the heights

The rabbit little knows the eagle's woes;
The burdens they endure could seem impure.
The views from dale and plain cannot explain
Perspective from the heights keen to the kites.

dancing with the dragon

Excuse me, I was dancing with the dragon
In my dreams. If my disheveled hair
Is savage, well, they wrestle as they rock,
But it's good fun, and exercise to boot.
I may awake exhausted, with a bruise
Or two, but I'm exhilarated now.

an asshole for one's love

No, change is difficult and dirtying.
It's arguments with relatives and friends.
It's causing wide discomfort and unease.
It's making bad mistakes while meaning well.
It's wrestling rather than the nod of head,
The friendly handshake. It is risking war,
And fighting it with honor and with grace,
And often stubborn clumsiness and angst.
It's scars and wounds and letting time heal them.
It's bearing through the bitterness and loss.
It's screaming at the sky for loss of friends.
It's giving up and coming back again:

Retreats, sabbaticals, back in the game.
It's being tough, an asshole for one's love,
And paying up the price, for all its cost,
But having faith it's worth it in the end;
The strife is worth the while all along.

the cannibals of men

These savage hags, the minions of Defarge,
Who snarl with their schemes of dark revenge
(They fancy liberation in their gall),
Are creatures of their sad and lasting wounds.
I would for pity join them in their quest,
But that they are the cannibals of men,
And would be wolves on meat within their packs.
Alas, I love the maenads, and would have
Equality for all, but such is not
Desire of the crippled ones who bite.

carve out canyons

You have to carve out canyons in your heart
To fathom all the pain of being Black,
Before the joy can enter in your soul.
But we still stay at skin above our flesh;
Our souls are superficial surfaces
Whose cracks barely allow those anguishes
To penetrate our conscience to its core.
We must let tears then excavate our hearts,
Which hardened like the Pharaoh on his throne,
For we held back the Hebrews from our love,
And they are all who toil in the hells
Of any pharaoh, any time, on earth.
We yet have the capacity to feel;
We struggle and we writhe against the truth.
A single drop of that entrenchant pain
Is more than poison we can bear to take,
Which they have had their oceans we neglect.
But till we take the surf upon our eyes,

And ache and wretch against resistant vibes,
New hollowed that the space to feel is real,
No healing shall we find here in this place.

lay aside the hero's tale

The price that I must pay for cowardice
Is love itself, its loss, where I might have
What beauty touches me so quick to skin
It shivers to the hearth of my own heart.
What these own craven fingers let go loose
From me — I broke the promise never uttered
Uttered by the heart I would not heed.
What price, no wonder that my heart's a pauper
Now — I failed — and so I live the loss.
We must if we would ever be mature
Learn lay aside the story that we tell,
The hero's tale, which edits out the worst,
And face our irresponsibilities,
The sinful foolishness with which we close
The door upon the angel of our dreams.

fragrant, subtle calendars

We mourn the seasons in our sicknesses,
Our sniffles our unconscious lacryma,
To mark the poignant passages of time;
The exudations of the woods and herbs
In ebbs and flows through nostrils into lungs,
In fragrant, subtle calendars, do pass,
And we, in reminiscence, sad review
With joy the shadowed reveries of youth.
It is the soul, for whom such precious times
Are heirlooms of our life, that seeks to weep,
But we resisting, then the body must
Obey, and all our sinuses rehearse
Our melodramas, most against our will.
The body feels the pathos with our soul.

Jerry Springer of the web

No literature of any great import
Will ever come of Facebook or its kin,
That shallow Jerry Springer of the web,
That turns all dignity and grace in men
To rot and strife and brings their friendships' end.
As every tombstone has initial date,
Parentheses embracing ending too,
I most look forward to its final date,
This vulgar, superficial vacuity.

your palms pulse Handel
for Elizabeth of Night

They made your hands in heaven, angel-swans
Of downy fingers soft as velveteen.
Your palms pulse Handel as they light caress
My back, and turn my skin to dreamy fleece.
You shape my curvatures as seraphim
Sculpted in flesh, a luscious faun adored,
And you are lullaby of heaven's heights
That melodies your tenderness on me.

rusting me with fiery tears

Trapped in the loneliness of merest me,
My once-ability to merge deterred,
With which I felt the melt of you and me,
I'm just this flesh devoid of ecstasy,
And such solidity's idolatry
To me. I once was cheesecloth, and I moved
Between the lines, expanding to embrace
The more-than-me, and felt exquisitely
That oneness! I was hardly merely me,
But more — and I was vibrant in that more!

I thrived in that suffuse togetherness!
I was so lost in love I felt for all,
My tenderness sustained me, and good will
Was just my nature! Now, however, I
So seethe with disappointment and with rage,
In being trapped in nothing more than this,
Transcendence starved of me on which I fed,
I'm but a puppet holding back my thrash
Of sad resentment. Now I simulate
The me I used to be, and act as kind
As I once felt, but rarely do no more,
And long for when benevolence was me,
And simple bonhomie was natural.
These days I'm so damn scared of everything,
A future where the soul is torn apart
By digital enhancements of the genes,
And freaks escape their own humanity
As if it were a curse and not a gift,
And seek to wreak their dreams of full control,
My hope's a tin man wound up without heart,
Shell-shocked, and rusting me with fiery tears.
Where are my wings? Where is that power to soar?
I'm just a lump, the merest shit of flesh;
I seldom find the spirit anymore.
With ease I blame it all on Donald Trump,
And that has truth, and that has goddamn truth,
That man has wrecked and thrashed my life for years,
And torn the fabric of my country's hope
To shreds, and left us all divided, bruised,
Abused, and buffeted, and broke as hell.
That's part of it. That's simply part of it,
A great deal of it, but it isn't all.
O for a future I could fond believe!
O for a dream and not a nightmare's seed!
To be more than this body! To be love!
How can I clean the tar of sin from wings,
So they, no longer caked in filth, may fly?
I miss more than you know my dearest friends.
Their love withdrawn from me, it buries me.
I need to feel their love or I may die.

my Roman friend of old

Sometimes ambition aches within my heart.
I should be doing more, and reaching high,
Much higher than the heights I've scaled so far.
O for a slope that I could run and scale!
O for a challenge that brings true reward!
O Ovid, I know your unhappiness,
Condemned to backwoods banishment from Rome,
The very center of your glamor's fame,
Where accolades were natural and free,
And everybody waited on their toes
For that next spell you conjured from your ink!
Yet even there in Scythia, my friend,
You knew your wet epistles were received
Back home with great anticipation. Me?
I've never left this Scythia of mine.
My muse, I feel it drown in apathy
About me, and I feel so very quelched,
I hardly have capacity to breathe.
This hymnic voice, a curiosity,
A little tinker toy of no great worth
To any, something interesting but vain.
But something great in me is crying out!
Is crying out to come out, Ovid, yes!
This flesh is but its womb, and I its mum.
My genius squanders in this backwards time.
It weeps and weeps within me for its chance.
I die a little everyday it seems.
Where are those accolades my verse is worth?
Why is my little fay of Erato
So drably dressed in shivering tattered rags?
Why must she live in ruddy skin exposed,
A shopping cart with bags, and forlorn eyes,
A hovel made of straw the bears tore through
And left their gore and mud on porcelain
She crafted Hebrew blue and white with gold
Such figurines that even still, dance more
Than flesh, and kaolin seems angel-skin?
Behold her craft, it makes you delicate,
A child in her eyes of gaiety,
A newer breath that heals the scalded lungs.
Just hold that sculpted gypsum in your palms,
Behold, Ovid, you feel a fresher thing,

A new nativity; the glass she crafts
Is frozen tears of sudden, giddy joy,
Or maybe a distillery of wine
Shaped smooth as glacier in the master's hand.
To see this gallery to ostraca
Reduced by bully bears who tear through thorns
And slash the briar night neath drunken moon's
Too much for me, my Roman friend of old.
Lend strength, old pal, and teach me how a tent
You still transform to palace filled with gold.
How did you do it? How did you not drown
On briny rivers from your bitter eyes?
Or rather keep from dessicating dry
From tear ducts arid in their overuse?
I'm troubled, and I seek your help tonight.

the essence of my happiness

It seems I have no knowledge of myself
At times; it's melted into mere events
And flotsam, and that beauty I once knew,
Is lost, and how I wish that she'd return,
The essence of my happiness and self.
I'm like a creature lost in exile
From its own soul, longing for its return.

eyes have yet to see the far-off light

When she, the Muses' mistress messenger,
Farewelled me without even one farewell,
That moment, Gandalf said, we have no choice:
We now must face the dark of Moria.
For she might, with the aid of memory,
Have lifted me to sweet felicity,
And laughter of her levity and joy,
Connecting me to spirits I have lost.
She held a key to open up the lock.

But now, the door slammed shut, I must endure
The dark and dusty way without a map.
The long way without guarantees at all.
It's scary in this dungeonous expanse,
This dusk where even light of moon is faint.
I will not be a skeleton in webs.
I must press on, assured that splendor reigns
Somewhere, and it is worth the while to trek,
Though eyes have yet to see the far-off light.

a curse without the dance

By holding pirouettes in, I implode,
Lovely explosions of my leaping arms
Held in to putrefy my longing soul.
The body is a curse without the dance,
A coffin of the spirit, but ballet
Turns limbs to downy wings of levity!
Yes, what but rage may this Mercurius
Feel in his curiosity to soar
When bottled from expanding out in twirls!
But little wonder caged he may resent
Within me, pulling me inside his craw
So porcupined with arrows of despair!
But let some eyes of favor scan my limbs,
When they are melody of antelopes
In springtime pronk, and I am all restored!
A gasp of wonder may be the applause
That sounds the waterfalls of Eden's springs.
Don't call me vain when I but hunger, friend;
A pauper thieved of fame proper to him
Is temperate when he asks for his share.
I need the spectacle as if were life —
And that may be somebody's reading eyes,
If these bon mots are slippers that they trace.

Acts 4:36-7

Then onto skiff with hoard neath schooner's decks,

The glitter onto tossing teeth of waves,
The avenues of porpoises and whales,
And out beyond the coasts of Palestine.
Thus Joseph brought the common wealth offshore
To Cyprus, far beyond the Roman reach,
Beyond the seizures of the Pharisees,
Where it would be forfeit, the fruit of much
Repentance of the rich, who gave their all.
This was the treasure of the kingdom, now
Conveyed to foreign islands where was safe.
Now bounced the body of the bosomed craft
On white, light foam of skipping aqua seas,
And seagulls cried, while pelicans let loose
Their pouch of fish as gifts to those on deck,
For grace provides, and passage was assured
To those with faith to launch out daring risk,
For faith is farthingless without its risk.
Led now by bobbing humpbacks, figurehead
In maiden draperies thrown forth by breeze,
The ship, alike a knife through frosting, cut
Clean through the froth, dividing out the billows.
Doves, clothed in chitons of feathered white
That kicked up flowing pinions to the winds,
Exploded happily from Aphrodite's
Shores, and butterflied forthcoming docks
In welcome. Joseph heaved with sailors' help,
The golden hoard, in carved and painted chests
Onto the mainland, where he built a shack,
And humbly waited for the messengers,
Apostles of good news, when they would come.
Epistles pigeons carried on their claws
Came nigh to seven months or thereabouts,
Proclaiming many hundreds now combined
In one commune inside Jerusalem,
Where tongues of fire spit the splitting skies,
And scattered hordes of Babel now returned,
Confusion left for understanding, yet
The saints were poor and hungry. So he came,
Laid up the chests in pine-board womb of swan
Of harbors, led the schooner out, and threw
His confidence upon the jolly sea,
Which gleamed in laughter light might leave on waves
So cool-cerulean. The good trustee
Proved better mettle than Judas, and brought
Jerusalem the overflowing coffers

Dear Barabbas, Son of God, bequeathed,
In whose name he had come. The joy was sharp;
The festival was mighty, and the poor
Were rich with dancing and with singing feasts!
The castanets clicked merrily, and toasts
Were full of mirth, and glee was everywhere!
For everybody shared and none deprived.
The Master spent his years collecting such
In penance from the rich; such fruit was sweet,
And all sharpened their teeth on bursting juice!

fluids are Messiah's hidden prayers

Cities on fire in the desperation of night,
Struggling through the dream molasses towards their happiness,
A melancholy thumbing nose at death's encroaching creep.
They cry in naked tenements against fond bodies' heat,
Imagining that fluids are Messiah's hidden prayers.

shrieks of all the shanty towns

In bed we percolate the passions of our time,
The existential shrieks of all the shanty towns,
The rumbling in the dark that restless cries for hope.

your naked reveries

To love you while you sleep, to value you in dreaming,
While I soar in concepts in the livid dark,
The fever of the cooking night a sacrament.
The sweet delirium of half-awake broodings,
As spirit reaches out to all the world in love,
For zesty salsa of a solidarity,

And you, the beauty of your naked reveries
In ample flesh beside me is a comforting
Beyond the reckoning of time, a miracle.

the utter Aphrodite of your flesh
for Freya

I was some cursed abomination you
Uplifted from a swamp of ugliness,
And made me child of the Elohim
Again, a human, beautiful, with grace
And elegance. My voice was valued, prized --
My talent was of substance to your heart --
You loved the all of me, and I was floored,
On knees in worship of your high delight,
The utter Aphrodite of your flesh.
Are you a priestess of the highest fay,
Some avatar who wraps her flesh about
The goddess, given up in medium?
You are a wonder -- and you're in my dream.
O come into my life if you're my soul!
I've never been enchanted quite like this!
I know you are the soul of theatre,
Which is, or may be, yes, my very soul,
The incantation of the holy word,
Continual surprise in effervescent
Marvel what may spring from silver lips!
O let this low and monstrous thing I am,
This Svipdag in the marshy strands by shores
Become celestial and valuable
Again, an asset to be prized by you!
That you might come and bless me once again,
Where you, my soul, will ever be so blessed.

roasting marshmallows

The cops are learning, if you fuck with us,
Well, we fuck back. Your city's burning down.
I guess you want all of them to burn down.

Keep acting like a death squad: they'll burn down.
And I'll be roasting marshmallows in them.

an angel that I heed

But she could fly with but a single glance,
A wish, a gentle lift of feet from floor,
And she were slowly skybound in the air!
(I think that is an angel that I heed,
Some whisper of enchantment in my dreams.)
I do. I only have to will the loft,
And buoyancy's beneath my slippered feet,
And I am savor of delicious swim,
Swan Lake in levitate, this tender flight
Of flesh flamboyant twirling slow through air!
A train of billowed nonchalance of silk
Trails cape behind me, as I saunter steps
Above the floorboards with a sassy strut
Yet full of innocence and lovely grace.
Such subtle charm is but a natural
Accoutrement to my oblivious
Traversing through the beauties of this world,
A carefree, elfish tenderness whose wish
Is but to play, to let the spirit leap,
And follow with the well-composéd form.

a Stradivarius

Am I a Marsyas, my skin beflayed?
For I lack power to be touched at all!
I pinch, and seems that skin is on these bones,
But if I had such skin, I could be touched,
And yet there's nothing anymore that does.
Were I as sensate as a slab of wood,
I'd feel more than this heart of calluses.
But once this skin of mine were fertile soil
In which a thousand different blossoms grew!
The ruffles of so many petals thronged
Was oversaturate with every mood

That were a color or a shade on bloom.
But blow, and this fresh skin were shivered through
A wave of feathers plucked and I might sigh!
I was exquisitely in consciousness
Of every affect effervescent known.
It trilled through me, and I was daily thrilled.
And yet I lack such transport in a year
As once was mine upon the keenest hour.
This once and greener shoot dewed up with sap
Is now a gnarled wooden dessicate;
Where foliage sprouted green and thick on limbs
Is now the crust of brittle, senile bark.
I once was aloe in my juiciness;
I rasp for feeling syrup but am dry.
How can one live without a sensate skin?
How to endure without capacity
To be so touched I loft into the sky?
I was no less a Stradivarius
I could be played in every subtle mode
The virtuoso whimsied, but my range
Resilient on the tender sliding bow
Was any timbre the most sensitive
Of ears might wish, and I had more to give!
But let a soft vibration whisper low,
And catgut could arpeggio on me.
I was a protege destined for court,
A lately lad of promise, who might swoon
Whom I capriced to will if she might glance.
Let her but hear the musicality
Of words lifted up into instruments
Of song's ambrosia that the gods might taste,
She'd be enchanted as I was myself,
Adrift in what might drift through this my heart.
I had an otherworldly touch to me,
A hint and breath of seelie savory,
A twinkle in the eye that wouldn't let go.
But what once surged the very blood through me,
In rapture's pulse and rushing beat, is stone,
And not a jewel of dwarves, but some dull thing,
That fails to register at all what verve
Was once the everyday delight of me!
For then I hoped; ambitions were my hope;
Still yet a chance that I might break it big,
And burst upon the scene a wild child
Melting hearts but fainting right and left,

As I might stroll the runway in my train,
All joy, oblivious, yet in the rain
Of scintillate applause be dewed with tears,
My gratitude in disbelief and grace.
But when those showers did evaporate,
The dream dispersing vapor in mirage,
I broke, reduced to but a common thing,
An anyone at all, a flip a coin,
A royal bard condemned to miner's town.
Where fairy dust summoned in arch of hands
Could not be seen for nothing more than coal,
And all my elevations but a laugh,
Derided as pretensions though were gems.
The roadside thorns slandered camellias;
Who needs such nurtured delicates? They said.
I had refined myself beyond my use.
A Paganini in a barn is nought
But vulgar fiddler to the commoners,
For anyone will do, and men oft hate
Even the distant trace of angel flame,
Though it may cool and lift one heavenly.
Banished to Scythia, I fell to knees
And floundered in the dust of donkey carts,
Forgetting I had skin, for nothing touched.
Are there yet connoisseurs of miracles
Who crave gourmet enfanciment of words?
Do they exist? Or but a fantasy?
If so, come forward; lavish skin on me.

beloved nudity of ghosts

I'll pipe, and breathiness of this smooth reed
Will wake the mistresses of froggy swamps
To saunter upwards in their ribboned fogs
And gaze from haze that tickles beards of oaks
Upon the pewter ripples mirroring
The midnight's silent ivory above.
Once mesmerized by moon's own dizziness
The lilting merry waters bring to eyes,
They'll gather up their mist to manikin,
And fashioning through drizzle of the dew
Some web to wear simulacrum of flesh,

They'll sport in seeming nakedness but steam
Their giddy fond circumference in grass.
If ever were so pure some juvenile
Tenor in an echoed Notre Dame,
Then hold, you sweet sopranos, you surpass!
For such were glimmer of the Elohim,
Whose melodies were seven magic days,
Each spell of which was birth of some new kind,
And song were but a womb light fertilized
In night above the brooding waters' gleam;
And these breeze-incantations ladies hum
Allude devout if distant to such song.
Then I, who know but ordinary strum,
May stamp an image of discovery
Upon my fancy of diviner tunes,
And let my ears run silver with new life.
Will they cavorting then set out to kiss,
Their lips but giggles bubbling to touch,
A seltzer of delight that's nought but love?
I might then spy upon their orgy's sight,
And glimpse beloved nudity of ghosts,
Caressing of aridity of ice,
In swirls of smoke the temple's hierodules.
From this endearing mimicry of lust,
But pantomime and raptured sentiment,
The hoary carpets, all decrepit, aged,
But tawny tinder withered in the sun,
Come viridescent fresh again in grass,
And patient stalls now ripen into buds
Sky's fire roasts into a thousand blooms!
No Spring has ever come but from these games;
They dance, and Nature skips where it was lame!

an entourage of elegance

She walks upon the ramparts of the rain
Where they are cotton-soft, and waves her hand
To bless the luminescent icicles
Descending from that glacier round of night,
So those intrepid spears of lunacy,
Which jolly dolls of kinky straw ride rough
With wings of dragonflies, may fertilize

The sleeping soil wet with clay and seeds.
When she peruses in her gallant glide
The gala of the silent spectacle,
An entourage of elegance appears,
A coterie of votaries in white,
A lady troop made of the finest light.
They seem to chase the phosphorescent fog
As it recedes the stark horizon's edge,
Distributing benevolence abroad
Like lightest drizzle of confectionery,
Sweetest taste on tongue a newer luck.
And then, elusive luments, they elide
The liminal ascents of silver sky.

a pantheon of light

It's not an infidelity to awe;
We cannot help where wonder wakes our heart,
And cardium's a pantheon of light
Wherein our many luminescences
Sparkle in cavernous embrace of friends.
We are a panoply of many shades
Of awesome fascination, and we crush
Upon reflectionaries of the sun,
For consciousness is gleam of breathlessness.

nickeled dimes

We must insist upon our wonderment.
Banality's the greatest poverty.
I won't abide austerities of awe.
A hovel with glamour could be chalet;
The fairies filled their soulscapes with delight.
But if instead you let monopolize
These acres of abandonment and joy
The rank quotidians of cyberscrew,
And give your leave to pundits of applause
To then define the year and era, friend,
You give the treasure up for nickeled dimes.

malfeasance

I owe the Elohim a Sunday psalm
Each seven days, for praise is merriment
Of angels, and this panorama's price
Is wonder: gaze about -- the sight is lush!
The fields of marvel never fade but spread
Wherever eyes might go; the scroll rolls on,
And every fold is innovate and fresh,
Some creature of bedazzlement and strange,
Some spectacle of our encomia,
In script of cursive breath on vellum flesh.
It is malfeasance to skimp on praise.

a ballerina through the swamp

The failure of my muse these many years
Is nothing but my foolishness to write
While mourning: mourning my democracy
(How little I had known that love-affair
That ran so deep and underground in me),
Mourning my friendships Facebook took from me,
Mourning too many jenga pieces lost;
Long nights so alternating numb and panged,
Just stunned but then aching so very long.
The ink coagulates to viscous sludge;
The pen, once instrument of Mercury,
That skated on the smooth, inviting page
With virtuoso and Olympic grace,
With twirls and sudden twists and gasping leaps
Now bluntly scraped the slate in frictious drawl.
I've forced upon that sprinter of delight
A slow, forced march through sewers of my soul.
I've trudged through scum but still my pen aloft,
I've forced the quill at gunpoint to produce
In gloomeries and coalscapes measured verse.
It stuttered, sobbed, and blubbered, but I pressed,
An admiral in a septic fuselage

Where trickles were the currents of the stream,
Demanding "forward! Forward! Flow ye forth!
Scratch stain in cursive spill on parchment's tracks!
Eluct, lifting your boots through mud, and march!"
Yet motion mired through the traffic spikes,
Flat tires every seven feet or so.
The texture of my moods stood thick against
My inching forward; every millimeter
Ached, and riptides of my sentiments
Washed me aback a ways, wrecking my stride.
My feelings were gargantuan and spiked,
A field of century plants with pointed tips
That ripped my clothes and tore my tugging flesh.
Yet still I trooped, a foreman and a fool,
Forcing a diary through tedium,
Dragging a ballerina through the swamp
And asking her to dance while on the march.
Imagine then the spirit of such arts,
Impressed with sullen grief and prodded toil.

tethered to angst

If only I could just forget the rest --
The newspapers, the headlines that upset,
The sense of sheer despair out of control --
I could feel pleasure, yet it nagged at me.
I tried to read of things that brought me joy,
But read against the grain -- the leash would yank;
I was a tethered man, tethered to angst,
And powerless -- if only I could forget.

farewell my pouts

Despair hath little force against Chagall.
When grey and gloomy moods encroach on me,
And I can't find a reason to rejoice
(How many times this year does that weigh down!),
The color of his soul on canvas shines,
And all my grumpiness must fight to thrive,

Alas to no avail! Farewell my pouts,
A stronger force has energized my soul.

my windows boarded up

At some point I just broke. Said fuck the world.
It hasn't been the same, not ever since.
My wood is splintered, hickoried and rough,
My windows boarded up. I keep my guts
Inside with duct tape, and I patch the walls
With gum. I run simulacrums of me,
Photons through film in grainy dance on screens,
That smile on the silver celluloid,
But underneath I'm seethe and sewage scream,
A thrash that fantasies of violence
(Of one who's done, but keeps on marching on),
And have to wrench the ancient rusty brakes
To keep these limbs from flying in a rage,
And every evening nail my face of old
Upon my writhing maggot underside.
I shamble and I limp, bundled in string
And glue that barely holds my scrabbled twigs,
Patched up with nails and trash that was at hand.
I lost the measure of my happiness,
Faking to make it, yet still unconvinced,
A once beloved and unique facade
Running on automatic, suavest ghost,
While tears of sand scratch through my eyes beneath.

the rolling bath of Ranch dressing and dill

O, let us not drop rotten packages
Of cucumbers off highway bridges' heights,
To tumble careless long the ivory
Of Deco concrete Marilynesque legs,
To land by algae dens of raucous frogs,
Who own such hidden creeks they hopping haunt.

The smell alone of all those vegetables,
Their hearts forlorn in fall, their hardknocks hard
Upon the thud of moistened gravel beds.
There they just sit, in hobo's ridicule,
Got no respect, their destinies awry:
They diva dreamed of lounging most adored
In produce palaces, adorned in stacks,
The envy and delight of all. To dream
Of that first crunch of succulence once home,
Once taken by the highest buyer back
Into domestic intimacies! O
The rolling bath of Ranch dressing and dill,
Tomatoes and nasturtiums by one's side,
A set of wooden tongs of fork and spoon,
The cherubim of olive capers' coo
Mewing about, the slathered avocado
Everywhere about one's nakedness,
One's sylphan flesh of light-green moistened web
With softest seeds! And O to feel the joy
Of underside of teeth, and hedonism's
Gustatory raves, the tastebuds' tang,
The flavor-clitori of jolly tongue,
The feast of it! The Merlot wine beside!
The gathered friends, the ocean toasts, the surf
Of Santa Barbara outside the ribs
Of white gazebo stilted on the cliffs!
The gulls in nonchalance envy blue cheese,
And lick their bills, the pelicans are horny,
Taking out their fantasies on fish --
The moon is tusk and sliver in a bruise,
A silver slit in black and blue of night.
The evening is its laughter's prodigy,
The marmalade but flows from ice carafes,
Life is a smooth and giggling waterslide
From one delight to others in unfold.
To be the salad in the midst of mirth!
To have that final peak before one goes!
Each crunch eternity of relished taste;
I soothe-surrender to esophagi,
And in my last, before the dark, enjoy
From bellies' rumble their gathered guffaws.
My epitaph their lasting memory,
That savory salad fairy-maidens made!
But now such cherished dreams are soured sore!
Their fate upended by cold hooligans,

Who thought a prank of throwing cartons down
The highway's edge, hilarity! What booze
These teenage punks consumed, they reek with beer!
And here I am just rotting with the frogs.
Now stop it, I proclaim! Just stop it, now!
You do not know the dreams that you contude,
When you hurl cucumbers in gullies lewd!

gumball machine

I am a broken down gumball machine,
Left in some ancient carnival garage.
My paint, once gaudy, flakes, in patches, dust
A patina in scratches, my insides
Delapitated mechanisms, bolts
And nuts in clunking disarray, the gum
Long-melted solid glob of blue in globe.

subterranean and lewd

My heart is subterranean and lewd,
A troglodyte in glory of the dark,
A fish in seas of sleep in rolling black.
I am a pig in luscious mud of night.
I am the canyon in the midst of mounts,
My bones, the soft stuff in between of green.
I am the bat-ballet of twilight's sink
Into the bowl of moonlit ebony.
I am corroded limestone eons old,
Old temples countenance of sculpted bone.
I am the leap between these deep ravines.

architecture of the damned

Condemned to be an individual,
This dungeon of a self that holds me back

From that communion with all I adore.
Yet here within its belly late at night,
Mere torches, India ink, its granite blocks
The hue and smear of soot, I float adrift,
And love as best I can my inner pain.
This wretched frame is most beloved art.
I stroll through architecture of the damned,
In species of a wonder at this place
In which I'm bound, and wax nostalgic here.
The beauty of a being that is doomed.
The precious dearness of this lovely mess,
The long, extended funeral of time.

syrup on the page

The gourmet chef treasures the ephemeral;
Those vast artistic webberies of taste,
Their pleasures melting on the savoring tongue,
Are day's delight, and then are excrement.
Yet this daunts not the architect gourmand,
For whom those fleet and passing revelries
Are everything: tomorrow yet again.
Each day a masterpiece is broken down,
In gaiety of fond iconoclasts,
A wonderwork, and yet the chef baulks not.
Imagine reading Milton, then it's gone!
The act of eyes consuming have erased;
The ink is trace of syrup on the page
One's mind slurps up, and then is history.
The poet then must rewrite everyday!
Nature alone has confidence as this,
(Besides our chefs), to know the waterfalls,
Which weave of lightning made of dew such webs
Of celebrating spray, the baby's breath
Floral in air of alder's subtle scent,
Come arid times, but dry moss on the cliffs,
May with a wish of hurricane and cloud,
Come seasons tumbling in their dominoes,
Be yet restored to pageant's ribald rush,
In kinky curls of plunging angel-down!
But chefs know Fahrenheit four fifty-one
Each afternoon: the menu may remain,

But breakfast burns in bonfires of flesh.
And yet that is a foppish nonchalance,
A toss of fingertips and frosting, froth!
Dom Pérignon is glee of bubbles burst,
Each life and death of crackling foam, pure joy.
It's gone! In ecstasy it had its life.
It's Buddha's art for sure: his belly's fat,
Nonpermanence in adipose and grin.

fuck these damn fluorescent lights

Don't let yuppies control the narrative!
I'm not enduring bad fluorescent lights
To satisfy their fetish of the earth!
Goddamnit, give me incandescent blaze
Or darkness! They've designed austerity
For you and me, while they live on the hog.
Fuck them! And fuck these damn fluorescent lights!

a gaggle's fluff

The sparkling city lights by fairy night
Are like the charming women's eyes I love,
To bask in playful company they share,
And feel the ambience of luxury
A witty mind with sense of style brings.
I need fragrant, bubbling milieu of soft,
Gentle allure, enchantment, fond champagne
Of colloquy's bright musicality.
Escape of laughing fantasy and fete.
I'm such a swan who needs a gaggle's fluff
About me, in imagination's play,
Mischief's light tenderness, and levity.
I want to feel the common helium
Of glad hilarity and giddiness,
The missals of elf whimsicality.

aebelskievers made of verse

I miss the sweet enchantment of your lips,
The sparkling dust of icicles of wit,
The way we would for hours in glacé
Compose such aebelskievers made of verse,
And send them out electrically as gifts.
Ten years and more, Francesca; still you keep
Me banished from your fairy bowers, while
Your adolescent entourage abounds
In giggling, gaga worship at your feet.
But once I was your prince upon the horse.
Have I lost so much honor in your eyes
That two swift votaries of verse as us
Must always stay divided for all time?
Just hush your fickle lips a bit, I pray,
Permitting me to fantasize a time.

glassy snow-globe

You lifted me into a miracle,
A glassy snow-globe in your fog-drift sky;
I was a toy in your menagerie.
We frolicked in the breathless child-lands
Of minds -- we were enchanted innocence,
And theatre naive, mere marionettes
Of keen delight. I thought it was a dream --
Except -- I never had a dream so brim
With spell -- my lips created new by you,
My pen a magic wizard's wand of wish --
But wave, and tales spun out almost alive!
Only a small elite has tasted such
Ambrosia (and it's not to do with wealth,
But native charm of elfin) -- Then you dropped
That glass -- it shattered -- water and the snow --
The shards -- I fell headlong, consumed, to earth --
I crashed, a meteor from heaven's edge,
Outlawed from Eldar mistlands of the Sun,

Amongst a race who knew nothing of verse.
I'd lived a weird between familiar worlds,
A liminal expanse of reverie
And light and passing fog -- a glimpse intense
Of that pure, concentrated essence Irish
Poets labeled "faerie", luscious draughts
Of inspiration's nectar -- now was gone.
Where cloud-Merlot of sylphan breweries
Once wet my lips (just where that night you kissed),
Now dust asphyxiated this my cup,
And everything was dull and void of charm.
The natives on this lump of earth just stared
At me when I spoke my experience:
A body made of awe, no longer flesh,
Leaping from wonderment to wonderment,
An Ariel across jet ink of stars,
Where mischief was the potion poets sipped,
And instantly were feasting with the best,
If Homer, Pindar, Bragi, Skallagrimson,
Hopkins, Sappho -- we dined with them all!
And now like Ovid lost in Scythia!
The creme skimmed off the creme, hilarity
Of Rome, the city's darling, locked away
In boons where no one cared about his verse!
Alas, the mythic king of festivals
And odd, protean twists of vernal Spring
In nothing but the Ozarks of his time!
My dear, you made of me to taste his cup,
To cry for Rome (though citadels of sky),
Remembering the Forum (of your eyes).
How many envelopes was I to waste
Inscribed with betterments on Provençal,
A Petrarch tossing sculpted livid gold
Into the cold of night for vanity
Of you, and all your cruelty? Void were those
Most virtuoso crafts I mailed to you --
You never once responded -- though I sent
A singing telegram of verse I wrote,
The very virgin-pressed express of heart!
I left you lyrics worthy of Lalique
You flung without a second thought as trash.
You made a Laura or a Beatrice
Seem positively sociable and warm,
You were so glacial and left me cold.
But I can still recall these many years

The very taste of those liqueurs so rare
No wine has ever neared it in its charm --
For you were grape and must, and I was yeast,
And sleep was but a cellar where it brewed.
Still I can hardly countenance the loss
Two geniuses of elfin might create
You yet refuse -- refuse is just your name --
And I, polite, but patient, wallow sad.

sugar oyster

no more beautiful but the flowers in the rain, the soft and hungry sound of maple sunshine from your eyes.

love, the lyric of your lips is the melody of nightingales in spring, and oh, the gentle spray of rain in softer hours of summer!

sweet, sweet the luscious candy of your southern lips is like a sugar oyster on my tongue, and now I am forever your enchanted servant.

salvation is a lip-smacking marvel of vapor and dew, flesh oh! in what sudden flash now light of moonlit sky in ebony of midnight

I felt beautiful again

Tonight I thought of you -- at last for once
In too long, I felt beautiful again.
That image in the mirror pleased once more,
Instead of seeming ugly and worn out.
I was the kin of dancing sunbeams once
Again, my soul an iridescent sky.

votary of fleet Atargatis

I woke this morning feeling like a woman,
As I had so many other days.

I felt so delicate and sensual,
So made of aether, rarified, and silk,
So made of sparkling jewels crafted from ice,
My flesh the thaw of frozen mountain streams,
My body moodiness and labile cream.
I felt self-valuable, a treasure of
The goddesses that sky-toboggan clouds
And thinnest tracks of ice translucent, clique
And ghostly entourage of Lady Moon,
Companions other times of Mother Earth.
I felt the substance of the Elohim
In me, unshadowed by the crudities
Of rage or doubting sorrow; I could sense
The prana-stuff of Dionysus in
My bosom, separating from the filth
Of Titans' legacies, an atmosphere
Of mirth consuming me deliciously.
I felt like trash no more, but rosaries
Of royal jewels in flower gardens' plush
Profusions -- just a moment's respite from
The ugliness I often feel these days,
The residue of the polemical
Divisions of our troubled times, the wrath
That boils and foul putrefies in me,
Corrupting me with paroxysms' hate.
The fight has laid me waste, and ruined fanes
And shrines of roses; temples lay in smoke
And rubble, Doric columns crumbling
Amidst the owls and fleet hyena packs
That roam and desecrate my Attica,
Achaean plains, now prison uprising
Of starving Roman slaves, and Spartacus --
I was a gorgeous gallus in my homeland,
Votary of fleet Atargatis,
Mermaidic deity of Syria --
But now in Sicily, I but cut wood
And drag water on latifundia.
And yet a coal lies under this my tongue,
A vision of a kingdom ruled by slaves.
I can't abide these bridles anymore,
But bridals to my Lady I would have,
A festive throwing-off of bitterness,
Restoring this plantation to Dilmun,
To Eridu, to Ashurbanipal's
Floral botanicum at Nineveh.

These dreams stirred in me as I peaceful slept,
That waking, Attis's long heritage
Awoke in me in landscapes made of grapes
And trimmed camellias 'neath palms of dates,
Which one by one I plucked and put to verse.

jello of collective dung

We tangle in the macrame of lusts,
And wrestle with competing avarice.
In darkness towards our longings we each grope,
In blindness, shoving and then being shoved.
We schlep through jello of collective dung,
And in the viscous sewage gnash our teeth.

turns my skin into a wonderland
for Elizabeth of Night

It's you whose fingers soothe me in the night,
Who turns my skin into a wonderland.
At last some peace in this too stressful world,
Your loving fingers on my sighing back,
This little piece of paradise you share.

birds would cease to sing

The birds would cease to sing if Virgil ceased.
The aromatic mountain shrubs would fail
In fragrance if Ovid should dwindle off.
The zephyrs tickling the vibrant leaves,
And sunlight frolicking on skipping streams,
Would lose their compass without nymphs and fauns
(Who it may be are creatures of our soul,
Without whom she cannot perceive the world).
The genres of the Muses are the eyes
With which our heart perceives the ludity

And lyricism of the natural world.
What sings? What pipes? What lifts felicity
To sacrament of our delight but verse?
And first and foremost verse must celebrate
Festivity and silent faerie bliss
In woodland coverts and the village green.
Pastorals sound of Ian Anderson,
His fluting lilt and cadences, his touch
Of honey-melodies that smooth the ear.
No clumsy hymnody of moralists,
Its cadence caged in gloom, can do the job.

straitjacket of skin

Let me escape into your stranger's eyes;
Upend my dull familiarity
And strip me of this straitjacket of skin.
For nothing is more grating on my nerves
Than my identity. Your fresh new eyes
That read me reimagine me, release
Me from the cage of me, the burdensome
And wretched tedium of being me,
Allowing me a nothingness of bliss,
A brand new thing just infanted in you
Who drinks me in, and makes love to my verse:
Far sexier to me than lowly flesh.
But true delight at what my pen creates
Is better than the best of any sex.

careless play of innocents

These wild branches of my pagan past,
Long grafted into Messianic stock,
I now attend to, for the votaries
Of beauty that they were, the careless play
Of innocents no longer innocent
Yet celebrating their nostalgia
For Halcyon of youth. Their many arts
Of pleasure -- all the Muses' many limbs --

Enhance Shabbat, and speak of Eden's bliss.

measure out the deep

I shall remember you and call on you,
Hellenes of Sabbatine and leisurely
Amusement, for your gravitas is light
Yet weighty. I shall hang your laurels high
Upon my walls, and let you peer into
Contemporary mysteries of time
Through these my eyes, and thus I welcome you,
Poet to poet, dialing down my mind
To present matters, full of noise and strife,
And join you in your ancient verities.
I need not occupy this slice of time
So arbitrary into which I'm thrown,
But mind, more like Odysseus, may roam,
Where treasure's pleasures measure out the deep.

captive creatures of our awes

O Beauty, don't you know, whom you refuse,
The man will love you through another one,
His medium for this your florid muse.
Each is a pythoness and oracle
To each, the meeting place where many loves
Commingle. He can't help adore you, if
Afar or underneath his nostril's breath.
We are the captive creatures of our awes,
And lovers linger, most especially
The ones we never got a chance at all.
Each holiday he'll fill a glass with wine,
Gaze out the window wistfully at night,
And tip his glass to you, be sure of it.
In secrecy we have a dozen loves,
At any time, imagining our lips,
Our eyes, our clothes bare thighs beside their skin.
The orgies in the underneath of dreams
Are everpresent, for the heart's uncaged

At midnight, and the reveries are sweet
That congerie most unbeknownst round us,
A silent milkshake in the subtleties.
You spurn him, but he loves you all the same.
Imagination's free and can't be blamed.

savor of the shade

You, Anaid, are nothing but a dream,
A mistress of my reveries and trance,
Who visits me by night to bring me charm,
And yet are more real than concerns of day.
The alder of your river nymphoid bark
Exudes upon me savor of the shade
Whenever I inhale, and I am there
In frolic with you, through the willow brush
And cocklebur. You are an apple tea
I sip into my seams, aperitif.
I'm smitten with a kitten who is flame
On oil in the drowsy bounds of night.

how her vineyard tastes

I still remember how her vineyard tastes,
The flavor of her grapes, her smooth ravine,
The chaparral between, the way she's shaped
Like polished ivory, the savory
Of tongue on tongue, and lips beneath sweet hips,
Her honesty of eyes, the fond surprise
Of just how soft the pillows in her loft,
The silk of skin beneath her cotton trim.
I chortle as I say I do recall,
For in the truth, I never knew at all.

the first temptation

Satan.
I see you, languishing. You hunger so.
You've fasted now for almost forty days?
Yet I am wise -- not in the way you like,
But I discern the bread you lack the most
Is justice. There your hunger pines the most.

Jesus.
The people, turned out from their homes, are starved.
What is this fast of mine compared to theirs?
A little taste of passing empathy,
But when I want, I stop. And yet their pangs,
Which do not stop, pang through myself. I weep!
How was this all-abundant world deformed?
The earth is willing with her womb and gives,
Yet her largesse is locked away in stores.
If only they would take down all those walls
Which keep away the poor, all would be fed.
Say pity, how has it come to this point?

Satan.
Such walls are built with stones like at your feet.
But you are the Messiah: speak the word!
Such stones turn into challah, do they not?

Jesus.
If stones could weep, as once good Moses plied,
The ground were wet with pity's marshy swale.

Satan.
Yes, Moses, yes! He took his staff and struck.
So you. Take up your staff and strike the stones,
And here a garden where a desert stood!

Jesus.
It is a garden! Men have made it sterile.

Satan.
Bring it renewed fertility again!
The people crave their miracles, my friend.
You have the power. Awe them with your spell,
And triumph is a moment's ride away.

Jesus.
The magic yet inheres in every twig,
In every rock, in every leafy staff!
The miracle's about! Creation brims
With it! If that is not enough to awe,
A little parlor trick will not suffice.
If they are stupefied to wonder such
As all repletes circumferent and broad,
Astonishing but everywhere, in life
Abundant, that is miracle denied.
That is a sacrament in sacrilege.
The lesser cannot win where greater fails.

Satan.
Philosophy and bother! Trust your gut!
You hunger. So do they! Words will not feed!
They've had enough of fruitless thoughts and prayers.
Be done with sermons. Turn these stones to bread!

Jesus.
The stones that need transforming are the hearts
Of heartless men, who hardened to the poor,
Turn them away. If they would heed the Word,
That fair instruction you blaspheme as naught,
Then they would share their plenty far and wide.
It says, "There shall be no more poverty,
When you come into this abundant land,
So long as you will follow these commands."
Go read. It's where the Jubilee is praised,
Right after sharing tithes with vulnerables.
Bread is aplenty! Heart is much more scarce.
Without this liberating word, what heart?
We can't abide nor live on bread alone,
We are not beasts, and there is bread enough.
What's lacking is the Spirit for to share.
Enough of your prestidigitation, fiend!

the second temptation

Satan.
Come follow me and meet your destiny.

Jesus.
You take me to the Temple? There I've been.

Satan.
I take you to the Royal Portico.
Here, let us climb. The vista is to die for.
Just a little bit more. Here we are.
Observe : how far the eyes can see from here!
And gaze down in the Valley of Kidron,
A wondrous height, and fathoms to the floor!

Jesus.
It giddies me, to teeter here, to tip
Above such drastic leagues below my feet.
There is some strange, alluring grace to it,
Though perilous. The very air is thin,
And wavers. Autumn leaves might blow so smooth,
And simply saunter, in their rocking swing,
Gentle descent to valley floors below.

Satan.
Majestic, such sublimities. Yet think:
Below our feet, inside the portico,
That grand basilica that takes the breath:
Four rows of royal colonnades, in cool
And shifting shadow, light a furtive raid
Of playful beams retreating from advance;
The limestone lined with marble, and the sense
Of such immensity, the hall so high
And broad, as if within a legendary
Cavern-kingdom, Corinth of the dwarves!
Astonishing! And yet to think that here,
Within the very Temple's sacred bounds,
Within that marbled womb of awe beneath,
The votaries of Mammon do their trade!
I see that sneer; the sacrilege, it vexes
You! No wonder! Here? Is nothing pure?
Is nothing holy? Here? To buy and sell?
To trade the slips of title to the land,
To levy up the soil farmers work,
And play roulette with rents, which are but lives?
Those lives! Their living energies, their toil,
All that labor, nothing but a toy
To those below us! They may say they deal

In coin, but you and I both know the truth:
Their tokens are of sweat, but more of blood.
And nothing but a bargaining for them.

Jesus.
It seethes my sebum in my blazing skin.
We stand above a monument of sin.

Satan.
But look below, into the vast Kidron.
Its dizzy maw but welcomes for a kiss.
It beckons, does it not? Relief, a peace
Of billows, vast a sea of winged things
That flit and flurry here and there above!
My breath: it no longer is here within,
But there, in chasm's vertigo of heights!
It calls to you, I know it does. Give in:
Just throw yourself, just hurl yourself, just leap,
And soar, Jesus! The angels will aloft you!

Jesus.
This body hath not wings as once I did.
It falls alike to gravity as all.
That only would result in tragic death.

Satan.
And yet this world so pains you in your soul.
Perhaps is better to return again
To heaven, more the natural for you.
Just look around: the malice and the woe,
The treachery; and more than just the whip
At heels to profit someone living smug,
But no! The very whipped themselves would cry
The mountains would you take the whip away,
Then turn you in! This world's too rough for you,
Betraying even those who come to free.

Jesus.
I must admit the things you say have truth,
At least in half, and do tug on my heart.
How not to weary in despair of this?
The misery -- but more the love of it!
And when I do look down over this height,
The sight is too delicious to my eyes.
To just surrender to the emptiness,

To tumble, and in this, to say goodbye ...
To close the book on this most cursed tale,
And take my wings again to heaven's heights,
Where peace and pure serenity has reign,
Where justice is the very air we breathe,
Where love is fragrance and our nourishment.

Satan.
Yes, go with this! The cherubim will sail
With you to where the floorboards are but clouds!
Is true, a body there would be below,
Mangled in blood, but you would be above!
An instant! That is all that it would take!
And think : the poetry of that collapse,
If you perhaps leapt from this other side,
To leave a corpse and blood where they do sell,
What brilliant statement! What symbology!
The very blood and broken bone they deal,
Before their horrifiEd eyes of woe!
That says it all! Your message wrapped up neat!
Your mission and its prophecy writ red,
And staining all the stones that money bought.
They'll have to be replaced, as now impure,
The whole place reconstructed, business gone
And vacated, at least a time. And you?
Far from this wretched den of scoundrelly!
Aloft in atmosphere liqueur and sweet,
Your very breathing candy on your tongue!
A trouble? Not a memory, no trace!
A single step. A little, subtle step.
A touch of air, a mezzanine of breeze,
A bridge of breath and fog, a rapture's wading
Into zephyrs and their harpsway's soft
And elegant pan-piping, cool and pure!
Inhaling purity at last again!
Those ankles have the trace of featherous sprouts;
But give them wing! Breath is your element!
Away with difficulty, welcome ease!
So easy, is it not? To take the step?
But balance on one leg with me, and let
The other taste the wine of sunset's sigh.
Observe as now the grapes but spilt on sky,
The cumulus a dripping gore the vine
But runs and softly stains; there falls the sun!
Now follow it, and take a naked dip

Into this sea of air more drunken wine!
Release the sorrow and the broken angst!
Be done with toil of the anguished heart!
Abandon this establishment of tears!
A slip, a simple slip of oiled toes,
And then a banquet of relinquishment,
Eat to your heart's delight, and then no more!
I hear the gully calling out your name,
Alike a woman to her lover, hear!
She sends for you! Her breasts are soft and sweet!
Her lips the edges of the roses' bloom,
Her skin the tickling evanescent breeze,
Her arms majestic, wide, now go to her!
She seeks you in the empty, broad liqueurs!

Jesus.
Behind me, villain! Heel! Take this away!
I shall descend, but by the steps of men,
Back to my propheciéd destiny.
The scripture says, Thou shalt not tempt the Lord!
Would angels catch me? I would think it so,
In body or in breath, but either way,
I toy not with the heavens! But obey!
I knew this vale of violence were vile,
Ere I came, and here I am, is true!
You beckon me to give it up for ease.
What ease on latifundias of woe,
What ease the peasant, what the destitute,
Who lost of farms but shuffle in the towns?
What ease the utter loss of distant hope,
A hope ever receding, that it seems
But bitter tale the Pharisees recite
To keep content the populace with dreams?!
They've had their dreams, they're gorged with naught but dreams!
Their bellies empty but their fancies full!
A heaven in the sky when they expire,
Fantasies to keep them toiling hard!
Messiah, always far beyond their sights,
A taste for their descendants and their sons,
Perhaps their own descendants there beyond,
And on that hope recedes, beyond all hope!
The time is now! Get you aback, you fiend!
The time is now! I shall not squander it!
This precipice is ever here for me.
It waits, is patient, and there is no rush.

You wish me gone? Of course you do, I know!
Well soon enough, and not by this my hand!
If I advance, how careful I may be,
A thousand snares are spread out towards the cross!
The cross! That dread, malevolent idol!
Erected on the roads to crush all hope.
Here lies your rotting hope, the cross declares.
Here lie the ones who thought to free the slaves.
Well let it come, it shan't intimidate!
I come a second Moses, I shall free!
No doubt that cross awaits at every turn.
You'll have your wish but soon enough, you foe,
No doubt! But not until I've had my say,
Not til assay of all the possibles!
Not til assembly of the destitute
Across the land in flocks of resistance!
How far we'll go? Who knows? The Father knows,
None else! So we shall give the test our all,
Not testing him, but letting him test me!
A gamble as my gift, I'll play to full!
How far? How soon the cross? How short the path?
I'll take it far as it may will to go,
But it will go, a start is had at last!
A start is everything, how far it goes.
No more the wait! We leap and we begin!
Yes, I shall leap! And into nought but air,
The vast uncertainty of history!
But not this portico! I leap to start
The Messianic age you rightly fear!
The kingdom will be had at any cost!

Satan.
A kingdom, so you say? Now let us talk…

the third temptation

Satan.
You wish to propagate a kingdom. Well…
There's many kinds, there's many kinds indeed.
Come with me and I'll show you all there are.
Behold, the glitter and the glory; lo,
The palaces and privilege; yea, the might,

The majesty, the wonder: feast your eyes.
Consider all the jewels and all the gold,
But dressing, petty background noise; and look
Ye on the pomp and honors kings receive,
Ambassadors and messengers in turn.
Now I'm no fool; I know your heart abhors
This luxury, nay, sheer idolatry.
I feel your keen disgust as I now speak.
Let me articulate your hidden thoughts:
Those hoards of filthy lucre grubbed by kings
Might open up their treasuries to all,
And make a public paradise instead.
Of course, of course. But you are just a man;
In fact, I hate to say, a peasant, no?
How will you ever reach your hand to grasp
And conquer, so you may convert these hoards
To common use? Aye, there's the rub, I say!
But what if I could offer you a shortcut?
How? The Roman Emperor is mine.
Oh yes, he serves his gods most faithfully,
In outward garb and ceremony, and
If they were in his heart as in his rites,
Not bad conceptions of the Elohim,
All things considered, but his heart is void
Of all but power, and power he has!
Observe these petty kingdoms scattered round.
Despite their pomp they all bow down to Rome.
Bowed to, yet they will kiss the ring of one,
And heed him. But his heart is in my hand.
I but instruct, a secret whispered hint,
A hunch of where more power might be had;
He'll take it as if Jupiter himself
Had sleek commissioned Iris to his dreams,
And spoke the word. Consider this, my friend:
Suppose that he were suddenly to turn.
Suppose that he, upon my whisperings,
Converted to your gospel in its full!
Imagine that! He'd make you Pontifex!
Upon the Palatine, right by his side,
You could direct the Messianic shift,
The whole world in the sway of your new way.
I could maneuver it, and help you rise
Up through the ranks; and lend a governor
To hear you, so the province rings with you,
And then a senator, a broader spread,

Until the emperor himself must hear.
Position yourself skillfully, and all,
In time, will fall upon your holy feet.
Ten years, perhaps; twenty, at most. And best,
No cross! Instead a crown (or close to it.)
Rise up the ladder of the smart elite --
They like their Stoics and philosophers,
Their magic workers, and such miracles
Are nothing difficult at all for you!
You're eloquent, you have an earnest heart
Whose sweet sincerity's charisma wins
Whomever you might speak with. Think of this:
Why bother with the petty Pharisees?
These hillbilly provincials in Judaea?
Please, their ears are closed, and even if
They weren't, so? These pompous sideshow hicks?
Who listens to them? Rome is laughing, see?
Bypass them altogether: you be smart.
Blend in to Roman culture and move up!
That way's advancement. Now I know your thoughts :
The compromises needed for this plan,
The flatteries and careful bridled tongue.
A petty price to change all of the world,
Now don't you think? And just a few, a few.
A few will not corrupt you. You are pure.
I'll pull the strings at every stage, open
The doors, you play your cards, and when it's time,
I'll make sure that the emperor will hear.

Jesus.
How kind of you! Your generosity
Impresses me! And all for free, no price?
You'll hand over these keys from friendliness?
You've changed. I thought for sure there'd be a price.

Satan.
Well, that is true, there always is, I say.
But just a petty fee for you, my friend,
A token, nothing more. A little gift,
That's all. I don't ask much. Give not a thought.

Jesus.
But no, say more, declare your little gift.

Satan.
No no, let us not trouble with such things.
There's much more to discuss in this whole plan.

Jesus.
But I insist. I must know to prepare.

Satan.
Well, if you ask, it's nothing much at all.
A little bend, perhaps.

Jesus.
A little bend?

Satan.
A simple lurch, a torso sway...

Jesus.
A bow.

Satan.
Well, not a bow exactly, just a bend,
A little gesture, just in gratitude.
To tip your hat in grace, no more.

Jesus.
A bow.

Satan.
Okay, a bow, if you insist! So what?
A bargain, no? For all I offer you?
I'll clear the path to where your kingdom lies,
I'll do all that for you, what you could not
Were you to work a hundred years, and you
Think that a little swish is something big?
A soldier will salute his general, no?
A small salute? Nothing, nothing at all!

Jesus.
Saluting signals who's superior.
You make a most attractive bargain, but
The scriptures say honor but God alone!
You fool! That's why I won't salute these kings!
You think then I will bow before your kind?
Begone, you've done your best, but you have failed!

idolize the gutter

They took the stars down from the heights of sky,
And wiped the heavens clean of all its lights.
And said, a star, despite what beauty brings
It forward, has no relevance in sin.
A single sin sufficient to dethrone.
And thought this conquest marvelous and pure.
I watched with horror as the night was stripped
Of all her jewelry, as they judged the stars,
And gloated in their envy dragging down
The eyes to idolize the gutter, image
Of our truth: the sky is but a lie.

lotuses from mud

I.
He's more than this what crime he may have wrought
With fingers; he is Walt, and all his song
Is threaded through my sinews and my flesh,
And sings through blood of me, and is my blood,
And is the blood of us, America.
He's larger, larger than a smudge of soot.
He's myriads of lyrics lost in lands
Of vast confusions' parlors coast to coast,
The burgeoning of possibilities,
The cry of wonder in a captive state
Built on the bones and blood of Indians,
Where innocence was never in the cards,
But ever feigned and wished and counterfeit.
There can't be better in a land of crime
Than Walt; the serpent's sin insinuates
And chokes the very earth where whips were wrought
With wrath on kidnapped backs working such fields
That bullets raped from gore Originals
Once planted with their corn. What else than sheer
Delirium that ever lied to snuff
The murder underneath one's feet could be?

This cynical and stained experiment,
This drooling scheme of usury and lust,
This country corporate from the very start,
An artifice of greed whose natural
Must be simulacrum, has crazed denial
At its core, and calls this paradise.
We steep in long-fermented, reeking sin.
We sip our gin in crematoria,
And take our lounge in muffled, desperate cries,
That oil-seep in lurid canticles
Of noon mirages; we are but facade,
But paper on a frame with painted grin,
Clown makeup on a corpse, at heart perverse.
We drove the hearses cross the slaughtered plains,
And called this orgy of panghoulia
By name of pioneering, but was numb
And dumb display of mayhem. It commenced
With rum and sugar cane and trade in flesh;
Such are its axioms on which it's built,
And rum coheres, for only sloshed and drunk
May any celebrate consumed in sin.
This brutal circus of oblivion
And fever has its glory in its lies;
Then what surprise is tainted all its touch?
What beauty rushing rhapsodized in me
Through camaraderie's magnificent
Evangelist of bustling throngs purrs hymns
I can't resist, they permeate my cells
And steep the bougainvillea and the rose
Inside my pores, and Aphrodite wraps
Me in her sheer chiton of ocean foam
And petals, but a rapture in the mist
And Stygian marsh of Milton's antihero?
We are such. But Walt took plume to skin
Of bulrush, and in berries' blood he wrote
The heaven one might forge in Hades' midst,
And I am in that only ever dream
With all of us, we're implicated in
The song America's impossible
Without, that's in our very cartilage
And tissues of our intimacy; here's
One statue if you topple, all is gone,
The edifice is broken dominoes,
The house of Jericho is rubble, dust;
The lady laced in adipose is sung.

So endless sigh is serenade we know,
If anguish or if ecstasy or both.

II.
He nursed the soldiers in their rotting beds
With tenderness, and gave their hours soft
Of lovingkindness; and in every thick
Of shrubs and fragrance of the lunary,
Beyond whose vegetative fog grew worlds,
Whatever world of prairie, plains, or grass,
Or mountains, rocky valleys, redwood trees
And oceans, rugged hobos on the rails
The Coolies laid in rust and chrome and pitch
And railroad ties of tar, a star to guide
In shivering freight, the weight of shocks of wheat
In tumble time of heatstroke harvest hands,
He hallowed, if his hands were calloused, caked
In fresh manure of the pumpkin loam,
Mechanic's grease by denouement of gloam,
The overalls unloosed, the ranting runs
Through panting splashing in the cattail ponds.
Just let me blink, just let my eyelids shroud
A moment but a flash of taint and mar,
Say no, say no, let me descend a fish
In what pretends we swish to swim the night
And breathe, not suffocating in the mud
Of charcoal, coffee grinds, discarded rinds
Of fruit the bittersweet and weeping! O!
I cannot, will not, ever, ever, no!
But Walt! O Walt! I can't -- and yet -- I can't!
I might be Swanhild horses tore apart,
Each limb the loyal to impossibles
That wrench contrariwise. There is no bus
I could throw Walt beneath, and yet no child.
Wild is bewilderment with me;
I'm in the rain with Lear, and rioting
In weepstorm, wind and spluttering, the dogs
Are bankrupt in their howls beside my moans.
Shall all my loves be Goya's Saturn, gore
The maw in limbs mere stubs of blinded gnash,
Oblivious and horrible? But true?
No no, I shut my eyes! I said, I shut
My livid, reeling eyes! I clench my lids
And pray. Sweet Magdalene, is there not snow
So fresh its melt might dip in Jordan sins

The mentors bleed behind, and scrub what scum
Their hands might dunk in creeks not ripe to plunge?
But how could even snow withstand such sin?
Some stain is turpentine and mesoderm.

III.
If I must say goodbye, my sweet swan song
Shall linger in eternity of wist,
And I shall nought be but my fond farewells,
If bitter, broken-hearted, dashed befuddled
In my burning question marks; I shall
My shrieked indictments shatter on my song,
And cymbal on the sun my dianoose;
I hang there. And if I must needs forbid,
My ban will be a bridge that ever spans;
My shun shall long pronounce those golden hymns.
For if my condemnation were complete,
I must recite the evidence entire --
Let me stay in trial -- at the bar
I'll cross examine, tough, impeccable,
Forever -- jury, let us hear that hymn
Again, take in state's evidence and sing.
If shames be serious, then courts must span
The half-life of the crimes, and on and on.
I'll litany the sins, but they shall ring
In wonder of the blundering man of song.
And we shall hear the testimoans of drones
And cherubim, and even angels' scales
Will falter; as they oscillate, all time
Shall flutter by, and butterflies contend
With cankerworms. I am not done as yet,
And doubt I ever may. Then add the wails
As background to the psalmodies, and sobs
The underside of gentle symphonies.
Calligraphy in drear verse if you must,
To keep the sins in sweetness clear to eyes,
But let that book of dithyrambs penance prove.
The joys it wagers must against be weighed.
I shan't forget, but either way, I can't.
I can't let go, I can't hold on, I'm plumb
In bloody blubber, drowning, still in song
And ecstasy, now here comes agony
To add her vicious tones of dissonance,
And they must stay, and I must welcome them.
With sneers, with sheer refusals, with alarm

Buried in numbness, stupored mouth agape,
But I the door must open and let in.
You couldn't have gilded hell a better gold.

IV.
Excuses, leave us of excuses, stay
The weasel's paw that would casuistries
Render in heady relativity
Of time and context. Stop. Just stop. Face front
And gaze. We are bewilderment with legs.
We are amphibian as yet in swamps,
New limbs just fins so tentative and fresh,
So faltering. We haven't got our bearings.
Still the world is ill and grows from sin,
Our keenest beauties lotuses from mud.
Our geniuses still cripples, still the halt.
We are the agony of middledom,
Tugged forward by most beautiful ideals,
Yet tethered still to atavistic beasts.
Conclusion is such prematurity.
Yet that's the rub. Unripeness and its blood.
If I enjoy the harp's most dulcet strains,
Am I accessory to beauty as
A camouflage, or else a broken truth
In rubble of Corinthians and wine?
If crimes are fluctuate with effloresce
And scintil, incident to cinnamon
And Everlasting's maple-breath of scent,
What then? What then? If miracles of charm,
(The only reason to endure this hell)
The respite sole of tortured souls, are sin,
I quit. That's it. Finis. I'm out. I'm done.
I can't abide without enchantment's chime,
I won't. I must refuse. And if to sing
Invokes a background shame, still I shall sing,
For song is all we've got in this sad world.
I'll add the words "you're wrong" to his great song.
I'll say, "You've made a horrible mistake."
I'll criticize his boundaries, test his rules,
Put wounds before his face, bring up disgrace
And daffodils in flatulence and filth,
But I shall sing. You hear me? I shall sing!
(And weep. In willows' hollows by the creeks.)

a long and brutal brooding

For Obi-Wan to find that Anakin,
The protege he raised up from a boy,
And loved beyond the love a mentor loves,
Had harmed children, that was a crushing blow,
More than a dozen hostile Sith could land.
How long it took for him to reconcile,
None know. But in his heart, it must have been
A long and brutal brooding, where he weighed
The crime against the vault of good he knew,
Tormented every step along the way.
Condemning, then, yet then, but turning back,
And recollecting love, in common life
Together -- how to wipe this memory away?
His answer was one frequently employed:
Two names. He gave one name to whom he loved,
The other to the monster he rejects;
Divided them, so that the names sufficed
To first preserve what cannot be erased,
The love, but secondly, what can't be cleansed,
The stain. It's rare that we've devised a trick
Much better, to be true to all the truth.
When heroes fall, they fall so very hard,
Yet we have not the halos quite to judge,
For sin and virtue oft are intertwined,
Which only angels' scalpels may divide.
The rest of us are lost in bafflement,
A broken jury weeping in our laps,
Soft-pedaling as also we indict,
Lost in the back and forth, and we are hung.
Lucas asserts a good redeemable
Remains, if it will sacrifice itself
For greater good, and Luke asserts the same.
How will we ever sort out praise from blame?

something we might yet become

And we are left with beauty of the ghouls,
The shrieking remnants of inhuman times,

Before the modern birth of living soul,
Which we still midwife from the edge of dark.
How those poor wretches saw ahead of them
To some redeeming harmony beyond
Their own ability to live, astounds.
It was the breathless light within their night,
And we shall take gifts from these prototypes,
Almost human, and reaching towards that goal,
But never stepping to the promised land.
"Human" is something we might yet become.

anything at all is doable

Adam.
That serpent speaking is my very flesh.
It seeks an end of every barrier.
It seeks its freedom, consequence be damned.
Incest, the harm of young, and animals,
Whomever might be near, no matter who;
Dark urges justify themselves. I think
We ought to listen to this canny snake.
Ought we not eat that fruit it so commends?

Eve.
But Adam, God forbid! We cannot eat!

Adam.
I say, hand me the fruit, and I shall eat!
And if you love me, you will heed my word!

Eve.
I do not think this wise. Why ought we taste
Of evil? Here we know sufficiently
The good, and certainly in concept know
The wrong; then let it stay conceptual!
Disaster does not need to be explored.

Adam.
But aren't you curious? The snake has said
That many wonders wait, and what a lie
Forbiddings be: a world is held from us!

Eve.
A world of woe. Just follow it a bit
Within your mind, you cannot help but see
The consequences end in misery.
This bower is a better world than that.

Adam.
A nursery and gaol, when better waits!
The serpent asks what evil is, what good.
Is good not then to follow out what speaks
Within us? Who forbids but one who hates?
There's so much to explore if we will taste!

Eve.
I love you with the all of me, and yet
You ask of me to follow you to rue.
What then emerges from that darkened wreck?
Do we, exposed to treachery within,
Retain ability to really love?

Adam.
I do not ask but I demand of you.
Prove you your love and render up the fruit!

Eve.
Alone with great reluctance I shall yield,
Still wary that we enter barren fields.

Adam.
No longer is imagination caged!
Now anything at all is doable!
How great we might become with fetters off
Astounds me! Error is a fertile field.
It leads to new invention. We shall rise
Above divinities, and hold the earth
In gripping claws and make it ours alone.
Who needs the strict commands of one above?
Let us decide what's right and what is wrong,
Allowing what we want to be our guide.

Eve.
But Adam, look upon horizons! Steps
Almighty feet down here to our domain!

Adam.
We must retreat! He comes to murder us!
Quick, put these leaves upon our limbs of lust!

Jehovah.
Adam, where are you? Why secrete yourself
From open truth? Did you not heed my rede,
And to your sure disaster, eat that fruit?
I told you it was madness to consume!

Adam.
The woman, Lord, coerced my hand to eat.
I would not think of it but she prevailed.
I begged her to desist, but she imposed!
What could I do? I cannot lose her love!

Jehovah.
And even now the venom of the fruit
Speaks lies from lips just lately your own truth.
You think it liberty to throw off rede,
And tyranny to follow sound advice?
Go then! Remove yourself and find what world
Lies yonder wise restraint and temperance!
See what unfolds! Now you will know the good
Recedingly in keenly growing wist,
But evil know by hard experience
Each day: the tree is faithful to its name.
See if you know what's better and what's worse
Than Wisdom spoke to you in syllables
Of love. This Garden is her earthly flesh;
How oft, my children, will you yearn for her!
I weep for you as you decide your fate,
And make the lesser, worser choice of all.
That you would trust delight, and innocence!
Yet that seems too naive to you as now,
The poison seeps so terribly in you.
This cynicism now will dog your days,
While poets shall compose pastoral verse
In pangs of sharp nostalgia for these days,
And being your descendants, curse your choice,
Wishing the gates of Eden opened still.
Come horrors now, but welcome them to breast;
You did invite, and you yourself will see.
Trust not that serpent to your mastery.
It oversteps its bounds of holiness.

You will discover to your shock and woe.
Farewell, farewell, beloveds, precious fools;
Farewell to you we loved so dear in heart.

struggling to emerge from a latrine

We're struggling to emerge from a latrine,
A foul melange of wreck and turmoil.
Within which otherwise amazing men
Committed wrongs in their confusions, and
Assumed their own desires were enough
To justify most anything at all,
Incensed at any barrier to lust,
Proclaiming tyranny at any bar
That might inhibit their own energies.
To be a rebel for the sake of life
Is laudable, but for the sake of lust
Devoid of any personable love
That takes regard of highest good of each
Is scoundrel territory; there we are.

unclassifiable

I want to live as if I were a ghost,
A spirit, soaring on my downy wings,
Aloft, aloof, unleashed, in love with wind
And open space, no set identity,
A thousand names, no one to pin me down
To this or that, but free in multiplicity
Of me, a smorgasbord of varied moods.
Dead to society's requirements,
To slip between the boundaries and times,
To be unclassifiable and drift,
To row my boat and live as if a dream.

wrath in spasm ate at me

Too often I was tortured by sad thoughts
Ill-fitting to my charity and peace,
As if some monster seized my imagery
And made me cringe at violent ponderings
I neither wanted nor reflected me,
But frightened me as if I were a curse
To everyone, and made me fear myself.
The joy and peace that once lived in my soul,
Have they now soured in me, sorrowful
And ruined by too many hopes disturbed,
Or are they there still yet, beneath my thoughts?
Let me be other than this turmoil's son.
I got too angry at injustices.
I wished the very worst on evil men,
And wrath in spasm ate at me inside.
Has that crazed maelstrom, furious at harms
To innocents, lost me to vertigo?
Where am I, but a flotsam to this rage,
Shell-shocked and beaten badly, in defense
Of injured ones? Can I escape this cage
Of thrashing impulses that I've become?
That now lash out inside my mind at all?
What bedlam is this hard absurdity?
Do I have some allotment of true peace?
Send it, I beg, and let serenity
Be answer in my kindness to such wrongs
That I abhor, consoling injuries
With visions of the kingdom yet to come,
A kingdom all of love yonder all wrath,
Where joy is so resplendent, who resents?
Who has the time to punish iniquity
Long past, dissolving shade in happiness?
Let joy then heal the violent; overwhelm
With love that cannot be refused or stopped.

the country lost its flippin mind

The years the country lost its flippin mind

And lunatics commanded government,
As if the Joker was in charge of all,
The biggest mindfuck of our sordid lives,
The most pathetic spiral-down of time.
I've never felt so beat up in four years.
My spirit limps with scars. We're all abused.
Not citizens, but battered wives, us all.

a sacred shrine to self

Some people you will only get one chance
To enter what amazing world they hold,
Which if you blow, it's gone forever now,
And you could be consumed by your regret.
Most people live so roughly, riding through,
But some have made a sacred shrine to self,
Where faerie lives in specialness affirmed,
A fragile web so delicate and pure;
And for their sheer audacity to host
The genius of their birth, they carry wealth
In charm beyond the reckoning of fools.
Foolish themselves, but very careful with
The sacredness of beauty's heirloom gems,
Wherein the souvenirs of wonderment
Inhabit memory-space, they steward awe
Like priestesses no one appointed but
The wooed and swooning Muses they adore.
Their life is light, meticulous worthing
Of everything which ever brought them awe,
Surrounding them in turn with breathlessness,
And evanescent hint of Aphrodite.
Wisdom of the nimble trust they hold,
Awarded by the fairies for their faith
In gasping preciousness most denigrate,
And making self exquisite, where judgement
Might falsely judge a narcissistic waif,
But hold the rarest worth: to value self.
Not as an undeveloped thing enclosed,
But all the gifts that fortune has endowed
Brought to their blossom, beauty proud affirmed,
Facilitated fay-custodianne,
Exuding aromatically what grace

Is now the native to them. For to dare
Inspires admiration from above,
And from below in webbed nooks of gnomes.
So few treasure the temple implements
Entrusted in the texture of their soul,
(The most trampling into forgotten dirt),
That those who find a way to consecrate
These jewels of unrepeatable beauty,
And holding them as holy sacraments
They let no careless lout e'er desecrate,
Are deemed as special ones, agents of grace,
Appointed delicacy-hostesses.
Their quirky scarcity is pomegranate
Seed in brandish surrounding us.
But if you lose their charm and start to waste
Away in wist, become a votary,
As they are, to the wonder given gift
To you, and live your life a precious shrine
No one but faith and boldness authorized.
In time, devotion shall collect and bless,
If you allow no one profane the shrine,
And you will float angelic through such bliss
Few contemplate or think their lot on earth.
It's all in fond allegiance that you show
To moments creme le creme that ne'er repeat,
Without permission valuing their worth,
Making a silken tabernacle shrine
Where you reside and ever where you go,
To play the host to finicky and shy,
Exquisite fairy-spirits, so they feel
At home about you. Caution: cruelties
And ugliness abhor them. They require
Sanctuaries of serenity,
A heart of harmony and dearest faith,
Belief in odd improbabilities,
And ne'er-be-care of what normals might think,
But sheltering in cozy, kindly weird.
And never throw your pearls to any swine.
That is the way to drink their faerie wine.

your sweetest joy is mine
for Elizabeth of Night

If I could eat this cake through your mouth's joy
And feed on the delight within your eyes,
My own sad deprivation of all cake
Might soothe a little watching you enjoy.
For in that frosting-frillery of glee,
I would remember all the taste of cream,
And rolling texture of its honeysweet
On cake-delirious tongue-ecstasy.
To almost feel its flavor in your smile,
And commune your satisfaction's gulp
Could be an amorous and consummate
Sensation. For your sweetest joy is mine.

heirloom's gallery

The way to worth your soul is *pietas*,
To honor every precious moment given,
Not allowing memory to fade,
But giving shrine to miracle and awe.
Not asking questions, but wherever grace
Touched down on earth, marking with reverence,
And gifting names to spirits of one's life,
The animating courages and depths.
Agnostic, open, spiritual, and free,
A welcoming of ecstasy and worth,
Intrepid, gallant, bold in speaking up
For justice of the heart, and noticing,
Just noticing the artistries about,
In sunsets, mountains, waters, woods, and glades.
And never desecrating wonder's shrines,
But giving honor in commemorate
Devotion to the ones who blessed one's life.
Such sentimentality is frowned upon
By modern cynics; let them keep their frowns,
And bound instead in meadows of delight.
The proof's in pleasure which is innocent.
It needs no evidence but gasp and sigh.
Doubt is the enemy -- it always is;

Question with freedom and with plumbing depth,
To honor marvel, open forth its charms,
But keep your sour disappointments chained.
Feed them; ferment them; make them into ale,
And barrel them to giddiness and froth.
But they are dogs, and dogs do not belong
In fanes, nor dirty paws on precious gems.
The cleverness of doubters is disgrace.
They never will enjoy the temple's charms.
The soul is underground in winding mines
Where geodes hide in earthy corridors,
And blend with textures of adventures' touch.
Where soul is, there is heirloom's gallery.
If some consider that idolatry,
They're fools, and empty vessels of contempt.
The soul acknowledges its many friends.
It never will cavil at honoring worth,
Whatever its odd origin may be,
And leaves debates on multiplicity
And unity to dull theologians.
It trusts its fonts of poignancy and depth,
Agnostically, without concern for name;
The simple blessing is its evidence.

allow no goblins to reside

Do not allow the goblins in your fanes.
Do not invite them with what media
Through which they would invade, for ugliness
Is everywhere, and sloppy carelessness
Ubiquitous and always has been. So?
Tend on your garden; that is duty's due.
Do not permit the vulgar ruffians
To smuggle bullying within your shrine;
Close up the curtains; light incense again,
And let the fools of carelessness abide
Brutalities of passing history.
It's none of your concern. At all. At all.
If you would speak your prophecies abroad,
To light where worth and worthlessness reside,
Excurse outside, but do not desecrate
The temple; peace is not negotiable

Within. Without, speak words of justice, judge
With fairness and with principle and truth.
Within, allow no goblins to reside.

I could be bubblegum

I could be bubblegum, if you would chew
And blow me big balloon to aqua skies.
I'd be so pink and mastic, aromatic,
Chaw fanatic, so pastel emphatic,
Sassy democratic, so Chagall,
With Jewish figurines floating through clouds,
With wedding veils and donkeys through the fog.
I'd ride polished menorahs through the air
Alike a Yiddish witch and stitch my stockings
Striped, and do the hora 'neath the moon,
While mumble-chanting Messianic psalms,
And live delirious in mystic dreams.
I'd ghost through waltzing wind so shabby-chic,
Sashaying watercolor ocean blue
Through snow-confetti you, accordion
And maple fiddle, griddle hotcake high,
With grinning fauns on floating flutes, and mutes
In mime, and buck toothed carrot heads in rhyme.
I'd serenade the schretels in their shrines
Of cardboard painted dainty with white lace,
And feel ecstatic expectation's dawn
In nippy night of cherry-frosting air.
I'd be the drifting jellyfish of zephyrs,
River-ribald rush of atmosphere
And weather-wist, a gist of flavor-burst
Of fruit immersed in berry mist, a lute
With wings that sings of wine and troubled time.
I'd limey up my feather-boned corsair
Of drifting ship, and whip the cotton-clouds
My sails against horizon's rosy lips,
And puppet show my paper soul with kites
And candy, Tristam Shandy's oddities
And vegan cheese, with purple tights, and bees
That buzz against kazoo of waxen sky.
Unwrap me, read my comic book, and chew.
Adventures wait in fantasies of you.

a scar I caress in lieu of you

You stand within the circle of my shrine,
And shine, though twenty years have almost passed.
I wonder, do you know how held you are
In starkest honor and in beauty far,
So very far, beyond all else?
I knew you in your freshest womanhood,
The girl still peeling from your molted bark;
But now you are some fairy soul so high
I can't the bottom of the pedestal
Quite reach! You are a noble elfin queen
Too high for me, too evidently high:
You will not speak to me, though I adore.
This love I have is friendship left in dust;
If only you could know how loved you are,
Bone of my bone, flesh of my history's flesh.
I so revere your every memory,
I can't imagine life without your touch.
Not fingers, though were soft, but your elan.
If you had never walked into my life
(Though clumsy you but stumbled in, I laugh),
Where would I be? Who would I be right now?
Some seelie godmother bestowed on me
A splendor seldom other than the angels
Taste -- a little spark of untold charm
The ages steeped in vintage dripped in you
No doubt since childhood. And I have lived
In ages when the gods still walked the earth.
You shattered me, and savored my sweet yolk.
I showed myself as never I have shown,
Complete of me in spirit's nakedness;
My beating heart pulsed in your youthsome hand.
It's not the pain, but mystery of you
That drew me, though you hurt me to the quick;
But that was nothing when you laughed -- all ice
Was thaw in giggling streams, and cloud noir
Wiped clean by sunshine's hand, and brindle straw
Came greenest grass of April. I was done
When you were done with me, so overwhelmed
With emptiness, I hobbled years in search
Of me, to find my way back to the track.
You left me stunned, in love and out of it.

Our love was fatal, and it left a scar
On me I so caress in lieu of you;
The rest is encore, and the accolades
Over the years in many bosoms speak
Of resurrection: I have lived such weight,
And Peter Pan's own levity, of life!
I've earned each wrinkle on this ponderous brow;
The years have made of me an aged oak.
I've much to take my pride in. But the prize,
My dear, the frosting on the cake, was you.
And given all the richness of that loaf,
The sheer garden of blooming flesh I've frolicked
In, the geniuses of beauty and
Of charm, but multiply the wonder, you
Ought truly feel the honor of my words.
I wish that you could peer into the eyes
Of all those smart and gorgeous paramours
I've had, creme of le creme, the choice of men,
The envy of all eyes around, for you,
In awe would truly feel homage I give.
And you would see the genii in my chest
Who first enchanted you has sung the spell
Anew, and woven such bewitchments, you
Would gasp! And taken the adventures far!
Oh, it's been hard, but less than marvelous
It's never been. I couldn't take of now
The sheer intensity of us in prime;
I like my soul unshredded, and intact.
For age has brought the luxury of bark
To these still-blossoming oak boughs, and I
Can rest within my calluses and dream.
Still what confection for to reminisce;
It is your conversation that I miss.

my paramours, the angels

O blessed serial monogamy!
I've had a glorious career of you!
Let me open my grand portfolio,
And show the greatest artistries I've made,
Those rich relationships of which I'm proud!
So proud, beyond all else : I've built a fine

Profession of exquisite romance, on
Foundations firm of friendship true and deep.
It is the conversation of our minds
That deepen hearts in curiosity.
It's true, I gravitate to beauties; still,
They had to whir and whip up cream above --
And it was that companionship I craved.
Each one, unique; each carved a masterpiece
With serious attention and with care.
Some day when I am welcomed into love,
But love itself, and set this body down,
I most expect to see my paramours,
The angels, welcoming me to that bliss
Which blots all consciousness in consummate
Reunion: but the light, and total love.

symphony of noise and beauty
for Ira Behr

She left. She was a symphony of noise
And beauty, and was gone. I sat noir
In cold and stony halls where shadows gulped
The scarcer light, my head in hands on lap,
And in the arid dim, moistness on palms.
The emptiness had introduced itself
In multitudes of spectres and regret.
Night was an endless longitude so bleak,
I sat and stared, and hoped the renaissance
Would summon to my hall and knock the door,
Perhaps some buxom floritude bouquet
In corset and full bustier, her grin
An offering of playful ample flesh,
But wind just whispered while coyotes howled,
And no one came. I sat and watched this show,
Set in deep space, a lonely outpost, far
From anywhere, just like my grieving heart.
And in the bitter solitude, it soothed.
Still sentenced to this monastery, faces
Came and smiled eyes familiar,
What archetypes of honor and of depth,
And lived me where the life should have abode,
But gravel slushed in dirty ice on knives.

How gently they removed those rusty knives,
And set the kettle on for honeyed tea,
And sat with me those years as I got through.
But lines of ink set out on simple scrolls
And read by orators, but they were kin,
They were such friends, who kept me company.
I had a rush of mythic life with her,
Where now was numb, but they brought me the myth
To poultice in the wound and heal the scars.
Where I had lost the vision, they brought theirs.
I think those people loved me very much,
Those writers, actors, and producers -- oh,
They didn't know my name; they knew my soul.
They made it for the every me there was,
In any form, who sat in empty rooms
And asked divinity impossible
Inquiries, and they dramatized the angst,
And someone knew. The human heart still lived,
Even if still anesthetized in me.
Where yet I was but embers, they brought flame.

a thousand terrible distractions

Pursue with singular fanaticism
All that brings you wonder. Though the world
May think you crazed or silly, go ahead.
The dividends, though not immediate,
Far from direct, often elusive, still
Will come. Where awe meets you, there God calls you.
You have no duty greater than this one,
And for its seeming ease, one most avoid.
It is the harder path to follow bliss.
Guilt bars the way and onus shuts the gate,
Then seriousness completes the wretched job.
But druthers are the Holy Spirit's voice,
Be they however strange or full of quirks,
Some path has its integrity for you.
A thousand terrible distractions wait
To soothe or spook you from your wonderment,
And chain you to the muddle in your soul,
That undeveloped place where nothing grows.
But works of wonder are your garden's seeds

From where your everything may flourish full.
It's subtle, odd, and low, but heed that pull.

the glass of placid Taedong

Blushing sun's descent to kiss the glass
Of placid Taedong. Fireworks of sparks
Rain on the river from the city's lights,
As tender-hearted murk of cooling eve
Embraces all. Curvaceous glide so smooth
But snakes the northern citadel with ice
Serenely rushing silver serenade
In cream magnolia as night deepens,
Distributing its welcome sighs to all.

my nightingale
for Elizabeth of Night

The fingers of my lover are divine,
And trace the traceries of breath and soul
On skin devout and listening. Her hands
Be-wing me, lifting me to heaven's heights,
And swirling me in cloudscapes where I drift.
She peels all disappointments from my flesh,
And helps me to believe in trust again.
She sings philosophies upon my back,
My nightingale -- her skin is heavenly,
And hums discourse that all will be ok.

song is the connubium of us

As freely as the air with wind doth breed
The zephyrs, so we intermix delight,
And soul to soul in rapturous embrace
Taste of each other delicacy's scents,
Exchange of pure aromas blent with love,

And where in ecstasy our given joy,
Native to each, expanded in the seek
We all pursue, comes forth as flavorful
Communion. All of this but in the breath,
For song is the connubium of us,
Ensemble of devotion that adores
In mutual adore that rises up
In highest praise. In harmonies we merge
In ways your clumsy bones and nerves can't know
In their approximate colliding: we
Are chime within the rhyme exultingly
In seraph psalm. What jealousy therein,
When everyone included in the song,
The sounding of our orchestra our love?
If two by two the creatures of the earth
Contend, we are instead a choirfold,
Polyphony of essence in one hymn.
In contrapunt's ebullience we ride
On swift crescendos through the fugue of us,
As fog throughout itself in cloudy swarm
Is intermixed -- thus one by one is touched
In labyrinthine dance philemically,
With but a blow of fragrant, flirty breath.
Our notes, where they may glide with assonance,
In interweaving union, this we feel
With all of us the each in its entire.
Similarly verse but permeates
Us to the threshold of delicious quick.
In such is smiling amity and joy.
What more than this when all else is but less?
For we caress no less than the divine,
For praise is but caress, and in that praise,
We each share in caress given by all.
Thus we are ever in each other's praise,
Cosignatories to that highest psalm
We ever in its variance shall sing.
What more in love than souls in symphony?
Your bodies are your flesh, but ours are song.

pick up a gun

We might as well pick up a gun

When we set mind to friendships shun,
For what is worse upon the earth
Than friends to say I have no worth?

just the pigs they are

But Circe only recognizes men
As just the pigs they are, and only brings
The truth to fore; who would then wallow in
The mud has little cause to her complain.
If one would let the hog inside squelch out
All spirit, mind, and beauty for mere food
And rutting raunch, how can one then complain?
Receive the body true to your own heart!
Enjoyment never is anathema,
But stomping the celestial in mud
Is ever sin; to drool and foully ooze
Upon the sacred for to make it crass,
To render it as dirty as yourself,
You're truly better than such envious crime,
And from your own suppressed nobility
May thus be summoned for to answer sin.
The noble man on Circe's island walks
Upright and free; the vulgar come to pigs,
And with a righteousness sole to be praised.

the bed became a town of ghosts

You left -- the bed became a town of ghosts --
I wisted for you, longing in my thews
For your extravagant and needed touch.
I dreamt you next to me, my warren-hare,
Curled up and cozy, yet your absence ached
Despite my dreaming, so I had adore
A distance, and content with kisses pale.

Flamingo
for Francesca

Flamingo are her bones, and feather-grass
Her wings; her skin, soft river silt and clay.
Her legs of hollow reed stilt in the murk,
Cloud-shadow pinions hovering above
The wetland mist. She seeks the saccharine
Of burdock sap to candy sip from straws,
And dreams of tart and sweet raspberry jam.
She saunters in the saline shallows, wash
Of inlet sea, surveying ripple play,
As light is wink and twinkle on its skein,
And afternoon gives shadows their command.
The wind, combing the droplets from the reeds,
Lends mimic of a drizzle in the shade
From lazy drifting fronts of fog above.
Then her exquisite beak spins gossamer
From dusty webs in bunchgrass thicket stands,
And from such strands, luxuriant, fine lace
She wraps a silken gauze about herself.
Whence in a language made of chimes and pipes
Only the thin-boned tufted creatures speak,
She tells such tales the water-babies thrill,
Enchanting with a mode of melody
Foreign and underwater peoples sing.
The waves are turning pages of her book.
In them, her eyes discern secret romance
And heartbreak, fables from the eerie depths,
Mudbottom gentlemen with paramours,
Their bodies inky-creamy in the drift.
She trills the catfish tragedies and lays,
And loons the picaresques of crawdaddies,
While lady trout, their handkerchiefs to eyes,
Wipe moisture from their lashes, lounging on
The junco-grass, unwrapping toffee rolls
And popping them in pouting cherry mouths.
The water-spiders skim and trace in swirls
Translations of the tales to gestural
Extravagance and graceful mimeries.
The wetland shamaness, mantled in down
Of herons and of mallards, carrying
Her pewter apple-branch with golden bells
She tinkles on the lotuses, sets out

A vial for donations: add your tears;
She'll drink them and transform them into rhyme
And fancy; watch your muted passions sing.
At last she lifts the silence from the sorrow.
Thunderclaps applaud, encoring rain.

the priceless value of his work

Haephestus must come out of his metal shop,
And gallery his precious jewelry,
Where all can awe in their great majesty,
And sheer sublimity of preciousness.
It's clear the hammer on materials
Draws him the most, but being secretive,
None know the priceless value of his work.

an elfin breath that swift enchants

The clouds have scent of sycamore and mint,
For fog clothes all the trees in its embrace,
And carries in its turbid zephyrs hints
From essences of bark and leaf and fleur.
Fog makes a Santa Cruz of anywhere,
And carries in metonymy the woods,
With all their elven sylvanries and pluck.
Fog is an elfin breath that swift enchants,
And rides its doldrums with a regal charm.
Gnomes whisper secrets in my ears in fog,
The traces of their herbal wizardries
And mineral researches in the deep,
Their libraries on air in fragrances
The poet reads with Druid clarity.

children of the zephyrs

Give then this flesh to clouds to clothe and keep,
To seep amidst the other foggy souls,
And in the freedom of the soaring air,
To frolic carefree in the gaseous flock,
A creature of our wonders not our frets.
What loops and flips and streaming through the skies,
Our interpenetrating essences
Commune, in awe and joy beyond the mind,
What things of levity alone, we leave
Behind our mortal gravity, and drift,
In bliss and nonchalance, as once in seas,
Before the Cambrian, the ocean sponges
Did in sway serene! What blessed boon!
No cogitation save alone of awe,
A wondrous stupor void of reckoning,
No strategies, no worries, no concerns,
But unbound play released from debt to time!
Simplicity of sheep in fleece of fog,
Etherium the meadow of our bounding,
Sheets of unseen linen swirling free,
The breath battalions oblivious
Of boisterous breeze! The eager puppies mist
Has made! Our gamboling at last released
From burdens of the aching flesh and mind,
New children of the zephyrs! Cherubim!
An endless infancy none can impede!
The mammary expanse of milky skies!
An innocence expecting fresh surprise.

thirsty for the open sea

Dissolve me in an omnipresent Love,
Nothing but love, but pure, unseparate,
But reabsorbed forever in the All,
The raindrop thirsty for the open sea.

gizzard breweries

My organs read as I read and partake
My thoughts according to their energies,
And in my gizzard breweries they dream.

no patience for wasted work

How quickly actions neutralize in time!
Their efforts most erased, they lie in tombs,
Frustrated, buried. Most colossal works
Within a span of decades all decay,
With remnants of their edifice in ruin.
Why should I then turbinate my peace
With fruitless hustling and uncertainties?
Why plant a garden others may tramp down?
I have no patience for such wasted work.
I know the temperament of this my time,
The faithlessness of people, and the odds.
Explaining sculpture to such ruffians
And vandals is a thankless, punished task,
And I have no such liking for more pain.
The time is rotten nor is ripe but wilts.
The best thing is to compost dung to soil.
This I do in hermitage away
From all unprofitable bustle. That
Is not a sacrifice that wastes but waste.
The theory is all putrefied and rent;
From there, regeneration promises.
Examples are but weeds; I seek the roots.
There is no day at all for us to seize,
But night to dream, and cast our wondrous spells.

council of the gods

Then robed in linen wrap lined all with gold,
Unfurling in Olympus' Aeolus,

Zeus delegated Themis to the call,
To summon to his council all the gods.
She thither went but everywhere about,
Crept into every warren and each lair;
Lit here on marble-polished fane, touched there
In vine-entwined haunts of hidden woods,
Alighted on the friendly-feathered fog,
And skimmed with skiffing feet the frolicked seas.
She slithered into labyrinthine grooves
Where in the excavated earth, fresh gems
Were wombed from magma slowly cooled by breath.
She skipped above the meadow-flower fields,
The scent of fennel, bronze of goldenrod,
And snuck through wild waving walls of weeds,
Wherein some slender shrine of polished pine
Drew forth the denizens of hill and field,
As everywhere her banner ran in breeze.
She sang to every rank in all the host,
From highest of the high to low of low.
She welcomed all the ripple skinned maids
Who ride the rivers' vapors as they steam,
And saddle dragonflies in flurries' flight;
All then the brooks and streams and tributaries,
Old arroyos, younger rivulets;
The Rhone, the Rhine, the Seine, the Mississip,
The Tiber and the Thames, the Volga, Congo,
Nile, Yangzi, Amazon, and more,
Respected dignitaries of the rills,
Beloved venerables of local plains
And regional expanses, honored all,
And eager in excitement to ascend
To their confederated capitol
That floated on a sea of sparkling stars.
These gentry from the Ozarks of the world
Were cinnamon and spritzer to abide
The Paris of the starry mountaintops,
Except the oceans, who kept to their beds
As duty to the mermaids and their fish.
But not a nymph from glade or rocky springs,
Nor grottoes' shade of mist-wisterias,
Nor gnome from under hill in beds of clay,
Nor moth-winged silken sheer of airy sylph,
Nor flamed efreet of fiery countenance
Was absent. All ascended elegant
On spiral stairwells carved within the rock

And lined with winding rails of ivory
Ringed round with silver etched La Tene with runes,
Until the airy arbor of the clouds
They bowed their chaplet-covered heads to bend,
And on the ramparts of the Milky Way
Gave billow to their bottoms on carved seats
Of webbed limestone tracery and gold.
Hephaestus proudly nodded at this craft
His hands had fostered from the elements.
Whence all excited hubbub came to hush,
When the Olympians assembled on
Their thrones, followed august by noble Zeus,
Commanding awe from but his presence. Pause
In silent stillness breath -- and then commenced.

lantern-lucent on my blessed bed
for Elizabeth of Night

What beauty bred from bowers of the stars
Lays down her morning glory flesh so silk
And lantern-lucent on my blessed bed?
What tender frame of roses' fame alights
Like gossamer and fragrance on my skin?
They made you in the heavens from what fleurs
They vine from dangled limestone cliffs in air,
And wove from petals this exquisite down
You call mahogany your satin skin,
Now didn't they? I see, and what a gift,
Priceless, unparalleled, the gods have given!

filet mignon of his nobility

He let his wrath become the most of him,
Encroaching steadily, until it ate
Away at all that was his very best.
That to his rage was most delicious meal,
Filet mignon of his nobility,
Until a heart of hollowness he was.
That wrath began with outraged righteousness,

Incensed at the injustices and wounds
The world inflicts. As he indulged, it grew.
It roused him and he felt expanded, high,
The very mouthpiece retribution spoke.
He gave it no resistance but full sway,
Inviting it to colonize his mind,
And counted it a virtue to feel hate;
He was a champion who it befit.
One day he woke to find his love was fled,
His insides ash and ruin doused in smoke.
His wrath was all for reasons of the right,
And yet it left him cold in empty night.

fond allures

Caesar.
Good discipline is one thing; a straitjacket's
Another. One must have his fond allures,
Whomever they offend. The anima
Goes where she wills, and where she wills, we draw.
We ask her not her reason nor her rhyme.
She follows what intrigues her. That's her charm.
There's only so far one can give restraint.
One must have one's indulgences in life
To feel alive, one's vital fantasies,
However they upset an ordered plan.
You may ask of us basic decency.
A further yoke you may not ever ask,
For mind and heart and curiosity
Are ever free, and we have our intrigues
We need at least investigate afar,
A fond flirtation from the barrister,
Where we stand proud and noble in restraint,
Yet dream. That is allowance none may ask
Deprived of us, for life is never smooth,
Never ideal; we make the best bet we
Can make, yet what remains has need as well.
Sometimes a hidden loneliness untouched
By who we'd will awakes at stranger's sight;
Perhaps forlornity of fathoms' eyes,
Secret enchantment most unfathomable.
That wakened, aching babe looks on, allured:

Are you the one who might so precious hold
This little pricelessness no one yet knows?
Are you the cradle that accepts the dream
That lives in darkness deep inside my breast?
I have so many pockets in my soul,
Where I had need to cubby sacred parts
Away from burning touch; that is my truth.
I hid them in the hollows of my heart,
In mercy of the quiet dark within.
There sleep, my inaccessible beloveds,
Whom I needed know they would be safe.
Sometimes they see in mimesis themselves
In shyness of a melancholy pout,
In pity that a beauty lends herself,
In all voluptuousness of pure charm,
And wish. They wish. Am I to stop their wish?
Who am I, that I might restrain them so?
For duty? Where was duty when they hid?
For decency? Where was that decency
When all melodic love was in its tears?
No no, there's only so far I can go.
I must allow these little ones to grow.

fond and yet forlorn

He who inseminated womb of dreams,
Bereft of me, with now my belly full,
On precious dawn of my delivery.
Whose sharp, mischievous eyes of playful depth
Would love the beauty that he childed
On me is far in darkness I can't see,
And so I gestate fond and yet forlorn.
The melancholy where the joy is born.

let the puritans complain

It's said it's pitiful for puppy eyes
To linger from a man already grown
At what has youth as yet with longing lure.

I have no part with such inhuman things,
That would condemn someone who but adores,
And misses something precious from his past.
We may not touch but we may always look,
For flesh sometimes has soul within its folds
A fresh adult just on the dawn of noon
May waken. Let the puritans complain.

no Mother Earth, no true theology

No Mother Earth, no true theology.
No fairies of the pasture and the glade,
No elfin hermitage in vine and leaf,
The children of her utter joy, no truth.
No honor for the Sun or for the Moon,
No mention of the Winds or of the Seas,
As worthy if subordinate nobles,
No fond allegiance from me and mine.
If forests have not nymphs and gentle fauns,
If gnomes do not peek out the rabbit holes,
If sylphs alike translucent butterflies
Do not sashay the hovered breeze in surf,
My soul cannot abide your arid world.
That Who in grandeur over all of these,
Though powerful, is kind, whose heart is good,
Demanding justice, hating slavery,
Encouraging communion, amity,
And charity, aligns with right o'er wrong
(Though as defined from more majestic heights,
Whose full priorities we do not know),
Makes sense, it sits well with my loving heart;
And that such high benevolence now plans
Rejuvenations of this world the Spring
Can only harbinge with its flowerings,
I trust; and that this vision has been sent
To many prophets over many lands
Diversely, each according to their views,
I reckon; but that all this earth's devoid
Of loving, holy Elohim replete
But everywhere, allied with the Most High,

Is a damned lie, as the attempts to smear
Them all as demons, that's another lie.
And my authority? My heart, my friends,
My heart. Call these the gentle fondlings
Of God's caresses in my tender soul
Beholding all of nature's majesties,
Each of the which in my delight I name,
And let their charm have personality
And flavor -- it is all the same to me.
If I'm a person, and I seem to be,
Be certain all these beauties are as well.
In fact, they person me their qualities,
And make the possible of joyful life.
Ingratitude in such is sacrilege.

I was made for old guild workshops

I owe my soul and spirit to Suger,
Who opened my interior to light,
And made a Paris of my wonderment,
That I might stroll flaneur along the Seine
Within my child mind with Madeline.
Hector Guimard's infernal libellules
That lead to labyrinths where midnight lives
Spellbind me in new infancy of eyes,
And from the muddled philistineries
Of Cowboyland's ennui deliver me
To times when craftsmanship was still adored.
I'm utterly displaced, for I was made
For old guild workshops where the masterpiece
Is laid, and nothing less than breathless will
Suffice! I live amidst admirers
Of grunts and crotch-grabs; I'm trapped in saloons
Where chewing chaw into spittoons is grace,
And gutter belly-skimmers joy to scoff
At any high-falutin elegance,
Where greater skill is greater the disdain.
So faithless to the filid faerie-smiths
Who understand that beauty's of the sidhe,
And once to taste, forever else is bland.

What's hymnody to morlocks in their lairs?
Why sculpture glass amidst a herd of bulls?
What use have oafs for sheer clerestory?
I am a turncoat waiting for my turn:
I'd flip these dullards in a half a glance
For real collaboration and a chance.

a Grecian tholos

To my most dear Francesca Lia Block,
Married a season, sole eternity
We had -- where all of life's fragility
Was perfect in its precious poignancy,
And the Shekinah seemed -- I do not lie --
To grace our missives with plasmatic prayer,
That blossomed as a nebula of flame,
Dissolving like a rain of powdered sugar
On our struck-in-wonder child tongues.
It was a season of a spell, what charm
A life never imagined it might taste,
Transported to an Irish-Yiddish realm
Where meydl-mariposa queens of fog
Composed enchantments made of nought but light,
The chiming of the dazzlements of dawn.
It was some nervous, fond impossibility,
So hyperreal each second -- I
Was rapt, was absolutely captured, caught
In webs of wondering cantrips, so engrossed
My life found teetering pinnacle of praise;
If seraphim whisper in pillow-talk
Amidst photonic Notre Dame on clouds,
They lent us then that language so adored,
For we were ever in discovery,
Each moment fresh, on threshold of surprise,
In fond devotion fed by laughter's springs,
And Easter was our every flirting wink.
Until it simply -- oh my God, oh no --
It simply disappeared, the all of it,
The portal to that incantantory
Domain -- it vanished, folded up -- since then,
Despite my literary loyalties,
My fond oblations in my best of verse,

No single word you've spoken, though I've done
No harm; in fact, I've tended this your shrine,
And polished it to smooth and marble sheen,
A Grecian tholos colonnaded white
By lakeside willows, rained upon by leaves
Of Autumn gold and saffron marked with dew.
And now you are my Emperor Augustus,
Leaving me to Scythian milkmaids.
I've galavanted with the cherubim
In shoji sky-pagodas hewed from light,
The likes of which Suger would salivate,
Swan Lakes of cavalier sashay and twirl.
I've translated my molecules to pure
Delight, subsisting on ambrosia's rhyme,
The sound of breath and sibilance, my toes
En pointe on rippling raptures! How can I
Subsist on peasant gruel in backwoods barns?
I've casually brushed elbows with the chefs
From near-celestial domains, where taste
Begins with the exquisite, and goes up
From there, where what desserts our royalty
Treasures are but the juvenile pranks
Of amateurs, a laughing snort's disdain.
I've tap-danced on the echoes of the dew
Before it has alighted on the grass,
And dosidoed with satyrs in the woods
To compositions of their panpiped joys;
Built me a harpsichord of different tones
Of ecstasy and played Chopin til dawn.
But now you say, well well, make do with dung,
And roll in it, and make your poetry
From annals of your deprivation's pangs,
I could not care! I shall not ever care!
Were you to send confections of the djinn,
The chocolates of delirious Rimbaud,
The lattes hummingbirds brewed sweet from clouds,
I wouldn't stop to deign to give it thought!
Come sit with me on edge of heaven's rim,
Now kiss your welcome to my ruthless boot,
And mind you not to crawl to heaven's gates;
I hold the keys, and you're non grata, lad,
A nobody, whose talent shall be smudged
Sarmatian in the mud, snuffed out in ash!
Now tell me, lady, is that piety
To all we shared? You know that it is not.

I never met a fickleness I liked.
When I am charmed, I show my loyalty.
You spit at beauty when you spit at me.

too flowery for you? go fuck yourself

My tender need for loveliness is real.
The desert schizoid of the Spartan heart,
The devil of the arid dunes, resents
What lush adornment, rosebuds in their splay,
Their open ruffled lips in seeking dew,
I need, the ointment beauty brings my wounds.
It's all "effeminacy"! I do claim
And clasp such to my breast as stuff of right;
I will not be divided from its soothe.
If that is too effete, then vulgar friend,
You are barbarian: taste my contempt.
Your head is meat and will not understand.
I long seceded from your shriveled state,
And gave allegiance to Aphrodite,
She who loves elaborate jewelry
And lush aesthetics. No materials
I need but rudiments of flowery verse.
Too flowery for you? Go fuck yourself.
You starve yourself of most exquisite things,
And think that desiccation virtue. Bah!
What melts me from within receives my vote,
What most endows the greatest gift, of tears,
That benediction of the very gods.
I fight for chivalry, for tenderness.
The warrior that's lost his heart is vain.
Who fights for less than love's a murderer.
I fight for the most precious right a man
May have, the right to femininity,
More native to our souls, more artifact
Of us, projection of our anima
(Let women be the persons that they are;
They can't always be mysteries we need) --
I claim it back, I take the treasure back.
I say it's manly to be feminine,

To almost swoon at gorgeous poetry,
To gawk at sunsets as we joy a maid,
To take our pride as gardeners of fleurs,
And have no shame, but rather greatest pride.
Such beauty is not luxury but need.

just once within all time

My convalescence, most against my will,
Has always been my mentor, and my aid.
How many libraries would have stayed closed
To me, how many poetries shut out,
If I had not been forced by fate to sit,
To lie in bed and tend my many wounds?
The heart begins with pity -- to oneself.
That's disapproved, and yet it is the truth.
One must learn one's regrets to say farewell;
Goodbye is the great art that we resist.
To say I love you to fragility,
To cherish in uncertainty ourself,
To learn through sickness what a precious gift
This life, which more the intimate to us,
Is -- yes, I hear you, O my weeping wounds,
And self, you have the right to mourn yourself,
To wallow in self-pity as a path;
You are an unrepeating miracle,
Just once, just once within all time.
Some say -- but then it's easy to just say --
A life to come awaits, or many lives,
But questions are apparent in our faith.
We are a lantern on the midnight sea,
Alive in undulation and our flame,
Surrounded by a thousand twinkling pyres,
But can see the flames snuff out as sparks
Also appear -- we know not but we feel
The poignancy of this we yet still are.
Who knows the hundred accidents I missed
In missing all I wish I could have had,
The vanities and sins. If I had had
The opportunities and honors I
Aspired to, I might now be a wreck,
Pathetic and successful. For success

Is awfully superficial, and more scarce
Than most acknowledge. It's the roll of chance,
And fortune ever is a fickle one.
I'm not a rat to scramble to the top.
But being ridden often to my bed,
What Virgil then without? What troubadours?
If I'd been traipsing through the world a fool,
One of my many sides had sabotaged
Me as of now, no doubt: my militant,
My fond philanderer... But still, I lie
If I don't say I wish I could have sung
More -- there my voice reveals my truer self,
And never did I feel more like myself
Than writing and performing my own songs.
O Fate, could you be kind, and let my song,
If melody or poetry or both,
Take wings on wind, delivering my heart
To many? What is deeper wish than that?
A convalescent in a studio.
It better fits than being on the road.
I'd love to live to hear a hundred lips
Recite my verse and psalmody -- I would.
How deeper of a prayer I cannot know.
To hear the recitation of my heart,
Reception of delight I've longed to lend,
To know these labors have proved valuable,
And cultivation was not all in vain.
This bed of pain was my own nursery,
Wherein what true sophistication I
May have was born. It hasn't been all ease,
Although it's here I've had to learn such ease.
I wish my life were different. Who doesn't?
Yet this mentor has been kind to me,
And after all, what choice was I to have?
To will it and to learn its lessonings,
Or be dragged kicking, screaming, anyway.
It's best for dignity to will it true.
But when I most feel sorry for myself,
It's then I most do love, and everyone.
How precious they become; already gold,
They are more valuable than jewels to me.
The ones that talk to me, and those that don't,
Though those have hurt me more than I can say,
And everyday I long to hear their voice.
But all I've loved I love so very true.

They are my heart, and I am theirs.
If stubborn, wry, cantankerous, and proud,
I'm theirs, and cannot ever be absolved
Of loving them -- they are my cherubim,
Whom when I close my eyes and seek some peace
From pain, it's their ensemble in my soul
That gives me joy and rest. That's gratitude.
I can't forsake any of them, my heart.
So convalescence's taught me many things.
The treasures: if my voice, my friends, my loves,
The classics and the soothing sounds of verse
(The very best of medicines and salves).
I owe it much of what I have become.

skein in skiff

O wind, so much you are my tender friend,
You soothe me in your sibilance of sough.
The gentle feelings of a poet flow
With you, I glow with you, inspired, high,
As if this soul were stretched out skein in skiff
Upon you, like a kite, and rode your drifts
In trance, as if in love, as if in love.

waiting for the cavalry to come

He's waiting for the cavalry to come.
It never does. He looks around the bend,
Perhaps over that hill, they're on their way...
He blows his bugle, fantasizes dreams
Of thousands charging, throwing down the walls
Of tyrants. Thirty years, and silence reigns.

a cow's life

This life, bucolic on the dappled lawn,

With yawning sunbeams through the sifting trees,
In bovine yoga, derrière on grass,
Belly to dandelions, not a care,
A cow's life: that's for me, a paradise.

Lenin but not Dherzinsky

Lenin but not Dherzinsky; Stalin -- with
A corset bound by stringent caveats!! --
But never Yezhov, and corrected, yes,
By Khrushchev, who for all his errors, worked
Towards dismantling the gulag-state.

wet for the wonder

Adam.
What I behold is more than all of me,
And yet is given to my weeping eyes,
Wet for the wonder; yet the more to taste:
The flavor of the fields, the sweetest fruits,
All given free! A hundred kinds of joy.
Here I but found myself in this full bliss,
All gratis. I am gratitude in flesh,
Flushed with a hundred kinds of ecstasy:
The lushness of the world, the fuller nest
That bowers us by rest beneath the stars,
The fascinating creatures at each side.

leaf collage in breeze

Sweet harmony of leaf collage in breeze:
The shuffle of the sun, the vibrant green,
The stillness of the air, the rooster's crow
Across the canyon, distant humming cars,
The humming peace of life in restful ease.

the muddled labyrinth of life

Lost in the muddled labyrinth of life,
Caught in the blur of flotsam and of ruts,
Adults often in eddies flounder, snared
In webs our habits wove against our will,
And we seek fellows to desperately escape,
But lose the easy touch of making friends,
So we oft make a most pathetic sight.
Without a compass out in tangled woods,
We long for highways leading out from here,
Yet fear the traffic as we peek from dens.
We ask the angels' friendly catalysts
To visit, then we fold away from prayers
And pine, trapped in our safer cubbyholes,
And genuinely don't know how to escape.
And so we make the best of hovel homes,
And spruce our Ozark cabins up a bit
To make the mess we've got something of good.
Send, angels, those who know the blessing-spells,
For who knows, we might have what they need too.

ink wet upon the page

To be there with Winstanley, Kelpius,
And Milton as they set ideas to pen:
The world held breath in hush in numinous
Anticipation, for such time was tense
With excitement, genius setting down
Its dissertations in a new creation.
Once these were not written yet at all,
But manuscript, ink wet upon the page,
The paper still as yet most empty space,
Where marvelous unfolding of the scrolls
Of the Akashic would set down its scrawl.
To be with them before the page was full,
The giddy electricity, the spark,
The crackling in the air, uncertainty.
Necessity, and pure contingency.
So we, the each of us, might be the next,

Might be the one confronting ancient men
And sages, looking through the telescope
Of time at far descendants bright in blur,
And channeling through wits and intuits
Some precious gift of treasure never seen.

November 3, 2020

I'm going to ease into this victory
To savor it, and let my parts believe
As they peek out to see the fascist's gone.
To shuffle off the trauma skeins and scars
From this frightful debacle of our times.

to sip the silence as its wine

That crow has everything I want in life:
To soar, to ride the winds above it all
And coast, to slide and glide upon the drifts,
To be but smooth and lofty, filled with peace,
And free -- to sip the silence as its wine,
To let its gentle fruitiness slip down
Its gullet easily as it may breathe.

the common touch of the divine

It being fragile, wonder must be nursed,
And nurtured with a tender, loving care.
Where genius touched its toes down on one's life,
Pursue -- discover everything you can;
Don't let it be elusive: follow it,
Back to the sources. Trace it to the well.
Study the circumstance of all who awe,
Until their sinews lay in fingers' grasp.
Whoever most intrigued you, find them out.
Some secret in mercuriality

Lies hidden in embedded textures' web.
Long years of contemplation draw you close.
And where your whimsicality is quick,
Keep that most quirky spark cupped to your breast,
Alive, and guard it with your very life,
Even if some say that is childish.
It has in common touch of the divine,
Which most hand over to the world's erosion
As they grow: build you a greenhouse, friend,
And let that delicate exotic thrive.

that is the sad of it

There's some so fickle, once you lose your charm
(For them -- your charm is usually intact),
They flee, and have no loyalty at all.
No piety for magic moments, not
A touch of reverence: their flighty self
Is gone, and you, for them, are but a has-been.
So much more the shame : they often are
Feathered most curious, these lovely birds;
One hates to lose the value they once placed.
It breaks ones heart. Often the awesome are
Capricious souls, who run on faithless whim,
And those who chase their crazes often drop
Who's not thus crazed; that is the sad of it.

the mountains know me

No one will ever know me; I'm alone.
I love that sweet aloneness; yes, I do.
The mountains know me, and the meadow's blooms.
The birds that come to sip the fountain know.
The gnarly oak with rustling twigs knows me.

the gutter as our citadel

We are not free, but flaccid, flabby, loose;
We've lost our tone and fiber. What was tense
And most expectant in us we gave up
For marijuana's drivel, and the slack
Of wastrels, having sold their dignity
For pottage. We have slipped our discipline,
Become mere swampy things that wallow low,
And count the filth our tongues dispense as gold.
No longer thinking we must raise ourselves,
Deaf to the higher stations that call us,
We've claimed the gutter as our citadel,
Despising all who wish the loftier.
Who do you think you are you hold so high
Your chin and gaze alike a peer at stars?
Skid Row is our Jerusalem, none else.

the citizens of sewers

My generation, in my eyes, are pigherds,
Slopping in the sty, completely lost,
And spurning cultivation for a blunt.
A fucking blunt! They'd trash the treasury
Of Western Civilization to get high.
Their atheism is the lopping off
Of everything above their vulgar hips.
They hate the heights, denying they exist.
Just let me curse and fuck and smoke, that's it,
There's nothing else to life, no higher pitch,
And let me bow to degradation's depths.
These are the beasts that some would call my peers.
They would be equals if they'd raise themselves,
But they're content to stay in Circe's pen.
What other generation's thought that diction
Is oppression? Frankness redefined
As vomit. Eloquence is tyranny.
How dare you mandate tact in my tirade?
Just let me mumble. Everything is base,
And beauty is a lie, celestial
Ascent a crock of shit. It's dog eat dog,

Just get your own, for ethics are for suckers.
Here we are, the citizens of sewers.

somatic whalesong in my suit of skin

O! This exquisite aching! This is life!
This tissue-symphony of poignancy!
This here today, uncertain of tomorrow
Flesh, inherited of billion years
Of sense and sentiment ephemeral
And all the more precious in consequence!
O deep, deep-feeling congerie of cells,
That seeks through aching for to touch its soul,
To mourn and celebrate its passing self,
I hear your most sacred biology,
Somatic whalesong in my suit of skin.

so soft it sifts the heavens

Give lip to Aeolus,
bough pine-sway
so soft it sifts the heavens;
limbs so gently
pan the night for gold
in milky streams:
Denarius in candlelight
behind a pin-pricked screen.

mahogany in moonlit dew
for Elizabeth of Night

Mahogany in moonlit dew --
her limbs in breathless sheathe of linen,

Bare beside me, water on my tongue --
I am a jellyfish of gasps, translucent,
Woven sighs in chainmail of iambics,
Suavity in midnight's still suspense.
These cheap anemone on sculpted face
Anoint their oil breath'd with steam
Upon her stream of clayslip skin
So curvature gourmet before these fluttering lids.

marinade of silence

the vivid frigid air --
umbelliferous canopy of pine --
the crosshatched ivory button in the skies --
the friendly frozen shadows --
sunk in marinade of silence.

Francis in the chaparral

Venta, linen enchilada, sandals but the breeze --
Cretaceous monoliths of sand
Arcade arroyo, Quercus agrifolia --
A Francis in the chaparral.
the livid trickle of the melted ice on pebbles.
Mormons, capitolul al patrulea, carte Nephi --
Fighting fires bare of foot.
The sagebrush rustling fragrance by the dormitory walls.
But 7000 feet away, a rotting sun
Held in aluminum.

lips are goblets dipped

Isolde,
    lips
are goblets
    dipped

in sweet
     of cluster's must
run river
    through dank cellar's dust
and eyes
     are globes of honeydew
each sip
     while staring into you;
your cheeks
     are clouds of oil
falling sun
     set fire-foil
that the breeze
     blew into purple night;
my fingers tremble:
     skin is livid fright.
There's orioles that sing
      within your irises
and tell my quill to touch
       your soft papyruses,
and write
       evaporating ink
with cursive sap
       and thence to sink
to lick the syrup clean:
       croissant with cream.
I'm liquid in the fire
        of a melting dream.
Are you a creature frail
      from feathered woods
where lily-linen nymphs
      bathe in the suds
of fountains?
        slippery as a fish,
quicksilver skin
       essence of wish
and hands' warm will.
     you are but glim
the whistle
       of a fleeting whim
the meadow flowers caught
      when sun did flash
and wrap your candy caprice
     in a cloak of petals' flesh.
  Open corolla

                delicate as silk
sweet fragrance in my nostrils
              tongue lapping up milk.
   However you are woman,
          O it radiates in waves!
recruiting me in dainty swoons
          while birdsong from my lips still raves!
    A touch of snow
              the Spring heat thaws
   yet while you glisten
              what are laws
To hold me back?
          I can't withhold.
   A honeybee in pollen's bounty,
              beauty-bold.
   If all the drops from sky were cupped,
       and gathered from the cloudy blue,
     they could not make a body such
     as ever would compare with you.
   If moonlight were skimmed off as cream
          and sculpted to a bust,
     what votaries of midnight hope
        to e'er attain your lust?
   if feathery foam from ocean's sighs
       were woven into lace,
    the bouncing unbound braids you wear
          would mock them in the face!
    Small spiders blush with envy:
        gossamer I might soon touch;
     if webs were soft as your sweet skin,
          how willingly the flies would clutch,
  and harp their cellophanic wings
      in dew-string necklaces of glue;
     whatever wondrous music made,
          would pale beside the melody of you.
    Your curvature's as question marks
          that candle in my eye --
  a doe-eye's desperate wondering,
      might I? ever might I?

garden of monoliths

The mystical garden of monoliths,
The cabbage patch of stones, the dental hills
Of clustered outcroppings of sandstone teeth
That wall Simiyi from Fernando dales.
Covert in canyons and ravines of shade,
Wherein serpents diverse coil and creep,
Metropolis of lizards, catacombs
Of ground squirrels, sharp rebukes of jays on wing,
A peppering of pepper trees and pine,
A wild acorn orchard on the slopes,
Lemurian mystique of lemonberry
Bush in nestled tufts lodged neath steep cliffs,
Where tuttering bursts of birds in splay are swift
From hidden nests, and flutter air like purrs.
Piedras that look longingly southeast
Over the Santa Monicas for sight
So soothing of the salty sea from whence
They once emerged. Where wind sleeps soft in caves,
And often with its offspring in debut,
Comes out to whisper musicals in sough,
Where pine and pepper leaves give light applause.
But sometimes, often in the midst of night,
The wind gusts forth a blust'ring wizard, wild
In fusillade of storm and streaming spell,
And makes the landscape bow to symphonies
Of howls making coyotes blush, and rants
That tickle hair electric into knots.
The area's replete with ghost stories
Of gore and cult and spattering of spooks,
But I brush these aside for fairy tales.
There may yet be maidens in linen white
Who walk and bless these monastery knolls.

quicksilver night conceals

The cool knife smooth through livid resin, rise
Upon the billows, maiden-busted prow!
Both day and night are liquid, passing waves;
The journey runs towards plural stars or one,

From stellar slosh to butterscotch in blaze.
The sea is sound in rhythm on the ears;
The creamy blur of dream in bosom-depths
Is motion in a lullaby of rise
And fall -- the rolling knolls of ripple-rills.
Whitewash fluorescent pearls that silver ski
The darksome seams in tremor, cloudy tusk
Who weeps sweet milk from heavens, sleet of light.
The waves are shingles of the scaly skin
Of glittering and unfathomable sea,
O massive fish quicksilver night conceals!

puttis

Chaste cherubim-ballet of soft caress,
Of fingertips to blush of flushing cheeks,
The tai qi regal cadence of the hand
In brush on plum or nectarine of face.
This oxytocin innocence of touch
So scintillating-clean of genitals,
Lustless yet worshipful in bliss of awe,
We adolescents knew upon the floor,
Cross-legged, facing-mirror and the bar
Aside, as we warmed up as intimates
Of eyes and angel fingers, leotards
And tights and leg warmers and salmon slippers.
Stretch, and let the flesh its spandex flex
Of Hermes-sinews feather-find its flight.
We leap to feet, horizon-hands an arch
Of falling handkerchief as we grip rail,
Flamingo-leather moccasins arrayed
Like herons in the estuary fog.
We are the buttermilk of gyroscopes
In orbitals across the hardwood floor.
And Wendy Michlovic, the very touch
Of grace in blur of tendons' willful whirr,
Our prima donna, humble in her mirth.
Then we take out our bible, Narnia,
Dog-eared, split into groups to wrestle out
Reduction of this tome to simple scenes.
And if but faun, with shaggy cloven feet,
And breathy reeds of pipes; or dryads, limbs

Stretched out to woody canopies of green,
And silken peeking through the webby gauze
Wrapped spindly round the trunk and through the boughs;
Or if a family of beavers, wet
But dapper in their furs deep in their dams;
Or elegance of evanescent glance
Of unicorn upon a grassy hill,
Against the glass of polished aqua sky --
We gingerly begin to morph and move,
Exploring muscles in alterity
Of mythic character, and find our poise.
She sets the needle on the vinyl's groove,
Our maestro, and then flirting limb to tune,
We try Tchaikovsky then Prokofiev
Then Copland each to match the scenic mood
And character, and let the dance unfold,
The words in whipped cream ruffles from our moves.
Each Autumn Saturday all afternoon,
In 1983, mythology,
And symphony, and limbs made liquid flesh
In feather-fretted heaven's gasp refreshed,
But most of all, that exercise of touch,
Doe-eyed tea-ceremony Artemis
Gave grace to fingers on the shivering face,
As we, transmute to Puttis, find our place
In burgeoning naïveté of youth.

Tiffany of poets

I'm not for everyone: oh no, I'm not!
I am the cursive letters' fond Lalique,
The Monarch Tiffany of poets, diva
Of adornment and fine tracery
Of assonance and jewelry of words.
That I'm too delicate for brutes brings joy.
Brains more of beef than blueberry cheesecake
May find my fine gourmet desserts too rich.
So let these troglodytes consume their hams,
Their bacons, and their hamburgers -- I'll string
The dew of nectarines in fragile webs
The tongue-tip cotton-candies with its lick,
Exuding from my syrup-skin champagne

That mists the breeze intoxicant and ripe.
I'll puff and ruffle feathers in my pride
Of craftsmanship, along the artisans
Of old, the greats, the priceless masteries,
And leave the swine to revel in their mud.
If lace of intricate beauty's too much
For you, go back to television, slob,
Adjust the Trump flag on your monster truck,
And let sophisticates envelop joy.

shakespeare's sonnets redux

make a xerox copy of yourself

I'll shtup you

when you get old, you'll be homely

better photocopy that beauty

it's fading as we speak

fuck

the wrinkles are gathering as I rhyme

when you're a hag,

you can look your daughter in the face and cry

"once I was this beautiful!"

yah? well, no more

let's knock you up

another Paris, and another Helen

Somewhere a landfill holds a treasury
Of love letters such as has not been seen
The world in its entirety; alas,
She tossed that pricelessness into the trash.
Some future archaeologist will find
This hoard amidst the rubbish, and be awed
That in a jaded age such as this one,
One loved with such an utter purity
That never faded, all those jilted years,
And wonder longingly, Who was Elyse?
And why did she commit this innocence
Into the earth, save as an offering?
A love too great for one soul to hold on.
Only the gods could live such paradise,
And to prevent their jealousies at such,
She put it in their hands, immortal gift,
Returned ambrosial bliss to Aphrodite.
She will say, that Cyprian, this was
The greatest grace I gave throughout that age,
Another Paris, and another Helen,
Without the onus of a Trojan War.
And Dante weeps for Beatrice; Petrarch sheds
The salten dew from reverential eyes
For Laura; both welcome me to their guild,
And weave the laurels through my flowing hair.
What honeydew meets snow on mountaintops,
She is the very pinnacle's ice cream,
The violets of the bluffs where Hermes lights,
With feather fillets in his golden hair,
And wing tips on his sandals; there he flirts
The briefest of the zephyrs' gyres high,
And winning contest of the pirouettes,
He takes a purple petal for his flights,
And sighs; her fragrance is astonishing.
She is a shock of valley lavender
That lingers near the quercus-shaded creek,
Lending aroma to the honey bees
Brew in the splashing frolicking of sun.
She is a hidden miracle whose ink
The vellum of her fond epistles leaks

Into the leaching soil; now those words,
Just as they fade, are but immortal breath,
Reconsecrated to the atmosphere,
The treasures of Olympus once again.

shy and flighty doe-eyed thing

I was a shy and flighty doe-eyed thing,
A lithe mercurial of liberty
In love with youth and dreading that it fade,
And so I shunned commitment like a curse,
Making whimsy my body's molecules,
And lavishing the bubble bath of life.
I was a dear and precious fool in love,
In love with life and everything its own.
I didn't stop to smell the fragrances
Of roses and camellias: I lived there,
In thorny mazes where the Muses stood
In marble bliss of meditative glee,
And hummingbirds zippered the golden air
Abuzz. I deemed as raiment these aromas;
I walked naked in the garden paths,
And pressed my lips to vitis vinifera
Where it grew. I sauntered in a trance.
I was the laughter of the light on dew,
The Aristophanes of stars on rills,
Utterly without seriousness atall.
And yet I brimmed in broodings of the heart,
Flirtations of my fancy's merriment,
And savored all that melancholic wine
The colic of a fit of sighs might brew.
Devoted here, devoted over there,
A creature of idolatries in turn;
Yet let the lightest tracery of locks
Be hinted, but the breath of vaporous chains,
I fled in fury of my protestations.
I was but each summer's day and eve,
The royal now embellished in its blush.
Taste now the sparkling sunset as it fades,
And wish upon a star for your tomorrows.
More than that I could not think to give.
If love repleted with its capers then,

The despotism of my caprice set
The reigning tone: what is more precious than
The evanescent? Be its votary,
And spend an evening in its passing shrine:
We'll toss our careless coins into the pond,
And ponder lilies cut as offerings,
Then let the membranes of our countenance
Find purling pearls of moist enchantment soft
Upon each other. Cooing in the eaves
Of Ficus canopies, our dallying
With tongues, the doves remark in reverie.
The moon is momentary wipe of fog,
An abalonial wink between the leaves.
Hold this in piety to Aphrodite.
Not our property: her mystery,
Her grace to share and then withdraw at will.
I lingered on the outskirts of her fanes,
Fanatical about those silver firsts,
For which I thirsted: passing ecstasy,
Again, again, each swan as she may pass,
Each plush of ivory and lakeside down,
A skim upon the skein in gelatin
Of lyric lunacy. Don't hold me down:
I am the elemental of this mood.
I'm but the preface in its cotton charm,
The very tufts of dandelion breeze,
The frozen dip of chins falling to lips
Repeated: this initial benefice
In lantern glass, a firefly in ice.
I am the Levite of the honeymoons,
The lips' incipience in caroled hymns,
The but this night no more enchanted priest.
Or so I fancied, but the charmer fell
Into his very spells, and was bewitched,
While they now flew from me, as I pursued,
"Let not one day be all that is this bliss!
But let tomorrows in their mystery
Reflect diverse, as Luna's lamp on lakes,
Last night's bewilderment of sudden love!"
But now they were the ones not to be locked,
And I discovered votaries are few
At sacred shrines. The singularity
Of charm is precious rare, does not repeat.
You lose your jewels when feet are all too fleet.

taking a shit to Sinatra

Taking a shit to Sinatra
On the bed
Into a garbage bag.
The dignity of 2020.

the coal, the stone, the geode lair

The clay itself inheres intelligence,
Asleep but dreaming of awakening,
And from below, in its integrity,
Without transcendent interference, grows,
Develops its potentialities,
And sets upon a journey none have planned.
It moves from density to porousness
To breath, and back again. It seeks sincere
Substantiality, the sublime concrete.
It has no time for tricks of the abstract.
It stubbornly resists all consciousness
With blathering of generalities,
But stays specific, as a saving grace.
It balks the flatulence of sophistry,
The airbag bloat professors heady belch.
It knows detethering's shenanigans.
It shuns such mania, content and still.
It loves the coal, the stone, the geode lair.
With great resolve, insists on immanence,
Inherence, what is in itself alive,
Indigenous, particular, as such,
Resisting any top-down sculpting hand,
But finding in its native synergy
Its rise. Egalitarian and strong,
So faithful to the tangible, so set
Against the jibber-jabber of the con,
So awesome in its Brechtian resolve :
Defiant, stubborn, beautiful, and pure.

to gaze at mammaries

Of one thing be certain : if I so choose,
A grown man, to gaze at the mammaries
Of any adult woman, simply for
It pleases me, there's not a force on earth,
Nor moral stricture that will stay my eyes
Or keep me from enjoying what they show.
You go on bitching all you like about
"Me too", or how it's inappropriate,
Or lecherous: I do not give a *fuck*.
I draw the line at what may please me; if
Your moral code frowns, it can go to hell.
I don't consent to live upon this earth
Without the soothing sight of myriad tits.
I'm flexible in other zones : not here.
It's medicine that soothes my aching heart,
And I will take my fill of all that heals.
And if you mind, please go and fuck yourself.

we must discover deeper roots

Of needs we must discover deeper roots,
That brush caressingly the aquifers
Which fathom in the percolative grit
Of silt and gravels, there to sip such pure
And honeysuckle trickles secreted
In bosom's bed of bounty-yielding earth.
For fortune, fleeting, often disappoints
The fledgling hope, the merest greening sprout,
Which young, naively thrashes in its grasp
For any passing wisp which dandelions
Fickle breeze with tantalizing fluff.
It must mature, that infant hope who trusts
What has not earned in least its confidence.
It reaches up; it cannot touch the sun,
Nor tender grope the feather in its flight,
But must sink down, which it confers defeat,

Yet in its tendrilous and capillary
Reach through darkened sediment no eye
May penetrate, it slowly in its hairs
And rootlets finds its inner sappy pith,
Its very self, and learns it must conserve
The essence of its bone-broth in its veins.
For every delicate and upward inch
It leafy whorls towards heaven's swinging blaze,
It needs must double down its musty roots,
So come what odd fortuities descend,
It has a dozen mysteries beneath,
Its crannied treasureholds it may at need
Tap richly to endure the winter's scant.
Hope and the earthworm poke the mealy soil,
Hope to barrel in molassan roots
Fermented sunshine, there to draw upon
When dessicate aboves are harsh with pain.
Then from beneath, as if from nowhere, springs,
Be it a slow and rationed drip, a strength
One does not have but which the earth yet holds.
So tested then, by season and by age,
Hope may, robust, choose steady, worthy ends,
Which do not faithless feed, and laugh, and flee,
But dividend their mutualities,
And find its hold against the bending winds.

reminders of the angels

That I must cater to vulgarities
Of gutter-culture, roping diction down
To stutter-parlance incapacitates
May mumble is insulting pandering.
I shall not feed the sad regime of grunts,
But nourish with reminders of the angels,
Who, in elevated rhapsodies,
Speak in supernal convolutes of sound
And helixed sense, requiring the ear
To step up in its keenest listening
To grasp but merest gist in beauty wrapped

Enigma for its celebrated awe,
Which only puzzles in their ponderings
May utter in an assonance of rhyme.
If such is difficult, arouse and rise.
I call out from the clean plateaus latrines
Know not, and shan't descend there to its muck.
Brush clean placental scummeries from wings,
And dry, ascend on billows with me here.
It is more pleasant and uplifts the ear.
My language is your spade; come plough, and reap.

leotard of birth

Flesh unimpeded by a single thread,
No shroud nor shadow over rolling curves,
In single surge emerges up from wet,
And lets the dripping advertise its orbs,
The smooth expanse of oil-sated skin,
Its full of everything to breath and sky,
The smile of its leotard of birth.

have mercy on my bruises

O Lady lambent Light of moonlit night,
O ivory figurehead on crescent prow
That shooes the tidal caviar of clouds
With gentle hands like oars through purling foam,
O negligee of mist and sequin stars,
O brewer of our dreams from midnight herbs,
Soothe me, your aching votary, soothe me,
Who calls you in the wink before the dawn,
When bruised within the heavens' purple hue,
You still pour down illume your creameries;
And being in the bruise of black and blue,
As day beats night in fisticuffs of dawn,
Have mercy on my bruises, aching like

The heavens ache at wound of rising sun,
And let that endless monastery zen
Of oceanic darkness phosphorus
By tickle of your fingertips you watch
Each night share with me but a molecule
Of its en-orbing peace, and soothe my wounds.
I hear you flirt outside my panes with wind;
The eucalyptus whispers of your tryst.
Share of your beauty's hint, and I am healed.

dormancies but dream in depths below

Satan.
Now come now, Jesus, you protest for peace
Your Father brings? Observe instead the wasps
And hornets, ever warring, every inch
Of hive they have continually fought,
Forever hard defended, often lost.
Is this incessant war caused then by men?
Absurd! It's in the nature that you love.
Consider then the mantises: what saints!
Their mandibles may never rest, it seems,
Devouring not only fellow bugs,
But lizards, mice, and frogs, nay, hummingbirds!
The zing and frothy-feathered levity
Of gardens, iridescent overcoats
Of tuft, the loveliness of flowerbeds!
Alive! While still they writhe, alive, limbs thrash,
The mantis chews away at flesh still quick!
Shall we then multiply examples, hm?
We might pedantically increase the days
With samples over samples of these crimes!
If nature is our model, robbery
And melee, nay, apocalypse is norm!
This vast array of cannibal horror.
If we, diverting, were to follow Greeks,
We could not say the father of this wreck

Were Zeus, but rather Ares, who is Mars!
Indeed, I look around: his handicraft
Is all but near ubiquitous in breadth!
Show me the weaponry he pays Hephaestus
Forge, the lances and the poisoned barbs,
The swords and axes, armor laid with spikes,
His magazine in full on battlefields,
You'll find it everywhere and more -- on flesh,
Incised and graven on the body parts
Of creatures that encircle us abroad!
While we here calmly discourse, wars are fought!
Do you not hear the pressing soldiers march,
In every click and buzz of background hum?
You wish to oust centurions of Rome?
But legions swarm in every hill and dale!
I do not see Isaiah's lions rest
With lambs as yet, nor oxen sleep with wolves.
The snakes have still to shed their poisoned fangs.
His all-encompassing disarmament?
Where is it? Anywhere? This is a dream!
A pleasant fantasy for fairytales.
One told by those whom soldiers' work keeps safe,
And privileged by security so won,
Imagine in their cloistered vanity
They have no need for warriors at all!
Like that: just give decrees of peace, it's won!
Such miracles this earth has never seen.
But old Isaiah saw! Or so he claimed.
He didn't see it anywhere about,
But vaguely in the future, safe and sound.
That is, if I recall, Messiah's task.
Oh, that is you! Or so the angels sing.
It's hard to tell. One hears some harmony,
But words are difficult to clear discern.
So this is your job! Wow! How do you plan
To bring these warring tribalists to rest?
Who have a dozen million years or more
Lived in their senseless cycles of melee?
On top of Rome, you must bring these to peace?
You like to harken back originals,
Creation's peace. Does nature testify?
The witness stills to silence suddenly.

You speak of Eden; nature holds her peace.
But speak of war, and hear her testimoans
Deluge us in their crying multitudes!
The vast papyri Alexandria
Now boasts have not the space for bloody ink
That would scrawl out the sagas of such gore
Each clan at arms, each species in its fort,
Has waged, is waging, and will wage again!
Your lovely vision is delusional.
I hate to pierce the bubble's levity,
Delight of your ethereal soiree,
The wished communion of your heaven's throne,
But Jesus, is there evidence at all?
What do the archives of biology
Declare? Do they assent to this your peace?
But if they speak of something else, then men
Will ever take that as their model, no?
Even your followers will know at heart
The score their loyalty must not admit,
And when they must lay down a bet, will know
The likelihood their faith will not permit.
You think me hostile, but reality
Is stubborn and intrudes even on good
And worthy plans. I'd hate to see you fall
Upon a splintered stake of wretched gore,
Because you could not calculate the odds
As shrewdly as the odds did calculate,
And die a criminal, but even worse,
A fool, who conjured evanescent steam
From vanity and hope, and thought it real.
O Nazarean, where's Isaiah now?
The larvae that will soon awake to war
Have long abandoned flesh that is but dust,
And bones their distant grandfathers did gnaw.

Jesus.
The eyes, as lovely as they testify
To beauties, cannot see what soul discerns,
And aren't proper instruments for truth
That goes beneath the surfaces of things.
But in the heart, there is a rebel voice,
That knows, against the bloody evidence,

That this is not how things should be at all.
It is the voice that cries for equity,
And justice, and it never rests for long.
It's not convinced by all the witnesses
You summon, in the spite of all it's seen,
And in its misery, it's seen it all.
Your pedantries are nauseate and dull.
The tomes are dusty, though aristocrats
Have levied them forever in their courts
Against the poor. Yet still their hearts are wise
To hopes that live defiantly against
The endless propaganda of your wars.
How can that be, if that's reality,
And nothing more is potent in its core?
Unless reality is more complex,
And dormancies but dream in depths below,
Deep roots unseen, that haven't sent their shoots,
Not even palest sprouts above the earth.
Call us but foolish swine, our nostrils know
The musty scent of roots still undivined.
Regimes ever are certain till they fall.
A well-built house seems confident until
A mudslide it could not foresee descends,
And in an instant, it is splintered ash :
Tomorrow in its midden grass will grow.
A garden might be planted there with gain.
Buried are boundaries of property.
So what is evident to all may fall.
You bring me competition's resume.
It's most formidable, I cannot lie.
It holds the upper hand in Earth affairs,
And scarcity its melancholy reign
Still plunders with impunity and wrath.
But then observe the heavens : endless suns!
Proclaiming their abundance, gifts of warmth
And light almost unending! Scarcity
Is scarce amongst their precincts. This we see,
Parochially, in this backwoods nook,
Is odd, is not the norm, does not reflect,
At least in full so far, the splendorous
And scintillating light of generous stars.
So we in shadow fight amongst ourselves,

The denizens of boondock cosmic caves.
Yet in this night, the dawn is brewing now.
The light is pregnant with its miracle.
Watch then the shadows flee as sun ascends.
Perhaps you have observed a paradigm,
A little model of another life.
Wherever there's abundance freely shared,
Even if relative, no surety,
That martial rivalry you revel in,
Amongst even the beasts, ameliorates,
And lessens, so that animals once foes,
Their bellies sated, learn to live in peace.
These are but sprouts of what will soon be trees,
And those trees soon a forest in their spread,
The deserts of our hopes soon greeneries.
You laugh and sneer at petty possibles,
For that they're small and insignificant.
So every giant ere their toppling fall.
Don't reckon me a fool. I know the score.
I know just where we stand. I know your hand
Still holds the scepter over many lands.
I know the shadow and its poverty
Still motivates the scramble for its sparse
And grudging harvest. But the light is near.
For we shall take the hoards of savage war,
And share resources freely out for all,
New conquerors with generosity.
That common share's the mystery we yield.
You're far too bound in your idolatry
To mere appearances to see the sign.
You can't imagine miracles may come
From tiny mustard seeds. But they will come,
Perhaps too inexplicable for you.
The world is living plundered regimens
Of hostile robbery and selfishness,
Beneath which buried Eden's creatures groan.
But when a newer order's evident,
When it surrounds and is consolidate,
The beneficial latencies will rise,
Potentials in the newly sated beasts
That few foresaw, and yet there always was
The rudiments of love, however rare.

Cooperation is the pinnacle
Towards which the creatures grope in dark of night.
Up to this point, each several brotherhood
Of species have reserved it for their kind.
The coming light shall make it general.
Scoff as you will, your pessimism's old.
Its cred is based on being old and grey.
But optimism holds the future, friend.
In its vast confidence I do have faith.
The night has had its say. But soon the day!

the poetry of adipose and skin

Recall the age of more abundant breasts!
When shirts with glee came off more easily.
It's not a pervy thing, but one of awe,
One's twenties, wonder to explore such flesh
In amplitude and in variety.
O, looking up into those several eyes,
Those quirky, eager personalities,
Their feisty attitudes, their curious
Experimenting, just like you, with lust,
And often falling further than one thought.
Sheer revelation, every time a bra
Was loosed, a naked priestess in one's arms:
Gazebo on the lake beneath the moon,
Antlers of stags in alpine greenery,
Smooth white of feather wipe on swan-sail skein,
Van Gogh of Rorschach fog in rippling steam,
A Shinto monastery, hush of breath.
And every nuance soft could speculate,
The castle swirl of cupcakes' frosting tip,
The poetry of adipose and skin,
The holy playground of the gripping hands.
Show me a temple that could rival this.

makes my heart to glide

Anchises.
She's swift, as wind is swift in lunary
Of midnight abalone on the boughs
Of whispered pine, and makes my heart to glide,
A spinner on the surface of the ice,
Arms offered to horizons east and west.
She's softer than the smoothest petals stems
May whorl about them pigmented in hue.
She is a livid flame atop a hill
Unfurling like a flag in rapid breeze
Who lights the darkness with her luminance.
Her mouth's a hidden nest of flocking birds,
That when her lips divide, a burst of song
Escapes on eager feather through the air,
And chocolates rest upon her dewdrop tongue.
Her skin is ripple of a tantalance,
A shiver and an evanescent hint,
A wish withdrawn, night's candle on the sea,
A mystery, like soft forbidden silk.
She is a tease upon the amber waves
That fingers send as envoys of intrigue;
A mere assortment of the alphabet
In apparitious conjuration baits
My fading, fonder curiosity;
She wakens, then she walks away again.
She's swifter than the fingers may abide:
She's phantom-fleeing filigree of mist.
I kissed the steam of breath fled far away
With wist, and wondered where her hidden haunts
Enveloped vanish of her modesty,
Surrounded by her glitterance of jewels.
Her cellophanic feathers faded fast
Before my aweing eyes, their phosphorus gloam
A subtle lume before they disappeared.
And just the tracery of melody
Her murmuring lips of chalcedone
And waterfalls left lingering on the air
Remained. I was lagoon and swoon in flesh,
A fibrillance in tingling chill of skin.

I canticle to call her back again.

Glendalĕ

Ionos.
She's my Anne Hathaway and AOC
Rolled into one, with hair of burgundy
Strewn through with snow-white blooms, and Camelot
Her dreamy homeland in the land of fog,
A shepherd-maiden lounging on a hill
Beneath an oak with Bronte on her lap.
She's awkward and she's proud, demi-divine
With wings Elizabethan from the Court
Of Seelie Sidhe, nobility in wounds
She weeps beneath her sunshine-bursting grin.
She's wine on willow vines to wishful eyes.
She's laughter strung on silver necklaces.
She's strength in gentle mercy to the lion,
Southern belle who tames the beast with charm,
Her Heathcliff of the moody moors and bogs
(Yet lingers with her Linton to this hour).
Two decades out, she draws my loyalty
Afar alike a Laura sonnetted
Eternal by a laurel-headed hand
That whisks the fluffy quills from passing geese
To pomegranate-scrawl her beauty's trace
On looking glass of vellum; or a guide
Through ivory-luminescent paradise
A Florentine once glimpsed in chapel pews,
Whose eyes, never forgotten, charmed his heart
A jilted lifetime in his reveries.
I too have joined their lonely laurel club,
Unfolding fame from memories long past.

to each a time, a pinnacle, a peak

To each, a time, a pinnacle, a peak,
When everything converged, reflecting soul
Just perfectly in this imperfect world.
Oft full of troubles too, but full of light,
Light more the brilliant as the years rush by.
A sign, a symbol to remember long,
When in one's prime, one felt the all of self,
The thriving of fruition in the life.
Loves more intense, one's opportunities,
With friends abounding, bountiful and rich.
The decoupage of soul and zeitgeist, time
And one's desires, all at zenith pitch.
Nostalgia is the welcome-back of heart.
Quite unrepeatable, the pinnacles.
Yet pulsars sending out those frequencies
Which nourished us, and may again, if claimed.
They are the lasting revelations life
Bestows infrequently to guide us through.
Good fruits, that we ought juice to the last drop.

myrhh of heaven

Food of the angels, honeydew and mist,
The myrrh of heaven, lammas bread and meal,
The sustenance of butterflies and birds,
Ambrosia light-deposited by fog,
The texture and the taste of harpsway's sound
Essenced in scattered loaf-crumbs, sugared snow,
Evaporate of sap, the meadows' milk,
The Feta cheese of hidden valleys' oats,
The caviar of air and running gum,
The lick of deer and nuzzle-meal of goats,
The ladybugs' delight, the crystal cream
Of antelope who run through clouds of dawn
With free abandon, gamboling in mirth.
No blood, no flesh, no slaughter of the prey,

But pure originals of nourishment,
The herbage and the edibles of earth.

I've known the very vamps

No doubt you have progressed forward through time,
Abandoning the past to be the past;
But I abide where you have left behind.
I live, at least by half, in that old place,
And never left, a juicy nectarine.
I am elastic, stretching far from here
Back to the origin, and keep my faith
To better times, and let the bitterness
Be accidence, while better moments rule,
Be they the decades past, their royalty
Eclipses newer upstarts, with a pluck
The feckless generations since decline.
I pledge allegiance to that pluck of mine;
I'm married to my mischief and its loves,
Its harlequins and fairy pedigrees,
Its aristocracy of whimsicality,
Its confidence in rolling dice.
I've mated offspring of the very imps,
The naughty nixen-maidens by the shore,
Who take the bodies of the misfit gals,
Whose blend of spunk and spite invites them in.
I've known the very vamps, of fur and lure,
Who linger in the shadows of men's loins,
And haunt their hearts with longing's hunger pangs,
And called them friends and confidants of yore.
I've lounged in their velour-lined lairs and laughed,
Sipping the cinnamon of cream, legs up
Diagonal in dim alcoves, striped hose
And buckled shoes, and learned their mysteries.
I have these fond epistles from the past,
Wrapped ribbon in glissade calligraphy,
And folded in the scrapbook of my heart,
My pixie grimoire sigil-etched in sap,
Keeping the ceremonies here and now

Established in the days of moon-flamed fog,
Vigil allegiant to what has been,
So if comrades of yore should knock the door,
They'd find the fires lit as yesterday,
A yesterday I keep as if today.

wonderment a child knows

Hans Christian Andersen.
It is a hopeless, therefore harmless, love,
One-way, an admiration from afar,
An unreturned, unnoticed sacrament
I keep alive for that it is a pure
Species of wonderment a child knows.
There's no betrayal in futility.
There's not a chance she'd ever wish for me.
But if you love, you say to me, do not divide
Your love between the unattained and she
Who loves you truly now! Be fair, leave off,
Do not lead on when you still feel allure.
My dear, I'd wait eternities in voids
If I would wait for those who spark my skin
Electric for their brooding misfit charm.
I must live now, and let the fantasies
Be nutmeg that may mint my longing dreams,
And meanwhile make the best of it in time.
Without regret: the love I have is *fine.*

a room of puppy dogs

I once lived in a room of puppy dogs,
Nigh twenty-five, and gamboling in fuss,
Clothes here and there in tatters from their teeth,
A laundry room beneath the basement stairs.
We snuggled up at night, my head on pelt
Of bellies, sounds of licking in the dark,

And silence. When through boards salvaged from ships,
Warped, splintered, weathered, piny-pitched and rough,
The sun broke through in foggy shafts of dust,
A peeping tom insouciant with torch,
The dogs might howl a bit, and scratch their butts.
Some were but months from babes, but others teens
(In canine reckoning of time), and all
Somehow, mysterious to me, had learned
To train their functioning a'down a chute,
Which in a corner stood a darkened hole.
I too had use of such, and yet the scent
Was dominated by detergent smell,
Aside the balmy footwear scent of dog,
With which it blended quite a wonder, that.
Each day, by creaking of an upstairs door,
Kept locked, an old curmudgeon of the sea,
Beard fur of feathered frost, would throw down steaks,
Slathered with gravy, and a carrot-top
Or two. The dogs would scramble fierce with growls
To claim with cutlery of teeth, their chunk,
While I dipped carrot-top in gravy sauce,
A certain delicacy for cellar fare.
Strange was the spastic carousel of legs,
The lanky whelps would soccer in the round
A ragged teddy bear with slaver's grease
Upon its scalloped brillo fur, and fight
To tear its seams some further scathing holes,
And this all day the entertainment held.
We spent nigh thirty months down there alone,
Until the old man died, his bloated corpse
An odor neighbors could not well abide,
And officers of law came by to see,
Releasing us from Hades' laundry room.
Those were the days, and though I look back now
With fondness most unusual and keen,
It's true, life must go on, dogs or no dogs.

single sip of drunken fingertips

Romeo.
Your skin seems but evaporate of musk,
Whose sweet aroma fingers strangely smell
On first caress. A burgeoning bouquet
Of ruffled peonies release their scent
In seizure of the captivated heart,
But single sip of drunken fingertips.
But eyes eclipse such raptures with the breath
Absconded of a sudden; lungs are still,
Yet tingling, then they rush to pant and heave.
The bellow mellows quick to whisper's husk,
And silence is a rhapsody of verse
That glues two pupils star to star in gleam.
Then lips which just before were green come ripe,
And wax to wettened bulge of juice and pulp,
The very shape and scent of plum on air.
This single fruit an orchard worth of sweet,
My feet step forward silken for to taste.
In wild woods of mouth, my feral tongue
Is frantic, smooth, anticipant to lick
The honey's dew upon your cheek's ripe fruit.
I long to gulp but sip to savor, sauced
On your ferment a spiced aperitif.
What lace this paper shuck and violet crepe
That soft cocoons your shea-softened skin!
Concealing fruitage secretive that waits
Unveiling with the teeth of subtle breath.
My eyes already peel pellucid rind
From thee, and dive into your traceries
And part like fog your plaited linen folds.
Yet patient hands abide impatiently,
Suspended by the grace of yay or nay
Your sighs, your murmured mews, enchanted eyes
May utter in a moan, the escapee
Of lips imprisoned helplessly on mine,
As I am sealed beyond my will to them.

chrysanthemum

chrysanthemum
petals blended cream and rose
fold
on splendid
multiplaited
fold
crisp edges
tender,
fluffy core
the fragrance
like the marriage
sun
and wind in Spring
held for the elements

how soft we all might be

A flower tender-nurtured in hot glass,
Exotic from the Eastern zephyrs' clime
(Or rather seeming so, yet grown at home),
And carried high above the thickets' thorns,
To keep its soft fragility alive,
In this a vulgar world of callous toughs.
Am I aught else but this? I am, I am,
For I have rind and sure bravado's edge:
How well I mimic hardiness that yes,
I have, but only in the half of it.
But though these limbs grow bark and thicken up
To keep the scathing bristliness at bay,
Sometimes I feel that petals are my flesh;
My heart carnational in fold and bloom,
Unlike the weedy, wooly roughs about.
But is this so? Are not all hearts as soft,
As petal plait jabot beneath it all?
I think it, yet experience dissents.
Though we begin as such, how quickly fates

Diverse according to their clime divide,
And make of us as separate though one.
The ginger sproutling learns to grow a coat
Of gnarly thistle-splay and hardened pith,
The tender shoots soon savaged in sharp teeth.
Yet I, my petals like unfurling flag
Held high above it all, serve to remind
(To elevate, not prick) how soft we all
Might be again if we remake this world.

success

Success? It can be many different things.
To be alive, to bear the several weights
And burdens, to endure, to meet with cheer
Adversity, and keep spirit alive --
This is success. Each chapter has its load,
Its moral one's obliged to reckon up.
That is a task that holds its share of work,
And if achieved with dignity, success.

the People's Chamber Halls

Lightning and sparks profusely from my head
Thunder: the traitors called Republicans
Have sold their country out and down the stream
To plebian assassins in the pay
Of demagogues, who smash our Capitol,
And piss upon the People's Chamber Halls.
Give me a gag and I will muzzle them,
Each every one, a happy censor proud
To shove their throats with axioms they balk.
Some things you must agree to to be held
A citizen, and if you won't, goodbye,
Deported or to prison, either one
Is fine with me: enough. Enough. Enough

With mad delusions vying for the state,
Declaring their equivalence to sense
And sanity and reason: just enough!
We badly need an Information Reset,
Blackout on all untrue axioms,
Until the sane ones once again outweigh
The crazies, who've been put back in their place.
A garden's crops must dominate the weeds.
A few weeds can be tolerated, if
The crops are in command, but if they're not,
It's time to mulch and crush and stamp them out.

traitors and retards

A "Libertarian": a synonym
For racist, fascist sympathizers, who
Defend their liberty to be an ass,
A loose cabal of traitors and retards.

A species of champagne and opium
for Elizabeth of Night

If I am abstinent from alcohol,
What need? Your lips are my carafe of wine.
Each breath a sigh; each visit to your shrine,
A subtle, vibrant ecstasy; each gaze,
A melting. And to touch you is to know
A species of champagne and opium.
Your lion's breath beside me in the bed,
To feel you here, a wonder and a joy.
You are the flagrancy of merriment,
Adventure of our curiosity,
The coo of doves intoxicant with love.

delicious poltergeist of haunting beauty

Butthole Surfers, Cherub
Jacob Holdt, American Pictures
Greyhound bus, I-5, through the Grapevine to San Francisco
Delirious poltergeist of haunting beauty
Surfing on a surfboard tongue through a windstorm,
Rhyming the gales in rhapsody.
King City, locusts at one's feet and everywhere
Dark blue Camaro, Richmond Bridge to San Rafael --
Skyline Boulevard, Doughboy fingers of milky moon
On frosted furrows of San Andreas Lake:
Darkness in glory of silent green of mountain meadows,
Pure sigh skating on cool of lunar train-tracks.

world's burlesque

The crows skim the spread sheets of wind.
Seaweed stalk-sways here on ocean's floor.
Applause crowds and fades and gathers again;
Hotdogs and crackerjacks in the sandstone bleachers.
Shadow pantomime of sun's flirtation.
Window is a peepshow of world's burlesque.

allodial of fraud

It still is 1492, today.
We still are there. The scathing diatribes
Las Casas furiously scribbled still
Are resonating. Gilgamesh is crazed,
And subjugates whomever may remind
Him of his Enkidu. The ink is fresh

On flayed skin's vellum Bartholomew witnessed.
Is Europe the lone well of living souls,
The others soulless, servile denizens
Of lesser destinies? Still yet we ask
This sinful question, though we may cavil.
The powerful have luxury to cringe
And weasel, if it serves to keep their reign,
But they are proud, however they may bow
To placate rising masses. Still this land
Is brutal bodies' excavation site,
The deed written in gore on leathern scalp,
And made a thanatopic title claim;
The inexhaustible springhouse of ghosts,
Yet writhing in coagulate of blood,
Offer contrary testimony still:
Illusory allodial of fraud.

this is our birthright

Do not discount the vision I have had,
For I've found something more delicious yet
Than all the orchard pommeries of plum
And apple, nectarine and citrus, grape
And apricot, or loquat dewy in
The sun, the sparkling Spring delight of sun,
Light dancing sun a gentle child's play
On bough and tender leaf of sprouting green --
A world beyond our world, as beautiful
And luscious, but one more refined and pure,
A higher frequency, where there's no loss
Of love, where possibility is not
So often wasted, where fulfillment comes
More easily, where kindness comes as grace
Effortlessly, where all one feels in love,
The buoyancy, the skipping on the clouds,
The endless adoration, and the trance
Of mystery unviolated yet
Explored with gingerly excitement comes
With every fond pursuit; where ought is is,

Where heartful sensitivity is strength,
Where cultivating all one's lovely gifts
Is honored rather than seen as effete;
Where ordinaire brutality is rare,
As rare as mountain air on cloudswept peaks,
And cannibalism of every kind
Is but a nightmare one once had now gone.
I've seen these things as clearly as this hand;
I've felt them as reality par none.
You cannot know what living is without,
For now that I have tasted life as such,
This world of disappointments pales and fades,
It chafes, it scrapes, it bruises-- and for what?
What is the point of this deceptiary
Fraud, this hint of what could be, this tease
Meant for nothing but goading us to reach?
The beauty that you see is Ariadne's
Thread out of the brutal labyrinth!
We aren't this sad approximation, but
The bright reality its sign portends!
But what assuages me stings me as well,
For now to see a touch contiguous
With that astounding beauty, that withdraws
Again to turn back towards normality,
That grey degeneration most accept,
Is ay acutely painful. Here and there,
The spheres may intersect, original
And copy; in such times, we feel sublime,
We're on the mountaintop, the world feels right,
The talents in one's heart welcome with worth --
But this fraud of a world says such are dreams,
Evaporate, ephemeral, and false,
Not to be trusted -- so it fades to dreams.
Our soul, which only thrives in beauty, shrinks,
And sinks from waking life to 'habit sleep.
The daylight world endured a dull impasse,
A prison to get through with stiffer lip
(Resentful, melancholy, but resigned),
And only in our dreams by night to thrive.
Before you pass your verdict that condemns
This all as fantasy, inquire more:
Question the children. Every child seeks

Vitality as such in rampant play
Not but by night but in the every day,
And only when eroded down forgets.
But peak experiences come to wake
Us from the stupor we've been ground into,
To bolden us to claim again such life.
A child swinging on the swingset soars.
A child running is nothing but blur
In flickering grin of untold happiness.
A child longing for a friend is fond
As fond can get, and when they may return,
Bursting bouquets of adoration's mirth.
It is our failure we don't keep this pitch,
That we discard this timbre, but reserve
It to our revolutionaries, who
We count fanatics, as we slave away
Before our third-rate idols who command
Our life a grey and spiritless expanse,
With dull rewards sprinkled but here and there.
I tell you I have exited the cave,
This grave, these catacombs we misnamed life,
And seen the sun of beauty up above,
Where heaven twinkled in the radiance
Of scattered raindrop iridescence, bright,
Resplendent with delight, angels in flight,
The levity of helium so light
And full of elegance and ease of grace.
And I have seen that this is our birthright,
Our claimable true destiny to grasp,
If we but will, and put shoulder to wheel.
It's not some wish of vanity, but truth,
Reality more vivid and more real,
The purest nutrient of this our soul,
Without which it but languishes and wanes,
But with it thrives in vibrancy and mirth!

in Eden's primal lens

She's not my manic pixie dream girl but

She is a pixie all the same no doubt,
A life as full and rich as can be had,
Of which I got a three year passing slice.
If I've made her my Laura, I know well
The angel I oft call upon is mine,
(Or I am hers), while my dear pixie lives
Her separate chosen life of ample worth.
But being shut from privy to that life,
And ay respecting privacy, I have
Alone my memories, the best in life.
It's best to not look too close at such times:
The charm fades to a mixed reality,
And I prefer the charm in purity,
The one that didn't injure me and run.
My part is simply editing the mix,
And concentrating all that ample charm,
Both magical and real, while leaving out
The pain as equally as real. This reel
Leaves that discarded film upon the floor,
To make the classic version, as it should
Have been, as seen in Eden's primal lens.

the fire and the lace

Still I in spellbound drift return to you,
Narcotic neural daze of sultry you,
The dizzy ways of knowing vixen you,
The violet trace of drizzling mane of you,
The pain of manic maze in pleasing you,
The pleas in desperate chase of fleeing you,
Confusion in the phase of having you,
The bronco bucking haze of filling you,
The fights and weeping days in loving you,
The jealousy in facing fickle you,
The fire and the lace when leaving you,
The longing in the waste of missing you.

the sugar of the sky

When you can sip the sugar of the sky,
But everything is bland and all too dull.
When you know how to feel the flight of doves,
But cloddy feet hold flesh on desert sand.
When you have licked the wonderlands with tongue,
But cotton candy landscapes fade too far.
When you have known such vibrancy few dare,
But all that sharp and focused feel is gone.
When magic is the trademark of your name,
But life has grown mundane and too banal.
Then crave, you crave, you craven crave a taste,
A flagrant flavor sour-sweet of life!
Piquant, mischievous, and citrus-spiced!
An end to hibernation! Hail to life!

my Peter Pan is weathered but alive

But being fifty, I'm no more the youth
Of twenty, and my body testifies:
The spirit wills to hop the fence and leap,
As once we spritely did, but sinews balk,
Sinovials protest, and they have force
To render their petitions competent.
Youth is alive, but in its elder prime
In me: I have the rugged look of age:
The twinkle in my eye is dominant
As yet, and kinesthesia expands
To throw myself to soar on heaven's heights --
But ligaments do not believe my faith.
And though I pluck with fury, white subverts
My efforts, peeking through to shame my hair
With frost beneath my hazel manly mane.
I have the regal look; the provenance
Of decades shows itself with gravitas

Upon the textured vellum of this face.
I have the testament of grief in me,
The weight of some defeats beneath my eyes,
That balances my levity with bulk,
And measures all my victories with shade.
Well, one needs shady grottos as one needs
The sparkling sun, so it has reason in't.
The will, indomitable, is our source
Of spunk and charm, which stem from lively spite
Of things, the thumbing of one's nose at time,
The countering of grey with color's crown.
I have such diadem upon me yet.
Sometimes the nozzle of my eye defies
Its former keenness; still my rapier beams
Its brightness in my fancy badinage.
The call to war arouses me my strength,
Where once pursuit of dallying did draw,
For there is much to joust about and win,
And we must win, for there is poppycock
Alive in mischief's foul shenanigans
The youth now take for granted as if good.
The brilliance of my fire's not as dead
But burns in tungsten fireworks as bright
As ever: try me with injustice: you
Will see -- beware the glare, for it will flare.
My Peter Pan is weathered but alive.

in shadows I was wounded

They raped me. How I wish they hadn't raped.
I wish those memories were not in me,
Confusion and abuse, and far too young.
How I've attempted to deny, in vain.
Of course it didn't happen to me, no.
Except -- it did. The clarity of that
Is undeniable between the times
That I'm pooh-poohing. O I wish, I wish,
I wish none of that happened to my boy.
I wish it didn't stay with me this long.

If I appear entitled, this is why.
Nothing can compensate for such a crime.
And if I've run to women for a cry
Within their naked arms and milky breasts,
My anguish acting as the alibi
Of this my hidden passion, I've had need,
And still I feel it, for to lose myself
In desperate comfort, anonymity
And sudden love, more antinomian
And pure, beyond proprieties --
For what was proper in my snuffing out?
In shadows I was wounded; there I'll heal.
If still I'm tempted yet hold back, the lust
-- Not for the animal or for a prize --
But for to find myself in losing self
In newer eyes that promise resurrect
When my heart's six feet under in the ground
Is what appeals -- if I refrain, it's hard.
I do. For though the liminal's the place
Where hurt happened, and healing must be found,
Still there is honor, uprightness, and love.
But often I would run and fly, escape,
To find another friend through eager lips,
To let my mischief be my suavity,
My wounded eyes the call to wounded eyes,
For only wounded ones may heal my love,
Betrayed ones nesting innocence midst pain.
To find one who will understand and trust.
But decency holds back my greater need.
Yet emptiness is honor's recompense
At times -- my anguish aches -- I need to run,
To find new eyes to say it will be fine,
To find in me their special wanted joy.
And make a world where that just never was,
A world so beautiful it's all in tears
Of wonder -- one can wish. There is that type
Whose melancholy leads right to their loins,
And in our secret sadness, there we find
Our intimacy; there, sublimity
Makes renaissance in creativity.
I wish they hadn't raped. O how I wish.

rippling plum

Black Corinth, sour to the sweet on lips,
Wine's preview bursting in its skin petite:
Sun's waterfall on rows of verdant vine.
The sibilance of bubbling Perrier
In redwood slats with steam atop the tub,
Beneath the arbor where wisteria
Mimics clusters of grapes in delicate
Crepe-paper folds of faded lavender.
Sicilian silence on her pursing lips.
She drips, skin sweltering in caviar
Of bubbles, and uplifts, a towel in hand
To wrap about her glistening rapture's ripe
And pearling rind, and stares on rippling plum
Of moon-whipped whitening on twilit lake,
Auburns and burgundies on cumulus
Above, as sun, a poppy comet, hurls
In heaven's flames to dive beneath the sea.
Her glance is sudden Siren trance of swoon,
Loon on lagoon, escape in sail on ghee
Of melted lunacy on warbling wave.
I am the spritzer's colloquy of sighs;
A dozen doves release in spray of white
On wing in feather-clap from out my heart.
I am a swift librarian of awe,
Perusing folios her lashes shed
Coquette. Sonoma rendezvous is fresh
In all-around-me aromatic breeze
Of wistful pollen gusts, and I am stirred
In tongueless still of all my heart's content.
With look of nonchalance, I stand transfixed,
As if the flirty splash of milk on green
Of vineyard's nighttime bashful-shadowed leaves --
Or old Cyrillic on the brandywine
Of alternating-luminescent lake --
Could be as wizard-beautiful as she,
As pythonesse-astonishing and pure,
As gypsy-bride abandonment of skirts
In tossing air of Volta virile swing.
I am in manifest of open prayer,

The fruit of longing's long gestation shared.
I am the fleshing-forth of laughing joy,
A smiling boy inside the suavity
Of man bemused by miracle and musk,
A smirk of flirting masculinity
In mischief's eyes. O heart, digest this dream,
To make its blessings ever part of me.
I'm spellbound in implausibility
Of she with me here in the champagne shell
Of trellised moonlight, basking in risqué
Of glances perilous: a daydream's nymph
Breath's boundary away from trembling lips.

the darling daredevil

Where stands the weight of clemency in hearts?
My friends have exiled me, for many years,
For peccadilloes, nothing more than that.
Each gambled for my heart, and tore a piece,
Each to their separate ways, and left me cold,
Here shivering in snow. Let it be told:
The price of being brave's to be alone.
One doesn't make friends easily this late.
The math's subtraction, not addition. Once
I was the cutting edge, the darling daredevil,
Admired for convictions. That
No more. Now I'm the one who's cut, cut off.
I shave away the edge as yet, alone.
Once I could feel the chorus of their love
Behind me, strengthening my firm resolve,
But pioneers go way too far for most.
To fight for decency against the daze
Of conscience is an uphill war of wills.
Sometimes they kill you, sometimes starve you out.
The price of bravery's too high for me.
Where is their clemency if I have sinned?
Is this sentence proportional at all?
If this is common justice, there is none.
What then the basis for a higher sort?

Forgiveness is a word the tongue adores,
While pledging in its heart severity.
And writing this is vain and changes none.

let the face talk

Sometimes I look upon your photograph
To see that face that you won't show to me,
And let the face talk where the words will not,
Drink up that once beloved, friendly sight,
So bitterness of this my exile rests
A moment or an evening or two.

a diva in the heart of dwarves

There is a diva in the heart of dwarves;
As solid as they are, they're sensitive.
They sour quickly when integrity
Is lost, withdrawing where wholeness has slipped.
Their hearts are deep and mineral, but keen.
They live no-nonsense in fidelity,
Expecting groundedness and clarity,
And turn their backs where fickleness is found.
They're not won back as easily once lost.
But faith for faith, they give selves lastingly.
They're artisans whose love is in their work,
Whose seeming stinginess is to reserve
To those who value them their masterpiece.

perceive the colt and not the man

A colt, cavorting amniotic-fresh
From mother's loins, the sun gleaming on dew

Of windswept fur : its springy legs bounce up
And tilt exhilarating air with joy!
Once more, once more, a taste of passing flight,
An awkward, mirthful gallop in the grass!
Muscle and sinews spirit's ministers,
Instant facilitators of the will,
The agents of the heart's abounding play!
Inside I still am this athletic colt,
This gymnast of the grass, but limbs revolt
And decades mutiny against my will,
So something spry is caught in something old.
Let eyes perceive the colt and not the man.

the angel-glimpse

The hopes we have for others are our gifts,
The angel-glimpse from Eden of their souls.
Alas, too often Eden's but a trace,
One soft and muffled many do not hear.

Oak and Avena

for Elizabeth of Night

Dark as the Oak, light as the Avena:
Two skins in intertwined caress of love,
The woodland and the meadow, grass and bough,
Desire in the wild floral limbs,
The petal-flame of lurid, living bloom,
Sunlight at dusk between two seeking lips,
Palm aubergine in nectarine of palm,
A soft and cherished grip in stroll of eve.
Fingers in wool and palms on cheeks, the hands
In straw, and almond eyes on irises
Of mustard-spangled blue in twinkling fond.

your beauty shrinks from me

Antony.
Defy exquisite scription in lithe verse;
Defy the ecstasy of syllables,
The catalog of roses wrapped in lace;
Defy the melting heart its finest praise:
You will not find the literature of love
That lauds you as I have time and again.
I thought you beautiful beyond all words,
The breathlessness of skin and awe of eyes,
The mirth of comedy in irises,
The touch of but petite of the divine,
A figurine of porcelain and rouge
Surprising Aphrodite made with clay
And breathed her rose aroma into life.
But beauty is a quality of soul
That thaws the wax and mask of brittle flesh,
Endowing it with some transcendent touch;
It is an inner poignancy and poise,
A loveliness born from its heart of love.
But though your form is flawless in your shape,
Your sculpted face, your soft mahogany
Of smoothest hue, the smile you possess,
No beauty can belong to one so cruel,
For ugliness then mars your perfect grace,
Deforming from within what from without
No doubt remains impossibly inspired
With a fountain-spray of subtlety,
The trace of heaven's holy touch and truth,
A statuesque near-immortality!
To take celestial form but not intent,
To spurn the inner loveliness the sky
Impregnated within your fairy flesh
Is not a beauty but mere vanity.
Deserved no doubt, but petty and untrue
To fingers of that goddess of the foam
Who plied you from the Niger's river-clay
And made you sign and miracle of her.
Your body, made of wonder's wish and touch,

Signals, but do you represent her heart,
Do justice on this earth where she's unseen
Except in baby's breath and peonies,
Except in tossing froth of ocean's spray,
Except in Spring's increase of nested eggs,
Except in flames of Turneresque sunset,
Except in lovers' mews on balconies
Where midnight and the moon cloud-intertwine,
Except in prodigies of feminine
Exuberance and most ebullient grace?
Do you with honor do her embassy?
What shaped you I of needs but do adore;
But do you foster forth these qualities
In care for those who worship at your shrine?
Your beauty shrinks from me when you decline.

between a son and mother

There are these love affairs -- between a son
And mother -- of the heart, and not the flesh --
A sweetness and devotion -- full of soul --
A healthy, wholesome love society
Ought heed and not deride -- a beautiful
Commitment, and establishment of joy
And care, a tender tending of them both --
A testament of all that's best in love.

ideals have proven inconvenient

We have the means to pry, and so we do.
So immature, that what we can, we will,
Because we can, and so abilities
Disable us. Capacities undo
Our frail integrities, and petty sin,
Now magnified by our technologies,
Transforms our meddling busybodying

Into a vast surveillance state of all.
Our precious privacy is but a quaint
Antiquity, a laughable pretense.
The foremost of our rights, our cloistered thoughts
And intimacies between confidants,
Are moled with tattletales and little spies,
If hackers or if spooks or corporate bugs,
Alerting advertisements to our talk.
Our sins have caught up with our grander claims,
And proven that our pride dissembled us;
For all our talk of sacred liberties,
We sold them out soon as a buck was made
The more in selling them, and so we prove
Our loyalties: to what is vile in
Our breasts, our principles but cover-ups
To gild our sad depravity with sheen.
Our deeds reveal our truer faith to us,
And atheism is but shedding skins
Of our hypocrisy, and letting go
The values we abhorred as we upheld.
Ideals have proven inconvenient;
We are so wicked we indeed believe
They're ink wasted on paper, pretext, fraud
In frillery, the currency of fools,
When principles, if followed, lead to grace.
When wholesome, they are guides and lead us through
The fog and darkness, our telemetry,
Which we at times must trust, and follow blind.
Shallow empiricists and pragmatists
May balk, but without trust in our ideals,
And readiness to sacrifice a time,
To lend the credit principles need most,
And time for our integrity to grow,
We falter. Power becomes destiny,
A nightmare of our jealousies and doubts,
A craven, snarling gambit of mistrust.
We amplify our rudest tendencies,
Then celebrate our grand ability.
The id is in control of what we make.
Forbidden Planet? Look around and see.

auctioning Messiah's clothes

Auctioning Messiah's clothes -- the jewels
Of Jews, the festival of massacre,
The volunteer militias, pumpkin pie
At lynching parties, relics from the bones,
Gold teeth and rings from crematoria,
The spectacle of torment at the cross.

that ruffle round the whorl
for John Kemmerer (1945-2021)

Full lips, lips ripe with dew and puckered pink,
Crisp rims of red that ruffle round the whorl,
Exuding musk of distant ripened fruit,
And held by twisted limbs of green with thorns,
In sway with gentle borealis touch;
Behind which rise, like sun-reflecting ice,
Smooth beams of steel and glass clerestories
That pierce the fog of Philadelphian clouds.

restored, released, renewed

Freed now of bodily impediments,
The pain and thrashing, decades' steroid use,
At peace at last, and flying free, a dove
United once again with source of love,
His essence, trapped and handicapped in flesh,
Now all of him, restored, released, renewed --
Out from the fog and smoke into the clouds
Of heaven, ecstasy in being free,
Embraced by all he loved in total love.

sunset's cobweb scene of fading flames

These then, the razors of the domey blue
He loved, giving clean shave to beardy clouds,
The building blocks of sunset's cobweb scene
Of fading flames, the frame of hickory
In thicket through which black of midnight played,
The long blue tongue of Schuylkill lapping up
The skyline, made of obelisks and sticks.
Here Franklin set his printing blocks in rows,
Here Michener resurrected Iceland's art,
Here Coltrane redefined the saxophone.
Here someone, generous with his own loins
To let me live, was born, and lived, -- and died,
A man I hardly knew, an intellect,
As fond of his own books as I of mine,
And crippled in his gizzards to the blood,
The blood of it, which wounded him to waste,
The guts at last reclaiming him to soil.
Stranger, here and there, and in and out;
A human being, troubled, like us all.
A thinker : "God's the sum of all of us."
I wish him well. Serenity and peace.
The scent of Laurin's paradise of rose.

army of a man

So often lonely I have fought the fight,
My single self to seek the stolen right,
I've not the ease of those on stable ground,
Who smoothly may defend their turf and bounds.
I've been a scrapper, army of a man,
No prisoners, without a single fan,
But trusting in the prophets old of yore,
The ones who fought for justice long before.

I dwell in jaded ages with no guts,
Where heroes are denied as too much fuss,
Where prejudice is just the way it is,
And every man is looking out for his.
I shrug the times, defying all the trends,
Defending losing causes that offend,
Yet still are right and still should have defense,
Even if opposition is immense.
I can't afford to be genteel and mild;
With one against a hundred, I am wild,
And I win, though I've got scars to show.
Sometimes it feels they go as deep can go.
I ache at night, my all of skin is scraped;
Sometimes my heart feels like it has been raped,
But on I fight, and hunkering down, I gear
Myself with arms of knowledge to strike fear
In those more ignorant who have no clue,
Yet bully with impunity -- they'll rue
The day they struck the underdog near me:
Their tail between their legs in infamy,
They'll bolt and run, the cowards, stripped of rank,
No money left in their poor knowledge bank.
I find the goons who guard the bounds of sin,
Who think their cause a holy one they'll win;
I siege their fortresses and storm the wall:
Like horns at Jericho, they all will fall.
They bow before their masters while they gloat,
But fall the same as those on whom they dote.
I have a streak of Joshua in me,
Yet solo like King David, must defeat
Goliath on my own with but a sling.
Yet when I'm in the dance, I have wide wings,
That whirl about the battlefield, and sing
Magnificats to humble down the proud,
The Spirit's whisper drowning out the loud.
A lonely task I wish already won,
But if it takes me, then I'll be the one.

the foxes still roam freely

How close the condemnation hath eluded us!
How sharp the edge just inches near!
How all surrounded by the peril we
Have slipped by barely, almost trapped by sin,
As many of our fellows fell, and hard!
How lightly we just skirted lips of cliffs!
How far hath wickedness been sold as good,
And danger as but freedom! Here are fiends,
With immorality's casuistry,
Ready to peddle to the hapless youth
Their gleeful sociopathy as truth!
The fox is made the shepherd of the hens.
Those who get through unscathed aren't innocent,
Just lucky, one foot shy of falling off,
Or worse, just never caught. How close we came!
That razor's breadth serves not to reassure,
If then to sigh, and pray for our good luck.
The foxes still roam freely in the pens.

makes reason validate his wickedness

The words of wicked men long resonate,
And incubate in caverns of the mind.
What we release has no impunity,
But circles good with pandemonium.
One ought not have an open mind to ill;
The fox, allowed to speak, will justify
His malice with a smile as innocence.
Untruths declared as truths poison the mind,
And ill reports by measure slant the heart.
That man is rational is flattery;
He rationalizes, and with abuse,
Makes reason validate his wickedness.
Our modern laxity is no defense,

But cowardice given apologia.
Prejudice is rash and buys the press.
The Constitution lies: our tongues can sin.

misty strip-tease on a summer's night

She was the kiss of lava on cold ice;
The steam surrounded her like foggy clouds
Fur-draping naked shoulders of the moon
In misty strip-tease on a summer's night.
My eyes were ooze, but molten pools of blue
On viewing her. I was a liquid doll
In dizzy cartwheels of the spellbound mind.
She was as flighty as a nervous doe;
One twitch, she ran; one hint of love, she fled.
But cool and slow and smooth one had to be
To catch her in her negligee of night,
And pass a slow aquarium of eyes
In underwater wonder, moment's pause.
But melancholy, soft communion stares
That helpless lingered sad before she ran.
She was a shy, ephemeral ghost of grace;
One glance before she disappeared, you're hooked,
And moments pass quotidian in blur
Until she surfaces, quite on a lark,
Again, and all the grey is colorized.
Insipid tastes undull and ripen sharp.
The blood has found its cruising groove again.
Life seems a wizard miracle of blooms,
A sudden labyrinth of rose and dew
That greens the barren desert where one lurched
So parched too long, but now oasis, if
Mirage -- for when your hope is fresh, she fades.
The paradise peels back its folds and frays.
The black and white in which one's color raged
In vain to break the tyranny of grey
Returns, and she is naught but wincing taunt

That wounds with silence as she stays away.
One's nothing but infrequent thought to her,
While she rules in ruffled monopoly
Of baby's breath and lilies in one's thoughts.
She keeps an empty throne she never takes,
But saunters by and slinks about a glance,
To stay the place she'll never occupy.
She's haunt of breath and lips and glimmering loins
That burns her tease upon the memory,
And whispers spells in silken dialect,
Phonemes just as mysterious as her.

papyrus singing birdsong

In vellum, whispers may assuage my angst,
And visions spilt in ink, the emptiness
Dispel: these bring to me society
Deprived of me, for which my life has longed.
Deprived, though I have needed. Gathered here,
Papyrus, singing birdsong through the panes
Of this my prison, where the life I wish
Is banished, now restored to me in scrawl,
Trifolia of winged feet on ink,
Collage in alphabet of outlawed dreams,
Here where the revolution is taboo.
Alas, for lack of this, I were but lost.
Surviving the Reaction in my books.
The life I love but hypothetical,
The camaraderie I crave abstruse,
The Pentecostal frenzy impolite,
I summon in the future's looking glass
I find on foliage marked black with glyphs.
Here conferences of arguments abound,
Here laughter of the ages riles grins,
Here all the best and beautiful confer,
Here daring pushes dullness to the side.
Without these visionaries' rhapsodies
Beside me all about, what grey would rule,
How rude my convalescence, parched and dry

The desert air, how lonely all this pain,
How lacking in magnificence and pomp,
How colorless, how callous, how inept.

O for a slam-pit

O for a slam-pit these my aged limbs
Could bear! I cannot walk but I would mosh!
How frenzy in my gusto longs to thrash!
What makes a spine disdain the crowd's embrace?
How can these knees banish the riot's thrill,
Or keep from me my skipping through the storm?
I am a gallop in unwilling flesh,
A running barren of its lusty legs,
A superhero grounded from his flight.
O where are webs that might stretch me to skies,
And let me vault on canopies of mist?
Whence fling of flitting flesh from pole to pole?
For but a bounce sublime of buoyancy!
I hobble in this hovel's lubberland,
Bereft of heaven's sylphan dance on fog.
I was a cellophanic dragonfly,
A neon whir through night, now but a slug.
If Muses could but condescend to touch
My tongue, too plucked of feather, and restore
Its plumes, then I could fly without my limbs!
But as it stands, both limbs and tongue are lame.
I could not lift from dusty rock if tried.
Anxiety's too careful vigilance
Towards caprice of ache, or where the next
Of strain and sore, well, how to lift my lilt?
I stutter to distract, and jerk through fits.
But once the adolescent flesh was free;
Once limbs to lilies' meadow-summons met,
And hormones hallowed impact in the pit!
There where the molecules are miracle
Of clash, there where the whirlwind gathers meat
To spirit's rush, there where baptismal sweat
Of frolic fêtes! Ah, there, if I could be!

If I could be!

San Francisco
a poem even Francesca Lia Block had to admit was pretty

Queen Annes in aqua-blue and lavender,
The lyric of the hillocks' rise and fall.
The nip in poprock air of misty sea,
A shimmer-city sitting on its dreams.
I knew loa that feather-sift the streets
With breezes' gaiety and levity,
And ride invisible the trolleys' rails.
Outlandish visions' elfin citadel,
Where all impossibles of elsewhere thrive.
I ran my Ariadne's labyrinth,
The narrow streets, the corner grocery stores,
The rooftop gardens, Nellies in their nests,
And lisps in swishes' sway; the poets' moots,
The Leftist ecstasies, the Jewish thrill
Of Messianic discourse in abstract
Of secular enthusiasm's tomes;
The homeless characters, eccentric bums,
The seagulls, and conspiracy unspoke,
The secrecy of heretics in dens.
I loved their pizza, and tofu satay,
Their cabs and burlesque-era theaters,
Cake-slice townhouses with their limestone steps.
I loved adventure's air in love's ménage,
The desperate, hopeless longing to possess,
The poignant melancholy's bittersweet,
The mystic daze that came with being stunned.
I was so stunned, I was delirious.
I sipped the interstitial space of texts,
And savored wine of my refusals' grapes.
Refused and yet adored, a potent brew.
I summon fireflies to irises,
And flint the glint of pupils' dancing sparks
So I may be adored, yet with allure,

Yet with the chase is never quite yet done,
The courting years-continuous and long.
I'm but a dumb romantic, sad and glad.
The city spoke to me, menagerie
Of fin d'siecle ghosts from yesteryear.
The history was syrupine and thick,
And dripped in crannies of the musty boards,
The sailors' silent reveries on streets,
The souvenirs of sleet and rusty rails
Of Turneresque sea-storm on lonely ships.
North Beach, an Asian blonde, her cozy loft,
With Ma Vie En Rose on video.
I met her in the stacks, flirted in tongue
Of misfit intellect, and got a date.
Against the Fall of 1998.
And Elfman sang to Sally as I drove.
The houses were mirage of sculpted mist.
Did we then kiss a single swipe of lips?
If so, it wiped my memory more chaste;
And yet the air was crackling with lust
I savored more in sweet abeyance, ah!
The magic of the evening replete.
Shapeshifters, selkies, gender-bending lads,
The mermen of the wharf's sea-polished pine,
And skipping brownie-boggins leaping rails
Of picket fences, leaving mischief-dust,
The meal of shooting stars, on porch and step.
That was the city that I loathed and loved.

plaster putto

Were I a plaster putto pissing wine,
Sweet Chardonnay of clarity and zest,
I'd rest more statuesque with levity.
A Cheshire's grin on boyish lips, to splash
The cobalt-tile tides in frothing sun,
As geysers rise hibiscus fresco-fleurs.
This light Muscat, diaphanous and pure,
Is nitrous oxide liquidine with laugh,

And I am bubbles in oblivion
Of mist. My fist fondles a noodle -- watch
It whiz -- it drizzles fondly on the breeze,
And birds look quite askance as it may spray.

the frolicsome brocade
for Freya

She is fluorescent zephyrs' merriment,
And bees' entranced bewilderment from fleurs.
The winged nested ones take song from lips
She bursting-bud in crimson sheen reveals
When she makes debutante her pearly whites.
The beasts bound in the frolicsome brocade
Of lush meadows that sprout with lupine blue
And poppy's livid flame when she walks by.
She's Flora's looking glass and Maia's maid,
Regalia of lilies in their lanes.
The blossom-bashful seeds, asleep in beds
Of cozy soil, wake when she is near,
And twine her calves with color-furling vines.
Is it the Spring? Or is it her? The same.
They write upon the heart same signature.
They lift the breath to loft upon same clouds.
They foster both delicious fragrances
That salivate the lips and wet the loins.
O maiden of Floralia, come near!

night restores

Anchises.
There is no alteration that could steal
Your beauty's fond preeminence from you;
Subtraction from infinity is nil.
Nor age nor sickness holds the might to rob
Your formidable gorgeousness from you.

You simply are high Aphrodite's gift,
And she bestows, against the very world.
What she has given, nothing has the touch
To abrogate; her charms are permanent,
As evidence of eyes proves yours are too.
Let temporary haze worry you not;
No touch of tarnish can unsilver you,
But like the Huntress, light's ecdysis peels
The dusty film from nakedness of moon,
And all the clouds misting her pewter fade.
Winter may icicle the pedestal
Of Venus; snow may frost her figurine
A simple season; Spring shows her pristine.
She sheds that snow as pearling dew in sun.
A garment may be soiled in the race;
The river runs all stains to clarity.
And no chiton undoes the shapeliness
Of fondest paragons, despite what rips
May for a day in thorns tatter it through,
For she is evident in eminence
Throughout, and all her graces sew those seams
To seamlessness. What burglars think to take
Comes apparitious in their grubby hands,
Revealing she as jewel-endowed as e'er.
She scintillates with stars about her neck;
If day obscures, no matter: night restores.

apple-sweet

Her beauty wavers balmy on the breeze;
She is her own fragrant rosarium.
I could be an intoxicated bee
Within her petals' pistils, shivering
In daze of adoration, nuzzling
In pollen ecstasy and nectar bliss.
One gaze from her unparallelèd face
Is pure ambrosia, clear and apple-sweet.

Phidias in rue

Anchises.
Her skin, if marble, could not be more true
A monument, she is so statuesque.
But sculptors weep to see her, envying,
Praxiletes and Phidias in rue.
"Alas, that I carved Venus short of her!
How now may Aphrodite give me grace,
When she may have been gifted with her face?"
Pygmalion lets go his ivory,
And leaves dull Galatea in the rock.
He soon concludes his eyes are fraudulent
Humbugs who seek to hitch him for a scam,
Yet still he dizzies in the gaze of her.
"I wilt before intimidating bloom
She nonchalantly carries in her eyes,
Upon her lips of ribald mischief, cheeks
Of dusky rue." Hellenes are pink with blush
To think they loaded foaming ships with spears
Over that second-hand and homely lass
That Paris craved, when they behold this beaut.
"What was that strife, over that counterfeit?
We see before our eyes the unveiled sun
Of which that woman that we worshipped was
But haze and dreary smoke! Alas, our wounds!
Away, vain arms and empty-hearted spears!
Why mothers weep by missing graves for her?
At least if it had been this shining sun,
This evident perfection, that had worth!
But we unfleshed ourselves and wasted blood
For penny-ante plain Jane Menelaus
Once mistook delirious as wife!
Alas for this we ever lost one life!"

song aplenty in the blood

The very river clay of red shouts out
In silent whispers from the weeping walls
Old Spirituals' baritones of woe
That sing from out the clinging ivy vines.
Foundations of the lowest who built treasure-
Cities for the Pharaoh, mud and straw.
But two true understand the pyramid:
Those at the very apex, and the base.
Those at the base more truly comprehend.
Whomever are the Habiru know well.
The hated, whom their skin speaks of the clay,
The poorest of the poor. No college text,
Except it share this testimony's truth,
Has understanding like they do in bones
That ache by midnight of the working day,
The burden of projected bigotries.
I place my hands upon the bricks and squint
To listen for the ghosts once living flesh
Who raised the edifice and poured their blood
Into the baked clay's pores, for there is song
Aplenty in the blood, that echoes here.

from soil such as this

Where Persian plows churned up the soil, Greeks
Grew crops that took on flavors of that clay,
And Jews chewed on the fruit, and laid their plows
To Cyrus, stirring up their Hebrew soil
With the leaven of the Saoshyants,
Which fertilized the Prophets yet anew,
Through Messianic dreams that did awake
The Habiru within, and it resurged.
From soil such as this, Christ had his birth.

Platte Bridge

Smithereens, the splintered wood and steel,
The fire burning -- ah, the chasm down
Three stories to the river down below:
Plummets the train, and hovering above
The dark abyss, but starlight on the skein
Of ripples on the river, dove, as if
An iron mermaid in slow motion fall,
The locomotive, with its passengers,
To wreck of bone, and shrapneled flesh, and death.
The saboteurs from the Confederacy
Skulked and gloated in the night afar.
How swift that slowest flight through faithless air!
In ruined pulp of shattered gore, the flesh
A hero rallied once to Harper's Ferry,
Then through brush and bush by night escaped,
Stood still and silent in the glimmering
Too-gentle gold of river sand by flames
Sparked in the shocking zen of river flow,
The aqua blue in shadow reddened now.
Here by the Platte, the neighbors still may swear
In early Fall, a merman-shimmering ghost
Is heard sloshing the shallows, Barclay Coppock's
Phantom humming abolitionist
Anthems -- and then the frogs croak in the reeds,
And there is haunting silence once again,
No trace at all of 1861.

Eucalyptine masques

Eternity of theater and dance
Amongst the trees, and blowing leaves in breeze.
Here Eucalyptine masques so gently sway
Ballet in Maxfield Parrish ruddy gum.
The pine needles baleen the tidal air,
Where clouds cavort in mischief and disguise.

sonnet her immortal to the nations

My love was given to me by the earth;
Declared to me, this is your lifelong mate.
Her face was stamped in hope upon my heart.
Alas, my Gomer wandered where she strayed,
And stayed a settler in a foreign land.
But love her in her freedom, I was told.
Learn how to love from distances afar.
Learn love as exiles cherish native lands.
Be her Petrarchus, tying laurel leaves
About thy cowl and locks, and sonnet her
Immortal to the nations' pining thirst,
Who'll ask, Who was this modern Helena?
Alas, I shall not summon thousand ships,
And stain the Trojan lands with blood,
For she has made her choice, and love shall heed.
A thousand letters I shall send to Troy,
Each more the beautiful than that just passed.
Let then her Alexander gloat as will,
For I shall hold the silver of the quill.
He loves her for a single life;
My words make her perennially fresh.
She comes to me as Aphrodite comes,
In longing and in dreams, the dreams of youth,
Alluring, holy, friendly, intimate,
The one who knew me in sincerity
Of second childhood, the very best,
When all I was was heart and thinnest skin.
Then in the chutzpah of my bounding life,
A fool, the concentrated spark of spunk,
A mosh-philosopher, a bold naif,
A cynical utopian and fop,
A ragamuffin Romeo and sage,
An Abba royalty upon the floor,
Both spaz and style in my suavity,
The heart-throb essence of the stunning svelte.

I had the looks, the moves, the charm, the brains,
A madcap New Romantic in his frills,
The very pulse of fun, and mischief's son.
How could she not then fawn, as I was fond?
She was a diva devotee of me,
A votary of this my sylphlike shrine.
To praise her is to praise who loved me too.
To call to mind our capers is to gaze
In that ecstatic mirror of such times
The ancients spoke as miracle and grace,
Intense and magical and singular.
So singular, that though in fact they ached,
And being maelstrom, if then fabulous,
They had to end -- a lifetime in a spurt --
They linger, haloed with a golden dust.
To tell the stories fills my heart with joy,
And through them, I may share my very soul.
It is a gift, an invite to the shrine,
The days when I was cause of many swoons,
Both innocent and cocky in my way.
To speak of her is to recall myself,
To speak the index of those holy days,
Those mad and sad adventures of my youth.
Such times feel like a lasting oracle.
I swear the earth spoke to me in my heart,
My hormones, and my winking quirkiness.
The glory of those times will not come back,
For other blessings offer up themselves.
My misery has blessed the slut in me
With many fruits of many flavorous lands,
And given me at last my quietude
And mirth, love sans adrenaline and pain,
But full of frequent laughter. Still, that lass
Still tickles me, and what may tickle you,
Stay true to, in your odd and wildsome way.
In fact, she was amusement, lemonade
And pink and fizzing, fascinating, strange,
Infuriating, wondrous, whimsical,
A spectacle, and zany to the max!
Leave off the empty generalities
Of romance; she was full of content, spry!
The things I said of Helena are true,

Yet I suspect Helen was boring; not
Elysia! She vexed you and she hexed you
With her goofy, dorky, darling charm.
I got a kick from her each passing day:
Now what malarkey will she pose today?
What brilliant insight in an airhead speech?
What cockamamie campiness and shtick?
What child-wisdom from beasts' oracles?
What folie-a-dieu to taste tonight.
She didn't fit; I didn't fit; voila!
A perfect match, made not to last but thrill.
I'm Pan as marvelous aristocrat
Of middle age, a salt and pepper Peter
In a tux, a catch with pretty paunch,
An elven secret mystic in my eyes.
If Wendy walks the bourgeois London streets,
What of it, meh! I had the best of her,
The most imaginative quantity.
I keep it treasure, fairy's flour-gold,
And sprinkle when I will, but eyes are fire
In my silver days the same as old.
More seasoned, rugged, sculpted, lips a scythe
Of lunacy and sharpened merriment,
I caper and cavort on crutches still,
An undiscovered Muses' marvel-well,
And how I ladle liberally for all!
I got it, and my Emmy's in the heart,
My Grammy then whenever I may sing,
Academy Award of poetry
With single scribble of my stylus.
Would I have waxed champagne as this with her,
Without this yeast of longing bubbling up
The mash and must in me, that now I vine
A wonder in pastoral hillocks' dales,
Sweet master wine to lips illumed with moon?
I doubt it; there's the price the Muses ask.
I labor at their lyrical fond task.

possessed by purple

Possessed by purple: velvet, eyeliner,
Corsets, fishnets, chokers, black lace, dracar --
Seduce me with accoutrement like this--
Bring back that 90s chic, late night, downtown,
Dark lights, highlights, eyesights of lasting charm
And fatal beauty, bustiers and webs,
Thick draperies, and legs in shapely gauze;
Entranced in strobe-light dance beyond all laws --
A leash: what femme fatale will lead me forth,
Bid me to lick her curvy vinyl skin,
Walk me, a heart-throb quadruped in collar
Down the midnight boulevard in dim
Fluorescents? The enticing essence of
A passing shadow's crush? The sudden hush
After the club when lips waver to touch,
And hesitate and sigh -- she takes you back --
To classic architecture now run down --
Old pillars, stunning stairwells, stonework, frost
On crafted panes, the stain of lipstick run
On neck, mascara smeared with sweat, corset
Unsnapped and brazen, gazing in the dark--
The window open to MacArthur Park --
Shadow puppets on walls ballet the moves
Of serpents sloughing skins, the spin of limbs,
Whirlwind of wish and wist that swirls each kiss
To heaven's swoon, a sweet annihilation's
Boon, a moonlit titillation's tune;
A mix of flesh exposed and gauze and sheets --
The sound of mourning doves down on the streets --
The careless splay of adipose and bone --
The stumbling out of bed to shuffle home --
The dawn's cool air, the stare of blazing pink,
Splashed water on the face home at the sink,
A slinking smile, scent of hers on hands --
One sniffs, and once again's in foreign lands.
Possessed by purple wrapped in ebony;
Mirage, bring back this luscious reverie!

midnight masques in candelabra glow

I wouldn't go back -- I simply wouldn't go back --
And yet my mind wanders along that track
So frequently -- allure and magic charm;
So much enticing pleasure mixed with harm.
So much confusion, thus a clinging close;
So much intrusion -- thorns -- and yet the rose.
This age of LEDs will never know
The midnight masques in candelabra glow
That kept us nooked in alcoves dark with shade,
The caverns lined with velvet, silk parades
Of capes and lace, the charcoal on the face,
The skin beneath the gauze so sweet and glazed,
The faerie glamour of enchanted days!
The city slept; we danced, we leapt, we crawled!
We teased our hair, and ripped our skirts, and mauled
Our blouses, though they billowed, tore our tights.
Stayed out til 4 AM on Wednesday nights,
And Friday, Saturday, and Sunday too --
Kontrol Faktory on Mondays, or Club Blue,
Or Nocturne; then the World on Thursday night,
Perversion; Velvet, with the naughty sight
Of go-go girls and tranny lads in wigs,
The catty badinage and vicious digs.
The faux-aristocrats in airy silk,
Edwardian and New Orleans and the ilk.
Guy in his wedding gown with gauzy train;
Dark habit of the sulking nun Shermayne.
The snazzy Britpop punk of DJ Split;
The spunky tongue of (un)leash's sharp wit.
The Frankenstein and Sid of svelte Rich Bitch;
The coven of the thirteenth vampish witch.
Those days are mist, and melt into the drift
Of moonlit fog -- a curse, and yet a gift.
These dingy digitals have not the taste
To relish those sweet years of blood and lace.
It folds up into time, and takes its bow.
Still stunned, and still seduced into its wow.

I miss the Castro like I miss my life

It's difficult to always be around
So many straight people. It squelches me.
They're unimaginative. Lovely, yes,
In their own way, but never fabulous.
Not magical enough. Obsessively
Too partisan for quote reality
Unquote. Too passive with their fantasies.
A person should be half delusional.
If more than that, it's dangerous; if less,
It's quite pathetic. People whom I've loved
The most insisted that their dreams were real,
Against the very world, without a doubt,
But visionaire intensity applied
To mandatory playfulness and style.
The spirit starts to starve without this stance.
And people say "pretentious", as if that
Were not the virtue that it truly is,
The childlike pretend that resurrects.
Austerity has no appeal to me.
Begone with ruggedness and sparsity.
Give me eye shadow, scarves, accoutrement
Of theater, ingredients of play.
I miss the Castro like I miss my life.
Suburbia is hardly life at all.
It lacks the catalyst of fantasy.
It's sterile to the point of being dead.
Too serious. Too tied to management.
Life never should be managed, but released
In bursts of color and of glamour, sparks
And mischief, spunk! It drags me down
To be amongst unfestive folk like this.
I think of all the saints' days down below
The border, folk who center all their lives
Around their festivals. But normal bores
Consider that extravagant and waste,
For everything must be as dull as them,

As plain, as ugly, unimaginative.
They lack effulgence. Trickle-folk. Without
A fountain in their soul to glory forth,
Without a thought of profit and of loss.
Bohemia is also pitiful,
The drugs, the lack of boundaries, the sloth,
The carelessness with love, the overuse
Of their patchouli, and the sloppiness
Towards ambition of their fantasies.
These culdesacs around me! Such dead ends!
Too mellow. Give me zen that crackles forth,
Not droops. Flaccidity of spirit, no!
Give me flamboyance and audacity,
That flaming derring-do that so annoys
The overmasculine, and makes them feel
Uncomfortable. To watch them squirm is gold,
The tables turned! Give me a festive queen
But anyday above a soulless bore!
I've been too deep in undercover work,
Too much a sleeper cell in zones of grey.
But feel that San Francisco Bay's cool air,
The spirit of adorned Victoria,
The bustle of the gaiety on streets,
The swish and wink and flash so unrepressed,
Now there's a place where I can play at last!
Where possibility still seems to brim,
Without impediment, where nonsense wears
A worthy crown, and struts as royalty,
Where dreams are unnegotiable but claimed!
Where I am tickled pink, mischievous
And marvelous, where life's a musical,
Where madcap battiness is beautiful,
So different from the madness squelching brings.
So different from the madness squelching brings.

the Belladonna belle of yesteryear

She's Primavera's fond original
Of peonies and violet candytufts,
Of karma chocolate and anenomes.
She's fresh as freshets in the April thaw.
She's everybody's wedding -- elegance,
And poignancy in ceremonial
Effulgence, goblets' essence of the grape,
Effusive floral urgency and splay,
The lingering of eye on worshipped eye,
Wisteria on iron arbors, wing
On snowy wing of bursting doves released,
The sunlight winking on the teary lake,
The papillon that flutters by the bride,
The burgundy of bridesmaids' melancholy
Satin repertoire, the vaporous
Suspension of ephemera in wist,
Petite eternity in deep amor --
Take everyone of these, and boil down
Their beauty to quintessence, that is she.
She is my very youth in Southern smile,
The Belladonna belle of yesteryear
And ever, slippery still on the skin,
Escaped, majestic silent salmon, lost
To weeping rapids roiling in the sea,
Where she now frolics fondly -- fingertips
Still feel her whispered trace, and I can hear
Her donkey-laughter, and her abalone
Grin, her mischief dalliance and spin,
Her sly and ludic lips, her pondering trist --
Manon of caprices and goldenrod.
Her name means light, Lucia, and the bliss
Of heaven's heroes' isle in the West.
Titania's afoot: the cantrip folds
Bouquets of decades in a pinch of time,
A lasting punctuated fragrance, rhymes
On rhymes of her first poem on my lips.
I wake, and recitatio returns

From dream the honeyed murmur of her verse.
Her vow: to make me love her; well, it worked.

Easter, 1995

Strawberry on the teeth from fingertips
That love, and smiling lips yet berry-red:
Las Vegas, Easter, 1995.
Wisecrackers, clowns, hillbilly Goths in love,
Security upon their playful tails,
Two bunnies in MacGregor's cabbage-patch,
And giggling in the curtainage of Caesar,
Slipping through the fountaineering spray,
And groping in the shrubby colonnades.
She told me then, teardrops, that she would leave,
Head north, to Santa Cruz, or Golden Gates.
She was impossible held in the hand,
A slinky volatility in flesh,
A sadness sly and laughing, clinging close
Yet elsewhere, ever shimmering, with mist
On lashes, sashes round her burgundy,
And velvet about her bosom, buxom plush.
Coitio dashed here, a little there,
Bouquet of chortling kisses in the bush;
Take to the dance floor, dance all night, two geeks
In bliss, who didn't belong, and therefore did.
Why sting me with such news? That cruel coquette.
She was the fling that lingered, each kiss chance,
Every embrace a gamble, mercury
In groping hands, intrigue and mystery
How long would last, an instant or forever.
"Well," I said, the sting of Scorpio
On mischief's teeth, "if you must go, there is
Another lass I've eyed at the Goth club --
You could choose her as your successor, hm?"
She was not pleased. Touche in badinage.
The thorn's prick made her love me all the more --
But she was leaving all the same, no doubt.
What kind of craziness dressed up as love?

I loved it! Pure adventure and uncertainty,
The footing never fully clear,
Therefore ice skating, grace, and slide, and soar --
Full wings, abyss, broad span, adrenaline,
A constant wondrous daze, a shaking head
That rolled its eyes each instant -- yet adored.
I held her naked in the hotel bath,
Her bladder pained, the Urised not yet
Dissolved in her; I cherished her, I loved
Her as a treasure ever in arrears
(A fast account shared out too liberally).
The tenderness, the sweet concern, the force
To hold two magnets, same polarity,
Together: wow! The force field in embrace,
Devotion spelt contra naturam, thrill
In our unlikelihood, and yet our fit.
Oh, there were fits, and maudlin theatres,
Coy temper tantrums -- what a mess. And yet
That circus-scintillating carousel
Of sex! My God! My Goddess! Ecstasy
And comedy entwined. It was a farce,
A delicate ballet of poignant farce,
Sweet farce, buffoonery's elysium.
What plays in Vegas, stays -- within my heart.

a playboy and a loon

I'm a loyal fellow; decades flow,
The letters fade, but fondness still remains.
I pledge allegiance to the ones I love.
They linger in me, flavor fresh as first.
Each tartness of those flapper tarts still rings.
It sings. It buxom brings me happiness,
And clings to me. Those lovely troubles, ah!
Those passing flower-flings of yester Springs!
Those harpy harlots, wit-endowed and dear!
I jest, in half; those geniuses I loved,
Those motley dolls, those femme fatales on stilts,
Those broken harlequins of poignant charm.

I do love William Shatner, yes I do.
He taught me how to kiss. This is a man,
Strength and a human vulnerability,
With horseplay in the eyes, and sadness too.
Assertiveness and satire all in one.
Each episode he had another gal.
And I, laid up in convalescence here,
Recall, in peering in the looking glass,
I did as well, a playboy and a loon.
And now, a 52 year old buffoon,
A sly old coot, a never-has-been star,
A shy celebrity of torrid verse,
A card, a winking knave, a greying sage,
I let them butterfly before my eyes,
A pageant of the birds, a cinematic
Spectacle of garter belts and lace,
Of promises and jiltings (most not mine).
I count the sighs as paramours of mist,
The zest of spritser in the summer sun.
Shatner lives on forever, like fine wine,
Each year the better, mentor and a friend.
Those capering affairs are like the years,
But memories -- and yet the stuff of life!

a handkerchief to wipe my tears

My women were my alphabet of yore.
What spry neologisms I did coin!
I rhymed them, lacing them on necklaces,
The soft brocade of lyrical cascades,
And sang each name, a miracle of charm.
A comfort in the moonlit solitude,
A handkerchief to wipe my many tears.

a little Eden now, tomorrow more!

How in the shadows' mufflement of light,
The lair of howl and haze and gnashing teeth,
This night too long, may we imagine dawn?
How can this world of morals' gossamer
And straw -- how flimsily it falls apart --
Hold up our yearnings from the cardinal depths
And colonnade our dreams to kingdom's heights?
How may the fetid marsh hold splendor firm?
We quake, anticipating all is sunk.
How much of Eden can we e'er restore?
As much as fiery fortitude of will,
As much as our imaginations dream,
As much as we endure hard obstacles,
That inch by holy inch, we fight for ground,
A little Eden now, tomorrow more!

Negar

In shadow, she is lithe, elusive, thin,
Fragile and tall, gentle and aquiline,
Shy eyes that glint against the strobing dark.
Black lace hangs willowy down sylphlike limbs.
Demure but savvy when you first converse,
Her mischief bright but sour on her lips,
Until she bursts in ravenflight-like laughter,
Cynical and innocent the same.
Her name's "Beloved" in her Rumi-tongue,
And those who get to know her would agree.

Our Lady of Conculia Capilli

What I most miss of that mistress of youth,
The poignant maiden of the lilac mane,
Is her thoughtful, unique counsel, her rede
Of animals, Arthurian wicca,
And her Pre-Rafaelite aesthetic eye.
Her counsel, thoughtful, strange, is what I miss.
I often wonder what her thoughts would be
On this or that, and sorely yearn my friend.
All hail to Aphrodite, but the bond
That lingers is the friendship fond and dear.
As if she were but fingertips away,
My thoughts, as though the decades were but web
Dissolving in my hands, turn sharp to her,
Discovering her absence with surprise,
As if she were a sibling of the womb,
Whose abscess is my cherishment of her.
What harm from time to time to tap her mind?
I never was a beast to her but friend.
I am a votary priestess-deprived.
How often others urge I let her go;
Who cancels treasuries even in trace?
If these mere rags from her once splendorous
Array, aside their wist, bring me pure joy,
A specimen unlike I've ever seen,
What fool abandons trove of fairy coins?
Her thoughts were silver alloy of sheer gold,
So quizzical, so full of riddling wit,
So unexpected, I can't emulate.
The source is almost dry, and yet the well
Still lives in aquifers forbidden me;
I drink dry dust in memory of wine.
I could be filling goblets with her must!
Divorce became a cruel obituary.
Who officiated and wed us?
Castro and Market were their names, and Grove,
Who met Divisadero, as their aids.
The witnesses? The amphitheater
Of Queen Anne's relatives, the foghorns late
At night in Bernal Heights, the olive trees

And tall magnolias along Gates Street
Near Cortland Avenue. Our Lady of
Conculia Capilli lacks a shrine,
Save in my heart and in my fervent odes.

surely I were Catholic

If Jacaranda tresses dressed the head
Of Mary, surely I were Catholic,
In melancholy of devotion's shrine;
Cut flowers fresh, the fingertips in dip
Of sanctus aquam, tapers lit each night,
A chapel placed along the Panhandle,
Beneath the sprucy Eucalypti boughs,
Those sites where something touched the heart for good.
No doubt that Tony Bennett was correct.

the wisps of jellyfish of sky

The clouds are cupping the orb of a rising egg. Perhaps it will hatch a mighty falcon of the sky, with silver tufts of wings to drink the wine of midnight. O drunken bird whose feathers are the drifts of clouds, illuminate the star fields with the splendor of your span! Give birth, O egg, to hope, and spirit's longing for new life, ye spawn of Spring!

O second sun, O glow of ivory in the wisps of jellyfish of sky, call then your mistress of the silver bow, who rides the stag of starry tines through ebony to morn, and ask that holy Artemis to bless her namesake down below, and bring her strength as she calls down the cavalcade of stellar nymphs who tend their maiden, fairy friends to tend her as she heals, may it be so!

our star, how patiently it spins

Last night, I felt something so long deprived
I thought I'd lost, the main chance slipped and gone.
You made me feel again I could be great,
That greatness lives in me as yet despite
The cripplings, the damages to heart
And mind, the missing audience, friends lost.
That some amazing spirit lives in me
I have the honor to facilitate
If only it's inspired, and I'm true.
I stopped believing in myself a time.
The ones I hold so high had let me down,
Would not give me the time of day or glance.
I thought delusion I could rise above --
But nobody, and nothing else at all.
A hack who painted lipstick on a pig.
But what I felt, that some things can transcend,
And something waits our welcoming, is true.
There's wonderful, ripe blessings deep inside,
Ready to blossom, with our loyalty.
And mischief, lovely in benevolence,
Winks at us hints of grace cubbied in time.
We must believe in possibility.
We must expect queer opportunities.
We must know when it's dark, the dawn is near.
The lies you looked into your mirrored eyes
And uttered, that you were but ordinary,
Nothing special, just an everybody,
What a stinking load of cods-wallop!
We aren't just dirt. There's levities about.
There's spindle-threaded dew criss-crossed with pearls.
There's weightlessness and subtle thrill of flight.
There's floating in a swift hot air balloon
And skimming mist above the shadowed roofs.
There's rungs which rung by rung ladder us up
To taste the nipple's nectar of the sky!
It takes faith in improbabilities,
Relighting sparks in sullen irises,
Belief in miracles but imminent:
If we await on tippie-toes with haste,

We may, while it spins by, touch that our star,
And hitch ourselves to its velocity
And flame, and soar the heavens spherical
With sweet jouissance and childlike delight!
And every time it circles, other chance
To lasso it and ride! And if we miss,
Ah well, a spell upon the ground a time;
It soon returns, and welcomes us again.
Such is our star, how patiently it spins,
Offering superlatives and elevated
Visions ripe to berry-pick if we
Might dare. Our daring is invited thus.
It never is too late while life has breath.
We may forget, but it remembers well.
It knows our true potential, and it winks
As it oft twinkles by, to let us know.
There's silver water cinematic spells
Of rippling light and flaming film noir,
Greatness by gratis, spectacles of joy,
And grandeur, giddy universe in play.
Inviting us, if we would like, to join
The ludic whirligig of nonchalance,
The sport of moment joined to perfect time.
It bids us climb above the dissonance,
And taste honeyed harmonics that revolve
In sweet suspense of mercury and stars,
And then resolve, with Aphroditic sighs.
You wiped away amnesia, that forgot
The Muses aren't angry, but amused,
And glad if we ascend to bring them wine.
Sometimes the animal may hypnotize,
Our eyes opaque that see just what is there,
And nothing else, the flesh is but a lump
Without its levity, stuck in the dark,
Believing sluggishness our destiny.
The star would have us soar and not to graze
Or gaze at dirt and call it destiny.
We have a home in heaven's villages.
Amazingness in you awakened mine.

miserable and comfortable

Mean to the angels who bring energies
You need to feel alive, 'cause they don't match
The incomplete lifestyle you've hobbled together.
Oft they came, and oft they went, for this,
But now they seldom come, because of this,
And life is miserable and comfortable,
Because it fits, but what you need doesn't.

lackadaisicality on wing

Sheer lackadaisicality on wing,
The reign of whim, no care but here and there,
Pure flash and strobe of hue and blotch on breeze,
The sunlight dancing on the papery blur
Of watercolor flapping, flit and blink
Directionless through leaf and round thick boughs,
And blending in the green grass oatstraw patch,
Emerging with capricious dalliance,
And on its merry way to who knows where.

invisible and winged

She is but flowing cloth inhabited
By air, that strides in gliding gusts that walk
The drifting clouds; she is but web and lace
In sheer with snowflake mesh, a warbling scarf
So silken in the wind, alike a torch
On shaking seas of brandywine and brine.
She's starfields in translucent lines of flesh
That teases breeze with hints of living glass.
Look through her: she is whisper linening
The breath with goosebumps, and her voice is flutes
Of mountaingoats that pet the zephyrs' fur.

She is a whirlwind stilled to sudden hush
That tingles in the desert oily air.
She's ecstasy invisible and winged.

your ugly, shitty soul

Gag white people. I've read their goddamn scrawl
On YouTube in the comments section: fuck
These white-trash motherfucker racist pieces
Of shit! No joke, just gag these useless mouths.
Free speech? Fuck you. Have something worthy to say,
And then we'll talk freedom of speech, you lout.
Your nasty cracker-ass privilege shows
When you open that filthy mouth of trash
And show us all your ugly, shitty soul.
Sit down, shut up, and let the humans talk.
You racist honkies need to zip your lips.

topsy-turvy land

The data has a backache, I should think,
It needs so much massaging, and the best.
When sophists run the handling of the facts,
How easily they turn to upside-down.
"I know your eyes, and all the instruments
Say one thing, but our mathematics say
Another. Put it through this model, and--
Voila! What you thought up was down, in fact."
Welcome to topsy-turvy land, my friends.
Accept the fully reconfigured facts,
As they're presented isolated, but
Do not demand consistency between
This fact and that fact over there, ok?
Leave that to us, the lawyers -- I mean, experts.
Yes, the sky seems blue, but that's your eyes.
You have to know the mathematical

Equation to determine its true hue.
Today we say it's green. We never said
It was violet -- at least we never say
That now, and that is retroactive, hm?
You can't believe old newspaper reports.
That was the truth, but policies have changed.

I live emotionally as I will

"Emotional fidelity" is bunk.
It's immature, control-freak craziness.
I live emotionally as I will,
Share with whomever I may wish, at will,
Live open-heartedly, have tender friends
Of either gender, open up my thoughts,
Confide in my concerns and theirs as well,
Enjoy great intellectual concourse,
Be playful and a goofball as I am,
And fountain forth the life-force that I have.
Whomever would imprison this is sick.
I don't believe in astronautic love:
Shut out the world, hook up your life support
Exclusively to one another, and --
That's it! What an impoverished kind of life.
More fitting to the cloistered world of veils.
To give to jealousy the guarantee
Against the physical is all it gets.
That's it. Whomever would deprive of friends
Is an Inquisitor who wants to jail,
And lock the heart up in its iron maidens.
Not for me. Not now, not ever. Nope.
I never will agree to such cruel chains.

bring me the feminine

Bring me the feminine in rose bouquets,

In bursting butterflies in rainbow flight,
In water skiing with a bridal train
Of lilies laced in silken thread behind,
Upon a lunar-candelabra'd lake;
In feathers of flamingo fluff-tufted,
In crystal carved to naked waterfall
Of arms-exultant nymph shaped by Lalique,
In melting for sublimities of eve,
Blue wounded bruise to falling ebony
With snowflake stars that dust the canopy.
Bring me sweet tenderness that touches hearts
With subtle gasp and mist of steaming eyes,
All unashamed, but lilting through the world
With symphony of lambent sentiment,
The glory of the human being's heart.

homeland of the foam where toes first danced

O undulate and ludic sea of froth
And iridescent furrows gloamed with lune!
O roaming meadows of the jellyfish
Where flesh translucent ripple-blooms ballet!
O swordfish frolic leaping o'er the waves!
O whipped and frothy cream of moon on sighs
That wrinkle surface gelatin in rows!
Ah, teeming avenues of bustling fish,
Naifs of fin in open-eyed lagoons!
O octosylphan serenade of arms
And suction cups, the mollusk-harlequins
Of sandy deeps! O long and lanky threads
Of kelpin forest, strands of sunlight bathed
In blue and amber, loom of weaving trout
Dart here and there in oily-hued cascade!
O homeland of the foam where toes first danced!
I jet skiied on an abalone dish
Across the buttermilk of waves to shore,
And there my glory, pearling-wet, revealed!

Come, toes, then, from the laughing lather-play,
From omelette of the sighing skillet tides,
And test the sand with carousel of thighs
And Julie Andrew spinning arms in grass!
Walk, doffing spray for mere of silken skin,
Godiva-lively; perspiration, drops
Of honey: grass grows hives and blossoms both!
O petal-plush of blossom-ocean, lush
And fragrant on the meadows! Scent is all
Of breath's eternity! My nostrils are
My only body! Herbs and blooms pervade
My sweet aroma-essence! Color blinds
My eyes of worship with glare of adore!
O ruffle-ribald bursts of bleeding rose,
Exploding pink on shrapnel-spackled cream!
Carnation-cousins whorling petal-froth
Tuxedo in their little crimson cups!
O duck-flesh smooth of white and wing on mug,
Magnolia! O stolen from the foam,
Fresh Baby's Breath! O glory of the dawn
In dusty cobalt saucers laced on vine!
O Jacaranda rain of bruised membranes!
O honeysuckle beak-sheathes hummingbirds
So come to linger bliss within with whist!
Proliferating budding joy of bees,
O pollen acres of ambrosia,
Delight of black-striped yellow leotards
On golden-dusted glycerin of wings!
These things I sing! Now that the bursting sea,
And meadow-fleurs with honey-hives are seen,
Life is complete! Beauty abounds; the rest
Is afterthought. But weave me pheromonal
Suites of Spring in pockets of the woods
Where lovers build their nests of goldenrod
And clover lined with reeds -- and skin will sense
The rest of pleasure's duties. That conceived,
I lounge on laurels: poetry will come,
And then aesthetic soul will save the world!
Clouds, make me now a downy bed of fog;
Seduce me, dreams, into a sultry sleep.

Svipdag's descent to win the sword

Then mountain down the foggy peaks of snow,
Below to smoky rivers swirled with haze
And ash, that howled with angst of ancient wraiths,
A vale of choking, fires long since burnt,
But charcoal held as yet on frigid air,
With echoes of old screams of bygone fright,
The world turned white with endless plains of ice,
Obscured alone by flurry drifts of smog.
What whispers taunted, teasing out deep fears
From slumber in the heart of this brave elf?
What mortal ever gazed his eyes upon
This after-realm of misery and lived?
Only the doomed, only the very damned,
Never to see the meadows green and lush,
Stamped by the golden lips of blissful sun,
But marked for horrid shadow froze in ice.
He shuddered. Still his inner eye could see
The beauty of the mossy trees above,
And he intended touch those lichen boughs
Many a time again beneath the moon.
An icicle alike a spear of light
Seemed then to gleam from towering clouds above,
And could he swear, if not hallucinate,
He saw the moon wink at him as he passed
Aloft in tracery-carved ivory,
His crescent ship that sails the heavens' seas?
Perhaps was token of a gift of luck,
A sign that hope was not as yet full fled.
He needed it. His store was running low,
And every crumb added bolstered the meal.
Forward, and only forward was the rede
His mother gave him for these sleety climes,
Regardless of the mood that said no chance.
Just foot in front of other shuffling foot,
And through -- what happens in between no weight --
But out, that is the answer, come what may,

But out and through and back again to life!
That was the truth to which he now must cling.
All this about? The Lie wrapped in thick smoke,
Deception and illusion seeped from souls
Drowned in the livid tar of it, the Lie,
Condemned to what their actions pledged they loved.
Now flesh thawed out a groove from walls of snow.
He headed south. Turned then in disbelief
And saw the smoking dungeon of the damned!
Ensconced in gleaming shelves of glaciers, heads
Of once-colossal cannibals poked through,
Their tongues hung out their rotting mouths of gore.
How like a city made of broken glass
And shrapnel sheets of jagged iron gates!
How then the flame-eyed vultures, merely bones,
Did gyre gloomily above with bats!
The screeching sounds of giant rusty saws
Dismembering the monsters down to size,
Enormous slaughterhouse of carnal ghouls,
Ground down, given the centuries, to dust,
To fertilize the Tree with their manure.
Sewage suffocated retching lungs;
The slime-fields of ordure and putrefied
Intestines' reek filled up the gasping nose.
He saw the wretches, size of mountains, cast
Upon a giant mill and bladed down
To sand and gory strips of falling clay.
Forward, keep moving forward, he recalled.
He heard the sound of rushing maelstrom slush,
And saw the icy rivers haunting flow
Down Mount Hvergelmir and all about.
Nearby the ears seemed catch a den of snakes,
In icy slither, venomous and cold,
And full of malice. Quickened up his pace,
To put some mileage in between himself
And this windy phantasmagoria.
He saw in thickness of the shadowed fog
The ember-eyes of tundra wolves peek through,
In stalking taciturnity and prowl,
And thought he heard them lick their famished chops.
At last he came upon the Elivagar,
Frigid river marking out the edge

Between the barren damned and all the rest.
One side was none but bleak, the other grass.
How then to cross this icy treachery?
He donned the skates his brother gave to him,
Then as if treason lay not neath his feet,
He glided out, and twirled upon the ice,
Pure sail and laughter, pirouetting there,
His sudden elfin joy defiant strength.
The blizzard-dragons, daunting, stopped their flight
In fright of this display of innocence
In wicked climes, and terrified, turned back,
The buzzards, spooked, upon their icy tails.
He gave himself to rotary delight
And spirals, skidding spray of frozen foam,
And homed upon the distant line of grass.
Where then this mischief in the corridors
Of darkness of the world emerged from him?
Once there, his playfulness scared off the every
Orc and goblin, yet was strange, this mirth,
Pure beauty in abandon of a slide,
A soar across the glacial expanse,
Till all was silent: not a howl was heard.
But smooth of poetry upon the ice,
But ecstasy of twirl and circle-eights,
In corruscating cursive; flakes of snow
Were tongue-snacks, evanescent taste of wet.
The breeze was fiancé upon his face,
Betrothal in the tundra, grin and thrill.
The sibilance of skates on frost like glass.
At last the meagre green of wilted grass
And scattered reeds was on him. Doffed his blades,
And fell to knees to kiss the grateful grass.
A living thing! At last! Though it be pale,
A living thing, a growing thing, a sign
Of vegetation! Here was lichen rock
Set pile across a reedy stretch of marsh.
He leapt from stone to stone on pointy shoes
Of elfinware, across the shallow swamps,
Somewhat monotonous, and yet with bounce.
A patch of grass between the mossy rocks
If here or there, reminded him he'd crossed
The ghoulish zone of smoking skull and bones.

At times, he thought he caught a glimpse of gnomes
Beneath toadstools, in their petite workshops,
Just tinkering away, then they were gone.
On one high rock, he looked; the view revealed
The marsh turning riparian and clear,
The reedgrass thickening along the banks.
But glance and flee, a passing deer to stoop
And gurgle tricklings' refreshing drink,
From growing stands of birch that waxed to woods.
He peeled the corklike bark of blemished white,
And folded, folded, til he had a craft
Of elegance, a sleek papier canoe,
And knifed two spindly boughs to shapely oars.
Then slipped his svelte, mercurial flesh in,
Alike a comely foot in slipper-silk,
And pushed off down the giggling crystal stream.
Sailed by, white birches, cedars thickening
Behind; sailed by, reedgrass, adorned with ferns,
Like shy divas with feather-tufted fans;
Sailed by, in conifers colossal, nests
Of eagles, mother took to cloudy wing.
The sky was overcast yet cozy, soft
And full of drizzle. There deep in the woods,
The silent lumbering of a grizzly bear.
Water was purling. There deep in the woods,
A family of raccoons might shuffle by.
The craft sailed further. There deep in the woods,
Crowned with a rack of shaped mahogany,
A small cohort of elks might graze and go.
No land of death, but some quaint bestiary
Reservation full of teeming life!
There yonder by the banks, an elephant?
There browsing in the distant oaks, giraffes?
What kind of strange, enchanted place was this?
Looked up, and wing-chatter was song on wind,
But beak-chorale corroboree in flight!
Toucans, macaws, with wild-colored bills,
And other birds he'd never seen before
Were thick in aerial conversation-squawk.
The otter and the mink splashed by the banks,
The beaver built his ziggurat of boughs,
The beetles crept the sawdust forest floor.

And little furry things with rotund eyes
Scamped up from burrows, curious, then dove.
Svipdag lay back against the spongy birch,
Eyes to the cloudy heavens, and relaxed,
The oars beside him, letting stream's intent
Lead on the way, wherever it might will.
The salmon sermoned bubble-serenades;
The trout painted the eddies rainbow-dash.
Now crickets merrily began to bow
Their spindly violins on grassy shoals.
He'd half a mind to slip into a dream,
Yet here was dream and charm abound to boot.
He half lost breath and melted for to see
The downy drift of snow-white winged owls
In slow majestic soar from crown to crown
Of emerald canopies. What miracle
Of frills folded up feather broad in flight!
He heard a rushing sound of sudden hush,
And coming upright, saw his stream and more,
A hundred streams, converge around a round
And mystic bank. Around this island's edge,
If island such a broad expanse might be,
Poured waterfalls from heavens' holy pores,
A chaplet made of spray that drizzled down
And prismed in its dew the gleaming light,
Whence then a rainbow arbor-spanned its banks.
Svipdag was swift bouquet of fleeing sighs:
Had eyes ever beheld such holiness?
Now beast, now bird, now bunny from its lair,
Now elephants in trunk self-shower in
The wading river-sand, now dragonflies
In arabesque winged macaroon of swirls
Through reedgrass -- all attend, and set their gaze
Upon this island's glory tinged with awe.
Beyond the fosses' beard-dew was a wall
Of ruffled ferns obscuring further view,
And yet inviting curiosity,
Svipdag's virtue and vice. And so he oared
His fleet papier-mache canoe inwards,
Towards the swirling river ring about
The island shrine, and when he'd reached its banks,
He folded up that skiff into a pad,

And pocketed it in his shoulder bag.
His slender hands were swim through waves of fern,
Which, lined with veins of gold, suffused like sun
Upon a meadowgrass. The fog grew thick,
A Sycamore-like scent to circling mist.
A mystical advance, each further step.
There under bracken, dwarf-laid brick appeared,
An ancient royal road through redwood stands.
One followed it by faith; eyes could not see
Three yards ahead -- but somehow silence gleamed
And crackled, gravitas descended thick,
And all the brume was colonnade and loft.
He circled then it seemed around a canyon,
Rough-hewn stony staircases of red,
Sedonic in a Santa Cruz like way.
The redwoods leaned in, listening intent,
As he passed by. He shivered. All the mist
Condensed around the canyon's lip to drops
That dripped and then rushed pumpkin-cool in fosse,
Down dozen rivulets by cedar-paths.
The elf descended, wary yet intrigued.
At last a plain of hundred Doric columns,
Rising from the reeds and ferns to clouds
Appeared; on every one, a riddle marked
In runes, an arcane dale of questioning
And fog. He arched his slanted brows and purred,
In simmering contemplation. Brick laid path
Laid long along converging river streams,
And slabs of marble on which whirligigs
And sundials lay were strewn across thin marsh.
At last the spokes of brook and stream found hub,
A grotto made of tourmaline and quartz,
Rough set in rocks alike a set of skulls
In polished ossuary; gold-carved stars,
And silver trinkets of the cutlass moon
Hung there in glitter. He looked down, eyes wide.
As far as eyes could see, the ground was gems.
A thousand scintillating gems a yard,
And more the gaze horizoned right or left.
But there within the grotto, circled pure
With marble smooth as glacier-glass, and hemmed
With tule green as mallard's neck, there was

A well -- clear pond, pure water, salmon-swum
And dipped with bobbing apples dripped in chrome
Of misting rain. A mystery. A well
Of wisdom. Hung there on the side by hair,
A giant head, its lips in dribbling sip
Through wild beard of that lagoon of awe.
It opened eyes which ogled round about,
And thundered in an ancient tongue now lost
A dozen puzzle-puns, each one wound thick
About its eerie syllables of yore;
Each assonance significant, a rhyme
Each phrase and breath, in perfect metre-speech,
If one could understand. He summoned now
His mother's charms of unpuzzling tongues,
And hoped that once he grasped, he'd have the wit
To answer, and with eloquence in verse!
So this the hazing, this the price to pay
To ask a question: first he must answer.
His mind became a gymnast, fresh with leaps
And suave agility, with dexterous flips.
It tested all his cocky cleverness
To sweat. How many had heard rumored hint
Of Mimir, Sage Below, the Well's famed ward,
Yet let alone discovered him, yet let
Alone confronted him in chills and beads
Upon the brow? Not many, he was sure.
Those hoops of word-brocade he leapt with skill,
One by the one, the charm answering the task,
Until it was his time at last to ask.
"I seek a sword for She who keeps my gem
In walrus-boned carved coffers, beating bright--
She takes my breath by night, and if by day,
The sunset winks at dawn at my lost trance
In her, conferring with the swans of dusk
About my dumb and silly fits of love!
She is sweet seance, spirit-steam and scent
Of fresh camellias, and she is dressed,
Skin-seamed, with peonies, her lilac hair
Is studded pewter with the midnight stars!
I swear she hovers on her shapely heels!
The simplest, briefest peek is effervescence,
Sparkling mead in chalices of quartz.

My sole remorse? That everyday I miss
To whist and feast upon her apple eyes
Is waste, a squandering of treasured gold.
She is the charm of every woman's face,
The lily-lace and shiver round their legs,
The coquette potter of their shapeliness
And spice, their inner beauty's edelweiss.
She is the taste of cherries dipped in cream,
The dreaminess of honey on one's tongue,
Essential oil of the moon by night,
Fragrance of sunrise, bowers' potpourri
Where lovers kiss in eglantine twined vines
Amidst the musky cedars! She is glass,
An idol of the lake, a pinch of heaven's
Nectar sprayed on sultriness of skin!
She is alive! And all that lives is her.
I am but footnote of her dissertation's
Sweet intoxication rede on love!
What is more lovely? Blue lobelia?
Compare her irises and weep, O fleur.
Hydrangea? But her skin is such soft stuff.
She purrs when she is pleased, and with such ease.
Without her incantations, Spring would cease,
The bunnies barren, ewes would spurn the ram,
The mare no longer awed by stallion,
The hens would yawn at peacocks' dalliance,
And sense of subtle romance would be lost.
I pray she pines for me as I for her.
If silver edge of iron sword she wills
To give her luscious nuptials willfully,
Say then, great giant, lord of wisdom's well,
Where I might find this blade, or how to gain?"
This Mimir shared the guardian's locale,
A dwarfen son of his, was Mimung called.
Shared then the secret of his guile, wished
The lad his luck, and closed his ancient eyes.
At once the elf repaired to hidden lair,
And followed his instructions: with a trick,
He seemed invisible, and tied him up,
While he retrieved the silver sea-etched blade.
Then merry as a madcap wit, he skipped
Through meadows prairied thick with honeyed sun

And goldenrod, displaying gleaming sword
Against noon's glare, and laughing. Sauntered south,
And sometimes galloped freely through the lanes
Of apricots and sunny lavender,
Where noble patriarchs and matriarchs
In august robes held their ancestral concourse.
Little did he care. He was in love!
What wisdom missed, what adages dismissed?
He could not be more lackadaisical.
He passed, twirling the point on fingertips,
And jigging to his private hoedown tunes,
The regal court where dooms of souls are judged.
What is such gravity to levity
As his? He'd seen the monuments of gloom,
The fields of terror and of toxic smoke.
So long, farewell! O nether fields below,
His star was rising! Then he came upon
The bridge made out of stars, and climbed thereon,
In wonder gazing down its curvy bow
To steep descents. The slope ran further up,
And as he elevated in ascent,
The copper-feathered valkyrie of sun
Sailed by on unseen winds, her chariot
Horsed forth by neighing flame. And shaking dew
Of fiery butterscotch from brows, she waved.
Down in the atmospheric seas, the moon
Tipped up his captain's cap in grinned salute.
"I'm going to meet the heaven's cardial queen!"
He thought. "I'm going to wed Freya! Wow!"
And all the underworld was afterthought,
Adventure in the after nether lands.
He counted all that voyage but for nought,
Except the sword, and only as the price
For her! For her! For only ever her!

her skin is tamarind
for Elizabeth of Night

Her skin is tamarind, as sweet to taste,
As exudacious of a tender dew,
As calming as the night is sweet and fresh.
Her almond eyes drip maple sap on gaze,
Her hair a coffee-tisaned Spanish moss,
A lush hung Clematis Romantika,
A neck bouquet of jet-black Hollyhock.
Her lips Aeonium and succulent,
Zwartkop, crassulan sweet-meats, honey gum
To tongue and begging lips that long for more.
Her mangos are the queen of papill fruit,
Her hips curvaceous to the hands' caress.
I must confess, when she is flowered in
A mesh of silken lace, her sultriness
Assaults me with the gentle craze of night,
And stare is light of torches flickering
Against a deep madrone so smooth to touch,
I gasp, again and yet again, I swear.
Calipha of oasis stands, who fans
Her thin-embroidered veil with mantid wings
Mounted on ivory, come-hither eyes
Goetic to my salivating dwale.
I sail my fingers on her sleek Medjool,
And Braille of it is nectarine I taste
With skin alone, and so I drone her name,
Its syllables soft phonemes of my joy.

a new bounce to her gait

She ran, her bridal gown behind her tossed
By sea-winds, down to where the tumbling brine
Was wet applause upon her dashing toes,
And peeled the webbing of her angst from arms
And shoulders, licorice in lace, and wept,
Each lily petal shingled on her dress,

She tossed, a melancholy offering
Into the ocean, falling down to knees.
The tangled kelp embraced her in its grasp,
As sea was lacrymal and splash on her.
The roiling clouds of thunder dark rolled in,
Asperging her and lashing her with sleet.
Blossoms like lily pads floated amidst.
And all her anguish fell upon her then,
What she had been through, all her loss and fears,
Nights worrying, and aching from her bones.
Defeated, so she seemed, she sullen lay
In salten stew of stirring, rocking tides.
The black drew out the blue of fading day,
Until her downcast eyes caught jellyfish
Lumescence of the water's oil lit
By ivory fire of the gracile sky.
Looked up and saw the slender, silver fern-
Fronds of the willowy chiton the sylph
Maiden with pewter bow and shafts of light
Wrapped round her bare and milky-lucent skin,
And she was staring at her, eyes intent.
A gust rose on her face and salten hair,
And lilies undulate in gentle waves
Flouresced in gleaming bath of showering moon,
Who seemed, arms stretching up, to dowse herself
In silken beads of phosphous waterfall.
She peeled the clouds aside like zippered veil,
Revealing apparition of the night,
A vision: porpoises saddled by nymphs
In ribbon-fleured florettes that knit the sea
In bobbing surge of rushing sunlit tide,
And tossed out gold and candy on the waves,
And one foot each upon the back of them,
The jilted bride, clad now in gown of dew
And sparkles, smiling, all restored to grace
And strength, her limbs suffused with life and light,
No care or wish, but lasting joy's delight,
Triumphant on the Triton-stallions.
Then Lady Luna drew the curtains back
Cream-steaming swirl and swishing backlit clouds
To soft Shabbat of cool black-sari'd night,
And twinkle-winking crescent-irises,

Clothed lunar nakedness in passing fog,
And faded finger-strand of mossy mist
Into the air so elegant and cool.
Below, the one who'd wept took glance about:
Manila blooms she'd stripped from jilted dress
Were fading foam, her limbs au naturel.
Her kelpy net had sunk into the deep.
But on her hair, now body thick and tossed
On shoulders sensuale, a chaplet laced
With ceanothus froth, and soft to touch.
She rose, and tear-stuff of the purling waves
Fell faucet-rush and running droplet gush
Down sleek, curvaceous limbs and starlit shape
Of innocence restored in sight of hope,
And off she walked, a new bounce to her gait.

this grudging world has cleaved us

Adam.
She sleeps beside me, yet I cannot feel
Her with me as I did in Eden once.
There adoration was abundant well
Of day by day refreshment, and I felt
One soul, two bodies: ventures in delight!
Each day, discovery, and sudden bursts
Of laughter. Now I know I weary her,
Here in this barren wasteland of a world,
Where once fresh air is choking dust, where trees,
Once frond-fond verdant friends surround, are sparse,
Where once cool winds that whistled pleasantly
Are stagnant gasps of sweltering, where all
Is hard, resisting us, a trouble, toil,
Struggle, pain, where once such harmony
One can't imagine here was ease and breath;
All things cooperated: who lacked love
In such a lovely floradise of fronds?
It seems a cruel, lost dream, a thorn that taunts.

I never yearned for Eve, for all was well,
But crippled now, I long for her so keen.
I've made a mandolin of palm and jute,
To trill my longsome serenades to her.
She forces up a smile from her frown
That ever reigns -- but I touch not. I can't.
Even when fingers skin-ascend her shape,
There is a distance never there before.
Her eyes, her mind are elsewhere -- as our mine,
Of course, both on the Eden that we've lost.
It's no use sitting here and pining angst
For her while she still sleeps; let me close eyes,
And for an interval more merciful,
Return to floral unity I had.

Eve.
The morning sun caresses eyelids mine
And beckons me to wake. Adam asleep?
Ever he sleeps, has not the time for me.
I never had desire, having all,
But now I thirst for how he used to look
On me, and how it made me feel -- oh God!
May any here feel quite as keen as there?
This atmosphere is handicapped and torn.
We scrape for meagre scraps. The earth resents
Us, and she shows it. Weeds, our heritage,
And bramble all about. How have we lost
A good thing for perfection, which, mirage,
But disillusioned? Now that humble good
We took for granted seems the highest thing,
Most unattainable, perfection we
Once had, but greed for more robbed us the more.
For my part, I was curious and wished
A promised wisdom -- that seemed worthy, no?
The serpent whispered prudence could be ours.
He didn't lie. A bitter kind, too full
Of crestfallen remorse, diminished hope:
What use such counterfeit of wisdom? None.
I would a foolishness that had its joy,
Though I wished wisdom, in itself still pure,
To this collapsed and utterly dismayed
Pragmatic prudence, born from stinging thorns.

I waste my breath. It won't win Eden back.
Surely to labor he will shortly rise,
And I shan't see him til the eveningtide.
The toil and the time, the muscle aches
By dusk, have all but separated us,
Who once inseparable, were special joy
Most unimpeded. Now we live apart,
He to his realm, and I to mine, but bed
Between us, and a passing meal, no doubt --
Once he fed fruit so sloppily and wet
To these my playful lips which sucked the juice
In savor, his kind fingers in my mouth.
Once every litter fall of fallen leaf
Was in the midst of waking bed to us;
Love in the orchard, cool wisteria
Like purple frost and rain, the kudzu fosse
That tickled canopy of every tree,
The mink and otter friends we understood
Not with our words but here within the heart!
How foreign now all animals to us!
How hostile! Here all things live in mistrust.
Observe their claws, their fangs, their horns, their hooves,
Ready to run, ready to fight or fend,
Each to its own, against the rest, if prey
Or predator -- a horrifying world.
Where now the ivy soft from tender fronds,
Where now the crystal, purring, stirring springs,
Where now the rivers' still serenity?
But most of all, where are those loving eyes
That once were worship of the earth with me,
And endless praise of heaven's bountiful
Abundance, stars, and comets, angels, awe?
The rough resistance of this grudging world
Has cleaved us, more divided than before,
Like separate species who were once but one.
Now all I do is long, for him, for there,
For anywhere but here. I wish for him
When he is gone, and yet when he is here,
Absent in ache, exhausted, I disdain.
He once had energy for me alone!
Each day, excursion of a different sort.
These days he's old, and so am I, worn out,

Before our time. Our labor siphons soul
From us. The earth slurps it into its depths,
And we are spent. Oh, will a savior come?
Who might that be? O Lord, please rescue me.

something giddy reigns

Atimes something so special comes to life,
Blue-lunar and uncommon, whimsical,
A dash of color, spark of twinkling light,
That all of life is lifted higher up,
A kind of breeze, oblivious and glad,
A season of delight, a most peculiar
Wonderment, where something giddy reigns,
And in that haunting kingdom of the strange,
Some joy imbued with mischief lives in us,
And that feels more like living than most days.
Life isn't real without such fantasy,
And days are dull without the fabulous.
Reality without some glamour? Grey.
A mystic moment fleshed out brings us mirth.

a worldwide technocratic takeover

Gaslit by the Establishment: abused,
Confused, and rused; my liberty, confined;
My fellow citizens, brainwashed -- one year,
That's all it took! The hallowed golden calf,
The sacred priesthood of idolatry,
One year, that's all it took! To hold the line
Of common sense and reason, heresy,
And we were treated as the heretics
Once were: reviled, ridiculed, and blocked.
One year we had our choice, the next: no choice.
A worldwide technocratic takeover.

A new totalitarian regime,
And any who can't see this are complicit.
It was frightening and harrowing.

such wonders are of Antichrist

Establishment science is not science
At all, but Babylonian priestcraft, run
By bureaucrats who tow the party line,
And slander all who question their dogma.
I owe such no allegiance. Do they wield
The stunning miracles of artisans?
So what? Such wonders are of Antichrist.

has-been hack

An awful thing occurred last night to me.
I had to see that ugly bigot's face,
In 2021, that has-been hack,
That piece of shit I never want to see,
That hateful, awful man, that can of trash,
The man who wrecked this country with his lies.
Good riddance, and good riddance, and goodbye.

where now stands praise we yearned

Have ecstasies accumulated dust?
Have raptures run their course and lay in bed?
Is passion convalescent, hopes but vain?
Where cubby strong enthusiasm's thrusts?
Where once applause imagined itself rain

The rootstocks slurped and thirstily drank up
To verdantize the meadows with fresh rugs
Of rye and prairie grass -- or so we dreamt,
So much we longed -- where now stands praise we yearned?
Where prospects of a lofting buoyancy,
Where audience and poet flush in love,
And swoon together drunken on sweet words
That carry them together to the skies,
For nothing but the pleasure of it all?
Where has it fled, that more I could have been,
I could have seen, I could have heard or felt?
Where has endless potential wandered to?
That plus sign that I crave, where is it now?

emotion on emotion

Emotion on emotion, skin on skin.
The epidermis by itself no good.
If I can't feel you, I don't need your skin.
Skin must be where the spirit opens up
Effulgently in full communion, or
Forget it. Let me feel your wild self,
Your soulful vulnerability, your heart.
Let skin be site where feelings find each other.
Our arms are cradles where our babes may meet.

a lion

If I'm close-minded in an age of filth,
Well, praise the Lord and hallelujah, lads!
I've reached escape velocity from ill,
And spoken mind against corruption's tricks!
You realize that "open-mindedness"
Is the seductive cry of every wolf
That sought a little pig to open doors?
Your open mind, his open, gaping jaws?
"But see things from my vantage point." No thanks.
You're flotsam, pulled by every noxious tide,

Without a center, lost, no anchor, toy
Of every trend, no more than creature of
Conditioning, a bauble of the age,
Forgotten roots, a faithless hollow straw
Whichever wind that comes, idolater,
Who bows obeisance at beck and call,
A puppet for the fascists behind the scenes
(Who've had their network since the days of Gehlen).
Is my mind closed to pernicious trends
And fads that make dehumanizing seem
The latest chic? That pleases me no end.
I am a tyrant, proudly, when it comes
To violations of humanitas.
A stubborn hardliner, I hold the line,
A Guardian, a lion : hear me roar.

Lesbia

Keep moon-loom weave diaphanous and bright,
A phosphorescence softly hung as cloth
From arms, that runs as rain towards the earth.
Let sheer and shadow interlope obscure
In innuendo of a fleeting shape,
A set of soft, curvaceous physiognomies
That blur in teasing play of shade and glow.

as delicate as flight
for Elizabeth of Night

You bring me wings the singing feathered things
Do soar upon in blush of sunset's flame,
As delicate as flight is soar and fling,
As lofty as the heavens' cobalt fame.

if I were rose

But breath of Goddesses' perfume, the rose,
More vapor in a whorl of crepe and pink.
The lumancy of lovely levity,
A puff of blush and fluted taffeta,
Flamenco in aurora's rising flame.
If skin as downy soft as this, what bliss!
These swooning nostrils were a paradise.
I shudder but to think: if I were rose,
How all-adored in every curvature,
In every ruffle, every hint of scent;
Mademoiselles would bring me to their lips
To breathe me in and touch me to their cheeks.
They'd toss me towards cerulean escape
Of clouds and feather-play, from verdant hills
Where they pinch skirts and frolic in the herbs
While skipping forth; then like a parachute,
That softly gradual returns to grass,
They'd laugh and watch me, giddy with delight,
Once more their fingers of empyreum
Upon my slender, sveltan stem of thorns,
And pull me wistful towards their flushing face.
Their sweet riparian hearts would gurgle forth
And throb in thought of touching me to brow,
Descending down the nose and swirling side
To cheekbones down to lips, to drink me in,
And I would be the darling of them all!

The daughter Beauty had with Grace

Anchises.
You are the daughter Beauty had with Grace;
And sister to sheer Suavity, who swooned
On looking on you, such is your elan.
You are the hammer Beauty forged in flame
To smash the senses of who gaze on you,
But perspiration and evaporate,
But steam that longs, and melts into a fog.

Make me but puddle redolent with drool;
A breath, a hope, a hopeless wish, a prayer.

morning canticle of winged ones
for Elizabeth of Night

These scoops of ice cream pendulous from flesh
You offer me to sweeten lips upon,
Makes every now the miracle of dawn.
The sheets are soft and silver-white with silk
Of sparkling starlight hovering in suspense
Before debut of morning canticle
Of winged ones, and I am pawn of awe
Who gazes on you, and these frosted gifts.
I cup their fond, smooth mystery with palms
That hallow them, and weep to joy on them.
To feel you thrill to shiver shudders me.

peacocks as my entourage

I now recall my preternatural
Charisma, and call back to me my charm,
That all may frolic with me in the spell
Of genius in its marvelous cherubim
Of sheer creation. Let them be now awed
By me, and dazzled by my golden pen.
Let fainting sickness be my passing mark,
As I glide by, and they may petal-toss
Upon my flowing hair their gentle pink,
Bringing me peacocks as my entourage,
And gospel-gilded disco darlings' voice
As backdrop aaahs, with boots of pastel fur,
And space-metallic belts on satin shorts.
When I cavort, a cavalcade of fays
Shall Dionysian follow-fawn on me,
Delighting in the beauty of the hour.
Come, Nonnus of Panopolis, again;
Again the hour sweetens into wine;
Once more the fragrant potpourri of pine

Is twined with ivy wrapped round fennel stalks.
Once more Green Men shall strut to India
To seek Bhagwan amidst their floral friends,
And Silenus flamboyant in his cups.
Your tongue, uniquely celebrant, is sought
And ay adored; now lift up pen and pour
The brandywine of ink scriptoria
On vellum, which is singing skin, and spin
A tale of veridite enchantment, psalm
Of siren seeping through the weeping grape,
A festival in giddy, metered breath.
For festschrift is upon us, from my verse,
A crystal-clinking merriment of sprites.
And I would woo with but a hint of rhyme.
Let them their undergarments, silky-smooth,
Bestow from fragrant legs towards my feet.
That is a floral garden I peruse,
And shake my shimmy as a gift in turn.
My skin is pointillist with tuft and fleur,
Which subtly fig my well-endowed cod,
While leaving dew-enscintillated flesh
The foremost, yet I toss out linen rags
I've tied to me, so that they may devote
Their lips to where I have perspired, sweet
And fresh. Creating atmospheres of fun
And let-loose, I adorn myself Lalique
In golden dragonflies with iridesced
Gems polished candiline, and manly fur
That dews with musk and brine as I incline
From dancing, having twirled the brazen pole.
If Mercury, if Presley, if Rick James,
If Bolan, I keep company of kings,
A court of charismatic angel-kin,
Who glory in the glamor of their crowds.
Come taste this century's most rarified
Splendor, in dandy new romantic ruche,
In frosting to the fingertips from rhyme.
Untimely prodigy in your own time.

who cannot trust himself, let no one trust

Your love is tepid, such a fickle thing,
It barely has a pulse, it's pale and grey,
No deeper than your epidermis, weak,
A sickly straw, so hollow, impotent,
Incompetent and undependable.
Whoever pleases you, you love that long,
Because you're pleased, and should they fail to please,
Should there be struggle, even for a month,
You flush devotion they offered for years
Down the latrine -- that's what love means to you.
A Nestle's Crunch, as thin, as quickly gone,
The wrapper, trash. With that, you then are done.
Unless more stimulating sweetness comes,
Completely unadulterated by
Mature reality or loyalty
Through thick and thin -- if it maintains your thrill,
You might then deign to let it stay a bit.
The bottom line : you have betrayed yourself,
So everybody else is now fair game.
Your reigning bitterness is so complete,
That sickly sweet alone can compensate.
And any trouble, any stress at all,
And in this disappointment called your life,
You jettison immediately, hm?
Even to whom comes with the dungeon key
And offers purest flight of cherubim,
Because you've kenned the prison destiny.
Your life is duty. Thriving has been lost.
You've given up. How easy then to spurn
Whatever's not an instant, lasting joy.
Who cannot trust himself, let no one trust.

whirlwind made of leaves

Her body is a whirlwind made of leaves
That eddy in curvaceous woman's shape,
And crinkle as the tossing leaves collide.

She's hint of ghost and remnant of the trees.
Her voice is hollow of a columned hall,
Her lips mirage and blur of blowing air.
She comes out in the gales of lunar night,
And haunts ravines and canyons where the trunks
Of tall riparian sycamores lend shade
To trickling water with their shadow-hands.
She transplants separated bunnies back
To warrens where their mothers fret for them,
And hides the frogs beneath the hanging leaves
Where swooping talons of the owl can't find.
She sweeps the gold within the running creeks
To keep it clean and safe from any stain,
And shelters silver veins exposed on hills
With ferns and dudlia so they stay cool
And free of glare, their shyness lit alone
By starlight, and she polishes the caves,
Maintaining majesty within their shade.
She sings to pebbles whispered lullabies,
Tucked snug within their blankets made of moon.
Who would take anything from here must first
Secure her leave, observing courtesy:
Setting out candles in a ring on stone,
Offering up incense and a drop of wine,
Then giving reason why another place
Has need of what was placed within her care.
If she judges the cause is reasonable,
She'll temperately share, but if it seems
Unworthy of her treasure, woe to him
Who takes it after she's decreed her "no".
Assigned the eons back to this locale,
She tends and prunes the energies for good,
Letting no ill find rest, but giving it
What alchemy it needs to find its place,
Transmuting into something usable.
When full moon fades, she vapors into air,
Leaving her leaf-litter upon the ground,
Until the lunar clock strikes full again.
She's always there, but only then is seen.

caressers

"'Caressers', they call 'em. You only feel
Them touching you, but cannot see their forms,
Except upon the river at full moon,
And then they shimmer silently on waves.
Whom they caress gets loaded up with luck
And joyfulness, an energy of love."
"What is their purpose?" "They caress the trees,
The herbs, the stones, the doves, and wild deer,
At Winter for to carry them to Spring;
At Spring to lend them energy for love;
At Summertime to wax them in the sun;
At Fall to ready them to hunker down.
The flora and the fauna feel their touch
As if the hands of heaven hallowed them,
And surely, as the tale goes, they bear seals
From the celestial franchising them
To bless and keep and guard best as they can."
"Then they are good?" "Whoever doubted such
Has never felt the goodness of their touch."
"Are they angels?" "They aren't angels, no.
When long ago, the straying ones did fall,
They knocked the angel-eggs off of the edge,
Those embryos translucent Ruach laid
Upon the seventh day while Elohim
Took rest. Displaced, they fell to earth confused,
Unbrooded, therefore not celestial,
And changed their shape to match their own locale,
If hill or dale or cave or some ravine,
If tunnels in the earth, if windy cliffs,
They each took on the nature where they fell,
And never knowing any other way,
Took on the essence of their birthing place,
Where they first hatched, unparented, save for
The elements, which they slipped on as cloaks.
They are but simpletons of innocence,
Perpetually as young as eggs they were,
And yet mature as depth of love they give,
Which is sincere, and all with earnest heart.
Around these parts, to feel them on one's skin
Is counted miracle to be envied.
One knows a bliss beyond the marvelous.
They're only found in natural abodes,

And hidden deep past thickets and in glades.
Those who go wandering into such haunts,
If they came talentless, return with skill,
And feel the beauty on their instruments
Just humming to be harvested at will.
They grant the great naiveté of grace,
Rechilding, rejuvenance, and breath.
But we ought not disturb their hidden work,
But let them be about their business, eh?
It's crucial labors they're assigned to meet.
For us, let us leave offerings of mint
And fennel, alder leaf and nectarine,
Then be about our way and through the woods."
"If only I could feel them on my flesh."
"Someday, perhaps, laddie, someday indeed.
For now, just let it percolate inside.
What's meant to be will surely be in time."

carnival of sylphs

Through pitter, splash, and patter, one might hear
Across the river hubbub of delight,
Unseen to eyes but sheer elan in air.
There palaces of silken river-film,
Taken dew-cellophanic from the streams,
And woven into tabernacles bright
And sheer, whose seams were sewn with algal thread,
Housed festivals and festschrifts, where the wise
Sported with puns and riddlecraft and rhyme,
And fancied burlesque parodies of tomes
Beloved, laughing as they catalogued
Its themes, and studied motions of the grass
And treesway in the breeze to choreograph
Their papillonic wing-ballets, renowned
As far as pleasant rumor percolates.
There verse, that dehabituated eyes
From weary dullness, wakened lasting awe,
And pleasure was in gorgeousness of sounds
Repeated variantly, making gasp
An existential stance, and overwhelm
Of word-evoked sensorium on tongue
A delicacy, and a honeycomb

Of dripping phoneme-echo and the play
Of fond, obscure allusion -- this was bliss,
The gaming atmosphere of carnivals
Beneath rich canopies, taken an octave
Up, a more celestial mirth, a joy
In silliness with footnotes. Garden tours
Where sudden ambush of performances,
If little masques or flurry of ballet,
Leaped out the sculpted flora, were delight.
There livery was varied, bright, and chic,
With everyone rejoicing in surprise,
And fabrics draped the walls for anyone
To take and wrap about and spin around.
Long conversations in the halls till dawn,
On lovely themes that tickled fancies full,
Old travelogues, or ancient rites and games,
Or bestiaries full of fauna lost
To time but vibrant in imagination,
Favorite fairy tales, or new unearthed
Collections. Or the mild rivalry
Of serenades amidst camellias,
As lovers jousted wooings with fair words,
And spectators, scattered through herb and bush,
In couples, feasted on hors d'ouevres and kissed,
A mild breeze from pleasant streams about,
The temperature of dusky eveningtide.
And everywhere, fine ornaments of craft,
Garlanding glass and sprigs of greenery,
Were dangling from the marble statuary,
Prodding strolls to take the sculpture in.
Some vied to rung the branching bridge of trees
Across ravines of water, leaping forth
One arm to tender tines with shaking leaves,
The other to another, shimmying
Above abyss, or tumbling wet below.
Some jumped about in burlap sack races,
While others tried their hurling arm with balls
To win a furry prize, while others scaled
Surrealist scaffolding that kissed the clouds,
And jungle-gymed their way back down again.
Then there was harmony of instruments
In elegance and uplift everywhere.
A festival of merriment alike
One never saw (and did not see indeed
But only heard) -- but then those ludic sylphs

Unseen packed up their gypsy bags and left --
It all were glamour and a cantrip's spell --
Leaving the silence of the croaking frogs
And crickets on the yonder rivergrass.

feather-fall of snow-drift fuchsia

I'm shower of the cherry blossom breeze,
A denizen of Spring, in petal-shed
Of fragile overwhelm of falling pink,
Extravagant and soft proliferate
Of red run cream, caress in feather-fall
Of snow-drift fuchsia, ocean-swirl in air
Of carefree bloom, moment's eternity
Of lush serenity, a gaiety
Of joy in Primavera's crème de crème,
Her debutante's fresh blush, the adolescent
Rush of bud to exhibitionist
Magenta gently lackadaisical
In sail of silent wist of breezes' kiss.

every open way

Anchises.
A plethora of rabbits all about
Whenever you alight upon my heart.
They scamper each and every open way,
Grass-glorying in wettened morning sun.
They burgeon, Springtime softnesses in blur,
When thought of you is surfing through these veins.
I cannot help devotion that I feel for you,
Spontaneous as waves upon the shore,
As constant and dependable and true.

a moth to every Muse's torch

Phryne.
Some say my heart's a slut; it isn't true.
It's most selective, even if quite broad.
Crème de la crème in every flavor I
Draw to my tongue so cosmopolitan.
I live in constant taunting, which abounds.
My discipline's as tight as sentiment
Is gushing, and it is the river Rhine.
I am a moth to every Muse's torch;
My greatest flight and flitting round their flame.
Some hearts are one-string lutes, but I am not.
My heart's a Celtic harp, as many strings
As fairies may abound in hidden hills,
The tunes as varied as the spells are lush.
I cultivate my trances; I am dazed
Deliberately; I live to be one stunned.
Sobriety is tiresome to me:
I am a fleur who breathes to fawn upon
The sun and wind and water and the earth,
Devotion pantheonic to the pure.
I am a temple courtesan of old,
In furs and feathers, practiced in the dance,
An acolyte of candles, reverent
And mystical, star-bright, who heeds the runes
On whom the deities select their choice,
And free to hearken to their majesty,
I minister their loves to whom they deign,
The fluttering in my heart their tea-leaves.
From whom I might fancy upon my own,
They choose, according to their scheduled times,
And I am bride, and wed as I am led.
The bridal chamber in my loving heart,
In utter secrecy and sacrament.
Such is my discipline, and difficult
Blessing; I live upon a balance beam.
I'm not promiscuous; I seek the best,
For excellence is ecstasy to me.

the age's total mockery of faith

Mendacity is normal fare for us.
Authorities have lied so many times,
And I mean the professional experts
More than the government per se, mind you,
That nothing is believable at all.
First this, then that, then back to this again.
It's airborne, but it's not, but yes it is.
It magically just disappears on food,
But everything you touch is dangerous --
Well, wait, it's not -- at least not very much --
Well, better hedge your bet. And on and on.
Hands down, the most totalitarian
And thorough propaganda in history.
If fact checkers say something isn't true,
I know it is, and if they say it's true,
It's likely that it's false. But who can tell?
Half-lies are skillfully mixed with half-truths,
And little dupes of the Establishment
Will swallow everything, while looking down
On those who seek alternative viewpoints,
The only way to ferret out the truth.
The age's total mockery of faith
Has made them true believers of the State,
And its official priesthood, scientists.
I'm jaundiced towards it all, for profit mars
The very possibility of truth,
And all our regulators have been bought.
The best that can be said is if it's said,
It might be true, at least in slanted part,
But then who knows? It's folklore at the best,
And folklore serves for something half the time.

thank God for Spiderman

My life is purely theoretical,
A wonderful idea. I'm quarantined,
I cannot get about. The windows are
My only outlook, save my state of mind.
Therefore, imagination is my life.

I must play-act my joys to bring them close.
Thank God for Spiderman and poetry.

farewell to Baals

Jesus.
We wait in moonlight of the shadowed cool,
In silence of the olives, still as steel
We hold by anxious hilt, for multitudes
Who come at Judas' bidding, as I have called,
The Lord's Day, when the evil stewards fall,
When demons from abroad are tossed to seas,
When we shall cleanse the Temple of its blood
Coagulated into signet gold,
Idolatry of Mammon from our midst.
Tonight is shade and fog; the moon but speaks
In parables of drifting clouds and mist;
Tomorrow dawns a brand new day for all,
The culmination of the Passover:
We let go Mizraim and the Kittim.
We void their titles and their holding deeds,
Declaring forfeit all they claim to own,
Reconsecrating it to the divine,
Who loves the poor, and lends it to their use,
Free use of all, for all, for all of time.
We'll tell our fellows in diaspora,
Bring this new commonwealth of liberty
Back home, foreclosing on the landlords' wealth,
And stripping merchants of their hoards of gold,
Spreading this joyful news around the world.
We'll force an exodus from out the shrine,
And then from out of Israel itself,
And finally from out the larger world.
Farewell to Baals and all who overlord;
Farewell to money and its locked-up stores;
Farewell to all impeding love's domain.
Our fellow peasants called from far and wide,
Whom we have gathered with our strident tales
Of casting out to shadow wicked Lord's
Shall come, as Judas runs the roads between,
And gives the sign we all agreed upon.
Then torch, and pitchfork, adze and mere stone

Shall come to animated hand, and us.
When they arrive en masse, arrayed with such,
Our prayers are answered, and we may proceed.
But let the cool wind now inspire prayer;
We ought be silent, listening to God,
Who shares in cryptic hints his mysteries.
Much of what may unfold is still untold.

she had the eldritch air

At the first outset, it was magical;
As years recede, it grows more magical,
The very elfin gemstone of my youth.
That's no conceit, nor fable told to brag,
But where my life touched fairytale for real,
Where some unusual enchantment came,
Reserved most times for stories, and touched me.
Her hands were clay of porcelain and rouge.
Her eyes were fixed on foreign sites unseen.
Her gait was awkward, silly, and unsure,
Most reminiscent of a little girl
I met when I was but a boy myself.
The girl had in her room a wooden fort
Draped o'er with cloth. The room was shaded dark.
It rose up ladders to the ceiling's height,
And wrapped around the room. She had a set
Of leather-bound folktales. She knew them all.
A party that my parents took me to,
Some friends of theirs. She was their only child.
She had the eldritch air, believed in spells,
Felt that the tunnel to the otherworld
Was somewhere within reach of seeking arms.
I never saw that little girl again.
Except the woman with the searching eyes
Seemed strangely like the girl if she had grown.
They both instinctively knew differently,
Askance, as if a curtain's draw away
From the uncanny, as if second sight
Intruded blurry on their sense of play,
And showed them glances of an otherfolk,
Some figures from the dreams of Mother Earth,
Her playthings in her slumbering naps of love,

Her tickled fancy from the forest floors
And highest firs, whom she adores in clay,
And hollows of the moths in infancy.
When she may drowse, she oft personifies
In trance sensations of sensorium
Within her body vast, and these fond souls
In sweet of dream are faerie. Children oft
May glimmer into glances of her sleep,
And see through haze the creatures of her mind.
These two, the woman and the girl (if they
Were not the latter butterflied into
The former), had slipped many times, one saw,
Into an other place, where Nature spoke,
As if pretend were just a little more
Involved than other children's make-believe,
As if the whispering from sheltered creeks
Spoke alder-tongue and lisp of cocklebur,
As if an odd and friendly face looked back
When one gazed on a tree or river leaf,
A cloud, or backyard viney hideaway.
I knew of none of this when we first met.
She half-intrigued, but partly vexed, and vex
Is but beginning of a wondrous hex,
At least at times, and this was one of them.
I'd leapt into my second childhood,
(My first sore interrupted by a wound)
And made nightclubs my playground-theatre,
So that the first we met was in such play,
A feline and a canine in the dark
Of twitching strobes; we spoke as animals,
Before we Englished, flirty shapeshifters.
She touched my heart at once with how she played
Without a hesitation, laughing eyes
That sparkled as she hissed in mode of cat.
The images between come blur to me,
With sudden shifts of brightened vividness;
I leap from flash to flash of swelling dream.
I'm now in bed with her. I'm weeping, held
By her compassion in my loneliness.
She is the kindly Lady of the Lake,
The fay from Avalon in velvet green.
Her kindness in my lostness makes me fond.
She seems an injured innocence like me,
Who wrapped the wound around the inner core
To keep it pulsating alive, and safe.

She has a strange forlorn endowment, sweet
And melancholy, covered o'er with cheer,
Like glittering glass strewn over sunlit gold.
She has a knowledge that she radiates
Through her uncertainty, and not from books --
Well, if from books, then Bronte, Austen, Grimm,
Or Monmouth's hoary bard of mystic Wales.
The jewel still twirls its facets in my hands.
She spoke to animals and backwood streams.
She dreamt of being a chef, and what delights
Of artichokes and cream, or vegan fluff
Of light French toast, or avocado wrapped
In sprouts and mustard round a Tofu Pup
She served, proved well her skill. Those days were each
A bafflement and a discovery.
You don't know you're on grounds of Fairyland
Until the time has passed, and what's banal,
A boulevard in upper Thousand Oaks,
Peels back its peeling paint to underscapes
Of dream, where temples house themselves amidst
Some silly architect's high middle-class
Pretensions, and I've always laughed at wealth,
So I was fond in mockery and jest.
Yet underneath my feet were fairy roads,
Were wild berserker running paths, were wisps
Of Chumash shaman-journeys, trees alive
A thousand years that once were voyagers
From Northern lands, when every plant and beast
Followed the eagle on migration-trails.
The Kinkade houses were but shimmerings
Of Rivendell on rolling sunset hills.
The 23 by night but river rush
Of Doppler whoosh and evanescent flash
Of highbeams, with the powdered snow on wing
Of one lone barn-owl perched above on lamp.
Her trace is faint of now within these haunts,
Though lingers still; I've bloodhounded her scent
In walkway and by roadside, where we stripped
And whoopied in my car, and on green hill,
By Grecian marble benches, looking out
The vast Conejo shire, where she loped
The sycamores and hung there upside-down,
A vivid livid changeling of the soil.
The hidden doors resist me sans her key;
The place minus her capers seems forlorn:

A landscape loves its vibrant dreaming-maids,
Who animate its features with their luck
Of youth's sweet escapades of fablehood.
It was so long ago, it's buried deep.
A generation has arisen since.
So few are so askance and so attuned.
The many droughts we've had because their tears
No longer bless the land with ballad-play
And dolls much more alive than adults think.
Too few observe these witch-paths anymore.
Unless some newer generation wake,
Who will to live the elfin way again.
Children at times still glimpse, but then are whisked
Away by electronics, when the trees,
And all their creatures, if unseen or seen,
Need them and yearn for then. The children are
The dryad-maidens and the pixie-lads
The shrinking woodlands need. Too few now come,
And less remember when they come of age.
But she did. And who knows? She might as yet.
How can I know? I am anonymous
To her, a poet stripped of name and fame
And friendship, though I've been loyal to her.
I am the melancholy left outside,
The yearned-for one impossible to catch
(I need no catching; in my slip, I stay),
The past that haunts for it is full of blood
That beats relentless from the blooming heart,
And therefore banished, lest her Edgar rue
A ruddy mountain Celt who ghosts her heart,
No doubt, as yet, which is the why the door
Is so stone adamantly shut on him --
That's me, the heart-throb elfin wizard one
Who new-romantic haunts her longing heart,
Though she will never say or dare reveal.
I was the slippery one who got away,
And she is similarly mackerel
To me, my mermaid, and my fairytale.
But most of all, the friend I dearly miss.

world is wet from embryo

Anchises.
But every feature of her face is bright
Alike the heavens by the blush of morn,
That every freckle is a star to me,
And every curl of hair a miracle.
Each hue and shade of hue an heirloom's touch,
Each inch a sign of adoration's breath,
Each glow, the rose of dawn, as I am struck
In fascination: what is perfect but
The atmosphere of this her beauteous face?
I look on her and everything is well:
The world's ills heal, and tarnish wipes away;
Rust comes to gleam and chrome, and light comes web
In beauty of the shadows, amber-rich
Through tinted glass, a phosphous gossamer.
The light is creature, reaching tendrils through
The umbrous cotton of the afternoon.
When I look on her, seven days are fresh
From Genesis, the amniotic dew
Still pearls on each and every life, the world
Is wet from embryo and bright with sun.
There is no flaw nor fault to anything:
The wars recede back into blushing bud;
The crosses fold back into blooming trees;
The ocean, yet to salt with tears, is fresh.
No cries, but awe is currency of all.
No trick, for when I see her, I am midst
Gihon, Pishon, Tigris, Euphrates, lush
With nymph-sprayed greenery. No serpent creeps
The orchard-paths to tempt; the nakedness
Of Eve, accentuated web and leaf
Stretched sheer about her curves in light of day,
Is Eden's splendor, daughter of the sun,
Magnificence of skin and peony
Of glabrous lips; the golden ratio rests
Upon her bosom and her flanging hips.
The artistry is bubble-blow of gasps.
There is no sorrow in her gaze's grasp.
O fountain Ponce de Leon sought to drink:
It is her eyes, they are a juvenance!
Omega fades, and alpha rules the day.

eager for life's diorama

O lime of sky on freshest fruits of youth,
A lemniscate of flesh the herbs surround
In meadow-garlands, yearning in one's first,
The pupils eager for life's diorama,
Ready, fauna of the glands alive,
The road so open, unexplored, and new,
The pallor of too fallen crests unseen,
A keenness to the woundability
Unwounded yet, the wax recently poured,
Awaiting open-armed impress of world:
"Come stamp me, I am longing to receive
Experience; let love's enflorate quill
Write Romeo upon my chest!
I lie Persephone in prairie grass
By springlets trickling over my toes,
And look out towards the burnished bronze of East
For him; let him arrive and activate
What verily ripe stews in dormancy
Within these wishing tremble-lips!
Call forth from me my waited true response!
Oatstraw and wind alone clothe now this form,
And welcome you, for love is breathlessness
And goosebumps if by day or torrid night!"

now broken up with grass
for Jade

Those many things you said still live in me,
Ringing throughout my belfry, though the tower
Now is old, and cattle feed where once
Parishioners were celebrant with faith,
Those stone-laid floors now broken up with grass.
Empty, in ruins, yet it still holds faith.

the mead of thirstiness

Bosom of buttercups that frilly whorl
About their curvy pendulums of flesh,
Spellbinding irises to lip forth sip
Of sights that are the mead of thirstiness.

Wild Eadric

this tale was first collected by Walter Map in his 12th century De Nugis Curialium

The moon has harem-maids of mist,
Whose flesh is vapor and but gist,
A glint of light in beauteous shapes,
That sprinkle luck on earth's landscapes.

They hide in haunts and stay unseen,
Keep to themselves in shadowed scenes,
Unless by waxing wide of moon,
They leave to swim in sky's lagoons.

One night when moon was drunk and winked
Through rolling clouds that never blinked,
A huntsman and his knave were our,
Searching the cold to shelter scout.

They came upon a leafy lodge
Into which they had hope to dodge
The rainstorms; but they had to gasp,
When gazed into that window glass.

For maidens made of moonwebs swept
That hall with grace, so that they wept,
The men, for beauty so intense,
So keen and true they had to wince.

If adoration came to flesh,
These women in their linen mesh
Of lambent light were it, for sure:
Never had eyes beheld so pure.

They all did dance, they all did sing,
In foreign tongues that seemed to ring
Of heaven high above the sleet.
They glided on those hovering feet.

But of them all, these phantom beings,
One stood more gorgeous yet: their queen.
Her bell-sleeves seemed to wheel the air
When she moved limbs so lovely-fair.

The hunter knew he had to grasp
Her hand within his wedding clasp.
Forgetting fear or courtesy,
He broke into their fond soiree.

He held her hand, and went to go,
But those mist-maidens wouldn't let go,
And clawed, and scratched, and left their scars;
Despite, he soon had slipped off far.

There on the wettened leaf he lunged
In hunger on her flesh, and plunged
His pleasure in the midst of her;
Three days he kept at this pleasure.

At last she spoke, and gave her leave,
As she rolled up her linen sleeves,
And gave her blessing's happiness,
So long as he might pass this test:

"Ask not of me
To ever see
The fairy dance
Nor come to chance
On grove or glade
Where we may raid
And ride the skies
With wings of sighs
And seasons seal
With our good weal;
For on that day
When you may pray
The mysteries
Make history

Through pry and peep
And peering deep
Then telling tale
Of how we hail,
That day you weep,
Awake or sleep,
And dwindle fast,
Mourning your past,
For I shall fade
Into the glade
And you shan't see
The likes of me
Within this life,
But live in strife
Of what you lost,
And what the cost.
Keep secret now
And take the vow,
Nor ever break,
For what's at stake."

This cantrip told, he fell to knees,
And vowed his heart for all to see,
Never to ask her privy ways,
Not once in all their many days.

She wove the falling snow to veil,
Collecting flowers from the dale,
And petalled legs, and petalled wrists,
And gave her rosy lips to kiss.

Beneath an ivied arch of gold,
They wedded with the oaths of old,
That all were present were but awed
At beauty given by a god:

For softest glare did gleam her edge,
And charm her features with its pledge
Of moon in fullest from her skin
And melting eyes inviting in.

None doubted then her elfin blood
That radiates in beauteous flood
That captures every heart that sees,
And makes the darkness turn and flee.

How many years they loved and lay
In softest beds of petalled hay
None counted, but they had a son,
The greatest jewel they ever won.

She wandered as she would in haunts,
But he would never dare to flaunt
Her butterfly-like absent flight,
Nor ever seek bring it to light.

But skin was gold, and eddied bright,
Releasing flesh to livid light.
A spirit in communion deep
With trees, she fell into a sleep,

A kind of trance, a dryad dance,
A whispering woodland breath-romance,
And with her sisters, wooed the leaves
From Winter of which they had grieved.

The seasons were her business
She wheeled with weal of elfinesse,
But what the spells or nakedness,
Within the leaves, she wouldn't confess.

Once when she wended towards the trees,
He spied a shepherd, as she fleed,
His eyes on her, and jealous grew,
Suspicions boiling in his brew.

When she returned, his eyes were thin.
"Just where were you, this afternoon?
Don't speak to me of "sisters' lair"
To cover rendezvous held there."

He opened lips to rail yet more;
She was already out the door.
Then skin to angry tears then mist,
She vapored into naught but wist.

His horrored eyes slashed him awake,
As flooded formidably ache
He knew would never leave him now,
For treachery of his once-vow.

He called her name, he spoke in tears;
His mind spun with his dread and fear.
He spoke his heart, tore him apart,
He never thought they'd ever part.

But barn and shed and wood and glade
Spoke nothing but that he'd betrayed;
No matter where he looked, was gone
That lady on whom he had fawned.

He traced her back to where they met,
But all that filled his heart was fret.
The spell was broke, the charm was fled,
And what rushed through him now was bled.

The light grew dim, the colors grey,
A grimness where they once had played
Took over, and he lost his taste,
Good flavor gone, fallen to waste.

What hope, what happiness, what joy?
What sweetness made him feel a boy?
His youth, one instant, ran away,
Leaving his hairs but white and grey.

He turned to stone upon his knees
There in that glade amidst the leaves.
The statue may be seen as yet,
A testament to pure regret.

His son placed flowers on the stone,
Now that he found himself alone.
And in his age, he withered too,
Until he found way to renew:

A saintly shrine he bowed before,
And vowed if he might live some more,
He'd give his self, and all he had
Richly inherited from dad.

That child of the sylfan sprite
Who bathed the trees with all her light,
Gave up all of his earthly goods,
And lived a hermit in the woods.

Some say, by night, as yet, one sees
Before the starlight has all fled,
His phantom laying flowers down
Upon his father's woodland stone.

one yearns to touch that softest skin

The only thing that brings me rest
Somedays are a sweet pair of breasts,
Which soothes and lullabies my nerves
With adipose and rippling curves.

It's natural for such to balm,
From birth they offer babies calm.
When troubled times arrive again,
One yearns to touch that softest skin.

It's sweet, it is not aberrant
To long for their soft labyrinth.
With so much pain within this skin,
Those wonder-orbs are not a sin.

ghosts in command

So much do injuries reign us that ghosts
Live these our lives more than our very selves,
And that's no vain conceit, for look around,
Observe couples about us: memories,
But half-remembered through a haze, do war,
The ones who hurt us long ago in joust,
That we are frankly ousted, and our lives
Become arenas for the phantoms' escapades,
Which eat us, and eat at us, robbing us
Of space to be, and spontaneity.
We are but pawns in someone else's war,
Who owns us -- yes, we sadly are their slaves,

And do their bidding, calling it our own,
Allegiant, yet with casuistry
That spins the facts to seem like we're in charge.

now but copper change

I once the corporate airs that scrape the steel
Of heaven's highways in their glass breathed deep,
And held the multiples of Mammon myriad
In skillful hands -- but now that fond
Roulette on which I spun turns Russian -- dart
Where all my heart is, lucre -- and I fall
From eyries where the moguls wing their eggs
Of gold and brood the waterfall-cascade
Of numerals, and find myself below.
If once a solid wad of bills, I'm now
But copper change, whose clink but serves to mark
The emptiness of this my porcine bank.
If money were my home, and it well were --
I'd gleeful live as mansion in a vault --
I now am homeless, and the dirty streets
Must shuffle in despair. My resume
Is flames; what could my letters say but ill?
A cardboard box but suits me very ill,
Yet it's a place where one can sit and drink.
Indeed, the fluid ounces rival now
Once ample savings, but my gut's the bank.
The grape and grain are made my ministers
By clement yeast, and so I take their alms
With blues' enthusiasm, drowning out
My fury with their flood. But now what coins
Did pity me, withdraw from me, servant
To brewers, leaving this my cup as void,
A sin. Have you known Icarus? With wings
Of Grant and Franklin I once flew the blue
Above, and slipped Santoni leatherware
Upon the snowflake boulevards of drifts.
Alas, the paraffin that held my notes
Against the wind became incontinent
In flames' proximity, and dripped, then gushed,
Then treacherous released my verdant wings.
See then the smoke of this my ruined crash

About me, lingering in shaming taunt.
A janitor! That's all that I could land!
A janitor! Whom I from suites once mocked,
Mocking myself as now! In just two days,
If I would keep my cups full, and I would,
I must make broom and mop my ledger tools,
And scrubbing all my brokerage that's left.
Toilets and dirty sinks my country club,
My honor in the finger clean of dust.
Yet if a janitor, what dignity
Is native to the humble office, hm?
Am I the same? My limbs and fingers are,
If reft of their Armani; and my face,
If tardy in its shadow. I once was
The Ruthless, and they gave me that as name
On Wall Street. That nickname, not my accounts,
Is still intact, and so I pledge to be
As ruthless in my modest janitage
Here from my basement closet headquarters
As ever I once was when still above!
Take shield, ye filth, you've met your mastering sword!
I'll mop up as I once acquired firms!
I'll frighten clutter from its dens of vice!
I'll make them fear to mock this janitor!
Be tyrant from below as from above.

I chant shalom

Such weight of grief I must give to the world.
It is not bearable to any else.
None carry; all must shrug. Forever is
Too long to say goodbye. It cannot be.
I would these ears be cursed for hearing so.
I would these eyes be shut for seeing so.
I'd hold this brain as criminal to think,
And in that thought alone, save yet the fact,
To break my heart most precious to me. O!
My tongue is broken with my heart, and fails.
Fair friendship such as parentage should last.
In faith, who are companions trustier?
Whatever years that might have been ahead
Are plundered, that building burnt to the ground.

I'd have the dust from them, the splintered shards,
And hold them as a treasure. Did I say,
Did I declare, did I make clear my heart?
Did I communicate that highest worth?
It is the lonesome days that march alone,
Companionate solely with memory,
And not this grieving hour, that take their toll.
I'll ask the air, What would you do? And try
To hear your answer, though my greatest guess
Is worse by far than just your presence here,
In silence even. Often you were silent.
But your presence was a masterpiece.
Your absence is unthinkable, and false.
Yet months and years shall stubborn tutor me
To feel what truth I cannot feel as now.
You have forever's loyalty in me;
I seal the deal and stamp the ink with love.
So this is every child's bitter weight;
Why must but one alone carry this grief?
But everybody? Each will have this time.
It is maror alone, no charoset.
O star of David, with your infinite
Enfolded triangles, hold now this one.
Make way the couch of Abraham.
Adopt this orphan as he once did me,
And give him home to last the ages through.
Look here, these palms, they are a tablature
Written with gold, his lettering throughout.
I show these palms, and say he guided them.
He held them, and he lettered me, and read.
He gave the city's oldest gift in ink.
Long nights, long summer nights, the windows cracked
To cool the sweltering, he lay beside
Me in my bed to keep me company
Until the eyelids fluttered. Then the call
Of the garage returned to him. In sleep,
Afar, I heard the whirring and the buzz,
The beeps, the chirps, the static of his lab,
The toyshop of his happiness; so strange,
Exotic sounds in interim of dream
Became a watching angel. This same man,
The night before, a scientist, now held
In afternoon a hoe to work the land,
A hose to water, and the land was home
To him, a straw between his teeth. Outdoors.

"It's good to get some sun," he'd always say.
He loved the open air. He would recite
Baruch atah and Adonai each Fall
By candlelight. He loved astronomy,
Geology, physics of radio.
He could be mild-mannered, with a smirk.
He liked to poke and pun, yet when his tongue
Was loosed, he'd take you on a running ride.
He never thought a matter was too small
For justice, and oft badgered for it, now
Complaint, sometimes dismissal from his job,
But he spoke up. The city called a moot?
He showed. He loved the vote and jury box.
He was a civic patriot, and proud.
A Carter-style Democrat for life.
He was a decent, gentle man throughout.
Sometimes a grump, but aren't we all? He had
A heart in Shostakovich Aspergers,
And tender English horns of Copland. Brash
Eccentrically, and animated, quite
To blushing of my mother and my sibs.
At other times, warmly considerate,
And sensitive to what embarrassed me,
If then at other times I rolled my eyes.
He had quiet respect for independence,
Gave people their space, yet held the bar
For uprightness to win, and noted it,
Or saddened at its absence. That was hard,
Though good. More powerful than a rebuke.
He asked the best, though in an easy way.
Sardonic with an understated hand,
He liked to quip. He was voracious, and
Encyclopedic in his knowledge-base.
Quite liberal regarding sex. It seemed
A natural thing, to not load guilt about.
A private thing, and yet one of delight.
Before he greyed, his hair was everywhere
A rust, and freckled, like a Jewish Celt.
He was dependable, and prided self
As a provider to his family,
And he stayed true to that. Sometimes I'd store,
For lack of things to say at times, a stash
Of topics to discuss we both might like.
O words, that you might form a body, hold
Him in your images. But let him rest,

Or wander as he wills, and when he may.
If ever he is dry, my tears will keep
Sheol in rain, so that the greenery,
Where he shall garden, stays as lush and ripe
As California. Love keeps open doors.
Keep me, so easily to stray, to heart.
Be gentle in your watching, but do watch.
I'll keep your piety upon my lips.
For now, grief holds their utterance as still.
Adieu, an evil word, a needed word,
I will but whisper, but I chant shalom.

nectar of the springs

they follow you, the dragonflies,
for they hear rushing water
in your laughter,
knowing you as nectar of the springs,
and rainbows trail behind you, tracing wizard dust of gold

a duchess of abalone

if tears were pearls,
you were a duchess of abalone,
walking on treasure of milky-mourning shell,
and soft flamingos, fresh from wet lagoons,
commend you in their mercies.

sighs are snowfall

sighs are snowfall of breath
bubbled from a joyous release of sadness

rainshower of peonies

White dove in rainshower of peonies,
Slow motion wave of lily-whitened wings
Ascending linen-sail through scarlet snow.

not the rind

Yea, once upon a May, the fairies seek
Lend fickle eyes of mortals one deep peek
At how the soul, and not the rind, appear,
So beauty from within becomes more clear,
And not some simple dressing from without,
Whence superficialities have clout,
But kindness and the spark of spunk take rank
Above appearances, and we can thank
Their peering power to behold the truth:
To see within the old esprit of youth,
Discerning shapeliness in the rotund,
To find resources in those lacking funds,
To wipe away concern with hue of skin,
But scorn a beauty that conceals a sin.
Thus midnight's mystery calls out from sleep
Unlikely pairs of slumberers, to steep
And winding moon-paths leading to the woods,
And there, under enchantment, find their goods.
The lad who henceforth only sought the thin,
Discovers more alluring charm within
A maiden blessed with rippling adipose,
And seeks to bring her company more close.
The fond coquette, who used to scorn the short,
Finds her jouissance now in such merry sport
As one beneath her chin may bring to lips,
And follow easily down to her hips.
The husband, who would jilt his older wife
For some young thing, now craves what vital life
Her loyalty and honesty shall bring,
And vows renew the spirit of their ring.
The shallow man, with eyes only for white,
Is overcome with wonder at the sight

Of creamy-dew mahogany on skin,
And falls for dignity of his new friend.
The pranking elves make mischief on this night
With spells of glamour that restore the sight
Of unimaginative mortal men
Within their lunar-lambent woodland den.
But single taste inside a mystic trance,
An opportunity in passing glance.
When morning comes, their mortal eyes awake,
Those eyes deformed and for their culture's sake
Too narrow to perceive the inner worth,
And fairies watch to see if there's a birth
Of something much the more and beautiful
Within the soul that is more dutiful
To love's sweet nougat unseen by the eyes,
Or whether blushing, they will now despise
The one keenly adored the night before,
And in the loved one's face shut tight the door.
This is their test, if magic reigns or not,
If one can learn to see with eyes of heart,
Instead of loving what will please the eyes,
Rejecting value for an empty guise.
And many fail, too many flunk the test.
The fairies shake their heads at callow guests.
Yet luck has might as well, and many part
As couples who can see each other's hearts,
And keep the glamour in their soul alive,
For from that font they both ever shall thrive.

never have doubt

for Elizabeth of Night

I hide my lacrymality within
When you depart, but underneath this skin,
Brine brews, although I smile and I kiss,
No poem can express how much I miss
You when you're gone; of that, never have doubt.
I do my best, but when you are without,
Where are those eyes, that skin, laugh I adore?
Sometimes I hopeful look towards the door
To see if it is you come back to me.
Although I work to wait so patiently,

My eagerness is riled in my heart,
Where you ay live, and there we never part.
It's circumstance; there's none of us to blame,
And yet without your limbs, I feel more lame;
Without your eyes, a haze alike the blind;
Without your lips, nowhere softness to find.
Without your heavenly caresses, scorn.
Without your truer counsel, more forlorn.
But if the anxious lips and loins await,
How fonder on each other they shall sate!

icicles like cigarettes

we smoke icicles like cigarettes,
exhaling fog and sparkling breath,
exuding steam from glacier-blue skin as smooth as glass,
and sigh, ecstatic elves of living frost,
electrical and sassy.

this living silk as gift

At times, I know my pricelessness of skin,
The magic in the flesh, the zealotry
Of special elfin genius shared with few
Selectively, and as a blessing, yes.
The knowledge of nobility within,
Self-evident and iridine with spirit.
Valuable as such, no mendicant,
Weak application for a purchased worth,
But primal confidence in what divine
Fingers set to embroidery of skin,
Infusing us with elohim within.
Most have forgotten this elusive fact,
And so I share this living silk as gift,
A revelation: we are palaces
Where genius in its embryo resides,
Awaiting waking: touch, and wonder comes.

a princely fish

I am a princely fish replete with scales
Of royal iridescence lined with gold.
I am as sleek, and move as smooth and swift,
For water is my everywhere ballet,
And I am fabulous Baryshnikov
In beauty of a salmon's glassid flesh.
I'm as mercurial and fleeting, fond
Of silver-quick retreat, but I return,
On call of whimsy. I lay older claims
To thrones and underwater colonnades
Than any regal human, for my kind
Inhabits and darts through the palaces
Of aquablue Atlantis under waves.
Let me inform you: things of classical
Antiquity take on a greater grace
In liquid prism of the blue-green sea.
There is ephemeral eternity
In noble wist of marble columns cast
In bottom sand as silky-fine as flour,
And we flit amongst them, over tile
Pink from faded rubies and a blue
From turquoise mermaid-polished with caress.
These ancient temples wrecked by waves seem right
For sea-aristocrats such as ourselves.
You baby-beings lately on the land
In hubris think yourselves the pinnacles;
Now, please, my darlings, let aside this lie,
And recognize your elders: look at us.
Compare our skins: there simply is no match.
The sun has either bleached or baked you, but
The water has left traces of caress
On shingle-iris of our haughty skin.
We love what glimmers, being natural
To us, so sometimes when we see the gleam
Of what seems silver (but is really steel),
We grasp at it to taste (not then the worm,
As you mistake), for beauty is for us;
Then catching us, you think us low and dumb.
But what pernicious scoundrel uses thus
To foul-entice an Epicurean
Of scales with some aesthetic majesty,

Who wonders at that curving question mark,
That glyph of mystery in argentine
You call a hook? Of course an aesthete bites,
You vulgar, fresh barbarians! Now please,
Take not such pride to hunt aristocrats
And think yourselves the clever ones! Indeed,
The salty-sweetness of our lives resides
Here in the glistening pink of our fine flesh,
Which you find tasty, but imagine, lads,
What taste the life itself you cannot see!
But I expect from vulgar landlocked scruff
Appreciation of the awesome depths!
A passing foolishness, I do assure!
Now take this miracle of briny luck
To heart, and let it grow in you some taste.
As for myself, I now withdraw to shrines
Where all is trance in molten cobalt glass.

happiness were deep-sea fish

if light were woven thread,
your countenance were sunshine
through the prism of the moon,
and happiness were deep-sea fish
in pure delight of your shafts
through murk of the fathoms,
Arrow-argentine queen of glowing twilight-meadows;
Your name, O maiden bathing in the falls of moon,
is bow-Diana of the heavens;
light is soft fabric of your chemise.

sap asleep by night

the bud is sap asleep by night;
each petal were an eyelid
wave by dozen wave awaking to the morning;
flower is the orb of sunlit eye
flirtatious with its breeze-blown petal-eyelashes.

falling gamelan to mud

rain is
wet
wind-chime
falling
gamelan
to mud.

just a little craze

There's charm within petite delusion, just
A little craze, enough to incandesce
Imagination, just enough to soar
Above it all, a tad beyond pretend,
A kind of vital, total playfulness,
With one eye wild, but only the one,
The other grounded in reality.
Charm's lost in full delusion, or too much
Immersion in reality; between
Is where the sweet space is, a little fae,
A little firm. A bright conspiracy
Between two whisperers to make their lives
More zesty with a vibrant secret, say
A pact of whimsicality, a spice
Of fancy lending glamour to a life.
It must be played with diligence and care,
But never losing sight it's a conceit.
It borrows from the lunatics their craze,
But measures it with careful theater.

maiden hidden in the soap

You are the maiden hidden in the soap
The paring knife reveals as it peels back
The bar. You are curvaceous as the soap
Under the hand, inviting smooth caress.
Your solid form is as a meltedness

Just barely frozen, carved by Corradini
Or by Strazza, veiled in rippling cream
Of moonlight shaped to stone. You are that rare.

Dialogue Between A Monk and Mage

Monk.
Standing in robes, within the circle bound,
What is it that you do, exactly, hm?
What good may come of this? What benefit?

Mage.
Communion with the depths and utter heights
Of broad divinity, and filled to brim
With majesty and its authority,
A vessel of its right to lay command,
And like Lux Fiat, all must be fulfilled.

Monk.
Communion? What a lovely word to use.
Perhaps inflation is a better word.
Enthralled with power, feeling it fill you,
Mistaking grandiosity for God.

Mage.
Have you the poetry of lakes and woods,
Of stars above, and ocean floors below,
Of cardinal directions every way
Extending to infinity, enjoyed?
An elevator to the heavens! That's
The circle! Have you felt celestial
Expanse and presence of the angels' wings?
Has your faith given you this grandeur yet,
That every time I step within the round,
Comes inundate and blissful to my mind,
Suffusing all my heart with utter awe?
Let mages do no else; that were a boon.
Let all else we intend be vanity;
That infilling of majesty is rich,
A welcoming of all benevolence,

A chance to let transcendence touch us deep,
That every mage were mystic, lapping up
Divinity's integrity and love,
The vastness of Creation's holiness.
Let that be but a taste of what is grand,
Humble metonymy, but some petite
Reduction of the whole in visionary
Sweep, I'd say that is a worthy faith.

Monk.
But is that not a mere conceit to serve
A darker purpose of manipulation?
Don't you intercourse with vileness?

Mage.
The raw and raucous lower forces hoard
Their stolen knowledges and secret lore,
With which they only mischief and wreak ill.
Yet once those treasures were the domain of good.
We are the royal summoners of God,
Handing subpoenas to the criminals
To show themselves, returning what they stole.
We then can use these lost abilities
For good things, that will benefit our kind.

Monk.
Are they not tarnished with the years of filth,
And carry foul intentions deep within?
If these pertain as yet to demons, if
Through residue alone, if not more deep
And sinister, if you appropriate
Such compromised, corrupted merchandise,
Are you not smirched with all that lay within?
If these belong to God, do you usurp
Possession of the heavens for humankind?
God can, no doubt, deliver anything
Of scum and tarnish and impurities,
But how can you keep poison, drip by drip,
From slow contaminating you, until
It has its hold on you, not you on it?

Mage.
The circle's where we ask profundity
To flood us with benevolence and good.
No venom may withstand such purity;

It's washed clean in an instant! And the fiends,
Who would demand, we yet interrogate
Instead, surrounded as we are by signs
Of utter holiness and mystical
Enthusiasm. In that circle, all
Is pure, is first Creation as the first,
Is Eden in its opening to skies
And stars and wisdom of the firmament.
No serpent enters in that paradise.
Besides, we keep them in a banishment.
They come in chains, and have no freedom here.

Monk.
How do you then attain this bondagement?

Mage.
We keep them in a triangle we etch
Upon the ground, at distances afar
The circle, separate and bailiffed there.

Monk.
A triangle? What's then a triangle?
A geometric form etched in the dirt?

Mage.
An old tradition of the magic mind,
A strong convention representing lock,
And jail, and prison, holding strong and firm
The foul, so that it is a captured thing.

Monk.
And yet you do invite these things to come.
How strange they would consent to such a deal.
An invitation to a dungeon? Odd.
But why should they observe conventional
Designs in chalk? What are such glyphs to them?
An etching in the sand, and you believe
That gives you utter power over them?
A little mark, a scratching in the ground?
Suppose we summoned to us ruffians
From some benighted neighborhood of men,
Where life is rough and hard, but then we drew
Geometry around them, and forbade
They leave this academic penciling,
Declaring they could do no harm from there?

Fill then this amphitheater with laughter!
They would mock you. Yet the devious,
Observing this your gullibility,
Might nod, and make as if were truly cowed,
Remaining free despite to roam and prowl.

Mage.
I thought the Trinity a sacrament
To you; if on all sides, the walls are shut
By that same Trinity as guardians,
Who shall escape? Who would pretend to dare?
If I inscribe the triple names of God,
The very fortress of divinity,
I am not frightened by some weakling wights.
Were they to storm the heavens -- that is here,
Within this circle, distant from abyss
That separates this ring from triangle,
They'd be rebuffed from thousand angelkind!
Inside this glowing ring, you realize,
I'm in empyrean citadel above,
The very mansion of the cherubim,
The fiery seraphim in ring about!
Here is but grace and courtesy and art.
A cosmos. Chaos has no standing here.

Monk.
Who could deny the grandeur that you speak?
Is full of wit and wonder. Yet how strange
That all of this but serves to ferret thieves
Or treasure, finding things forgot and lost;
Or casting fascination of a love
Upon disinterested or scorning ones,
Often in wish of some adultery;
Or worser yet, flattering malevolence,
By promising a vengeance with a curse!
How may God condescend to tinker thus
In pettiness and its illusions, when
Such narrow, bothered wishes are but wind
Of paltry bickering and nastiness?
That were far from the grandeur worthy God!
Would he not pity and then remedy
Such quarrel-sourced, sclerotic visioning,
Replacing thus with something wonderbound,
Rather than sad indulging stuntedness
And its injured and angry trivia?

Assuming you could grant such vulgar spells,
Such noxious vanity from cantripped lips,
Why would you want to? Is that not a curse,
To answer trifling, ornery prayers of fools?
That only will but magnify their lot
Of itch and scratch and irritability?

Mage.
What harm if God shares his effectiveness,
Even in little drops, with the assailed?
Shall not communities expect some good
From deity? Shall justice always wait?
Is after life the sole domain to hope?
What harm if hope is then dispensed a bit?
Shall we do nothing but console their lot
With visions of a higher consciousness,
And beg them be content with such aloof
And apathetic grandeur, too withdrawn
To help at all? What loyalty shall cleave
To such uncaring, haughty purity?
They have their hopes, little as they may be;
If I may make them feel more opportune,
And grant even an echo of a joy
Into some sad and miserable life,
Why would I not? I give no promises,
But rather do restore their sense of chance,
Their worthiness to ask the dice for luck,
A blessing. May that not bring light to them,
However dim their wishes might begin?
To climb the ladder of desire to prayer,
With lower wishes being nought but rungs
That lead to higher things, but needed rungs,
Convincing them of mercies to be found,
And finding mercy, able then to give it.

Monk.
Mercy? How is vengeance mercy now?
The enemy is cursed, the thief is caught,
The once denying mistress punished ripe
With lashes of her wish-coerced desire?
How does this improve humanity?
Justice for Capulets and Montagues
Is Hatfields and McCoys ever in feud,
Pretending even ghosts demand vengeance!
A madness. On and on it ever goes.

A hungry man crosses a fence to take
A loaf of bread from those who have surplus,
Perhaps a coat or shoes deprived from him.
We call him "thief", neglecting those who steal
His needed mercies, blessing stinginess
As just, but feeding self amidst plenty,
A crime. Who then impoverishes the poor?
The landlords and their sheriff-warriors,
Who rent them of their very rags and rice.
But who calls such nobility to task,
As robbers rife with weapons at their hands?
The poor, in their assymetries, then fight
Their quarrels, not with whom the lion's share
Demand, but with each other! Shall we then
This farce of petty thievery condemn,
But keep the robber-barons clean of charge?
Here, let me use my bright capacities
Of wonder to help you to apprehend
Your neighbor, bringing him to stand to hang,
A gift of gallows. Now his sullen kids,
Bereft of father, wallow in their tears,
And marinate in wretched misery,
But none the richer, desperate as yet,
Grow worse and mean, and thus the problem grows,
From curse to worser curse, that is the way!
Call it justice, but someone low is hurt,
And injury, if multiplied, brings more.
Four thieves where there was one, and orphans now.
But take the wished-for woman of the man.
She hasn't wished or wanted him at all,
Choosing her singleness, or some one man
She really fancies over him, but no,
Let's magically coerce her to give up
Her will and agency, and puppet forth
To him, to be his slave of lecherous love.

Mage.
You have a talent to portray as dark
What often is but innocence alone.
Come now, if you critique our great estates,
Then you would know how seldom choice has reign
In marriage; parents, and their will for wealth,
Tsunamis over what the daughter wants.
But even were they free, how free is whim?
How often stubbornness and fickleness

Impedes commingling of beauty's limbs!
How often does a headstrong, rigid will,
From pure pigheadedness, reject some good,
Some wondrous good, outside its small concepts?
Mere mulishness has not the dignity
Of liberty, nor raw contingency
That merely marks the arbitrary sign
Of random wanting! Slaves of chance called free
To let their slavery determine them!
Come on! How often is a destiny,
Bestowed by loving providence, refused?
But every day, but every single day!
What ill is multiplied by shutting doors
On gifting angels! Evil is where good
Is impotent, and will not strengthen self.
If but a spell, a lovely little trance,
Can wake the dreamer from her nightmare stance,
Arousing her to better dreams that bless,
I should feel guilty, for an agency
That is no agency, except in name?
The words are rubbish. I unlock the will
Caught in a dungeon, that it thought was home,
And let it entertain undreamed-of chance,
Its mighty flow of opportunity,
And from that vantage point, then make its choice.
Coerced is what she was before the spell,
Capricious, turning right or left for what?
She now can see from out a different light.

Monk.
I spoke in symbol, for I don't believe
In all your haberdasher's foolery.
You spoke of Fiat Lux. Yet when you speak,
The world spins on oblivious and dull,
Revolving as it would, to no effect.
These rituals may be some theater
Of marvel, but for all their bother, fail
To bring results. Please, no true Scotsman, please,
Let's speak of ordinary, cold results.
Grand, robed within their circle temple-grounds;
In life, but bumbling nobodies who preen
At glories not their own, but count as luck
Paltry coincidence and shallow chance.
"I got that job." "I got that wench." Well good,
I'm proud of you. And I see you enjoy

Intimidation, camping up on fear,
And reveling in threat. Without a sting,
For sure, but you can play upon belief
That evil is more powerful than good,
So prevalent, and people then will spook,
To the delight of your fat arrogance.
Say you command the bogies, then they bow
To you, a king of their anxiety,
And you keep them in line with chains of fear.
Do not object -- you may be more than this,
More noble, higher, more benevolent,
And yet other practitioners of this
Fine Art you champion are certainly
Characterized, accurately, as such.
It all is poofery and poppycock.
A fun jaunt in the charming fields of play,
But little help when life has gone astray.

Mage.
I thought we might respect our dignities,
And reach across the bar of enmity.
But you seem most intent on your contempt.
I shall not on these insults pitch my tent.
Adieu, I say good day to you, farewell.
I stand in heaven's ring and not in hell.

you're in cactus

If pain were needles, you're in cactus now,
And if I could, I would remove each one,
Needle by needle, for I know so well
The hundred stings that knock one to the ground.
And if I could, you'd never be in pain.
Oh, not like this. Oh, not at all like this.
But let us soothe ourselves to know in time
Each day, by day, we'll pull those needles out,
And this ordeal will give way to new bliss.
To think of you in bliss brings me to bliss.

effeminate and lovely Son of God

Effeminate and lovely Son of God,
Millinered with the curving horns of ram,
Nebrided in a spotted pelt of fawn,
Long, flowing, curly hair netted in lace
Of silver-strand and woven trains of blooms,
His buskined calves, relaxed, raised high on chaise
Of chariot, dispensing casually
To crowds about blossoms dipped honeysweet
In glaze, and rose-confetti, grapes at lips,
Both purple-pleasing, riding through the gates
Of New Jerusalem triumphant, palms
Waved wondrously inviting him within,
Messiah-maenads dancing in the streets
To timbrel and the cymbal, flute and reed,
To welcome new King David clad chiffon
In fuchsia, rouge and eyeshadow of blue,
His carriage pulled by braying Apuleii,
The psalms of sweet Isaiah on his lips,
The good news to the poor and animals,
The end of slaughter, strangers holding hands
And nuzzling noses, masses donned in fur
Of fauns and lively rags, the common wealth
Distributed to all with fanfare flourish,
Shofar in the streets, the Torah wrapped
In peonies and sprinkled dust of gold
Held high with hands, renewed with tzedekah
Of public love, the Purim spirit splayed
In masque and fossed chiton and merriment,
The end of despots, carrying away
Of landlords, new ptochoi soviets
Assembled on the sidewalks scattered hue
With iridesce of Holi dust to moot
The newer dispensations of the land:
At last, the revels of the exalted poor!

we get the Puritans that we deserve

We get the Puritans that we deserve,
When we neglect responsibilities.
For they are nags, and we are lazy sods,
Who've left humanitarianism behind,
And scoffed at pressing needs for reparations.
Schoolteachers who press a ways too far,
Precisely just as much as we have lagged.
They are our needed moral drill-sergeants.
We've shirked, we've shrugged, we've mocked at bleeding hearts.
And though our calls for joy and ease have worth,
The younger generations are our scourge,
And have no patience for our daintiness
And slob-luxuriance in face of wrongs.
They want correction now, and they will have it,
Over you and over me, right now.
We've held the Gospels up for centuries,
The Good News to the Poor, but we have scorned
This heritage the young ones now lift up,
Demanding Messianic goals and dreams.
They're shrill, they're thin, they're sanctimonious,
They've lost ability to listen well,
They've no respect for elders: such is youth.
And they are vengeance for our apathies,
Which we deserve, we certainly deserve.
Don't try to slough it off on foreign memes,
Don't try to blame the universities.
Look in the mirror: you're the very cause.
Assume responsibility for once.
Let us surpass our justice warriors,
And they'll admire the wisdom we have gained.
We can then, hand in hand, reset the scales,
Returning to the balance we have lost.
It's quite ok to shake some rods at them,
The staves of discipline and bucking up,
But they will shake their rods at us as well.
Do we have visions of sensitivity,
To make the world a lovelier abode,
To make it fit for those with open hearts?
If not, we cannot fault their "victimhood",
For we're at fault for normalizing pain,

And closing eyes to rife brutality.
Like it or not, this world is now for them,
So if we want to save the Renaissance,
With all its Greco-Roman antiquity,
We'd better make the case it complements
Isaiah's dreams -- and it is solely vain
To blame it all on Marx, for Marx is but
The faithful herald of Isaiah's dreams.
We do not have the right to pray in church,
In synagogue, in mosque, on temple grounds,
And contradict that in the outside world.
We have no right to claim the heritage
Of Israel if we spit on its worth,
Denying it its cultural domain.
We get the Puritans that we deserve.

800 million people

Contemporary laziness now scowls
At China : cue the crocodile tears,
Melodramatic hand pressed to the brow,
"The tyranny! The awful tyranny!".
You shop the same at the 99 cent store.
Meanwhile, they've lifted up from poverty
Over 800 million people. There's
A word for that: it's liberation, not
The despotism hypocrites accuse.
First you must do the same before you charge
Another as a despot: who've you freed?
For poverty itself is despotism.

[the actual present # is 853 million people lifted above the World Bank definition of poverty. If any Christian scoffs at this, let them rip the cross from off their neck, break it in two, and trample upon it.]

taste of peach

fingers, who limb from out the fog of dream,
know you are rabbit's fur and taste of peach,

maple of everlasting to the scent,
a tongue-full of vanilla frosting's fluff.
you are the wish that wistful wishers wish.

the scars a tribesman sports

Sometimes the longing in my breast for her
Is ache, and ache, and mist of eyes, and ache,
The yearning of a little boy she touched.
The dates say quarter century ago;
The heart says yesterday, and every day
Asks "Where is she?" and "When's she coming over?".
No use telling me I should forget.
She's stamped on me as surely as the scars
A tribesman sports along his face and neck.
O flame on verdant pinnacles of leaves,
O Golden Rain Tree, Corte Cancion.
Bare feet, long linen skirt in Renaissance
Apparel, skipping through the chaparral,
With Bronte underneath her underarm,
A shepherd girl amongst the bourgeoisie,
Oblivious and gypsy-eyed, a fae...
I act the fool. How many times could I
Have been there in the span of 6 short months
Before she moved away to San Francisco?
I pretend it was eternity.
Suppose it was a couple times a week :
At most, far less a hundred times by far,
And likely less than that. We likely saw
The Probe on Highland Avenue more often,
In our midnight eldritch masquerades.
And fading memory conflates a nest
Of reveries, and how it felt within.
That's all that matters, all that stays with you:
How all it made you feel, how cotton-soft
In cozy fog of feeling, how content;
For me, how safe I felt to float and drift,
To lose myself, and be found in her arms,
To let my inner airhead hammock-surf
The waves of pure devotion. And when I
Dissociated after sex, and curled
A ball with limbs, unsure which one I was,

Forlorn, young to the core of me, she held me;
Understood. Just understood and held me.
So I bonded with her very deeply.
You can't show that craziness to all.
They'll push you far away and leave you cold.
How few, how very few can you entrust
Such utter, earnest vulnerability?
Who see the toddler, beautiful, in shrapnel,
Still with sliver of his fragile trust?
It's more than gratitude, for sure, but I
Am ever in devoted debt to her.
And that small one, the one they hurt so bad,
The one they bruised, the one they spun confused,
To tweak and make of him an ultra-kid,
Remembers her, and calls only for her.
For from that little boy, I found my leap,
My prance, my gallop from what secret store
Of joy he stashed away from everyone,
He aquifered beneath the stream of tears.
She hopped and skipped and matched me in my joy.
That's life, you understand? That lasts a life!
She will not reminisce with me, dear friends,
So you must be my audience of love,
Help me to light this theatre of verbs
With ambience of all that mischief-play.
I've met adults. They never keep that joy.
They always lose the most of it to age.
So eager to grow up, they lose their self,
And find their fun in sad perversities,
Or simply languish, thinking that their lot.
She made me feel just like a prancing dog,
A soft Golden Retriever, eager, spaz,
Relaxed, excited, and oblivious.
A dancing queen. We lived the Abba life.
The timbre of those times you cannot know,
You have not dreamed, you've never felt the pitch.
I lived it! Now you know my yearning soul,
You know why I so long at times for her.

Artemis in bronze

If lithe were copper curvature of form,

Outstretched with slender arms and recurve bow,
But wrinkled drapery about the hips,
And otherwise what Actaeon once saw
In balneum of moonlight's fireflies,
As nymphs caressed her skin with froth and sponge,
A goddess captured archetype in pose,
Then Huntington gives Artemis in bronze.

silliness were brandywine

Anchises.
To say you are out of my league downplays
The truth of it, for my feet walk the ground,
While you're in beauteous stratospheres above.
You put to shame the star celebrities,
Whose looks and grace take second prize to you.
Such gorgeousness as you command is more
Than eyes can drink, even when parched with thirst;
It is a power overwhelming hearts
With dizzy awe and trance losing its balance.
Where are all those sober plans I had
Before I laid my eyes on you, and dove
A thousand leagues of giddy wonderment?
My drizzling pen won't cease in sight of you,
Although my treasury of words is sparse
For all I've lavish spent in praise of you.
If fawning silliness were brandywine,
When these eyes, chalices, are filled with you,
I were a lush, as hopeless as the hoboes
On the dirty curbs of downtown streets.
I'm someone else in every thought of you,
Someone more noble, given access to
The penthouse where the angel poets play.
Out of my league as well, I pose it up,
The ticket that your eyes give me in hand,
And schmooze in verse and improvise my psalms,
The jazz piano plunking to my beat.
When you muse me, then I amuse the choir,
Wingbeats in applause, though you don't know.
Or do you? You may sense my votaries,
But what Brisingamens I've jeweled for you,
You haven't heard, that I remain discreet.

The crushing cost of honor. But to dream
Of this Roxanne you are to hear my words,
Even anonymous from balconies,
And watch, even vicarious, you swoon;
Or say, the Swedish Nightingale, to deign
Give ear to these my humble mermaid tales,
And blush with flushed enchantment: rarest cream
Of sweetest cream of whipped and fluffy cream!
And such a taste is but a taste of you.

scent of inner sinews
for Elizabeth of Night

A real romantic thing, but seldom told:
When scent of inner sinews is the same
From many slides and glide of thigh on thigh,
So that, sweet to the nostrils, savory
Aromas vapor fragrantly for both.
Where she goes, there I am with her, between;
Where I go, pollen of her broth resides
Where she will slide again, and had so slid.
This scented brew that only we can make
Is a memento we keep secret in our thighs.

poem on a toilet roll

Writing a poem on a toilet roll;
A faint and quaint memoir of ancient scrolls.

naked, warm, and dolphin-wet

When I eat artichokes, I'm in the bath
Again with you: you're feeding them to me
With vegenaise, and all is decadent
And lovely, naked, warm, and dolphin-wet,
And woman-wondrous, pendulous and soft.

The steam is Scotland fog from porcelain,
The mirror clouded with the kiss of mist.
Our banter has that skipping, flirting tone,
Where laughter is the consonants, and awe
The vowels; our skin is every feeling-scape
Of flavor, rich and smooth and comfortable.
My heart adored and pampered like I've yearned
A thousand years it seems, and I can lean
My neck into your arms with total trust,
And let the bubbles mermaid-make us foam.

duty and beauty

Anchises.
O speak not to me of my duty
When I'm in presence of such beauty!
Such a trance may alter laws,
Inserting some dependent clause
That gives to Caritas her due
When her fond Graces come in view.
I fall not if I falter, see?
I do not break my loyalty
If then I pause and simply gaze
At what makes every eye to glaze.
If spellbound, I but hesitate
Before enchantment, such is fate
And not a fault, merely a charm,
But in such there can be no harm.
My limbs and lips are bound up tight,
Pledged to my word to do what's right,
But offering up the gift of rhyme
For any poet's not a crime!
The Muses, who are wondrous blithe,
But ask of us a little tithe
When they appear in any shape
That pleases them in our landscape.
If they then choose what's ripe and fair,
That's natural for those who share
Such gorgeousness in sound and verse.
For blessings I can't yield a curse,
But praise; and I but praise their gift,

In any form they choose to lift
From earth to skies to shine like stars;
A minstrel must raise his guitar
In psalm of miracles of grace!
Such is his duty when a face
Of Nature's incantation shows.
The pen is slave, and so it flows
To where the Muses give it wings:
It celebrates each blessed thing.
If ink alone is spilt, not limbs,
If words alone contain the whims
The Muses lend, that's not a crime,
But very purpose of their rhymes!
From whence, from whom, from when, not I
Determine where their mystery
Reveals itself; I follow there,
And where they work, my quill may dare.
My flesh abides within its bounds,
And arrogates not to abound
Against my honor -- but a glance
(With words that follow)'s not askance,
But adding to my repertoire.
It's not a sin to praise a star,
And dream of joining heaven's path;
That's worthy of nobody's wrath.
I keep my dreamy rendezvous
Within a stanza, and stay true.
If one would ask me shut the door
To inspiration's paramours
(Not mine but hers, but hers not mine;
She has good taste if they're divine),
This little well I am soon dries,
And my career is then despised.
I keep up with my craft's demands,
And follow where the Muse commands.

to feed you mint

The fairies won't disdain to feed you mint
And chocolates, the birds will bring sweet cream,
The dragonflies will leave lush nectarines,
The spiders will leave silver webs in hair,

Reminding you of pleasures in your pain,
And you shall lounge in pampering again.

lads of butterscotch-sunlight

Maidens with saris silk-woven from winds caress your peony cheeks;
Lads of butterscotch-sunlight twinkle raindrops of gold on you;
Undine salmon-sylphs sprinkle their cool, refreshing droplets, easing your angst;
Dapper mud-mothers clothed in Autumn leaf soothe all your wounds with porcelain clay.

baptismal on aching flesh

Egg yolk cracked from nest of morning sun
Pours down baptismal on your aching flesh,
And fills you to the brim with unguent light,
As eyes horizon-open to cool blue
Of cotton-wispy sky, which waters you
With ice cream turquoise firmament of breath.

oysters yielded but reluctantly

Anchises.
I'm simply paralyzed in love with you:
You are the ocean; I am powerless
Before your natural sublimity.
I'm drawn to you as to a wondrous sight
One catches on a cliff through sunset's flames,
The waves beyond the frilly canopy
O'er Neptune's porpoise-chariot of fish:
I'm caught in awe I have no strength to balk.
You are the spirit in a precious shrine;
I am but votary, and come with shells
And margarite, and peonies as lips

To brush so shiver-soft in scented wind
Against your own. You are pearlescent flesh
The oysters yielded but reluctantly,
For femming of the sky (who now wears skirts
Of clouds), who cast his lost fertility
To gasping basin of the drunken sea,
Who, sotted with his heavenly champagne,
Birthed you in bubbles of the brimming deep.
You wed the fashioner of gold and jewels,
The dwarf-lord of the dactyls; only he,
The son of Hera, genius-gifted craft
Of seelie elegance and trancerie,
Could translate your transcendent, beauteous flesh
To mirrors made of stone and crystalwork,
Adorned with argentine and webbery,
The stars your father held in spread of flesh
Now gleaming gems, just like your flammant eyes.
You shake me like the waves will shake the cliffs;
You shatter me like beating froth makes sand.
You birth in me the longing that the sea,
Relentless, pines in ever-reach towards clay.
Your beauty is a mountain, Everest
Of sibilance of sighs; you are the peak,
Where clouds, like cherubim, nurse on your pap,
And rest in valley slumbers as fresh snow.
Did wizards of the Welsh, from honey-horns
Of fluted petals, call you Flora, wombed
In Zantedeschia, camellias,
And lotus? Cells are driftwood in the wind
Of awe that is my gasping body now;
My atoms are the gilded dust the fays
Blow whisper-whimsically when mischief makes
Them caviar of giggles, epicures
Of rapture; I am lost, and happily,
In ecstasy of curiosity
About the everything of furtive you.
You are variety in unity,
An endless fascination, nectar-limbs
Coagulate sucrée in rich, deep cream
And jimmies, glaze of pastried skin
And starlight, lactate mimicry on waves,
The trace on slate-gelate of bedtime lamps
That line the necklaces of nereid Night.
You are the might of sights miraculous
And opiate and cool. My heart's a school

Of darting fish, which way and everywhere,
When you're about; I'm scattered swimming drift
And braided lemniscate, now shy, now bold,
Now bursting, now invaginate in veils;
Now telling tales, now forming alphabets
Of sweat and breathlessness, caress of gold
And peach-fuzz; I am summate of salute
In serpent-charm of baited breath and bows,
My heart oblate to you. You are the shrine's
Metonymy, the eloquence of rose
And dew, the envy of sophisticates,
Muezzin aesthetes' floral patroness,
The dear of darlings, starlings' wingspan soar
O'er roaring saltine surf, crepe-myrtle clothed,
Chemised in sheer anemone of blood
(Recalling priceless pearl-lips of your love),
Philanthropist of blossom-chic and silk,
The heart-throb bosom bounty of the gods.

the rabid poisons raped

Let us translate flesh to ambrosia,
So that the pith of you is nectarine,
A succulent, a pleasure-parlor's fizz,
A whiz of wonder-rush and giddiness,
Hilarity's inheritance, the trace
Of smooth serenity and gratitude
For rampant joy that hums in every limb,
Each membrane like the cellophane of flight
The butterflies embody in their strolls
Through grassy corridors of sunlit wind -- and not
The aches of bones the rabid poisons raped,
The shattered shred of weeping agonies:
Let those be still, let those now take a hush,
A nap, a breather, and let bitterness
Be washed away with sparkling honey-mead
Of tickled smiles cabaret with kicks
That hint the frill of petal-skirted thighs
In high of shaking spirits and delight!

Verdugo

Mountains resting on a swirling sea
Of flame, volcanic islands floating still
In sparkle against shadow of the eve.

illusions that you love

She'd swipe you with a knife at any turn,
Come on, get smart, she changed, she's not the same:
The one you worship's a Pygmalion
You made by bringing all the finest parts
Together, all intriguing charms, but that one?
Please. She'd swift corrode you with contempt,
And wilt you with disdain, then turn and laugh,
Happy to smash illusions that you love.
She had inspiring elements one time,
Long, long ago, but choices have their weight:
Who she could have been long ago was lost
For what she chose, and that's simply her choice.
Keep fashioning her better doppelganger,
But be savvy, keep it real, my friend:
She'd disappoint you with a savage glee,
And trample on your sacred principles
With utter disrespect, and ravage you
To tatters, spitting on your scattered rags,
And heaping dung upon you, tossing salt
On every wound she could think to evoke.
She's ruthless, that one, savage, shallow, cruel.
The woman you've made is a paragon,
This statue you've spent decades carving well.
But you have had to peel the stony heart
Back to reveal the one you wish she were,
And this one's better by the far than she.
You are forgetting all the friction: sparks
And scratches, fights and matches, getting burned.
The one you reach for lives inside of you,
Your better half, an aesthete and a femme,
Nurtured by fragments of that love she had,

That desperate adoration you adored.
So live in self-ensplendorate jouissance,
Affirming this your other side you've loved,
And let that harpy live in peace afar.

just dump her

If she is difficult, forget the rest --
Forget the beauty and the charm and sex --
I mean impossible -- just dump her, friend:
Admire from afar. You don't need that.
You think the sex is worth such rigmarole?
It's not. She's immature, a waste of time.
Find someone who is grown up, sensible,
Who loves as she is loved, not lashing out
At daddy or whomever. Don't need that.
There's much more satisfaction in a book,
Much more fulfillment in a worthy cause.
Leave her manipulations far behind.
Her sexiness is but a demon's mask,
A harpy's camouflage to hide her claws.
The joy she'll get in tearing you apart!
I'm telling you, my friend. Just take some heed.
A better woman, reasonable and kind,
Awaits. Not thrills at every turn, it's true --
But those are tricks to brainwash you a slave.
And love that's genuine is thrill enough.

columnar-sculpted like a forest glade

Crystal stained to color living light
As it stretches its web-like fingers forth
To penetrate the cavern carved from stone,
Columnar-sculpted like a forest glade,
With elm and beech and oak and elder-tree
In limestone etched with twining vines and leaves,

And marble ringed with turquoise like a pool
Upon the floor, and silver chalices
Filled to the brim with juice of grapefruit, peach,
And pomegranate. O what rainbow scenes
Illuminate the frosted panes of quartz!
What swirls of aqua oceanic splash!
And what a symphony of dark and light!
The shadow like a roiling stew, with steam
Penetrated by colored shafts of light;
The cool of rock and shade, the glacier light
Of leafy-dappled sun through rime of glass.
Herein an ancient ambience takes reign,
Primordial feelings rising from the stone.

as many of them as I can

Costard.
What marvelous creatures full of wit and charm!
What feathered birds of plumulous delight!
What floral fauna, gardenous and ripe!
These women, O these women, O these gems!
I want as many of them as I can!
I want to wash in wonder of them all!
To flit and butterfly through flirty crush
On each, to giggle with the gaggle, dip
My chip into such savory-flavored cream,
Such dream of incantation and repose,
Such levity in repartee, such joy,
Such silly riddles, such variety,
Such conversation, carbonated mirth!
To simply follow whim of women where
Each wish may will! To saunter boulevards
In dapper wear and pinned carnation, eyes
Oblivious in lovely drift of scent,
Such lovelies drawn to me, who wish to touch,
Adoring softy with their fingertips
My contours, full of praise, who lend their warmth,
Who share my fond aesthetic quick to melt
At every beauty, sighing through the town,
A promenade of sibilance of breath.
Yes! Why confine oneself to only one?
Did Dionysos heed such poverty?

He sauntered in the midst of myriads
Of lovely maenads, fluttering by them each,
In blur and temporary focus: that's
The life! Call it philandering, who cares?
A nasty name for something wonderful
Does not erase its beauty! O such life!
Just wandering through loveliness and scent!
Committed only to light flirtiness!

two curly-haired Davids

Lips of the sacrifice, of wine grape-spilt
On tongues of rapture, lapping up the must,
Two curly-haired Davids in marble white,
Beneath a waterfall with rushing suds,
The eager hands on slippery silky skin,
A feast of fingers, masculine and ripe,
A banquet of the bosom smooth and flat.
Brass zills a'clinging, aulos buzzing, flutes
So breath-devoted neath the quivering lips,
The maenads in their featherweight silk gauze
About their twining thighs, with jingling coins
Hanging from headdresses: they leap and bend,
They ankle-fly and bow to sweep the ground,
They kick each pointed toe to north and south,
While thick, cool steam arises from the pool
In which the lovers, grapes to lips, do kiss.
Eternity of wist in raindrop bliss.

Mystery weeps

I hear a midnight woman lorn and moan,
Darkness coagulated in fair limbs
Horizoning the moon in bosom's breadth,
With stars the halo of her hair and skin.
She's Mystery and weeps, for angst in bones
That burns, and crushes her to crawl the floors.
My heart goes out so helplessly to her.

If I could lift from tonnage but a pound,
Could cool mere inch of fire's savage breadth,
My aching care would have some weight of worth.

worms delight in gnawing at the roots

Come petty vengeances from narrow minds
To settle grudges, wager envy's lash,
And fraudulently claim the name of justice:
Old offenses buried, never marked,
Exhumed, and made the shaming death of fame,
So merit lacks its might for merest fault.
The worms' delight in gnawing at the roots,
To bring trees of magnificent height down,
Because as worms, such height is yonder them.
When all the forests fall, they'll squeal in dirt,
And claim that victory of leveling.

stretch the worse to seem the better

Make now society Procrustes' bed:
Lop off the excellent, and stretch the worse
To seem the better, or, the same as all.
One grey expanse where we may kiss the ground,
And call that crawling walking, to ensure
The lame take no offense at better legs.

Roxanne

Cyrano.
To love when you can't have, and have to hide
Your love from view while somehow getting it through
Is both devotion and a Tantalus
Beneath mouth-watering grapes so close to lips
One quivers for to taste, yet cannot have.
Each fortnight haps a drop of wine may fall,
Petite-intoxicant, on pining tongue,
So longed for, yet so little. One must do
With humble traces, rarities as these.
Ah sweet Roxanne, belonging to Christian!

the realm of prayer

Cyrano.
The things in life you have to bear alone
Because you made a choice you have to live,
And have to have the strength all on your own
To see it through, and keep it to yourself.
Perhaps you fell in love where you shouldn't have,
And have to keep it barreled up inside,
So no one knows at all, not even she.
(Vicariously, through another's lips!
She will not know, but she will hear my words!
Though one she favors speaks those golden glyphs!)
So what you go through, in the in's and out's,
The fleeting joys and lasting sorrows, all
On you. So if you hope, or if you pine,
You keep the zipper on your lips closed up,
And keep your pleading in the realm of prayer.

epiphany of Aphrodite

What pioneer displacing Native land,
Consumed in mundane toil, ever had

Themselves epiphany of Aphrodite,
Dressed entirely in blossom-wear,
And glowing like the sun in shaded glades?
Drab Jesus, that is all they ever had,
Dull idol, popsicle on faded wood.
Where were the fairies? I don't hear of them
In diaries of pioneers. How sad.
A broken people, who have lost the fay.
But why would elfin folk speak to such kind?
Who slander them as demons, storming in
Invaders, on the graves of Native bones
So fresh-interred? Yet I suspect some did.
They'd lost the language for it, but they did.
Some backwoods beatific vision, in
Some hidden grotto canopied with leaves.
They saw a deer, white deer, the twinkling sun,
The glint on molten glass of running stream,
And Aphrodite, apparitious, came,
Invested in the foliage and fleurs,
With wings and silk-chiffon, and when she spoke,
Gold-dust puffed from her lips, that when they looked,
Nothing was not rapturous beautiful,
And all consumed them with a sure delight.
They could not speak of it to anyone,
For fear of being called madcap and lost,
So they just said that God was in the woods,
The wild country. That's sole trace we have.

the roses purr

Anchises.
You are my wings, you lift me high above,
Propelled through stratospherical expanse,
And all is wave of cloud and rushing air.
Because of you, the flowers are more rich
And crisp in hue, so clear, and yet they blur
So far as I just melt adoring you.
They come alive, astounding animals,
The roses, purring as I saunter by,
And whispering hypnotically your name.
They pulsate, and their colors focus tight,
But little suns of pink and crimson lip;

They flush, they blooming blush, they reach towards me,
Because of you. Because of you, I smile.

Aubrey Beardsley wings

Antennae bobbing happily in breeze,
The chrysalis-reborn in drapery
Of sheer and spotted span that beats the wind,
With friendly nonchalance strutted along
Upon a sunbeam slowly spotlighting
An ancient oak, and as it flit about,
Its Aubrey Beardsley wings relieved the clouds
Above, against which merrily they played,
I noticed it, and thinking then of you,
For I was happily in midst of dream,
I caught it by the tail, and bring to you,
As fresh in flight and sheer delight as dream.

enlist in Starfleet

But how do you get out of Dodge when Dodge
Is everywhere? This hobunk nation blows,
This Ignoramusville, this Cowboy-Land.
Please tell me where I can enlist in Starfleet.
To the future! Let us take the reins,
So that the Federation comes at last.

to dance in zero gravity

But O to dance in zero gravity!
To float beneath a purple-tinted sky!
To gaze up and behold the double moons,
Each ringed, with comets sailing slowly by!
To awe at starry spread of Milky Way,
Ballet in weightlessness, the drift of limbs

In dreamy limbo, licking lips for joy:
An under-oceanic place of whim.
Delight beyond the starry-speckled rim.

behold you loving me
for Elizabeth of Night

Dessert of sweet approval of your eyes
Is honey; to behold you loving me
Is such rich pudding luscious to my tongue.
I am an exile lost in loneliness.
My nights are long and filled with only me.
To feel you giving me a stamp of worth
Redeems some of this existential angst.
I honor you, appreciating all.

tribal chief

The janitor who is a tribal chief,
Disdained by arrogant imperialists
For whom alone their values are of worth.
He's loyal to the council of his folk,
Who meet each moon in a fiesta time,
Which others see simply as party space.
As groundskeeper and gardener, he knows
The trees and plants, and how to tend the grounds.
The dull invaders deem their property
What is the sacred tenure of his folk,
So he allows them to hire his help,
That he may be present upon his land.
He carries the esteem of all his tribe,
And all the ignorant contempt of us.
And all that keeps us from beholding him
For that high dignity for which he stands
Is our dismissal of indigenous
Nobility, and Other ways and means
Of dignity upon this planet Earth.

Indigenous America

Indigenous America: the hues
Of turkey feathers and the Autumn leaves,
The forests full of colored foliage,
The rusts and browns and oranges of Fall,
The pheasant-feather plumes of sunset gold,
The partridge-tufts of rusty stripes and snow,
The denouement and decrescendo songs
Of the senescent seasons, as they wheel
From wist of weeping trees to winter-white
In cold Shabbat before the birth of Spring.
O Golden Eagle's paisley-plumage spread,
Tuft-shingled reddened earth and zebra white,
Haudenosaunee longhouses adorned
With husk and shuck of Maize, vines of Legume
Which tease and wind the corn-shoots with green spades
That shelter seeds, above the scrubby patch
Of pumpkin sunset-globes and gourdish squash.
These long eternals of the ancient place,
These colors of the flag original
To forest and to brake and preening plume.

the red-legged partridge

Red-ribbed, with India ink dribbled on snow
That runs from blood of eyes down to the breast,
Hued pigeon greyish-blue, beneath which rust
Is ruddy-soft with pomp, and up the neck,
A mohawk-cowl of muddy running brown,
Falling on pomegranate-reddened beak,
With legs the talons of a carrot-stick,
Such gentle grey and subtle brown to tail,
Such origami-white and hickory wings!

the cosmic cure

O Lord, let me assemble here my shards,
My yard of broken parts, amalgamated
Hopes, and nourish them, and cherish them
As broken remnants of my greatest loves
I don't know how to put together yet,
But you do, you know how to resurrect,
So let me lay these inert fragments on
Your altar, knowing that in time they'll heal,
And all original devotions find
Their cure; and in the meantime let me preach
Unto a world that breaches me your word
That total sharing, no holds barred, of all
Is your prescription for the cosmic cure,
And let me hold faith in this certainty.

you will at last command

O adolescent still in teen despair,
Hold on! You must endure through many storms
Before you come into your very own,
And then that most tormentuous prelude
Were worth it. If you kill yourself, no fruit,
No feast. You'll never know what you'll command.
And if you persevere, you will command.
I promise you you will at last command.
Take me: I cannot even walk, and yet,
My powers thrive, I conjure worlds to pen,
I've love in every form, and scholarship
Surrounds me like a team of rabbis, yes,
It will get better. But you must endure.
Sometimes this year I've lived on faith alone,
Not knowing what will come, or how to heal,
But through the all of it, a better man
Than I once was when I was floundering.
There's always challenges. Will ever be.
But you get better. More and more yourself.
Don't interrupt this for some cheap despair.
Despair should be expensive, vintage, rich,

A little folly of indulgence, not
A precipice. There's so much joy beyond
The fog. Keep going. You will find your way.

wish upon the tip of tongue

I am a bride in gown of mesh and blooms
That trails the swanfeathers upon smooth lakes
I hover over as I follow stars.
I am the genius wrapped within the fool
Who flutes and spins around the heaven's pole
To tickle giggles animal and child.
I'm quintessence of your wonderments,
Faun-curiosity of pond and glade,
Fur legs and quirky grin, whom you adore.
I am confetti, shooting stars' surprise,
A foaming fountain gushing everywhere;
I am the wish upon the tip of tongue,
The spell that lifts away in merriment.
I am the secret pantheistic joy
Hidden in sprout and bough and verdant leaf,
The echo of the laughter of first song
The dancing Eden-angels seven sang.
I am the pang of sudden, alluring love
The lovely Muses render for a rhyme.
I am the sundae-sighs wisteria
May shade in velvet gloves of zephyrs' doves
In wing-brush tender by the blushing cheeks.
I am the caramel, as beautiful
As skin of Sudanese, that drips from lips
That scoop the soothing smooth of honeyed ice.
I am the verdant peeking featherage
Of cobalt-breasted regal fan-flair birds
That fireworks with thousand tufts of eyes.
I am an orphan tossed from hand to hand
With hope each time this time I shall be loved,
Who lives in safety of a precious dream,
Who sails the stream the Muses whip with cream
Of whim and fancy as the froth shall splash.
I am mad dash of wishing, welcome all
To Julie Andrews' alpine carousel
Of arms, wide worship from the twirling waist

Embracing all creation's Springtime flush!

has name of love
for Elizabeth of Night

These bubbles are but giggles yet to come,
The caviar of laughter in a brew
The vine-philanthropists gave forth as alms
To dripping beggars of the sorrowed eyes.
More purple than the blood, more clean and clear,
More sparkling, more full of hidden joy,
More veil de-veiling, nougat's cardine taste
To secret-solvent lips that give away
In mascot motto of one's shaded soul,
And yet this wine to me has name of love,
With friendship as the grapes that yield their sighs
Of fizzing effervesce and do adore.
That is what takes me far away on wings.

monuments of mirth

The Five Year Plan, amazing, marvelous;
The Movement for Collective Farms, oh wow;
The Anshan Constitution, what godsend;
The Great Leap Forward, monuments of mirth:
These milestones shall ever nourish me.

consummated

The soul is not annihilated, no;
It's consummated! If that be its last,
In union with its love, all of its love,
That last is lingering eternity,
The taste of wished reunion and sweet song.
You say this is but vanity and wind?

You live your empty life, devoid of hope.
I choose a soulful life endowed with faith.

Mike Monahan

Who can live long without Mike Monahan?
One misses him as soon as he is gone.
And yet the echo of his dramatage
Persists with joy a lifetime's reminisce.
Those eighties Saturdays in Westlake hills,
The business park alongside verdant knolls,
Wherein his studio opened a stage
To whisked improvisation on the boards.
I'll live a long life with him in my heart.

an aquaman upon the land

To make life more akin to like a dream,
A waterscape of drifting through a daze,
Drawn out by feeling, whether here or there,
Receptive, and responding to the flow.
Deliberate intent and conscious work
Disrupt, and make the smooth a jerky ride.
I am an aquaman upon the land,
Who needs the currents moving me about.
Emotion is my ocean, I the fish
That swims in it, or tumbles, yea, I toss,
But in an ecstasy; the tepid streams
That trickle as arroyo in the sun
(Those meagre, dribbling leaks most men prefer)
Fail in their motive force: they fail to move.
Aridity as this I can't abide.
The merest trace of management is foul
To me; to seek control, manipulate,
Is gauche. Find rather then the river's side,
And live by all its grace of rush and flow.
A good cry is a spell that calls the sea,
That welcomes waves to carefree move by whim.

If that is sissiedom, that is a crown
A queen may don, and elegantly wear
In regal pride, dismissing with a flip
Of flippant and disdainful hand what dreck
Is recommended by the mass as worth,
That schizoid cowboy-puppet, tight-sewn lips,
Self-made and -motivated, worth a yawn,
Insufferable and dull. Give me a gush,
A rush of feeling, and an aqua flow.
To give oneself to what the dream bestows.

sweet sorbet

Anchises.
A taste of you replaces sweet sorbet.
You coat me like a blanket in the snow
With powdered essence of your honeyed lips.
I am a'glaze with you; my skin is slick
With sugar of your strawberry caress.
I am undressed with merest glance from you;
My petals close for shyness swift exposed.
I am a poem mumbled from a gawk,
Agog with you, engodded with your scent,
Sensation of a lifetime sudden swoon.
You are the moon, and I am lunatic
With lute, who paints upon a pluck your beaut.
Who scoots to suit you where you wish my flute,
Which breathy zephyr-trills on you volute
Upon the velvet ear. I am the deer;
You are the headlights. I am drifting kite;
You are the string. You sail me in the sky;
I'm ever high around you. I but float,
And saunter on a cushion of the air,
No cares, and galavant in caravan
Of butterflies that follow you so true.

upwards to the skies

It's dangerous to be too practical,
To reckon everything from what is real.
Reducing rhapsodies to bottom lines,
Dissolving poems into ledger sheets,
Adjudging beauty by the coin it yields.
Methoughts we were to cultivate our souls,
To elevate our tastes, refine our minds,
Make capable of delicate assay
Our hearts, adjusting upwards to the skies,
And not mere peering in the pointless mud
Like pigs self-satisfied with vulgar mush
And shallow, grunting lust, our gaze held down
With blinders to horizons. To the soul
Our duty lies, so that the heart may rule.

more to sleep as life

One may imagine for a lengthened time
Long sleep and sleep and more to sleep as life;
I think to dream is why we came to earth.
The more that soft oblivion surrounds
In wonder, ah, the greater is my life.

canteloupe exposed to milky view

But sliver of illuminated moon
Through shuttered blinds on strip of lambent skin,
A cantaloupe exposed to milky view
Of passersby, enticement of a fruit
Beyond the reach, me sleeping in the buff.

a mountaintop of cream
for Elizabeth of Night

Blackberry on a mountaintop of cream
And adipose that shimmies to my tongue.
Domain of marshmallow and butter-bob
That makes Monet to shiver on his pond.
O orbs demidivine, be my dessert!

show us the way to 2022

Diana with the crown of sunlit spikes
Holding the torch o'er Upper New York Bay
To streak the wrinkles of Monet with fire:
Shine the way, O copper-tarnished queen,
Deep color of the aqua-glacier sea!
Show us the way to 2022,
A dawning of new life and liberty!

CPSIA information can be obtained
at www.ICGtesting.com
Printed in the USA
BVHW040549260122
627124BV00024B/370